The Self
We Live By

The Self
We Live By

Narrative Identity in
a Postmodern World

JAMES A. HOLSTEIN
JABER F. GUBRIUM

New York • Oxford
OXFORD UNIVERSITY PRESS
2000

Oxford University Press

Oxford   New York
Athens   Auckland   Bangkok   Bogotá   Buenos Aires   Calcutta
Cape Town   Chennai   Dar es Salaam   Delhi   Florence   Hong Kong   Istanbul
Karachi   Kuala Lumpur   Madrid   Melbourne   Mexico City   Mumbai
Nairobi   Paris   São Paulo   Singapore   Taipei   Tokyo   Toronto   Warsaw

and associated companies in
Berlin   Ibadan

Copyright © 2000 by Oxford University Press, Inc.

Published by Oxford University Press, Inc.,
198 Madison Avenue, New York, New York, 10016
http://www.oup-usa.org
1-800-334-4249

Library of Congress Cataloging-in-Publication Data

Holstein, James A.
    The self we live by : narrative identity in a postmodern world /
James A. Holstein and Jaber F. Gubrium.
        p.   cm.
    Includes bibliographical references and index.
    ISBN 0-19-511928-2 (hardcover : alk. paper). — ISBN 0-19-511929-0
(pbk. : alk. paper)
    1. Self.   2. Self—Social aspects.   3. Identity (Psychology)
I. Gubrium, Jaber F.   II. Title.
BF697.5.S65H65   1999   98-31085
155.2—dc21   CIP

Printing (last digit): 9 8 7 6 5 4 3 2

Printed in the United States of America
on acid-free paper

For Suzy and Suzanne,
who provide us with selves to live by

Contents

Preface

This book has a twenty-five year history. It's not that we actually conceived it a quarter of a century ago, crafted it over the years, and finally brought it to fruition in its current form. Rather, its leading idea has been collaboratively simmering for a good long time, the notion being that the self is not only a "social structure," as George Herbert Mead put it, but also a valued social construction, reproduced time and again in everyday life. The idea has motivated several of our research projects, in which subjectivity in some form captured our attention. If the self, itself, wasn't always the leading concern, the question of the social construction of subjects and its mediating conditions in a variety of institutional settings was. It has been our habit always to deal with the question in terms of the ongoing practical activities of these settings, notably, the participants' shared understandings and the everyday work of interpreting actions and events of local interest. That long-standing idea has now, finally, boiled over into this story. The order of authorship, which we rotate, is irrelevant to what is a continuing joint venture to consider the interpretive horizons of social forms, the self among them.

Of course, biographical particulars flavored the brew along the way. For Holstein, it may have begun inadvertently with some innocuous observations he made while watching friends in the English department at UCLA evaluate student essays. The "graders" were working with rigorous evaluation criteria that included the names of the student authors being removed from the essays before they read them. But as Holstein watched and listened to the grading sessions, the graders nonetheless repeatedly constructed identities for the missing authors in order to make sense of the texts they evaluated. Try as they might, the graders couldn't erase a sense of the subject behind the text as they supplied motives, attributes, and other agentic qualities for the disembodied essays in front of them. It was evident that the graders were constructing the subjectivities they needed to do their jobs.

For Gubrium, it started in the 1970s in a field project conducted in a nursing home, which dealt with the question of how it was that nursing home residents' biographies and lives within the facility could be figured in such different ways. The idea that there were many social worlds of "living and dying" in the nursing home, with their respective subjectivities, helped to form an answer. Gubrium maintained this interest in the social construction of the subject and developed it in a variety of other settings, including a residential treatment center for emotionally disturbed children in the later 1970s, a physical rehabilitation hospital and the Alzheimer's disease movement in the 1980s, and family therapy in the

1990s. Looking back, it was evident that across these settings, the issue of the construction of subjectivity was always center stage in the research process; these experiences converge in this book on the topic of the self we live by.

We now take the opportunity to tell this story in the explicit terms of the social construction of the ordinary self, the social structure that Mead and others so ingeniously conceived decades ago. As we like to do, we broaden the traditional analytic horizons a bit to include the settings in which matters of self are addressed and discussed and decisions are made about those whose identities are in question. So we often turn to places such as nursing homes, courtrooms, and support groups to set the stage, but we also consider more mundane settings, ordinary households and friendship groups, for example. Our aim is to show how these locales and their going concerns shape the self we live by.

The story we tell is not as upbeat as it might have been early in the twentieth century, a time when progressive ideals presented high hopes for what we were, and could be, as human beings. Neither is our story as desperate or glib as the one told by some contemporary commentators, where the self is said to be socially inundated or merely a plethora of images of itself. Instead, we present a new ending for an old narrative that preserves the very social nature that the self was assigned decades ago, but embeds that nature in the many and varied self-constructive possibilities of contemporary life. The theme we develop for the new ending is that the self is an increasingly complex project of daily living. It is an entity that now ubiquitously embodies our subjectivity; in the course of everyday interpretive activity, we are more actively engaged in constructing the self than ever before.

Several friends and colleagues have helped us, either directly or indirectly, to formulate this story. Norman Denzin, for one, has been unflaggingly supportive. Norm read and responded to the manuscript early on and, while he wouldn't tell the story the same way we do, his own thoughts and projects have contributed immensely to the story line. His critical consciousness and always generous intellectual sentiments continue to inspire us for their contagious encouragement to move in new directions and not settle too comfortably within the bounds of theoretical membership. Norm—thanks for all the support over the years.

David Silverman also has been a great friend to this project. He probably wouldn't tell the story the way we do, either. Indeed, we're not sure David would figure that there was that much of a story to tell, about the self itself that is. But he sure would narrate its production superbly, and it's his consummate skill in that regard, as well as his equally generous openness to new ideas and interest in new directions, that inspire us. Like Norm, David has continually reassured us that intellectual and disciplinary borders, like other rules, are made to be stretched, if not broken. David—thanks for always being receptive and for recognizing that analytic inspiration comes wherever you might find it.

We also want to thank Pertti Alasuutari for reading parts of the manuscript and commenting on how we were presenting our narrative. He noted that the story, understandably, unfolds in relation to the American experience. The early pragmatists who formulated a social self were, after all, Americans, and those who responded to the pragmatists were guided by their kind of thinking in developing their own commentaries and research projects. But Pertti also pointed out that the story we tell has a much broader, international significance, resonating well overall with contemporary concerns over the empirical status of identity, in particular, and the postmodern debate on subjectivity, in general.

We are grateful to several other friends and colleagues, whose work in one way or another was useful to us or who otherwise contributed to the story line through related projects of their own. We extend our thanks to Malin Åkerström, Sylvia Ansay, Jun Ayukawa, Chris Corey, Mark Cohan, Bob Emerson, Chris Faircloth, Lara Foley, Carol Brooks Gardner, Steve Golant, Bill Gronfein, Haim Hazan, Matti Hyvärinen, Gary Kenyon, John Kitsuse, Doni Loseke, Amir Marvasti, Gale Miller, Mel Pollner, Bill Randall, Paul Rosenblatt, Joseph Schneider, and Darin Weinberg.

*The Self
We Live By*

Introduction

CHAPTER ONE

Restorying the Self

The self has fallen upon hard times. After decades of attention to self-awareness, self-improvement, and self-esteem, an embattled self cascades from all
quarters. Some claim that self-indulgence is society's downfall, with the narcissistic individual undermining community. At the same time, warnings that we
must nurture, sustain, and safeguard the self are giving way to new, playfully
dismissive signals that all therapeutic efforts are ultimately futile. Coherence and
constancy, it seems, don't amount to much any more in a postmodern world of
instantaneous communication, hyperkinetic consumerism, and electronically mediated imagery. In such a world, the self is everywhere and thus nowhere in
particular—fleeting, evanescent, a mere shadow of what it used to be. Once
viewed as a central presence in social life, the self, we are now being told, is arbitrarily "up for grabs," an "anything goes" entity, if not an insidious "con game"
(see Berman 1992, Featherstone 1992, Gergen 1991, Sica 1993). It's a seemingly
tragic ending for a story that started out so optimistically, but now finishes with
disintegration if not cultural chaos.

Still, there are echoes of renewal, even glimpses of a new kind of ending. Increasingly, we're hearing that our lives are storied (Bruner 1986, Rosenwald and
Ochberg 1992). Not only is there a story of the self, but it's been said that the self,
itself, is narratively constructed. What's more, we're told that self is ubiquitously
communicated (Gergen and Gergen 1986, Kenyon and Randall 1997, Sarbin 1986),
providing endless possibilities for who we are and what we can be.[1] Yet, as varied and inventively distinct as these are, they are stories "disciplined" by the diverse social circumstances and practices that produce them all (see Dunn 1998).
From the systematic details of ordinary talk and social interaction, to self's widespread institutional mediations, constructions of the self are conditioned by working senses of what we should be at particular times and places. For all our inventiveness and social combinations, we are still creatures of everyday life.
Inventiveness and diversity are always tamed by the social arrangements within
which selves are considered and produced.

Hopefulness versus disintegration; presence versus imagery; narrative inventiveness versus discipline. How can we reconcile these competing messages?
What's the point? Is it that the self continues to significantly inform experience,
but is now more narratively complex than ever? How can we be both selves and
the stories of these selves? What social processes make this possible?

These are the questions this book aims to answer, beginning with a story of
a social self that some say has now retreated from the spotlight of American social psychology into nihilistic postmodern disarray. It's a story told in many vari-

ations, but one that nonetheless teaches us how we came to think and talk about ourselves until recently. But contemporary circumstances demand a new ending, a new storyline that takes account of the self both as a familiar beacon of everyday life and as a light that is itself differentially illuminated as it moves from place to place in a socially variegated environment.

Some may disagree with certain details of the plot we develop; others may object to what we have left out. We are not suggesting that our story is the final word on what the self was or has become. Our aim is more heuristic than explanatory. We want to emphasize how pitiful the initially promising social self has become and to stimulate the consideration of another trajectory. Ultimately, we aim to present a different conclusion centered on the continuing relevance of the self we live by, because we view the self as an undeniable feature of contemporary social life, a presence that is more vital, dynamic, and necessary than ever. Our point will be that despite reports of the social self's demise, it remains a sine qua non—an essential element—of our current lives.

Opening Pandora's Box

The self of modern social psychology is a relatively recent formulation, born of a unique combination of individual agency, optimism, and democracy. We can trace its origins to the work of several intellectual pioneers of the early twentieth century—William James, Charles Horton Cooley, and, perhaps most significantly, George Herbert Mead—who laid the groundwork for a perspective that, in time, would be appropriated for "symbolic interactionism," a term coined decades later by Herbert Blumer (1969). We'll consider their contributions to this story in greater detail shortly, but we couldn't begin without crediting the forerunners in its opening chapter.

The story of the social self begins with a radical break in the way the self had been conceived in Western social thought. Once viewed as an idealized, abstract platform from which concepts and judgments emanated, the self transcended society, standing prior to, apart from, and philosophically above the everyday hubbub of life. This was the lofty—even haughty—*transcendental* self born of the European Enlightenment. Two centuries later on the American scene, however, ordinary social relations could not be dismissed; social democracy was the very essence of American character, retaining an indomitable egalitarian hope for the future, ostensibly unshackled from philosophical stricture. American social thought offered up a new vision of the self as a social object that was part and parcel of ordinary living, which, to put it in the vernacular, would readily "go with the flow" of American progress and ingenuity (see Crunden 1982, Feffer 1993, Rucker 1969).

This self was the virtual reflection of social participation, a veritable "looking glass" for us all, as Cooley would call it. Social life meant constant commerce with others. As society's members interacted, they took others into account. In the process, they developed a sense of who they were from how others responded to them; *individual* selves arose out of the *social*. As Mead (1934) put it,

The individual experiences himself as [an object], not directly, but only indirectly, from the particular standpoints of other members of the same social group. . . . [The individual] becomes an object to himself just as other individuals are objects to him. . . . it is impossible to conceive of a self arising outside of social experience. (Pp. 138–40)

This socially grounded self was dynamic, not a timeless philosophical position. It would change in relation to others' responses. Yet it was not intended to be a mere puppet of the social, for individuals were viewed as actively and intentionally adapting themselves to social demands. Individual agency combined with social feedback yielded a self that could move competently and confidently through the world, both reflecting and responding to changing needs and circumstances. As an object sensitive to others' responses and appraisals, the self possessed an experiential foundation that allowed it to adjust to the rapidly developing challenges of modern life. Not transcending the social, the self was subject to change for its own and others' good, for the betterment of both the individual and the world of which it was a part. This social self was remarkably versatile. Perhaps that was its most appealing quality in the context of the burgeoning aspirations and unlimited possibilities taken to be part of the American Dream: a mutable self was essential for complex and changing times (Zurcher 1977).

Social psychologist John Kinch (1963) tells a colorful story that dramatically underscores this versatility, showing us how the social can literally bring out the best in the individual. Exercising some editorial license, we'll present an updated version of Kinch's tale because it so vividly conveys the buoyant side of this very social entity. At the same time, however, we want to adumbrate how the social sources of the self represent a virtual Pandora's Box of possibilities that are not as positive as originally imagined.

As our version of Kinch's story goes, members of a graduate seminar in social psychology were intrigued by their first encounter with the symbolic interactionist literature on the self. Shooting the breeze after class, a few of them began to casually explore the implications of the approach as their conversation moved to a local drinking establishment. Talk shifted from the theoretical to the practical, if not the insidious. The discussion became quite animated when the group realized that this literature had something remarkable to say about the power of the social as it relates to the self.

"If all this is true," Emily ventured, "wouldn't it mean that if you could control enough of the significant social responses to a person, you could actually change that person's self, or at least their self-conception?" The question became a challenge. If they were to believe all those "old guys"—Mead, Cooley, and others—social responses could be quite personally consequential. Didn't that mean that the group itself might, on a small scale, play a role in shaping the social selves of those involved with it?

"Let's see how this works. We could pick somebody out, treat him like he was, say, the smartest guy in the program, and observe what he thinks of himself. We reflect an intelligent image of him and see if he takes on that image, right?"

"Right, interact with the guy as much as possible and give him the impression that we view him as a bright guy. Tell him how insightful and clever he is. Make him think we look up to him."

"Yeah, it might be a snow job, but what could it hurt? If this thing works like they say it does, it would be a change for the better, right? Wouldn't it lift that self up a couple of notches?"

The plan sounded intriguing, as many things do after a few beers. This would be more than amusement; it was actually putting theory to an empirical test of sorts. In fact, this is precisely what they were being taught to do in their research methods course: subject theory to systematic examination in the real world. It was the perfect opportunity; all they needed was the perfect subject. Whose identity could they experiment with? It had to be someone they knew, someone with whom they regularly interacted. The person had to care about them as a reference group or they couldn't expect to have an impact on the self. And it had to be someone in whom a change would be obvious enough to notice. After all, they weren't going to administer a battery of "self-inventory" tests to the subject.

The consummate candidate, they quickly realized, was right at hand. Shirley DeMure was a first-year student in their Foundations of Social Theory seminar. She kept to herself for the most part; since she was new to the graduate program, they figured that she had no real friends to speak of. She appeared friendly enough but always seemed to hang on the periphery, wanting to be part of what was going on, even if she wasn't the center of attention. Shirley was around a lot but one hardly noticed her. Mostly quiet in class, she sometimes had something decent to say, but nothing remarkable. Shirley was the perfect mark.

Here was the plan. Group members took it upon themselves to act toward Shirley as if everything she said or did was extremely intelligent and interesting. Respond positively to her comments in class. Hang on her every word in conversation. Ask her opinions, then laud her for having such intellectual command. They also agreed to expand the range of their interactions with Shirley. Go out of their way to talk to her around the department, include her in the give-and-take of graduate student life. But don't be obvious! Shirley was no dope. After all, she did get into the doctoral program, didn't she? Wasn't she Phi Beta Kappa at some small college in Ohio? Subtlety and persistence were the bywords as the group turned their understanding of symbolic interactionist thought into practice.

It really wasn't such a difficult ruse to pull off.

"What'd you think of the reading assignment, Shirley?" one of them would ask. "Hey, that's interesting, I never thought about Weber that way before."

"I can't make any sense out of those French guys," another moaned, "you know, Comte, Durkheim, Mauss, the whole lot of them. You spent a year in France, didn't you, Shirley? What's that all about?"

"Hey Shirl, let's get together after class and you can give us some ideas about how to write that critical theory paper, okay?"

A little interest, a little attention, a little admiration. The group filled Shirley's social "looking glass" with continuous appreciation.

After a few weeks, they took inventory. Had Shirley changed? Well, she was speaking up a lot more in class and she was becoming a bit opinionated. Why, last week she sounded like she'd invented feminism, for crying out loud. "So far, so good" was the group consensus and they decided to forge ahead. This was no big deal and the results could be intellectually fascinating.

By now, the challenge was building. Shirley was no longer the passive subject they initially conceptualized. She seemed busier, more active, more assertive. She was challenging group members' own opinions in class, in a friendly manner to be sure, but also with a self-confidence that was a bit intimidating. Some members of the group found that their questions for Shirley were not part of the act anymore. They actually wanted her input, solicited her perspective. Shirley, it seemed, was becoming quite the expert on classical sociological theory. Rumor had it that she'd applied to be a teaching assistant for the undergraduate theory course the next year. And didn't somebody see her having lunch with Professor Upton, who usually taught the course?

This wasn't all bad from the group's point of view, because, to a person, they'd come to like Shirley. It was no hardship to include her in their after-class discussions and they were almost eager to invite her to join them at the bar after Friday's seminar. For her part, Shirley seemed equally enthusiastic to join in. Indeed, after a few weeks, she was the one who suggested that they convene to a new coffee shop across campus.

Cooley and Mead must have been on the right track, the group concluded. "We've really brought her along."

Pleased with their analytic acuity and empirical ingenuity, the group was only a tad smug about what they'd ostensibly created, the product of their cleverly designed social responses. They'd done no harm as far as they could see, and learned a lot in the process. The project was over, success declared, and symbolic interactionism endorsed.

They soon learned, however, that social processes are harder to control than they'd figured. It seems the group hadn't paid that much attention to the fine details of Mead's pronouncement that self and society were *ongoing* social processes, and this one was now out of their control. Each member of the group continued to seek Shirley out for counsel and camaraderie but, bit by bit, each also noticed that Shirley was becoming just a trifle inaccessible, sometimes unavailable.

"I've got a big appointment right after class, Emily, see ya next time." "Sorry, Steve. Can't do coffee this Friday. Got some important stuff I have to arrange." "Listen, Karl, I'd love to help you with that paper, but I've got my own work to worry about."

The semester was ending. Shirley failed to show up at the ritual last class meeting and sherry hour at Professor Oldscul's home. Feeling just the slightest bit anxious about it now, one member of the group feigned nonchalance as he telephoned Shirley to ask what she was doing Saturday night.

"Would you like to get together at that new Afghani restaurant that just opened?"

"I don't know how to say this any other way, Paul, but I don't date graduate students. There's just no future in it. I've been seeing this surgical resident, but I think I'm gonna have to dump him, too. Good men are hard to find these days."

Silence. Had the phone line gone dead?

"By the way, Paul, could you tell the guys that I won't be in Contemporary Theory next semester. I'm the kind that has to do something productive with my life. I gotta get myself outta here. I'm goin' to law school."

So Shirley, evidently demure no more, packed her self-assured, self-motivated self off to Harvard Law, where, the story ostensibly has it, she met a Kennedy, went into politics, stood for election, resigned her elected post to spend more time with her family, and took a job hosting a daytime cable TV talk show.

This is the gist of Kinch's story, more or less, the point being that the self is socially responsive and undeniably malleable. Just as important, it is always open to new challenges and opportunities. To one degree or another, this view of a socially responsive self moved to the forefront of American sociology and social psychology at mid-century. It also became the subject of extensive social commentary. In the shadow of World War II, the sciences of the self flourished as the social self grew in prominence. That is, until critics stumbled across some of its more unpleasant implications: a malleable self needn't always change for the better or as we desire. It could just as easily reflect the unexpected or unseemly side of social life. The social emergence of self was not as predictable or auspicious as many had presumed, as Shirley surely taught us.

What would happen if this eagerly social self was subjected to too much influence by others? Social pressure, as we were coming to realize, had the power of a glacier. You might not see it working, but at the end of the day it had carved a little bit more of a niche in personal identity. What about these less sanguine possibilities for social influence on the self? Well, for one thing, viewing one's self in the social looking glass made one dependent on that reflection, didn't it? And to what end? Could the self be too much of a social creation, a slave to social valuation if not approval?

By mid-century, we were hearing faint warnings to this effect, that Americans were becoming progressively more "other-directed." There was nothing wrong with that per se, but this wasn't rugged American individualism, was it? The other-directed individual, we began to hear, took his bearings from those around him, molding his actions and presenting himself so as to "get along," to "fit in." This wasn't a bad guy, mind you, just a conventionalist, something of a conformist. The "organization man" was born, too, with a self that reflected the proliferation of organizational goals. And he married the equivalent of the organization woman, who took her cues from the neighbors on the block and the local PTA. While this might be good for the organization, what about the sovereignty of the self?

Even more frightening alarms reverberated when someone asked what would happen to the social self if it fell in with the wrong crowd? Pandora's Box was becoming the proverbial can of worms. Social deviance was a growing concern in the 1950s and 1960s, and many began to see the social self as both its victim and cause. What, for example, would become of the social self if a person joined up with, or was born into, a group that was widely treated as misfits, pariahs, or eccentrics? On the other hand, what if a person's significant reference group thought of him as deviant? What if the group reflected self-identifying characteristics that were unflattering?

Various theories of deviant behavior began to surface that directly or indirectly implicated the dark side of the social self. We were told that if a person kept the company of deviants—associated with a gang or criminal subculture, for example—he or she would likely come to identify himself or herself in like manner, becoming one of them in name, if not in fact. If we arrested, tried, or imprisoned an alleged offender, some argued that such a person might take the degrading judgments to heart and come to see himself as the "bad guy" the system labeled him as being. Treat individuals as criminal and they will come to see themselves as criminals, or so the story went. This posed a real conundrum for those interested in reform and rehabilitation.

In retrospect, it's clear that fortune smiled on the social psychology seminar experimenters when they chose to respond to Shirley as if she were intelligent. What if they had treated her as foul-tempered? What if they had acted like she was demented? Wouldn't she have seen herself that way, too? Might they have created a monster in place of a veritable genius?

Of course, these questions are exaggerated, but the literature on self and identity did begin to address negative possibilities. Ralph Ellison (1947) wrote of the "invisible" self of the black man living in a white society in his book *The Invisible Man*. Malcolm X (1965) told of straightening his hair and despising his blackness in response to the reflections gleaned from both black and white Americans. We learned from Robert Rosenthal and Lenore Jacobson's book *Pygmalion in the Classroom* (1968) that school children viewed themselves positively and performed effectively when they were approached with high expectations. Those subjected to low expectations, in contrast, languished. The emerging message was that the social self had a decidedly negative potential, a dark facet that we had ignored as we nourished its promise.

The social self was soon engulfed in high drama, a classic confrontation of good and evil competing for who and what it could become. But before the climax, the nature of the challenge seemed to change. From out of the postmodern avant garde came the accusation that, for better or worse, the struggle over the self was already over—if there had been one in the first place. Some said that contemporary life and its instantaneous electronically mediated images had simply blown the social self away, leaving in its wake only myriad signs of itself swirling about where substantiality once resided. Others said the self hadn't blown away, but was drowning in its myriad relations with others, inundated by the social. Filled to capacity, and then some, by the ever-increasing demands of life in a consumption-oriented, media-driven world, the self was still there, but it was overwhelmed by the legion of voices clamoring for its attention, deluged by endless sources of identity. This was neither good nor bad, necessarily. It was just a multiplicity of social callers that whirled into and around the space the self once seemed to occupy at a more measured pace. The social looking glass was turning into a "wilderness of mirrors" (Hazelrigg 1989).

A New Ending to the Story

Under siege or already defeated, it's clear that the social self has seen better days. What started out so auspiciously, at century's end has become a self so awash in the social that, according to its critics, it is no longer centered in experience. It's of little value to itself or to others. Still, it's hard to deny that this allegedly embattled social entity remains something that we constantly act toward; we speak its interests as we design personal objectives, formulate actions, and achieve goals. It's also an object we continue to act from; it provides motivation and justification for what we say and do. Nearly everything we attempt or accomplish today is done in relation to what kind of selves we are. From preschools and day-care centers to prisons, clinics, and hospices, individual identity is the basis for all manner of choices and decision-making that affect our lives. Cradle to grave, we perennially refer to our selves to make sense of our conduct and experience, and to guide related actions. The self, in other words, is not only something we are, but an object we *actively* construct and live by.

Let's re-examine the status of this self for a moment. The social self, as portrayed in Kinch's cautionary tale, arises from social interaction. Mead tells us that, as a product of social reaction, the self is experienced only indirectly, by way of the responses of members of one's social groups. It is social in every respect, continuously created and recreated in relation to its social reflections. Sheldon Stryker (1980) sums up the argument:

> [T]he human organism as an object takes on meaning through the behavior of those who respond to that organism. We come to know what we are through other's responses to us. . . . The manner in which they act toward us defines our "self," we come to categorize ourselves as they categorize us, and we act in ways appropriate to their expectations. (P. 116)

The social actor is an other-seeking agent, one who directs behavior toward others, whose responses, in turn, provide definitions of who one is. Conduct, therefore, is formulated in relation to a self that is virtually dispensed by the social. This being the case, the problems that beset the social self seem to derive from the rather passive acceptance of whatever the social has to offer. The implicit view is that while the human actor controls his or her own behavior, the self is more or less at the mercy of the social. Accepting whatever comes down the social pike, the self responds to the weight of others' expectations. It is the view of a self that wants desperately to live up to others' sense of who and what it is. More recently, it appears to have been battered into definitional oblivion by the frenzied demands of contemporary life.

It's not a pretty picture, but it's not one we have to concede, either. We intend to propose a new ending for the self's story, offering an alternate vision of a more actively formulated social self. We will describe a self that remains empirically grounded, but that is not so much a socially responsive entity to be filled or saturated with meaning as it is a social construction that we both assemble and live out as we take up or resist the varied demands of everyday life. This is an eminently practical and socially variegated self, artfully and deliberately built up in various shapes and dimensions as a basis for dealing with the circumstances in which it is located. It is a self that is able to both withstand and challenge the many self-formative demands of postmodern times.

As "self-interpreting animals" (Taylor 1989), individuals are subjects as well as objects to themselves. Self-interpretation involves social input, to be sure, but it's also a matter of interpretive practice, of putting forth the effort and engaging in the everyday work of orienting to each other *as selves*. As we thusly construct ourselves, we simultaneously indicate who and what we are to each other. Still, over the course of human history and across cultures, there has been no guarantee that the subject is always formulated in terms of an individualized self (see Carrithers, Collins, and Lukes 1985; Foucault 1977; Lee 1950; Rosen 1995; Shweder and Bourne 1984).

Human beings have activated myriad subjectivities other than individualized selves. We can see this vividly in Tobias Schneebaum's (1969) account of his experiences while living with the Akaramas, a tribe inhabiting the jungles of Peru. Accidentally stumbling upon the tribe, which had never seen a white man, Schneebaum found himself accepted by, then willingly inducted into, the group. Learning their language and culture, he realized that their way of life included no place for "the individual"; the concept was literally foreign, unknown to them. The Akaramas did nothing independently, working, playing, hunting, and eating together in small sets of same-sexed intimates. Indeed, they even slept together, piled into bundles for warmth and comfort, and reportedly engaged in communal acts of cannibalism and homosexuality.

As close and comradely as they were, however, when death claimed members of the tribe, their absence went unmentioned, seemingly unnoticed. Despite his total acceptance into the tribe, when Schneebaum decided to leave the Akaramas, he was convinced that they would not miss him; they wouldn't even notice that he was gone. According to Schneebaum's account, the Akaramas hardly acknowledged separate individuals; each member was fully—and only—a part of the collectivity. The group was the paramount subjectivity; there were no individualized selves to speak of. The self that Schneebaum brought with him into the jungle was socially dissolved as he lived with the tribe, all but obliterating the distinct "me" that Schneebaum had been previously. This ultimately terrified him and, finding it too difficult to practice Akarama subjectivity, he abruptly walked out of the jungle, leaving Akarama life behind as he retrieved his Western sense of individuality.[2]

Strange as this may seem, the individualized empirical self is also a relatively recent phenomenon in Western history. We haven't always looked upon each other in the familiar terms of individual subjectivity, in terms of a self that each and every one of us treats as the logical and emotional center of our life, as socially mutable as that is. Michel Foucault (1977), for example, tells us that it was not until the last few centuries in Western Europe that the subject was constituted as an individual, with its social, legal, and moral dimensions. Before this, "commoners" were largely undifferentiated from the groups and activities in which they participated; they were extensions of "the crown" and members of their occupational or kinship groupings. Bereft of individuality, persons were legally identified as members of other categories or corporate bodies; they lacked what we today might consider distinctive personal identities (see Sheridan 1980). According to Foucault, it was only with changes in juridical orientations and the development of the human sciences, among other things, that we came to envision people as having the sorts of individualized selves we do now.

As we conceptualize contemporary selves, then, we must regard them as a distinctive version of subjectivity. Currently, we actively engage in structuring our lives so they appear individually meaningful, organized, coherent, and responsible (see Garfinkel 1967). This individualized self is the primary, though not the exclusive, subjectivity game in town, so to speak. As practitioners of this form of life, we have distinct personal interests and related behavioral objectives. Of course, all practitioners of subjectivity take others into account, to be sure, but they don't necessarily embrace nor adopt expectations of individuality. Rather, they take others into account to construct socially useful depictions of themselves. Now, more than ever, people are interpretively assembled into individualized selves.

Subjectivity constitutes its own moral agency. By interactionally conjuring up a self, one implicitly provides reasons for why he or she may have acted in a particular fashion or interprets things in a distinctive way. The proffered self provides an account—"a vocabulary of motives" (Mills 1940)—for explaining and justifying conduct (see also Hewitt and Stokes 1975, Scott and Lyman 1968). Such a subject increasingly appears to be a prerequisite for action in our society. Its detailed construction provides grist for a broad range of responses, from formal assessments of its inner states to corrective actions for its distempers and disabilities.

While this subject is clearly social, its production is both artfully agentic and culturally circumscribed. Never the mere reflection of social responses, it is actively crafted in light of biographical particulars, using culturally endorsed formats. While early theorists of the social self alluded to its public sources, they didn't give us much sense of the skilled work that producing a social self entails, nor did they foresee how complex and socially variegated that work would become.

In today's world of proliferating sites and scenes of identity work, the self is increasingly an institutional project, something persons must continually manifest as a basis for making sense of their conduct and relationships. The self remains central to daily life precisely because it is envisioned as the leading agent (and audience) in our everyday social dramas. The social entity that Mead, Cooley, and others invented has become virtually everyone's business; it is widely produced to account for who and what we are, eclipsing those subjectivities—the sovereign, the family, the tribe, the community—that in earlier times were our primary beacons and moral agents. Culturally and institutionally, everyday actors in today's world expect selves to be at the center of their experiential affairs.

As a contemporary cultural and institutional requirement, the self must be skillfully fashioned in socially recognizable terms. But it is not automatically conjured up to meet the demands of the moment, the audience, or the situation. Selves don't simply "pop out" of social interaction. Nor does just anything go. Local understandings circumscribe, even if they don't determine, how these identities are presented. While culture cannot specify the actual working details of the self, it does provide a broad outline for the possibilities.

Now, more than ever, our lives are conducted under organizational auspices, which specify these possibilities. We live in municipalities, work in factories or bureaucracies, come home to families, send our children to school, present our spirituality in a vast array of churches, share our troubles in support groups, and convalesce in nursing homes. Each of these organizations is a "going concern" (Hughes 1984), a social institution with particular ways of doing and framing matters of relevance to participants. They offer distinct senses of who and what we are, were, and can be. As we act and interact within the shadows of these concerns, their working understandings of personal identities supply the interpretive materials and the general instructions for assembling the selves needed to function effectively in the immediate scheme of things. Participants use these codes and materials to forge the selves they must evince to get on with life under the circumstances. It's no wonder, then, that with the immense proliferation of institutional settings, selves are in greater demand than ever.

This demand is one basis for many of the current laments about an embattled self. The purported tensions plaguing contemporary experience derive in part from the belief in a coherent self that is forced to confront society's myriad needs for identity. But if we avoid the image of the self as a social receptacle, there is no reason to believe that it will overflow or become saturated. Nor should it necessarily burst apart under the stress of competing social definitions. Rather, we want to restory the self so as to provide it with opportunities for being diversely constructed. Local understandings help us assemble selves that fit various concerns that condition our lives, but they also present clear and present grounds for resisting them in constructive response to what otherwise befits our purposes. If we set aside the ideal of an integrated self, the multiple self constructions that emerge in various settings become the identity-bearing subjectivities that serve the interpersonal purposes of today's complex social environment.

Redirecting the story of the self in this fashion effectively restores the early pragmatists' sense of the self both as a vital daily enterprise and as a topic for sociological commentary. The object of this book is to apply a vocabulary that makes the self visible as a *project* of everyday life, whose local by-product is more properly articulated in the plural, as "selves." Our point of departure is the social self envisioned early in the twentieth century. From there, we'll trace its movement from its ordinary social conditioning to its current existential dilemmas and crumbling experiential moorings. Part I revisits, then revises, this story of the social self in detail, drawing upon both classic and contemporary commentaries to bolster the account. Appropriating an unlikely blend of theoretical inspiration from ethnomethodology to the genealogical analytics of Michel Foucault, we provide a new ending to the story. In the process, we formulate an alternate way of apprehending and analyzing a self-in-use. We will lay the analytic groundwork for addressing both the social mechanisms and the discursive understandings through which subjectivity is constructed. As we noted at the start, the aim is to restory the social self so as to highlight (and reinforce) its presence in contemporary life.

Part II presents the everyday technology of self construction, the complex social processes by which subjectivity is produced. The self is featured as an artifact of interpretive practice, as something under construction at every turn of social interaction. We also describe the institutional conditioning of the self construction process, elaborating our vision of the circumstances under which the self is assembled, from what resources, and under what auspices. As a result, the contemporary self is shown to be more socially elaborate and institutionally mediated than it was originally conceptualized to be. Finally, in Chapter 10, we conclude with a discussion of the moral climate of the self we live by.

PART 1

Envisioning a
Social Self

The self, as that which can be an object to itself, is essentially a social structure, and it arises in social experience.

—George Herbert Mead, 1934

CHAPTER TWO

Formulating a Social Self

T he story of the social self is a big one, a blockbuster of its genre. Our version begins with the American pragmatists William James, Charles Horton Cooley, and George Herbert Mead, who wrote and taught philosophy and sociology during the late nineteenth and early twentieth centuries.[1] As pragmatists, they oriented to the working features of experience, focusing on the provisional truths and knowledge of everyday life. Andrew Feffer (1993, p. 3) explains that "the pragmatist theory of truth [is] that knowledge is [not universal, but] relative to social behavioral 'situations,' . . . evolving as an instrument in the ongoing process of problem solving." One of the pragmatists' most significant conceptual breakthroughs along these lines came with what James (1961[1892], p. 43) called an "empirical" understanding of the self. By this, he meant that the self should be conceived as an entity whose existence in the world, knowledge of itself, and sense of well-being derived from experience. This use of the term *empirical* is rather different from what it has come to mean for many in the social and behavioral sciences today. While the term is now often associated with particular research methods, privileging measurement, quantification, and statistical analysis, the pragmatists used it to reference experience in general.

The social self the pragmatists envisioned was anything but cosmic, extraordinary, or otherwise transcendental.[2] Bringing it down to earth, so to speak, they situated the self in daily living; one could see and hear it unfolding in the social interactions of ordinary individuals, which stood in marked contrast to a European heritage of philosophical commentary. Terms of reference hearkened the commonplace: I, me, mine, you, them, us, other. Most simply, this was to be the story of the grounded, workaday self, whose plots and characters emerged as much from the persons and situations under consideration as from the authors and philosophers who added to the storyline in their own right. This story begins to unravel at twentieth-century's end when it is eclipsed by another, radically different, even destructive account that replaces the experiencing self with mere images of itself.

In this chapter, we trace the story through key texts, starting with James's, Cooley's, and Mead's classic contributions. Their work provided the impetus for related treatments that developed at mid-century. We emphasize, above all, how the pragmatist contribution to the story served as a basis for rejecting the existing transcendental or philosophical status of the self, offering up in its place a social self derived from, formed by, and changing with everyday life.

17

Turning Away from the Transcendental Self

Perhaps the quintessential image of the transcendental self resides in René Descartes's famous seventeenth-century dictum, "I think, therefore I am." With this pronouncement, Descartes established a *logical* place for the self, which virtually preoccupied Western philosophical commentary for the centuries to come. Whether called the "I" or the "self," Descartes's is the cognitive entity—the cogito—that he claims presents itself through philosophical reflection. As if to argue, "I know I am thinking, therefore the entity that thinks behind my thoughts exists as 'I,' " Descartes locates the self at thought's ostensible origin. The source of his thoughts, in other words, is an entity that is centered where thought begins.

This is a philosophical, not an empirical, exercise in self discovery. Self isn't derived from experience, as the pragmatists would later insist. Nor is it used to comment on the resulting vicissitudes of everyday life. Indeed, as Robert Solomon (1988) points out, this self is existentially thin, certainly not as morally rich and substantial as the entity Descartes's compatriot Jean-Jacques Rousseau discovers decades later strolling through the forests of St. Germain in France: "Self as such, the soul of humanity . . . the self that he shared with all men and women the world over" (p. 1).

Logically thin or morally rich, this self nonetheless transcended ordinary social life. It didn't extend empirically to ordinary working men or women and certainly was far removed from those at the margins of society such as the ostensibly crazed or stigmatized. It was, rather, a philosophical position from which social matters were considered and argued. Whether it was Descartes's Enlightenment cogito, which had decidedly rational leanings, or Rousseau's more romantic counterpart, it was a self placed prior to, or above, "the artifices and superficialities of the social whirl," as Solomon puts it. If Descartes thought and therefore was, the position from which he did so was detached from the swirl of social life. This transcendental self was disembodied, separated, and distinguished from the very corporeal body upon which it otherwise philosophically mused and cast judgment. If anything, social life and the body spoiled the logically envisioned, transcendental self; they certainly didn't participate in inventing or producing it.

While the cogito stood its philosophical ground for years, its experiential fragility is highlighted in a contemporary joke that casts empirical doubt on Descartes's assertion. As the joke goes, Descartes was once invited to a regal English tea party, where he was to be introduced with a flourish as the famous purveyor of "I think, therefore I am." Appreciating the attention, Descartes accepted the invitation, despite his strong distaste for English tea. As the party got under way, an unknowing waiter approached the great philosopher and dutifully asked him if he would like a cup of tea. Haughtily, Descartes responded, "I think not!"—whereupon he vanished into thin air. So much for the disembodied self!

Joking aside, as experientially fragile as this position later proved to be, what Descartes suggested about the self was nonetheless epoch-making, setting the retrospective and prospective terms for centuries of debate. While some, such as

Rousseau, may have romanticized a fuller self, and others, such as Augustine hundreds of years before that, painfully explored inwardness in relation to otherworldliness, it was Descartes who placed a separate and logically distinct self at the center of philosophy. This was a fully reasoned, not other-worldly, fulcrum for ensuing deliberation over the meaning of existence and the moral order (Taylor 1989). As Charles Taylor explains, "the change [effected by Descartes] might be described by saying that Descartes situates the moral sources within us" (p. 143), not somewhere else in the cosmos.

But as Solomon (1988) also points out, the self Descartes logically derived was never purely philosophical; it had ideological bearing. According to Solomon, Descartes spawned a "transcendental pretense." The story of modern continental philosophy, which stems from Descartes's *Meditations*, is not just about specialized problems in metaphysics and epistemology, but is also a dramatic narrative of the European self-image. The transcendental self was an equally compelling fulcrum for a Eurocentric view of the world, one that was at the time being explored, colonized, and hegemonically interpreted. In this narrative, Solomon adds, ". . . science and knowledge play an important role but only alongside the romantic imagination, unprecedented cosmic arrogance, continual reaction and rebellion, and the ultimate collapse of a bloated cosmopolitan self-confidence" (p. 3).

Solomon explains that the leading theme of the narrative was the rise and fall of "an extraordinary concept of the self." It served its adherents and national interests in a variety of ways, not the least of which was to provide a hugely successful logical context for understanding human nature, experience, others, and their relation to the cosmos. Its philosophers assumed that they could change the world, which, indeed, they sometimes succeeded in doing. And, Solomon notes, it was done with an extravagant lack of modesty, one that took for granted that the European scale for weighing reason and the sentiments was also the world's standard. The assumption was that the cogito or philosophically reflecting self not only had knowledge of itself, but, in that knowledge, knew any and all possible selves. What followed from this transcendental pretense was that everyone, everywhere, was principally the same. As Solomon (p. 4) comments,

> The self that becomes the star performer in modern European philosophy is the transcendental self, or transcendental ego, whose nature and ambitions were unprecedentedly arrogant, presumptuously cosmic, and consequently mysterious. The transcendental self was *the* self—timeless, universal, and in each one of us around the globe and throughout history. Distinguished from our individual idiosyncrasies, this was the self we shared. In modest and ordinary terms it was called "human nature." In much less modest, extraordinary terminology, the transcendental self was nothing less than God, the Absolute Self, the World Soul.

Solomon goes on to say:

> The transcendental pretense is no innocent philosophical thesis, but a political weapon of enormous power. Even as it signaled a radical egalitarianism, and suggested a long-awaited global sensitivity, it also justified unrestricted tolerance for paternalism and self-righteousness—"the white philosopher's burden." Philosophers who never left their home town declared themselves experts on "human

nature," and weighed the morals of civilization and "savages" thousands of miles beyond their ken. (P. 6)

The critique suggests what the early pragmatists were up against as they began to formulate the self in more mundane terms. Broadly speaking, they envisioned a contrasting kind of self, one enmeshed in the diverse activities and circumstances of daily life. This self was to mirror the reflexive consciousness of ordinary men and women in the world. While the pragmatists did not ignore the social self's logical relation to nature and the universe, theirs was not some idealized or abstract position from which one contemplated nature, the cosmos, and our place in relation to them. Rather, they were more interested in how selves operate *in* the world, especially how individuals managed their relations with each other as they reflected upon themselves and upon those with whom they interacted.

As the term *pragmatism* implies, adherents turned their attention to the *practice* of everyday life, an important concern of which was the nature of the workaday self. While the social and behavioral sciences now take this for granted, we cannot overemphasize how radical this reaction turned out to be. The pragmatist turnabout did not so much mean being realistic or expedient in consideration of the issues in question, which is a common enough interpretation of the term *pragmatist*. Rather, it meant considering issues in the context of ordinary living, not the transcendental world of traditional philosophical commentary.

While James, Cooley, and Mead often refer to the self in the singular—as the self or Self—its lived presence in the world of everyday life needed to be plural. James (1961[1892], p. 46), for example, called attention to the socially manifold self when he emphatically stated, "Properly speaking, *a man has as many social selves as there are individuals who recognize him* and carry an image of him in their mind" (emphasis in the original). For the pragmatists, references to the self or Self were more a manner of speaking than they were representations of a state of being. In contrast, it was much more likely for the European philosophers to refer to the self or Self in the singular, tellingly signaling that self's transcendental character. James's, Cooley's, and Mead's self was plural because their attention was concertedly empirical, focused as it was on the varied "we's," "us's," and "them's" we are to one another as we go about our daily lives. The social self was always the self-at-hand, the socially operative sense of who we are to ourselves and to others.

James, Cooley, and Mead also had a more politically modest self in mind than did their philosophical forebears. Their formulation coincided with an empirically democratic, some say distinctly American, view that selves belong to all of us and take their shape and import their substance in our everyday relations with each other. It was a decidedly non-European view. Several commentators have suggested that the pragmatists were in the unwitting "business," so to speak, of formulating a version of the self suitable to American bourgeois interests, less centered on imperial, universal reason than on a progressive, democratically dispersed working agency appropriate to the times (see Reynolds 1990). But, as William Skidmore (1975) cautions,

Some say it [pragmatism] was a peculiarly American philosophy because it took a disapproving view of pure abstraction for its own sake and because it put considerable emphasis on action, as opposed to thinking and logic, and in general, the mind. . . . But pragmatism, to its philosophical adherents, did not mean simply "If it works, it's good," as is sometimes said . . . pragmatism was a movement which used the traditional concerns of philosophy as a point of departure from which to defend a somewhat novel way of looking at these problems. (P. 201)

Whether or not the early pragmatists' self was intentionally formulated to resonate with distinctly American interests, their view did establish the grounds for a different approach. The selves that resulted could not be transcendent nor arrogant, simply because they were commonplace. They had no empirical warrant for being anything other than the ordinary subjectivities they were within the whirl of everyday life. According to Norbert Wiley (1994), this whirl was no more evident than in the vibrant and growing metropolitan cities of the time, where the fantastic diversity of immigrants and religious affiliations virtually demanded a conception of the self that could encompass the differences. If existing philosophical formulations were too conceptually distant, the popular psychological understanding of the self as a configuration of traits or "faculties" was also sorely lacking empirically. The pragmatists' social self, in contrast, was up to the challenge of the broad range of experiences.

Lest this sound too triumphant, it's important to remember that the pragmatists' formulation would itself be challenged in due course, both on the home front by commentators on the state of the self in American life (see Chapter 3) and by dissenting European heirs to the transcendental pretense (see Chapter 4). But, for now, let's consider in greater detail the social self in the pragmatists' chapter of the story.

William James's Empirical Self

In their discussion of the development of symbolic interactionism from pragmatist thought, Bernard Meltzer, John Petras, and Larry Reynolds (1975, p. 6) indicate that "a significant advance made by James was the removal of the concept of self from the purely metaphysical realm to the view of at least some aspect of it as derived from interaction processes in the social environment." Commenting on James's ideas, philosopher George Santayana (1957) refers to the European transcendental tradition's "genteel" intrusion into American philosophy, which James argued against because it stood removed from the commonplace experiences of social life. In particular, Santayana applauds the pragmatists' turn away from Hegel's absolute self.[3] In a speech given in 1911 to the Philosophical Union of the University of California, Santayana describes James's effort, emphasizing the value of taking into account the experiences of common men and women.

William James kept his mind and heart wide open to all that might seem, to polite minds, odd, personal, or visionary in religion and philosophy. He gave a sincerely respectful hearing to sentimentalists, mystics, spiritualists, wizards, cranks, quacks, and impostors—for it is hard to draw the line, and James was not willing to draw it prematurely. He thought, with his usual modesty, that any of these might have something to teach him. The lame, the halt, the blind, and those speaking with tongues could come to him with the certainty of finding sympathy. (P. 205)

According to Santayana, James's pragmatism "broke the spell of the genteel tradition," grounding intelligence and the self in the empirical world. Referring to James's views, Santayana writes:

> Intelligence has its roots and its issues in the context of events; it is one kind of practical adjustment, an experimental act, a form of vital tension. It does not essentially serve to picture other parts of reality but to connect them. (P. 206)

James's (1961[1892]) discussion of the empirical self begins simply, not with a philosophical problem, but with the self he and others experience in everyday life—the self of daily awareness that is formed in reflection upon itself. Using personal pronouns, he explains that awareness senses a source—"I"—and an object of awareness—"me"—of whom I am aware. While James's "logic" is reminiscent of Descartes's, it is important to note that its object of reference is intentionally empirical. James puts it this way in his book *Psychology: The Briefer Course* (1961[1892]):

> Whatever I may be thinking of, I am always at the same time more or less aware of *myself*, of my *personal existence*. At the same time it is I who am aware; so that the total self of me, being as it were duplex, partly known and partly knower, partly object and partly subject, must have two aspects discriminated in it, of which for shortness we may call one the *Me* and the other the *I*. I call these "discriminated aspects" and not separate things, because the identity of *I* with *me*, even in the very act of their discrimination, is perhaps the most ineradicable dictum of common-sense, and must not be undermined by a terminology here at the outset, whatever we may come to think of its validity at our inquiry's end. (P. 43, emphasis in the original)

From the start, James sets an "everyday" tone. In his very first sentence, he describes something each of us might well refer to "personally" and, more or less, be aware of. James wants to emphasize the commonplace, "an ineradicable dictum of common-sense." This individual reflexivity—a personal awareness of oneself—is so plain and simple, it seems, that its discussion needn't even be bogged down by a special terminology. As if to say that each and every one of us has and uses the words—words we carry around with us all the time: *I, me,* and *myself* in particular—James hesitates to insinuate himself into his text as an author, a philosopher, or a psychologist with a language of his own. Rather, he suggests that he is merely commenting on what each of us, more or less, already possesses.

The self, according to James, is not to be hastily objectified; it must wait for experience to do its work before it is realized. While we all use personal pronouns to refer to ourselves, and the point of origin of our self awareness (I) can be discriminated from the object of that awareness (me), James warns us that the "ineradicable" identity or unity of *I* with *me* must not be undermined by this terminology. James cautions us that to have words for things, such as the *I* and the *me* of the self, risks reifying them rather than sustaining their referential status as simultaneous facets of the selves we are. James is suggesting that the terms he, and we, use to refer to aspects of ourselves are just that, namely, terms of reference, not separate and distinct experiential objects. When we think ("whatever I may be thinking of"), we can—in mind's discourse—think of ourselves thinking. In that sense, we become objects to ourselves. Similarly, James informs us that when we communicate with others about who we are, we again inadvertently convey both subjectivity and objectivity. That is, we distinguish between the *I* and *me*, even while James admits that, empirically, "between what a man calls *me* and what he simply calls *mine* the line is difficult to draw" (p. 43). This referential entity we call *me* is not clearly distinct from what we and others claim to own, including our bodies and possessions.

Whether James is discussing thought or speech, he is careful to point out that the self and its referential facets are aspects of communication, either the inner practice of self-awareness in thought or the allocations of subjectivity evident in open references to personal characteristics—to you and yours or to me and mine. Self is part and parcel of the process of referring to ourselves, to others, and to the world, however that is accomplished. It doesn't exist separate from, or over and above, communication. James's aspirations for a psychological science, however, do lead him to concentrate on the interior of the communication process. As we will see later, it is George Herbert Mead who concertedly takes the self outside of itself, locating it within what he calls "social behavior." Still, while James develops a psychology, his discussion of the empirical self isn't mentalistic. His focus is always practical, beginning with people in their worlds, surrounded by others, whoever they might be, referring to each other and involved in the concrete affairs of daily living.

James concentrates on the empirical self, which he subdivides into the material me, the social me, and the spiritual me. His discussion of the social me formulates a decidedly social self. Emphasizing its everyday endowments and embodiment, James introduces the empirical self or "me" in the following way:

> We feel and act about certain things that are ours very much as we feel and act about ourselves. Our fame, our children, the work of our hands, may be as dear to us as our bodies are, and arouse the same feelings and the same acts of reprisal if attacked. And our bodies themselves, are they simply ours, or are they *us*? Certainly men have been ready to disown their very bodies and to regard them as mere vestures, or even as prisons of clay from which they should some day be glad to escape. (Pp. 43–44)

It's evident that James doesn't want to sharply distinguish the body and other material markers of who we are from the selves we, and others, consider ourselves to be. Indeed, this very lack of demarcation typifies pragmatist thought. The self is viewed as a working point of reference for ourselves and others that arises and gets designated within the course of embodied interaction. Our bodies and the material aspects of social interaction are important features as well as signs of who we and others are and, as such, feature our identities in practice.

Because the self is plunked down in everyday life, it shifts and is bandied about in the course of social interaction. It is formed locally, not universally. The social self emerges, grows, and is altered, within our daily affairs; it doesn't transcend them. If this self is at all extraordinary, it's extraordinarily mundane. If it has constancy, it is as stable as the patterns and accompanying material signs of our relationships. This returns us to James's comment that *"a man has as many social selves as there are individuals who recognize him* and that carry an image of him in their minds." This social self is not fixed, analytically or philosophically, nor is it finalized to accord with an idealized state of being. Rather, as James puts it, whether "me" or "mine," it is

> . . . fluctuating material; the same object being sometimes treated as a part of me, at other times as simply mine, and then again as if I had nothing to do with it at all. *In its widest possible sense,* however, *a man's Me is the sum total of all that he* CAN *call his,* not only his body and his psychic powers, but his clothes and his house, his wife and children, his ancestors and friends, his reputation and works, his lands and horses, and yacht and bank-account. All these things give him the same emotions. If they wax, and prosper, he feels triumphant; if they dwindle and die away he feels cast down—not necessarily in the same degree for each thing, but in much the same way for all. [I understand] the *Me* in this widest sense. (P. 44, emphasis in the original)

Charles Horton Cooley's Looking-Glass Self

Paralleling James, Cooley devotes two chapters of his book *Human Nature and the Social Order* (1964[1902]) to this empirical or social self. Like James, he begins with the leading personal pronouns. Terms of reference such as "I," "me," "my," and "myself" signal more than points of view; they are the commonplace communicative markers of the experiencing self. In the following extract from the introduction to the first chapter, Cooley almost desperately aims to leave aside ideas of a transcendental self. He clearly wants to locate his concern in the realm of everyday life, in the world of "common speech," set forth as a "self that can be apprehended or verified by ordinary observation," not in terms of what he thereafter refers to as the "abstruseness" of metaphysical discussion.

> It is well to say at the outset that by the word "self" in this discussion is meant simply that which is designated in common speech by the pronouns of the first person singular, "I," "me," "my," "mine," and "myself." "Self" and "ego" are used by metaphysicians and moralists in many other senses, more or less remote from the "I" of daily speech and thought, and with these I wish to have as little to do as possible. What is here discussed is what psychologists call the empirical self, the self that can be apprehended or verified by ordinary observation. I qualify it by the word social not as implying the existence of a self that is not social— for I think that the "I" of common language always has more or less distinct ref-

erence to other people as well as the speaker—but because I wish to emphasize and dwell upon the social aspect of it. (Pp. 168–69)

In one fell swoop, Cooley locates the object of his interest and, following that, designates a procedure for investigating it. The self he wishes to discuss is possessed by each and every one of us. It doesn't belong to metaphysicians or moralists. Yet, because it belongs to everyone, it also would include the object of metaphysicians' and moralists' own ordinary references to themselves.[4] Cooley notes that he's interested in what psychologists refer to as the "empirical self," but he qualifies this, explaining that what he calls the "*social* self" is the same entity, but with an emphasis on "the social aspect of it." Cooley thus formulates an object of study he believes to be natural and distinct from philosophy's counterpart transcendental entity, but which clearly registers a reality shared with psychology.

Cooley goes on to indicate that his way of viewing the self will not be philosophical. He throws his lot in with the scientific method, in particular, with what "can be apprehended or verified by ordinary observation." While Cooley's subsequent development of introspection is scientifically suspect, he nonetheless intends to proceed empirically, in relation to concrete experiences. His systematic observations of his two children's self-references at play are exemplary. Together with other observations, this serves as evidence for his claims and hypotheses. Consider how "factual" and perhaps somewhat snide Cooley is about this in the following extract:

> Although the topic of the self is regarded as an abstruse one, this abstruseness belongs chiefly, perhaps, to the metaphysical discussion of the "pure ego"—whatever that may be—while the empirical self should not be very much more difficult to get hold of than other facts of the mind. At any rate, it may be assumed that the pronouns of that first person have a substantial, important, and not very recondite meaning, otherwise they would not be in constant and intelligible use by simple people and young children the world over. And since they have such a meaning why should it not be observed and reflected upon like any other matter of fact? (P. 169)

Dismissing metaphysical and moral offerings, Cooley declares that the core of the empirical self is self-feeling, not philosophical categories. Self-feeling, of course, implicates the body. While originary self-feeling is hardly the social self envisioned as developing out of group relations, the body is the grounds of everyday self-awareness and self-control, according to Cooley. Appealing to James and Hiram Stanley, Cooley puts this directly:

> The distinctive thing in the idea for which the pronouns of the first person are names is apparently a characteristic kind of feeling which may be called the my-feeling or sense of appropriation. Almost any sort of ideas may be associated with this feeling, and so come to be named "I" or "mine," but the feeling and that alone it would seem, is the determining factor in the matter. As Professor James says in his admirable discussion of the self, the words "me" and "self" designate "all the things which have the power to produce in a stream of consciousness excitement of a certain peculiar sort." This view is very fully set forth by Professor Hi-

ram M. Stanley, whose work, "The Evolutionary Psychology of Feeling," has an extremely suggestive chapter on self-feeling. (Pp. 169–70)

Reflecting pragmatists' Darwinian heritage, Cooley then explains:

The emotion or feeling of self may be regarded as instinctive, and has doubtless evolved in connection with its important function in stimulating and unifying the special activities of individuals. It is thus very profoundly rooted in the history of the human race and apparently indispensable to any plan of life at all similar to ours. It seems to exist in a vague though vigorous form at the birth of each individual, and, like other instinctive ideas or germs of ideas, to be defined and developed by experience, becoming associated, or rather incorporated, with muscular, visual, and other sensations; with perceptions, apperceptions, and conceptions of every degree of complexity and of infinite variety of content; and, especially, with personal ideas. Meantime the feeling itself does not remain unaltered, but undergoes differentiation and refinement just as does any other sort of crude innate feeling. (Pp. 170–71)

To Cooley, crude feelings of self are instinctive, but are also shaped and transformed with our experience in the world. The self is embodied and visceral from the start, part of our natural human endowment. But it isn't immutable; original self-feeling is built up into innumerable self sentiments. With experience, self-feeling forms into the social self, with all the nuances and variety that experience can muster. The empirical self adds meaning, direction, and control to self-feeling. What is original for us as human beings, then, are the visceral sensations of our individuality, according to Cooley, and this provides the bodily underpinnings for stimulating our activities as social entities.

These are pretty solid empirical groundings, distinctly different from those offered by transcendental philosophy. How does Cooley convince us that this is a compelling source of the self, one that rivals the offerings of metaphysicians and moralists? For this, he turns to matters that would ostensibly be evident to anyone who cared to think about them. While Cooley indicates the empirical self by pointing to the common pronouns we use to refer to ourselves, he also asserts that there "can be no final test of the self except the way we feel; the self is that toward which we have a 'my' attitude." Cooley claims that "a formal definition of self-feeling, or indeed of any sort of feeling, must be as hollow as a formal definition of the taste of salt, or the color red; we can expect to know what it is only by experiencing it," again implicating the body (p. 172). The empirical self, Cooley argues, is most evident in the various actions we take, in response to events or conduct that cast aspersions on self-feeling, revealing the "my" attitude. Cooley puts this plainly:

But as this feeling is quite as familiar to us and as easy to recall as the taste of salt or the color red, there should be no difficulty in understanding what is meant by it. One need only imagine some attack on his "me," say ridicule of his dress or an attempt to take away his property or his child, or his good name by slander, and self-feeling immediately appears. Indeed, we need only pronounce, with strong emphasis, one of the self-words, like "I" or "my," and self-feeling will be recalled by association. (Pp. 172–73)

Whether or not we agree, Cooley is nonetheless presenting a story of the self that contrasts materially with those he "wishes to have as little to do [with] as possible." If he were inclined to make a related point about how to study the self, he would say that we must turn to metaphysicians and moralists' actual objects of concern, not the concern in its own right, in order to understand the selves we are. To emphasize this, Cooley recalls several literary examples of self-assertion, implicating both experience and self-feeling, which again prods his philosophical nemesis. This is followed by yet another illustration from everyday life to make his point:

> We all have thoughts of the same sort as these, and yet it is possible to talk so coldly or mystically about the self that one begins to forget that there is, really, any such thing.
> But, perhaps the best way to realize the naive meaning of "I" is to listen to the talk of children playing together, especially if they do not agree very well. They use the first person with none of the conventional self-repression of their elders, but with much emphasis and variety of inflection, so that its emotional animus is unmistakable. (P. 174)

In a much quoted passage, Cooley suggests that the self, while rooted in self-feeling, nonetheless operates in the imagination, drawing from, reflecting upon, and responding to real and imagined others. This forms Cooley's well-known "looking-glass self," which has three principal components: "The imagination of our appearance to the other person; the imagination of his judgment of that appearance, and some sort of self-feeling, such as pride or mortification" (p. 184). It is responsive not simply to itself, and certainly not to some transcendental category of meaning or morality, but to how it imagines itself from the standpoint of another. Here again, we glimpse the penetrating richness of Cooley's self, an entity that draws both from what it makes of itself from the point of view of the other and from the resulting self-feeling.

George Herbert Mead's Interacting Self

The self becomes less instinctive and more socially interactive when Mead takes up the narrative. With telling reference to both James and Cooley, Mead (1934, p. 173) discusses the place of cognition, feeling, and interaction in the formation of the self. He begins by noting that "emphasis should be laid on the central position of thinking." Self-consciousness, rather than feelings, "provides the core and primary structure of the self," according to Mead. But, most importantly, self-consciousness is the inner representation of what is otherwise an *external conversation* of significant gestures. Mead avoids a strict line of demarcation between inner life and social interaction; in his view, they are both forms of communication. Thinking is an inner conversation with oneself; social interaction is an external conversation with others. Both are socially symbolic and reflexively interactive. The empirical self is neither more nor less a part of internal or external life. Rather, it is an integral part of a working subjectivity, wherever that is experientially located.

Mead disagrees with James and Cooley's emphasis on self-feeling, because a focus on self-feeling viscerally essentializes the self, leaving it only secondarily social.

> The thinking or intellectual process—the internalization and inner dramatization, by the individual, of the external conversation of significant gestures which constitutes his chief mode of interaction with other individuals belonging to the same society—is the earliest experiential phase in the genesis and development of the self. (P. 173)

He then explains:

> Cooley and James, it is true, endeavor to find the basis of the self in reflexive affective experiences, i.e., experiences involving "self-feeling"; but the theory that the nature of the self is to be found in such experiences does not account for the origin of the self, or of the self-feeling which is supposed to characterize such experiences. The individual need not take the attitudes of others toward himself in these experiences, since these experiences merely in themselves do not necessitate his doing so, and unless he does so, he cannot develop a self; and he will not do so in these experiences unless his self has already originated otherwise, namely, in the way we have been describing. The essence of the self, as we have said, is cognitive: it lies in the internalized conversation of gestures which constitutes thinking, or in terms of which thought or reflection proceeds. And hence the origin and foundations of the self, like those of thinking, are social. (P. 173)

Mead turns skeptically to Cooley's looking-glass self, which Cooley claims to operate in the imagination. Mead's concern here is that—contrary to the title of Cooley's book—Cooley's project is more about an oddly unsocial human nature than it is about social order. Contrasting biological and social origins, Mead comments on the "advantage" of a more clearly social perspective. According to Mead, his own social approach, which locates self in ongoing social interaction,

> enables us to give a detailed account and actually to explain the genesis and development of mind; whereas the view that mind is a congenital biological endowment of the individual organism does not really enable us to explain its nature and origin at all: neither what sort of biological endowment it is, nor how organisms at a certain level of evolutionary progress come to possess it. (P. 224)

In a footnote, Mead succinctly discusses Cooley's looking-glass self. It's evident here that Mead is still astutely the philosopher, yet one who espouses a distinctly nontranscendental view. He focuses on Cooley's implicit solipsism, accusing Cooley of placing social interaction within the imagination of the individual, rather than the reverse. Mead pulls no punches.

> According to the traditional assumption of psychology, the content of experience is entirely individual and not in any measure to be primarily accounted for in social terms, even though its setting or context is a social one. And for a social psychology like Cooley's—which is founded on precisely this same assumption—all social interactions depend upon the imaginations of the individuals involved, and take place in terms of their direct conscious influences upon one another in the processes of social experience. Cooley's social psychology, as found in his *Human*

Nature and the Social Order, is hence inevitably introspective, and his psychological method carries with it the implication of complete solipsism: society really has
no existence except in the individual's mind, and the concept of the self as in any
sense intrinsically social is a product of imagination. Even for Cooley the self presupposes experience, and experience is a process within which selves arise; but
since that process is for him primarily internal and individual rather than external and social, he is committed in his psychology to a subjectivistic and idealis-
tic, rather than an objectivistic and naturalistic, metaphysical position. (P. 224)

Interestingly, Mead's terminology for the empirical self is the same as James's
and Cooley's, even while it is decidedly more interactional. Before Mead discusses
the "I" and the "me," he considers the social foundation of the self, again toeing
the line between the philosopher and the empiricist. From the start, he locates the
self's foundation in language. For Mead, the self is *part* of the process of communication. It doesn't exist before it, nor does it develop and come to be expressed
through it. These would categorically separate the self from the social, from language and communication. Instead, Mead begins by locating the self *within* communicative action. Self is that part of communicative action that reflects on itself,
either in the course of the inner conversation called thinking or as an openly reflexive product of social interaction.

Mead goes on to distinguish the self from the mere body.

The self has a character which is different from that of the physiological organism proper. The self is something which has a development; it is not initially there,
at birth, but arises in the process of social experience and activity, that is, develops in the given individual as a result of his relations to that process as a whole
and to other individuals within that process. (P. 135)

Then he differentiates the self as an object from other objects of experience.

It is the characteristic of the self as an object to itself that I want to bring out. This
characteristic is represented in the word "self," which is a reflexive, and indicates
that which can be both subject and object. This type of object is essentially different from other objects, and in the past it has been distinguished as conscious,
a term which indicates an experience with, an experience of, one's self. It was assumed that consciousness in some way carried this capacity of being an object to
itself. In giving a behavioristic statement of consciousness we have to look for
some sort of experience in which the physical organism can become an object to
itself. (Pp. 136–37)

Mead seems to be saying that in a Cartesian framework ("in the past"), consciousness in its own right was taken to constitute the self. In contrast, he argues
that consciousness per se cannot be the self's own object without substantive experiences to reflect upon, and from which we indicate to itself who it is. Experience provides the means and the meanings through which one becomes conscious
of what one is. Consciousness, in effect, is always consciousness *of something*, including consciousness of oneself as meaningfully something (some thing) or another.

In practice, the answer to the question of who we are to ourselves requires
that we first behave in the world. The "I" who eventually tells itself or others

"that's me," needs the communicative resources of experience to make this designation. The very "I" that is presumed to do so, itself only exists in reflexive relation to the "me" it indicates and specifies in the course of social interaction. Both "I" and "me" must wait, as it were, for the activity of everyday life to unfold in order to exist empirically. Mead's interacting self is in this sense an integral part of society; indeed, it can't be imagined, even described, without the meanings drawn from experience. To attempt to imagine or describe a self separate from experience would be tantamount to communicating without meaning. Such a self would be literally meaning-less, unrecognizable and nonexistent.

Because the self is "essentially a social structure" (p. 140) that arises in social interaction, it is an "object" that is dynamic, elastic, and manifold. If the self has unity, it is a unity derived from patterns of experience with others. Mead provides examples from everyday life.

> We realize in everyday conduct and experience that an individual does not mean a great deal of what he is doing and saying. We frequently say that such an individual is not himself. We come away from an interview with a realization that we have left out important things, that there are parts of the self that did not get into what was said. What determines the amount of the self that gets into communication is the social experience itself. Of course, a good deal of the self does not need to get expression. We carry on a whole series of different relationships to different people. We are one thing to one man and another thing to another. There are parts of the self which exist only for the self in relationship to itself. We divide ourselves up in all sorts of different selves with reference to our acquaintances. We discuss politics with one and religion with another. There are all sorts of different selves answering to all sorts of different social reactions. It is the social process itself that is responsible for the appearance of the self; it is not there as a self apart from this type of experience. (P. 142)

In this context, Mead then speaks of the normality of a multiple personality: if we think of the self as an integral part of social relations, it is reasonable to consider its separate personas. As Mead reminds us, "We are one thing to one man and another thing for another." In the course of everyday life, we become—separately and distinctly—the varied selves that we present in relation to whomever regularly participates in our affairs. The regularities of home, say, or the work place, provide contexts for the production and reproduction of particular selves. The indulgent and affectionate father of home life can normally reside alongside the strait-laced martinet who commands the office. Being a social structure, self is formulated in relation to the very conditions it responds to and, in this regard, it normally divides into different selves.

How does this manifold self develop out of social experience in the first place? Mead views the formation of the social self in relation to play and organized games. He describes the play of children with imaginary others to make his point. In the early stage of self development, Mead argues, children literally practice selves as they actively play out who and what they are with imaginary others, taking roles such as mother, father, teacher, and policeman. Mead refers to this as a kind of "doubling," in which one both plays a role and responds to it. We can actually hear doubling in operation as the child now plays the mother and then responds as a child to what transpired in the role of mother. The child, in effect, rehearses a pair of social structures—a set of roles and selves—and in the process learns how to "do" the mother-child dyad, in effect, doing interacting identities. In familiar phrasing, Mead refers to stimuli that "call out" such socially meaningful responses.

> In the play period the child utilizes his own responses to these stimuli which he makes use of in building a self. The response which he has a tendency to make to these stimuli organizes them. He plays that he is, for instance, offering himself something, and he buys it; he gives a letter to himself and takes it away; he addresses himself as a parent, as a teacher; he arrests himself as a policeman. He has a set of stimuli which call out in himself the sort of responses they call out in others. He takes this group of responses and organizes them into a certain whole. Such is the simplest form of being another to one's self. . . . A certain organized structure arises in him and in his other which replies to it, and these carry on the conversation of gestures between themselves. (Pp. 150–51)

His reference to "a certain organized structure" leads Mead directly to the games in which we experience and articulate varied selves at a later stage. He is referring to a socially shared kind of game plan, which can be played out once it is identified. Mead argues that whether it is playing cops-and-robbers or playing dolls, the organized structures of such games form particular selves. In turn, such game-activated selves reflexively direct and manage their related social actions. Once we learn the game, our selves and related actions are structured to elicit certain performances and not others, making us distinctly accountable to ourselves and each other. A child who knows the game can play its various roles, thus coordinating his or her actions in relation to other players. Mead contrasts simple play with what develops from playing games:

> In that early stage he passes from one role to another just as a whim takes him. But in a game where a number of individuals are involved, then the child taking one role must be ready to take the role of everyone else. . . . In the game, then, there is a set of responses of such others so organized that the attitude of one calls out the appropriate attitudes in the other. (P. 151)
>
> The fundamental difference between the game and play is that in the [former] the child must have the attitude of all the others involved in that game. . . . We get then an "other" which is an organization of the attitudes of those involved in the same process. The organized community or social group which gives to the individual his unity of self may be called "the generalized other." (Pp. 153–54)

Thus Mead leads us to a fully social self. While Mead isn't clear about just how gamelike the self is in practice, the term *game* is there, connoting selves that are collectively, not individually, structured. Together with the idea of the generalized other, Mead gives us an empirical self that is reflexively conscious of the working organization of roles that constitute it as a social structure.[5]

Symbolic Interactionist Contributions

Following the early pragmatists' formulations, the story of the social self we are recounting becomes increasingly sociological. In the 1930s and 1940s, Herbert Blumer (1969), one of Mead's students at the University of Chicago, began to organize Mead's notions about mind, self, and society into a distinct perspective that he almost casually labeled "symbolic interactionism" (Blumer 1969, p. 1). In time, the label itself contributed immensely to the unfolding storyline. Just as the term *pragmatism* both reflected and, in turn, conceptually secured a body of American philosophical thought around James, Cooley, Mead, and others, *symbolic interactionism* became a rubric for disciplinary identity within sociology. As the label gained currency, it became the hallmark of a particular set of ideas about human nature and social order and, especially, about the relationship of the individual to society. As Stephen and Jonathan Turner (1990, p. 169) note, symbolic interactionism became "a vocabulary that could be used to give quick, novel descriptions of [such] familiar material in a manner beyond common sense."

Symbolic interactionism orients to the principle that individuals respond to the meanings they construct as they interact with one another. Individuals are active agents in their social worlds, influenced, to be sure, by culture and social organization, but also instrumental in producing the culture, society, and meaningful conduct that influences them (Hewitt 1997, 1998; Lindesmith, Strauss, and Denzin 1988; Manis and Meltzer 1967; Rose 1962; Stone and Farberman 1970; Stryker 1980). The self is never far behind in this scheme of things. It is the agent that serves as the reflexive beacon of social interaction, not existing separate from, or otherwise transcending, social life.

The focus on the social self in an increasingly scientized environment inexorably led to the question of whether the self could be studied by methods of social science research. If the early pragmatists concentrated on formulating the *idea* of a social self, symbolic interactionists became as interested in systematically documenting its empirical manifestations. Over the years, two streams of symbolic interactionist thinking—the so-called Chicago and Iowa schools—took this in different directions.[6] Blumer (1969), who taught at the University of Chicago, became the central figure of the more process-oriented Chicago school, while Manford Kuhn (1960, 1964) and his associates (Couch 1962; Kuhn and McPartland 1954; McPartland and Cumming 1958; McPartland, Cumming, and Garretson 1961; Mulford and Salisbury 1964; Vernon 1962) at the University of Iowa were the leading proponents of the more structured Iowa school (see Denzin 1970 and Joas 1987). Their respective methodological emphases on firsthand qualitative observation versus quantitative measurement served to define the scientific meaning of the social self to both followers and outsiders for years to come (see Fine 1995).

Blumer (1969) summarizes his methodological position in what he refers to as "three simple premises" (p. 2), belying their complexity. While the premises are meant to convey his view of symbolic interaction in general, by extension they would also apply to the construction of the self. The first premise is "that human beings act toward things on the basis of the meanings that the things have for them" (p. 2). Blumer explains that whatever those things are—physical objects, other human beings, social roles, activities, or situations—it is not the things in their own right that mediate human beings' actions, but what they mean for them. If symbolic interactionists emphasize the "meanings" component of the premise, it is important to note that the meanings at stake are human beings' *own* meanings. It's not some independent or transcendent source of meaning that effects action, but what ordinary human beings themselves, in the course of social interaction, consider meaningful. Again, we can take this as applying with equal significance to the meanings attached to the self.

Blumer's second premise is that "the meaning of such things is derived from, or arises out of, the social interaction that one has with one's fellows" (p. 2). This draws from Mead's view that the social self is an integral part of social interaction, not an entity which stands separately from it. The self, as Mead puts it, is a social structure. The premise has methodological implications, suggesting that to know and document the shape and content of the self, one must observe the self in action. Secondary reports will not do. Nor will idealized or socially distant representations. If we are to study lives, including selves in social interaction, we must study them from *within* the social contexts they unfold, not separate from them. Blumer instructs his reader to study what is natural to the self, to view it and document its place within the actual process of social interaction.

Blumer's third premise is that "meanings are handled in, and modified through, an interpretive process used by the person in dealing with the things he encounters." This is cautionary. While Blumer directs us to human beings' own meanings and to the everyday interaction within which meanings arise, he also warns us not to take those meanings for granted. Human beings don't settle their affairs with meaning once and for all. Rather, they continually engage the interpretive process, including the interpretation of what they mean to themselves.

The caution is explicitly directed at those symbolic interactionists who, while they would accept the first two premises, are remiss on the third, employing highly structured methods that don't permit the interpretive process to continually show through.[7] Blumer urges us to view the human being in social interaction as incessantly involved in meaning-making. The methodological directive here is to document the articulation and emergence of meaning in rich detail as it unfolds, not in lifeless analytic categories and statistical tables. Blumer explains:

> The actor selects, checks, suspends, regroups, and transforms the meanings in the light of the situation in which he is placed and the direction of his action. Accordingly, interpretation should not be regarded as a mere automatic application of established meanings but as a formative process in which meanings are used and revised as [indigenous] instruments for the guidance and formation of action. (P. 5)

In other words, symbolic interactionists should describe how people form and revise what is meaningful to them, which we assume would include meanings that define the self.

Adherents of the Iowa school developed a more structured approach. While Blumer and those who followed in his footsteps emphasized naturalistic inquiry,

Kuhn and his Iowa school associates were concerned with measurement. Certainly, for them, as for all symbolic interactionists, the self was a social entity par excellence. But Kuhn and his associates also believed they needed to precisely pin down the meanings of the self before moving on to consider its relationship to other aspects of social life.

In a seminal paper, Kuhn and McPartland (1954) argue that, while the self has been a key concept in the symbolic interactionist approach to social psychology, "little, if anything, has been done to employ it directly in empirical research." Here, the term *empirical* veers away from having an experiential connotation and, instead, takes on a distinctly quantitative tone. From Kuhn and McPartland's discussion, it's clear that the emphasis is on the self as a meaningful object, not on the self as interactively meaningful. The aim is to designate concisely what each specific self under consideration is to itself, a goal that works against Blumer's third premise. This leads directly to the formulation of a method to assess self-attitudes, as Kuhn and McPartland explain.

> If, as we suppose, human behavior is *organized* and *directed*, and if, as we further suppose, the organization and direction are supplied by the individual's *attitudes toward himself*, it ought to be of crucial significance to social psychology to be able to identify and measure self-attitudes. (P. 68, emphasis in the original)

The emphasis on the words *organized*, *directed*, and *attitudes toward himself* is conceptually and procedurally telling. The terms are part of the vocabulary of a more standardized and ostensibly "scientific" approach to the social self than Blumer could abide. Kuhn and McPartland refer to human behavior as organized and directed, implying causation. Human behavior does not just simply form, develop, and respond to itself, but is organized and directed *by something*. Inasmuch as "the organization and direction are supplied by the individual's *attitudes toward himself*," self-attitudes can be viewed as causal agents. In other words, one's behavior will vary according to one's self-attitudes. From here, it is a short step to arguing that other aspects of human behavior also provide organization and direction, affecting self-attitudes in their own right. The working vocabulary stands in opposition to Blumer's language, which comprises terms such as *act*, *meaning*, *interpretation*, and *process*. The latter are part of a language stressing descriptive intelligibility and understanding, which eschews the logic of causation. Virtually specifying alternate empirical horizons and related research procedures, the respective vocabularies could not help but contribute to the development of opposing "schools" of the social self.

In perhaps its most significant methodological invention, the Iowa group developed the Twenty Statements Test (TST). As Kuhn and McPartland (1954) reasoned, "The obvious first step in the application of self-theory to empirical research is the construction and standardization of a test which will identify and measure self-attitudes" (p. 68). Reflecting the post-World War II trend toward quantification in the social and behavioral sciences, the term *empirical* also was being appropriated for the increasingly popular preference for "hard" scientific procedure. It was taken for granted that the Twenty Statements Test would indeed serve to "[do something] to employ [the self] directly in empirical research."

Described in numerous articles, and employed in countless research projects, the TST consists of a single sheet of paper, with twenty numbered spaces, directing respondents to do the following:

> There are twenty numbered blanks on the page below. Please write twenty answers to the simple question "Who am I" in the blanks. Just give twenty different answers to this question. Answer as if you were giving the answers to yourself, not to somebody else. Write the answers in the order that they occur to you. Don't worry about logic or "importance." Go along fairly fast, for time is limited. (Kuhn and McPartland 1954, p. 69)

Over the years, the exact wording of the TST varied somewhat, mainly becoming less specific in its instructions, but the format remained much the same.

Some researchers focused on the alleged causes of the resulting self-attitudes, hypothesizing that independent variables such as class, educational background, and age "organized and directed" self-attitudes (see, for example, Kuhn 1960 and McPartland and Cumming 1958). Others examined the behavioral consequences of particular attitudes, hypothesizing that self-attitudes "organize and direct" conduct (see, for instance, McPartland, Cumming, and Garretson 1961 and Waisanen 1962). In hindsight, it's amazing what a single research instrument produced in the context of times that stressed the scientifically rigorous study of social life (see Kuhn 1964). Perhaps as much as any research development, the TST objectified and concretized the formulation of the social self. It showed just how far adherents could turn away from the transcendental self and what could be scientifically accomplished in the name of the "empirical."

Erving Goffman's Socially Situated Self

If symbolic interactionists document the condition of the self in social interaction, it is Erving Goffman (1959) who takes the self full-tilt into the situations of everyday life. Goffman's self takes on meaning in interpersonal relations and, in that sense, Goffman agrees with symbolic interactionists. But he is also deeply concerned with the situated contingencies and rituals of interaction. As Goffman puts it, "[the] self itself does not derive from its possessor, but from the whole scene of his action" (p. 252).

Goffman would not object to Blumer's three methodological premises as they apply to the self, but he adds his own twist to the story by way of a theatrical language composed of terms such as *scenes, scripts, front stage, back stage,* and *performances.*[8] The language highlights the "dramaturgic" or scenic features of the social self, suggesting that self and social interaction are more patterned than Blumer's premises would give them credit for being. In Goffman's view, the self is not just social in that it develops from and responds to others in the course of daily living. Circumstances being what they are, actors take account of the setting where, and occasion when, self formation occurs. For Goffman, there is always more at stake for the self than ongoing social interaction; there's an "interaction order" (1967). Traditional terms of reference such as "I," "other," and "role" provide an important analytic initiative, but these are not situated enough to take account of localized contingencies such as who, in particular, might be cooperating with the actor in question to define the self. For example, one would think that it might make a great deal of difference if those cooperating were a loosely organized as opposed to a well-coordinated team, or whether they were responsible for appreciating or degrading the actor in question. If negative purposes have negative implications for self-attitudes and coordination makes a difference, then a disciplined team effort could very well be, say, situationally devastating (see Goffman 1961).

It's important to point out that while Goffman stresses the situated contingencies of social interaction, he does not lose sight of the working self. Like the early pragmatists, Goffman preserves a self formulated as both "I" and "me," performatively placed in the world of everyday life. If the interaction order is center stage, the self that is articulated in the varied scripts of social life nonetheless has room for improvisation. The self is not just a role player, a mere puppet of its staging, but works with others at its dramatic realization.

Goffman's self is dramaturgic in two senses of the term. First, it *presents* itself to others. It is actively engaged in its dramatic performances, mustering what it is capable of presenting in light of the social scripts of various occasions. Its engagement is moral in the sense that it commits itself, or is committed to, the ongoing interaction order of the varied scenes within which experience unfolds, and its performance is evaluated in those terms. As such, the selves presented are not simply given, but are "given off," as Goffman puts it, further revealing the effort that is put into its accountable production. Goffman introduces his approach this way in *The Presentation of Self in Everyday Life* (1959):

> The perspective employed in this report is that of the theatrical performance; the principles derived are dramaturgical ones. I shall consider the way in which the individual in ordinary work situations presents himself and his activity to others, the ways in which he guides and controls the impression they form of him, and the kinds of things he may and may not do while sustaining his performance before them. (P. xi)

The self is also dramaturgic in that it is *staged* to accomplish particular moral ends. It manages and successfully performs both small and large everyday dramas, whether they are as simple as a greeting on the street or as complex as international diplomacy. The self not only works to dramatically realize itself, but simultaneously engages in particular performances, which to some extent have a life of their own. Just as a theatrical performance has roles, a play, and the stage upon which actors develop their roles, everyday life more or less realizes its own moral scripts.

While the differences between the theater and real life should not be overlooked, for Goffman their similarities are vast.

> I assume that when an individual appears before others he will have many motives for trying to control the impression they receive of the situation. This report is concerned with some of the common techniques that persons employ to sustain such impressions and with some of the contingencies associated with the em-

ployment of these techniques. The specific content of any activity presented by the individual participant, or the role it plays in the interdependent activities of an on-going social system, will not be at issue; I shall be concerned only with the participant's dramaturgical problems of presenting the activity before others. The issues dealt with by stagecraft and stage management are sometimes trivial but they are quite general; they seem to occur everywhere in social life, providing a clear-cut dimension for formal sociological analysis. (P. 15)

In many respects, Goffman fleshes out the project that the early pragmatists began. The self, in his chapter of the story, is not only social and empirical, but circumstantially realized. It is a locally interactive beacon of experience and it takes shape within, not separate from, the various situations of everyday life. Time and again, Goffman reveals that each and every one of us has many selves, pertinent to the purposes of daily living, always part of, yet also reflexively separate from, the moral orders we share with others.

CHAPTER THREE

The Dark Side

I f the tale of the social self began on a progressive note, this was not destined to be the whole story. Tough times lay ahead. Adversity would not necessarily spring from a frontal assault, nor even by way of hostile ambush. More insidiously, the foreboding challenge was a product of the self's own sociability. The troubles that the self would experience emerged from encounters with the "dark side" of the social, the forbidding facets of its own emergence. These confrontations stemmed from the very same social processes that initially gave the self its hopeful prospects. As the self plunged into the social, eagerly seeking out who it was, it lost its earlier bearings, virtually foundering in a sea of social demands and reflections. Even worse, it sometimes fell in with the "wrong crowd." Indeed, what would result when negative input was society-wide? The social self, we've noted, could be a Pandora's Box of tribulations.

As we trace this part of the story, we turn once again to exemplary texts. Of course our choice of texts shapes the emerging narrative, but we think the selections reflect major trends in scholarly commentary on the self that also garnered popular currency. Following World War II, the dark side initially shadowed the American character, but also portended the organizational entities we were becoming. The rampant commercialization of feelings was not far behind with the managed self in tow. We also follow the social self into the seamy side of life by way of a literature on deviance that for decades captivated both sociologists and the public at large.

The Conforming Self

The postwar years saw sociology flourish as a discipline. From Talcott Parsons's theoretical edifices and Robert Merton's middle-range approach, to the myriad empirical studies emanating from increasingly productive research departments in the major universities, American social life was awash in sociological commentary. Perhaps the most important and enduringly insightful self book of the postwar decade was David Riesman's (1950) *The Lonely Crowd: A Study of the Changing American Character*. Read by social scientists, a staple assignment in a wide range of sociology courses, and one of the very few sociological texts of its time to be broadly appreciated outside academia, the work is so perceptive that when it is read at the start of the twenty-first century, much of it rings as true as the day it was written.

The Lonely Crowd is ostensibly concerned with what its author calls "national character types," but Riesman's arguments range boldly across topics such as social and historical change, politics, personality, morality, self, self-image, self-awareness, and autonomy. His primary thesis is that as societies change from a state of incipient population growth to incipient decline, social conditions give rise to important changes in predominant character types, changes in the selves that inhabit, if not dominate, the social scene. Riesman argues that as modernization, industrialization, and urbanization began to flourish, so did the "inner-directed" character type. Later, as these conditions became thoroughly ensconced, and the economy shifted from an emphasis on production to a consumption orientation, the "other-directed" man (and presumably, woman) began to proliferate.

While Riesman repeatedly assures his readers that he is not advocating inner-directedness over other-directedness, or that one is more "autonomous" than the other (see Bellah et al. 1996 [1985]), the comparison is sometimes unavoidably invidious. The mere cultural connotations of "independent citizen" and "conformist" are evaluatively charged in the American context, encouraging a reading that frames "inner direction" as morally superior to "other direction." Riesman's text repeatedly asserts, if only implicitly or in textual manner and tone, that the other-directed character type is somehow less admirable than its American predecessor.

This account is exemplary for its compelling arguments, empirical warrant, and unparalleled foresight. Riesman did not set out to explicitly critique the social self; the term *self*, for example, does not appear in the index of *The Lonely Crowd*. Still, the self is deeply implicated in his discussion of character and identity. For Riesman, the self is decidedly social, very much like the self that Mead envisioned. "Man," he writes, "is made by society" (p. 3). Still, Riesman (1968) also contends that the self is not entirely the product of social interactions; there is a hereditary element as well. Experience "begins at birth with a specific genetic endowment which in turn evokes differential responses from other people" (p. 446). Like James and Cooley, Riesman resists the vision of a self merely "refracting the expectations of others in what can become an endless circularity" (p. 447). While the self that inhabits *The Lonely Crowd* does its share of "refracting," to be sure, there is considerable variability in how much of the self is mere refraction, how much can be self-directed, and even in how successful one might be at adequately refracting desired images. As Riesman points out, one can fail at reflecting a desired image just as well as one can succeed (p. 447).

Riesman (1950) is explicitly interested in character structure—the American self, as it were—especially the character patterns that dominate society at a particular time in history. He defines *character* as "the more or less permanent, socially and historically conditioned organization of an individual's drives and satisfactions" (p. 4). The term is intended to be less comprehensive than *personality* or *total self*, which he takes to include inherited temperaments, talents, and biological and psychological components, as well as more social components that may be either permanent or evanescent. In his view, character represents those social aspects of personality that are learned in the lifelong process of socialization.

Riesman goes on to stress facets of character "that are shared among significant social groups" (p. 4). Drawing upon several writers from the psychoanalytic tradition, he argues that "social character" exists by virtue of society's needs, citing a key passage from Erich Fromm (1944) to crystallize the argument:

> In order that any society may function well, its members must acquire the kind of character which makes them *want* to act in the way they *have* to act as members of the society or of a special class within it. They must *desire* what is objectively *necessary* for them to do. (Fromm 1944, cited in Riesman 1950, p. 5; emphasis is Riesman's)

Character is thus socially conditioned and, according to Riesman,

> there is an observable relation between a particular society and the kind of social character it produces. . . . Since the social function of character is to insure or permit conformity . . . the various types of social character can be defined most appropriately in terms of the modes of conformity that are developed within them. (P. 6)

Riesman doesn't think social character determines individual behavior, however, and cautions against overestimating its role in the social process. At the same time, he warns of the perils of character and culture "overreaching themselves," suggesting that the character structure of a particular group may "swallow up" individuality and personal choice in the interest of shared group pursuits. In other words, what the early pragmatists opened the self to can, under the right conditions, engross the self. We are beginning to get glimpses of the idea that social life constructs the selves *it* needs.

While he only occasionally specifies *self* as his topic, Riesman refers repeatedly to those aspects of character that are known to, and seen by, individuals. He often writes implicitly of self as others (like Mead) generally conceive it, and even uses the term interchangeably with *social character* on occasion. Thus, much of what he explicitly discusses in terms of character, readers might interpret as implicit commentary about a socially produced self.

Riesman's thesis concerning sociohistorical change and the development of character types is grounded in the argument that changes in population and technology are the chief correlates of changes in the social character of groups and nations (p. v). Citing the historical pattern of development in industrialized countries, he explains that they typically begin from a point of population stability where the number of births and deaths are roughly equal, both being relatively high. The populations of such societies tend to be relatively young; the turnover of generations is rapid. Riesman notes that societies under these conditions face the prospect of "high growth potential"; their populations would dramatically increase if the death rate were lowered by technological advances. When such a society experiences a decline in the death rate, it may enter a phase of "transitional growth," in which births exceed deaths, and population expands rapidly. When growth subsequently slows as birth rates decline, society moves into a phase of "incipient population decline." With low birth and death rates, the society is dominated by middle-aged groups.

Riesman contends that each phase of "the population curve appears to be occupied by a society that enforces conformity and molds social character in a definably different way" (p. 9).

> The society of high growth potential develops in its typical members a social character whose conformity is insured by their tendency to follow tradition: these I shall term *tradition-directed* people and the society in which they live *a society dependent on tradition-direction.*
>
> The society of transitional population growth develops in its typical members a social character whose conformity is insured by their tendency to acquire early in life an internalized set of goals. These I term *inner-directed* people and the society in which they live *a society dependent on inner-direction.*
>
> Finally, the society of incipient population decline develops in its typical members a social character whose conformity is insured by their tendency to be sensitized to the expectations and preferences of others. These I shall term *other-directed* people and the society in which they live one *dependent on other-direction.* (P. 9, emphasis in the original)

The Lonely Crowd is principally about the transition and differences between inner-directed and other-directed character types, although Riesman is ultimately interested in another emerging possibility—the autonomous character. In terms of the central argument, however, Riesman is especially concerned with the growing prevalence of other-directedness among the middle class. It's not that the populations of societies undergoing industrialization are uniformly inner-directed, while postindustrial societies like contemporary America are other-directed. Rather, he argues that the distributions of these character types differ across developmental epochs, and that at mid-century in the United States, other-directedness is on the rise, while inner-direction is receding.

If the self is a source of direction for individual actions and interpretations of experience, then Riesman's typologies provide the background for a story of different possibilities for the social self. For Riesman, both the inner- and other-directed character types are social in origin, but in different ways. For the inner-directed person, *"the source of direction for the individual is 'inner' in the sense that it is implanted early in life by the elders and directed toward generalized but nonetheless inescapably destined goals"* (p. 15, emphasis in original). As social as its origins are, Riesman argues that this character type is more or less "self guided" once the foundation has been laid. Indeed, he likens inner-directedness to having a "psychological gyroscope." "Once it's set in place by parents and other authorities," writes Riesman metaphorically, the gyroscope "keeps the inner-directed person ... 'on course.' ... The inner-directed person becomes capable of maintaining a delicate balance between the demands upon him of his life goal and the buffetings of his external environment" (p. 16). While not on "automatic pilot," the inner-directed self is still more or less stable and relatively resistant to external input once it is formed. Whereas "signals from the outside" and "public opinion" in matters of conformity are always potentially influential, messages from the exterior and the responses they elicit must constantly be reconciled with the enduring, goal-oriented inner self.

In contrast, the other-directed self is more fluid across the life course. Riesman argues that societies characterized by incipient population decline, urbanization, increasingly pervasive mass communications media, and changes in families and child-rearing practices offer new sources of consequential social input. Schools, public institutions, peer groups, and the media at least partially supplant parents and family as molders of character. The character type that emerges is much more sensitive to the ongoing input that these sources exert on the more mutable self. For other-directed selves, writes Riesman,

> their contemporaries are the source of direction for the individual—either those known to him or those with whom he is indirectly acquainted, through friends and through the mass media. This source is of course "internalized" in the sense that dependence on it for guidance in life is implanted early. The goals toward which the other-directed person strives shift with that guidance: it is only the process of striving itself and the process of paying close attention to the signals from others that remain unaltered throughout life. (P. 22, emphasis in the original)

The other-directed self is finely attuned to ongoing external input. It is constant in the sense of being enduringly other-directed, but remains fluid with respect to how it reacts to the social. As Riesman puts it, "this other-directed mode of keeping in touch with others permits a close behavioral conformity . . . through an exceptional sensitivity to the actions and wishes of others" (p. 22). Riesman, of course, acknowledges that persons of all eras, living in all societies, tune in to what others around them say, think, and do. But in his account, the modern, American, middle-class, other-directed person develops an acute need for approval and direction from others—contemporary others, not one's parents or ancestors (as in inner- or tradition-directed societies, respectively). This "goes beyond the reasons that lead most people in any era to care very much what others think of them. While all people want and need to be liked by some of the people some of the time, it is only the other-directed types who make this their chief source of direction and chief area of sensitivity" (p. 23).

As Riesman develops his comparison of character types, he describes both strengths and weaknesses. Returning to his metaphorical imagery, he remarks that the internal gyroscope of the inner-directed self can be upset by competing voices of authority that resemble parental voices, causing the self to veer off course. But the gyroscope tends to hold steady even as external signals try to distract or impede it. In contrast, Riesman pictures the other-directed self as equipped with radar, implying that the other-directed person responds to a wide circle of others, far beyond parents and their surrogates. In this sense, he or she is quite "cosmopolitan" in orientation. The self is not simply a reproduction of the inner circle of family or intimates. It is "at home" in all settings by virtue of its capacity for superficial familiarity with, and sensitivity to, others. At the same time, the radar screen is constantly receiving outside signals, scanning new and diverse sources of social input in a seemingly endless process of monitoring the social environment and appropriately modifying the self in response.[1]

Despite Riesman's intent to be evenhanded, the connotations associated with the outwardly oriented social self are often dire. Riesman's metaphors and descriptions, offered in the context of the cultural and historical circumstances of the book's publication, strike a tone of alarm, alerting readers to myriad liabilities attached to a self that is overly eager to reflect its surroundings. Riesman simply can't avoid highlighting the dangers of other-directedness, of this dark side of the social.

Consider the tone and implications of Riesman's description of growing up and living in contemporary America. In an other-directed society, the account begins, there is "a heightening of awareness of the self in relation to others" (p. 49). Parenting and child-rearing under these conditions often amount to "installing" in children "something like a psychological radar set—a device not tuned to control movement in any particular direction while guiding and steadying the person from within but rather tuned to detect the action, and especially the symbolic action, of others" (p. 55). Children end up facing the requirement of "making good," but what "good" might possibly be depends upon others' opinions. For the other-directed person, "One makes good when one is approved of" (p. 49). Thus one's sense of good and bad, right and wrong, one's self, and one's self-esteem, derive from actual or imaginary reference groups.

According to Riesman, the child learns that "nothing in his character, no possession he owns, no inheritance of name or talent, no work he has done is valued for itself but only for its effect on others" (p. 49). In school, children don't learn to "accomplish" as much as they learn to "get along." Cooperation is more important than productivity. Intellectual achievement takes a back seat to relational skills. Schools play down competition for correct answers, good grades, and superior report cards, replacing exhortations to excel with queries of "Mirror, mirror on the wall, who is the fairest of us all?" (p. 61). In the context of an American cultural heritage that generally prizes independence and individual achievement, this is a disturbing development.

The fate of the self gets bleaker as Riesman's tale continues. The other-directed person, he argues, is increasingly channeling energy into the "ever expanding frontiers of consumption" (p. 79). When compared with what Riesman calls the inner-directed individual's relentless pursuit of "production," the other-directed self is shallow, superficial, narcissistic. This other-directed consumer is especially vulnerable to social persuasion because of his sensitivity to public opinion and his need for peer approval. What the consumer wants most, what he thinks is "best," is determined by what others tell him, not by what an independent self decides. And this situation is compounded for the other-directed self because in contemporary America, "the social" is more expansive and intrusive than elsewhere or ever before. With the proliferation of mass communications media, Riesman argues that the "peer group" expands, consumer referents abound, and there are endless sources of social input on what persons should like, should do, and should be.[2] It's not that the process of self-formation changes radically in modern times, but that the social sources of character virtually overwhelm the individual. The portrait of the other-directed self is not very attractive.

"America is becoming increasingly self-conscious," writes Riesman (p. 265), suggesting something more than simply a heightened self-awareness. The self not only scours the social scene for feedback on its appearance, but slavishly takes shapes that are known to be socially acceptable and valued. The other-directed person wants more than mere tolerance or acceptance; he or she wants validation (p. 264). Taken to the extreme, this self gives itself almost completely over to the other's values, merging the desires and preferences of the individual and the group.

Bland conformity is an unfortunate consequence. The other-directed person seeks security in the endorsement of others, not distinction gained by standing out from (or above) the crowd. The cost of this, Riesman intimates, is the sacrifice of excellence. The other-directed person wants "approval, not fame" (p. 282). He or she is likely to be ritualistically conformist, not innovative, self-reliant, or self-governing. This is a sociability that Riesman fears will obliterate individual autonomy.

To avoid this, Riesman urges readers to recognize the considerable power of active social participation, and not to let others simply wash over them. He recommends proactive measures be taken, positive steps to draw autonomy, not mere conformity, from social interaction. Ultimately, however, Riesman seems decidedly ambivalent about the social self, at once holding out possibilities for how it might be more autonomous, while simultaneously admonishing us to resist the quest for approbation so that we might retain more of what we are as individuals:

> If the other-directed people should discover how much needless work they do, discover that their own thoughts and their own lives are quite as interesting as other peoples', that, indeed, they no more assuage their loneliness in a crowd of peers than one can assuage one's thirst by drinking sea water, then we might expect them to become more attentive to their own feelings and aspirations. . . . The idea that men are created free and equal is both true and misleading: men are created different; they lose their social freedom and their individual autonomy in seeking to become like each other. (P. 373)

The Organizational Self

If Riesman portrays the social self as a conforming victim of its times, to William H. Whyte, in his book *The Organization Man* (1956), it's more of a "sellout." Less sympathetic and considerably more ironic than Riesman, Whyte claims that Americans are seduced into conformity as they blindly, blandly pursue the corporate, suburban American Dream. Written in the mid-1950s, the book's main character is the young to middle-aged, middle management junior executive. This person doesn't just work for "The Organization," he *belongs* to it. Solid members of the middle class, Organization Men have "left home, spiritually as well as physically, to take the vows of organization life, and it is they who are the mind and soul of our great self-perpetuating institutions" (p. 3). They are the patrons of suburbia, living with their wives and children in planned, prefabricated communities.

A writer for *Fortune* magazine, Whyte saw the Organization Man as the 1950s corporate version of Riesman's other-directed character.[3] Confronting the "pressures of the group, the frustrations of individual creativity, the anonymity of achievement," Americans of the time were looking for a way to navigate an increasingly bureaucratic world. The question they faced, Whyte observes, is this: "Are these defects to struggle against—or are they virtues in disguise?" (p. 6). Striving to realize the middle-class dream, Americans sought direction much as their predecessors had taken their bearings from the Protestant Ethic. What they found, argues Whyte, is a "Social Ethic" (p. 6), an ethos that could just as well be called the "organization" or "bureaucratic" ethic.

By social ethic, Whyte means "that contemporary body of thought which makes morally legitimate the pressures of society against the individual" (p. 7). According to Whyte, the social ethic comprises three main propositions: (1) the belief in the group as the source of creativity, (2) the belief in "belongingness" as the ultimate desire of the individual, and (3) the belief in the application of science to achieve belongingness. He offers the gist of his argument in the following terms:

> Man exists as a unit of society. Of himself, he is isolated, meaningless; only as he collaborates with others does he become worth while, for by sublimating himself in the group, he helps produce a whole that is greater than the sum of its parts. There should be, then, no conflict between man and society. . . . society's needs and the needs of the individual are one and the same. (Pp. 7–8)

The Organization Man (and presumably woman) is the character that cleaves to this credo. He or she puts the group or organization's interests above individual goals and priorities. This is Riesman's other-directed man taken to a bureaucratic suburban extreme. Be a team player. Find your niche in the organizational hierarchy. Strive for the mid-range, or just above, but never venture to the extremes. And above all, be "normal." While he appreciates the Organization Man's aspirations and contributions, Whyte reserves scant affection for him. "He will, in sum, be the apotheosis of the well-rounded man: obtrusive in no particular, excessive in no zeal," writes Whyte. "He will be the man in the middle" (p. 147). But to achieve this middle ground, Whyte believes the Organization Man sacrifices too much in the way of individuality, creativity, genius; he gives up too much of his individual self. We must *fight* The Organization, Whyte implores, lest we succumb to the conformity, mediocrity, and neuroses of life where society is valued over humanity.

The self's plight is implicitly chronicled throughout the book. Whyte contends that, above all, the Organization Man wants to belong, to blend into the group. He strives for corporate togetherness, for compatibility, for membership. Insuring this requires strict resemblance above all else. Therefore, wanting to reflect the best qualities of the organization and its membership, the Organization Man's self could hardly be anything other than the virtual mirror of its social surroundings. Normalcy and conformity are the bywords of the Organization Man, for better or worse.

Whyte intimates that the bad now outweighs the good where the social self is concerned. Its dark side is apparent in the homogenization of the corporate middle class. Individual distinction vanishes in the accompanying decline of personal enterprise and singular genius. The social self in service to the organization—one that desperately mimics the group in hopes of inclusion—is not necessarily pathological, but it is militantly monotonous, assertively nondescript.

Whyte tries to be compassionate toward the Organization Man and his reflecting self, but his preference is clear. Conformity and belongingness, he notes, offer the warmth and security of the tight-knit group, but the "double-barreled effects of belongingness" (p. 395) in the long run prove costly. Conformity, he explains, is not the problem in itself, but it becomes an affliction when one cedes one's self to the group mentality, gives in to the need for "alikeness." With specific regard to the self, writes Whyte, "the group is a jealous master. It encourages participation, indeed demands it, but it demands one kind of participation—its own kind—and the better integrated with it a member becomes, the less free he is to express himself in other ways" (p. 397). Surrendering to the group thus requires one to relinquish the distinctive, individual self.

While the group is a "tyrant," Whyte also concedes that it is simultaneously a "friend." Therein lies the rub, for "what gives the group its power over the man is the same cohesion that gives it its warmth" (p. 399). This duality mirrors the sanguine and sinister sides of the social as far as the self is concerned. The conformist self is socially cultivated and affirmed, while at the same time the individual self is "intimidated" by normalcy (p. 401). Adaptation to the social, argues Whyte, "has become more than a necessity; . . . it has become almost a constant" (p. 435). The Social Ethic is not just a guidepost; it is a moral imperative, something ingrained in the self so deeply that there no longer remains any question about whether one should adhere to it. It's simply the way the Organization Man *is*. This self is the prisoner of prevailing opinion, a hostage to conformity, but that's everything it wants to be.

The Emotionally Managed Self

Riesman and Whyte portray the self as a passive victim of its sociability, a well-intentioned, if bland, reflection of its surroundings. This self is all but lost in the "house of mirrors" that comprises modern society. But can't the social self resist? Can't it somehow sustain something of its own, even as social input virtually inundates it? Arlie Hochschild's (1983) book *The Managed Heart* offers us a sensitive account of one attempt the self has made to stave off cloying sociability. Echoing James's and Cooley's concern for the affective dimensions of self, Hochschild introduces readers to the "emotion work" done by airline flight attendants. Focusing on professionals whose job it is to keep others happy, she describes how emotions function as "messengers from the self"(p. x) and how the flight attendants try to preserve their selves in the face of the nagging demands of selflessly, cheerfully serving others. Her part of the self's story centers on how these workers attempt to "preserve a sense of self by circumventing the feeling rules of work, how they limit their emotional offerings to surface displays of the 'right' feeling but suffer anyway from a sense of being 'false' or mechanical" (p. x).

While Hochschild's is a narrative of resistance, in the end it shows just how con-suming sociability can be. To be sure, flight attendants represent a very special cat-egory of "emotion worker," yet they epitomize the way many people respond to contemporary conditions where feelings are commodified and emotion management is commercialized. In such a world, Hochschild explains, the "true" self is often over-run by false selves that have been mobilized to help ward off the demands of the social. As outside interests inundate the real self, it may retreat inward, leaving only its uncomfortable vestiges and false personas inappropriately directed toward oth-ers. Valiant as it may be, the resisting self is still victim to the social.

As central as the social self is to her story, Hochschild is somewhat evasive about its nature. She is decidedly clear on what it is *not*; for her, the self is some-thing more than the situated performances Goffman writes about. Hochschild em-braces the notion of "presented selves," but she doesn't let that become the to-tality of the self, as she believes Goffman has done (p. 217). She explicitly rejects the concept that the self's capacity to act "derives from the occasion, not from the individual" (p. 218).

Positioning herself closer to James and Cooley, and especially to Freud, Hochschild posits a self that can deeply feel, direct, and internally manage actions and emotions (p. 217). While the origins of this self are not clearly specified, we can infer a self profoundly indebted to the social, even as it retains consequential indi-vidual roots. Hochschild's appreciation for Freud is apparent throughout her book and her vision of self is far less socially emergent than is, say, Mead's. Still, juggling both Freudian and sociological traditions, she suggests that the self is both stable and socially dynamic. "Most of us," she writes, "maintain a prior expectation of a continuous self, but the character of the self we expect to maintain is subject to pro-foundly social influence. . . . our self and all we expect is social" (pp. 221–22). Hers is a multilayered self, laid down through psychosexual development and social-ization, one that has some sense of continuity and stability across situations, yet one that constantly adapts to its social surroundings.

While this self is neither purely a reflective social self nor one that is situa-tionally presented, it has its affinities. Indeed, while she conceives of a more or less singular, stable inner self, Hochschild also argues that versions of the self can be offered to meet situational demands. More precisely, Hochschild posits a "true" self and the possibility of multiple "false" selves (p. 194). She argues that a "false self" is a "disbelieved, unclaimed self, a part of the 'me' that is not 'really me' " (p. 194).

> [T]he false self embodies our acceptance of early parental requirements that we act so as to please others, at the expense of our own needs and desires. This so-ciocentric, other-directed self comes to live a separate existence from the self we claim. In the extreme case, the false self may set itself up as the real self, which remains completely hidden. More commonly, the false self allows the real self a life of its own, which emerges when there is little danger of its being used by oth-ers. (P. 194)

This version of the social self has many of the qualities of the other-directed self, but a "true" self manages to struggle against total inundation.

Hochschild does not condemn the "false" self, at least not all of its manifestations. She does, however, point out some potential shortcomings. Perhaps the most prominent recent model of the unhealthy false self, Hochschild notes, is the "narcissistic self" described by Christopher Lasch (1979). This self, she writes, "feeds insatiably on interactions, competing desperately for love and admiration in a Hobbesian dog-eat-dog world where both are perpetually scarce" (p. 195) This pursuit is ultimately unsatisfying because any success or gratification accrues to the false self, not the real self. In a sense, this is but another extreme manifestation of Riesman's other-directedness. In Lasch's view, such inundation in the social is ultimately destructive.

There's another form of other-directed false self that Hochschild finds equally troublesome: "the altruist, the person who is overly concerned with the needs of *others*" (p. 195, emphasis in the original). When overdeveloped, argues Hochschild, this false, altruistic self oversteps its boundaries, and begins to bond the true self "more securely to the group and its welfare" (p. 196). Whereas the narcissistic self may be especially adept at taking advantage of others for its own desires, the altruistic self is "susceptible to being used" (p. 196), not because it is weak or ineffectual, but because it is overly concerned with the welfare of others at the expense of the true self's welfare.

Still, in Hochschild's scheme of things, the false self can serve a very important, self-preserving function. In practice, the false self can set itself up in service to, for the protection of, the true self. It provides a means for the individual to accommodate the demands of social life, while not becoming merely the reflected image of the social. It serves as a sort of buffer between external demands and an internal core that may be at odds with such demands. In this sense, the false self is necessary for preserving the true self while living civilly among others. Referring to Rousseau's romantic version of the unfettered, feral self, Hochschild argues that

> the false or unclaimed self is what enables one to offer the discretion, the kindness, and the generosity that Noble Savages tend to lack. It is a *healthy* false self. By giving up infantile desires for omnipotence, a person gains a "place in society which can never be attained or maintained by the True Self alone" (Winnicott 1965, p. 143). (P. 195, emphasis in the original)

Thus, the true self needs the help of false selves to shield it from the onslaught of the social.

Hochschild's formulation suggests that emotions are beacons for our true selves. Every emotion has a "signal function," she argues (p. 29). That is, "it is from feelings that we learn the *self*-relevance of what we see, remember, or imagine"(p. 196). Emotions put us in touch with the inner "me," providing us with an inner perspective for interpreting and responding to experience. Social life becomes problematic, however, in that it often demands that we harness our feelings. This emotion management, argues Hochschild, intervenes in the signal function of feelings (p. 130), and often serves to obscure a person's sense of self (p. 136).

How does this work? Hochschild suggests that in contemporary life, we are increasingly unsure of our answer to the question "Who am I?"

> Ordinary people nowadays move through many social worlds and get the gist of dozens of social roles. . . . We still search for a solid, predictable core of self, even though the conditions for the existence of such a self have long since vanished. (P. 22)

Clinging to the notion of a true self, we confront diverse situations, are subjected to so much social input, play so many social roles, and offer so many situated, false selves, that we have trouble discerning who we really are. Hochschild argues that we look to our feelings to help us locate our true selves (p. 22). We rely upon their signal function to guide us, to put us in touch with our true selves. But to the extent that we intentionally manage our emotions, this "distortion of the managed heart" (p. 22) leaves us out of touch with our authenticity. The true self may not be destroyed, but we lose close connections to it.

Compounding the problem, in contemporary society we are increasingly asked to keep our feelings in check or, more and more frequently, to put the appropriate feelings on display. Asked to do this "on demand" as part of our jobs, we participate in the growth of what Hochschild calls the "commercialization" of feelings and emotion work. Putting ourselves "on the market," so to speak, further compromises our ability to discern deep feelings about who we are, obscuring important messages from the true self. Hochschild laments that

> it is precisely this precious resource that is jeopardized when an outside interest dictates the management of feelings for instrumental ends. As ulterior motives are inserted between a feeling and its interpretation, one loses the sense of what the true self might be. Not only does one lose touch with one's feelings, one loses access to the true self in the process. (P. 197)

With the commercialization of emotion management, Hochschild argues, we are asked to manipulate feelings and, by implication, our false selves, for purely instrumental ends. As this happens, those feelings and selves come to belong "more to the organization and less to the self" (p. 198). The result, claims Hochschild, is "burnout" and "estrangement."

Hochschild uses the emotion work of airline personnel to illustrate such costs. Flight attendants in the late 1970s, she argues, are not only asked to smile as they serve their customers, but are instructed to really feel and project a warmth and sincerity that conveys the smile as genuine. But with emotion management and the distinction between real and projected selves in view, Hochschild asks,

> What happens to the way a person relates to her feelings or her face? When worked-up warmth becomes an instrument of service work, what can a person learn about herself from her feelings? And when a worker abandons her work smile, what kind of tie remains between her smile and her self? (Pp. 89–90)

The suggestion is clear: the flight attendant and, by implication, the rest of us in our own ways and circumstances, are estranged from ourselves.

According to Hochschild, we are not oblivious to this plight, but awareness alone can't avert the process of estrangement. People know that "social engineering" affects their behavior and feelings; we know that each of us is asked to present images and emotions that don't emanate from our real selves, but are instead dictated by social circumstances, organizational policies, and the like. Mindful of the commercialization of emotion, we try to make up for it by correcting for, discounting, or reassessing the meaning of emotional displays, displays of self "given off" that are not genuine expressions of the true self. We do emotion work as much to shield our true selves and feelings as we do to manage social situations. It's a way of resisting social intrusions, a technique for counteracting the social demands placed on who we really are or should be.

At the same time, however, this resistance serves to further isolate and insulate the true self. According to Hochschild, "we make up an idea of our 'real self,' an inner jewel that remains our unique possession no matter whose billboard is on our back or whose smile is on our face. We push this 'real self' further inside, making it more inaccessible" as we mobilize false selves, appearances, and emotions to serve instrumental ends (p. 34). Ultimately, we have to look harder and harder, further and further inside, to find our real selves, to recover who we "really are." We don a "cloak to protect us" against social and commercial incursions into our true selves and emotions, but that cloak so encapsulates the real self that it becomes virtually unapproachable, all but unrecognizable, even when we search for it (p. 34).

If the social threatens the true self, it's our defenses against the social that can ultimately be the self's undoing. Hochschild, however, doesn't completely despair. She suggests several ways to manage the assault on feelings and the self. One way is to more conscientiously regulate the demands of emotional labor. The secret to success may be found in a "healthy estrangement, a clear and conscious separation of self from role" (p. 188), a conscious distinction between true and false selves. The key is adjusting one's self to a role in a way that "allows some flow of self into the role but minimizes the stress the role puts on the self" (p. 188). The social is kept at bay as the individual finds ways of resisting total immersion by intentionally separating self from role.[4]

Outsiders

So far, our story of the dark side has followed the self through the neighborhood of the socially acceptable, if not the socially desirable. The characterizations produced bland conformists, organizational sellouts, and the emotionally estranged. While Riesman, Whyte, Hochschild, and others viewed these emerging social selves as unattractive, they also pointed to their social functionality. If the social was engrossing the self, it was incorporating a willing partner.

A darker, less socially acceptable side of the self was highlighted beginning in the 1960s as sociology turned more and more to the study of social disorganization, social problems, and social pathology. Sociological champions of the "underdog" (Becker 1967) and "unconventional sentimentalists" (Becker 1964) introduced another chapter of the story centered on what was called "deviance," which continues to command the attention of the discipline. In some ways, it was a return to older themes, but with less of the progressive fanfare; the social was much darker now than it figured in an earlier era. This aspect of the dark side was a domain diametrically opposed to what genteel philosophical sensibilities abided or could envision the self to include.

The theme of this chapter was not that social life was commandeering the self, leaving in its wake mere conformist shadows and emotional robots. On the contrary, this part of the story told how social circumstances could turn the self *against* conventional society. Ironically, the social could produce the antisocial. This was not a radical departure from what came before, since it centered on the same social processes, but it did involve selves in the social construction of the unacceptable.

Peter Berger (1963), in his immensely popular book *Invitation to Sociology*, offers a familiar point of departure: ". . . identity is socially bestowed, socially sustained, and socially transformed" (p. 98). Turning to Mead, he continues, "The genesis of the self is . . . one and the same event as the discovery of society" (p. 99). Taking the role of the other is decisive for the formation of the self (p. 99). Significant others, of course, are most important, but, in Mead's terms, the "generalized other" also has his or her say. This generalized other provides *society's* input into the self. Thus, writes Berger, " 'self' and 'society' are the two sides of the same coin." Self and identity are not something "given" in some psychological sense, but they are "bestowed in acts of social recognition. We become that as which we are addressed" (p. 99). This, of course, also aligns with symbolic interactionist thought and doesn't contradict Riesman, Whyte, or Hochschild. "Society," continues Berger, "is not only something 'out there,' . . . but it is also 'in here' as part of our innermost being. . . . The structures of society become the structures of our own consciousness" (p. 121).

In this narrative, society is largely responsible for "creating" the selves that populate it, for better or worse. A society appreciating compliance and conformity breeds conformists; that's Riesman and Whyte's account, in a nutshell. Hochschild astutely adds that a society that commodifies feelings confounds the emotional self, threatening its authenticity. But Berger and many others see far more dire consequences. If a person treated with respect and dignity comes to see himself as dignified and respectable, one can reasonably ask what kind of self might a person develop if he or she were treated with ridicule, derision, or disdain? Wouldn't we then expect the development of a contemptible self?

Berger broaches such possibilities by creating an imaginary scenario in which a man is arrested and incarcerated.

> A man turned overnight from a free citizen into a convict finds himself subjected at once to a massive assault on his previous conception of himself. He may try desperately to hold on to the latter, but in the absence of others in his immediate environment confirming his old identity he will find it almost impossible to maintain it within his own consciousness. With frightening speed he will discover that he is acting as a convict is supposed to, and feeling all the things that a convict is expected to feel. *It would be a misleading perspective on this process to look upon it*

simply as one of the disintegration of personality. A more accurate way of seeing the phe-
nomenon is as a reintegration of personality, no different in its sociopsychological dy-
namics from the process in which the old identity was integrated. It used to be that our
man was treated by all the important people around him as responsible, dignified, considerate and aesthetically fastidious. Consequently, he was able to be all
these things. Now the walls of the prison separate him from those whose recognition sustained him in the exhibition of those traits. Instead he is now surrounded
by people who treat him as irresponsible, swinish in behavior, only out for his
own interest and careless of his appearance unless forced to take care by constant
supervision. . . . Identity comes with conduct and conduct occurs in response to
a specific social situation. (Pp. 100–01, emphasis added)

The plot twist that Berger introduces was there all along: the good, the bad, and
the indifferent sides of the social self derive from the same process.

This turn in the story was merely awaiting the emergence of the "labeling"
perspective to underscore its significance. This approach to deviance developed
the storyline vividly and with great passion and imagination (see Becker 1973
[1963], Schur 1971, 1979). Its central tenet was straightforward: "The deviant is
one to whom that label has successfully been applied" (Becker 1973 [1963], p. 9).
Howard Becker, more than anyone, has been associated with what he and others
have called "labeling theory," so we'll take his version of the perspective as exemplary.[5]

Becker begins with the fundamental observation that "social groups create
deviance by making rules whose infraction constitutes deviance, and by applying those rules to particular people and labeling them as outsiders" (p. 9). One
becomes "deviant" when one is labeled as such, Becker writes, *then* one learns deviant motivations in interaction with other deviants (p. 31). This reverses the motivational pattern, as it is commonly known, by placing deviance before its
"causes." Such is the counterintuitive attraction of the labeling perspective. Moving on, Becker notes that societal labeling is not all there is to the deviance process.
"Being caught and branded as deviant has important consequences for one's further social participation and self-image" (p. 31–32).

At this point, Becker's commentary gets sketchy as far as the self is concerned.
While he is clearly implying a close connection between social interaction and self
development, he fails to outline the social psychological process entailed.[6] We
must turn to others to fill in the details. Edwin Schur, for one, elaborated an account of deviance as a social process that he traces back to Mead's social psychology of the self. Stressing that deviance is a continuously shaped and reshaped
outcome of dynamic processes of social interaction, Schur (1971) made it clear that
the development of deviant selves and self conceptions was an important aspect
of the process and that this development could be best understood in the terms
Mead made available. Erdwin Pfuhl is even more direct, arguing that "the origins of the labeling perspective are found in the work of Charles Horton Cooley
and George Herbert Mead" (1986, p. 126).

Pfuhl takes up Cooley's view of "self-feeling" to elaborate the labeling perspective on deviant selves. People's self-feelings, he suggests, consist of three elements: (1) how they imagine they appear to others, (2) how they imagine others

judge them, and (3) the resulting self-feeling, for example, shame, pride, mortification, and so on. Next, turning to Mead, he argues that the self, especially the deviant self, arises as people take the role of others and see themselves as others see them. In this way, one develops and internalizes a self-conception based on the standpoint and view of others or society (as implied in the term *the generalized other*). Pfuhl quotes a noted symbolic interactionist, Bernard Meltzer (1967, p. 10), to elaborate this observation: "The standpoint of others provides a platform for getting outside oneself and viewing oneself as others do. The development of the self is concurrent with the development of the ability to take roles."

Pfuhl then explains how the "deviant self" is formed. When people consistently negatively label an individual, he argues, the label becomes the category by which the person is known. Through ongoing interaction, the individual comes to accept the identity and label, seeing himself or herself through others' associated eyes. Such individuals come to see themselves in the negative terms society assigns to them, and they develop the consequent self-concepts and negative self-feelings. This leads to what Edwin Lemert (1950) calls "secondary deviation."

Lemert's description of the process by which uncommitted, even random, deviation is transformed into a way of life is crucial to most of the interactionist writings on deviance, even if it is often unacknowledged. To summarize briefly, Lemert (1950) argued that there are different "modalities" of human behavior, some of which deviate from societal norms. These deviations are variably disapproved, and societal reactions vary accordingly. This Lemert calls "primary deviance" or everyday rule-breaking. It is not necessarily these modalities of deviant behavior that are responsible for the formation of "deviant persons." On the contrary, Lemert suggests that it's the degree of social visibility of deviant or rule-breaking acts, the nature and strength of societal reaction, and the individual's exposure to societal reaction that contribute to the development of deviant identities.

> If the deviant acts are repetitive and have a high visibility, and there is a severe societal reaction, which, through a process of identification is incorporated as part of the "me" of the individual, the probability is greatly increased [for adopting deviant roles and identity] . . . the "me" in this context is simply the subjective aspect of the societal reaction. . . . *When a person begins to employ his deviant behavior, or a role based on it, as a means of defense, attack, or adjustment to the overt and covert problems created by the consequent societal reaction to him, his deviation is secondary.* (P. 76, emphasis in the original)

The sequence of interaction leading up to secondary deviation thus involves societal reaction and the (primary) "deviant's" response to that reaction. Others' reactions, according to Lemert, may lead to changes in the "deviant's" psychic structure and revised "self-regarding attitudes" (1967, p. 41). The "secondary deviant" who finds himself shunned and stigmatized by normal society may then seek out the company of other "deviants," who serve as a further source of deviant self-identification. In this way, the deviant self is even further "validated" (1950, pp. 225–26). This "personal progression" can leave the "deviant" with "a distinctive self-image based upon . . . his image reflected in interaction with others" (1967, p. 50).

Goffman (1963) also describes the role that stigmatizing reactions can play in the development of self-conception. When individuals are stigmatized, he writes, whether as different, criminal, deformed, disturbed, or demented, they take on society's view of themselves; ". . . the stigmatized person learns and incorporates the standpoint of the normal, acquiring thereby the identity beliefs of the wider society and a general idea of what it would be like to possess a particular stigma"(p. 32). Reminiscent of Mead, Goffman goes on to suggest that ". . . the standards he has incorporated from the wider society equip him to be intimately alive to what others see as his failing, inevitably causing him, if only for moments, to agree that he does indeed fall short of what he really ought to be" (p. 7). Among the possible outcomes of this process, Goffman explains, are ambivalence about one's self, negative self-conceptions, self-derogation, and self-hate.

Secondary deviation is Mead's social self gone awry. Along these same lines, Lemert suggests that persons finding themselves in the midst of the process of labeling and secondary deviation can become "adjusted pathological deviants." "The adjusted sociopathic person," he continues, "is simply one who accepts his status, role and self definition" (1967, p. 69). In essence, Lemert is telling us that by responding perfectly normally to the self-shaping conditions of social life, one can develop a self and an identity that are acceptably pathological. This is, of course, the ultimate irony for the social self: the social process through which a sense of self is developed produces a self that one accepts despite its socially unacceptable identity.

Lemert provides an example featuring an "errant schoolboy" (remember that this was written in 1950). Out of childish exuberance, excess energy, or other similarly "innocent" motivation, writes Lemert, the boy engages in a relatively harmless classroom prank. He is punished for the offense but little is made of it. Soon afterward, however, the boy, out of "clumsiness," creates another disturbance. He is reprimanded again, but now others start to think that this may be a pattern, that there might be a "bad boy" here. The teacher, for instance, begins to refer to the boy as a "mischief maker." The boy initially resents what he sees as unfair treatment, and the resentment deepens as he is repeatedly singled out for attention due to similar "deviant" acts. Eventually, the boy comes to see himself as a mischief maker, too, and actually begins to derive satisfaction out of fulfilling the role and reaping the rewards (as well as the punishments) for creating such mischief.

There is a sense in which the labeling process encourages "self-fulfilling prophecies" of deviance. When a person is treated as a deviant, he or she finds nondeviant self-images and avenues of behavior progressively less available. Normal associations are shut off and the "deviant" is virtually forced to associate with other deviants. Under such circumstances, deviant behaviors may be increasingly valued and conformist behavior negatively sanctioned. Eventually this may lead the "deviant" to act like one because that is what others expect. This, of course, echoes an earlier suggestion by Frank Tannenbaum (1938) that "criminals" and, by implication, other deviants, are produced through normal responses to social expectations:

> The process of making the criminal ... is a process of tagging, defining, identi-fying, segregating, describing, emphasizing, making conscious and self-conscious; it becomes a way of stimulating, suggesting, emphasizing, and evoking the very traits that are complained of.... The person becomes the thing he is described as being. (Pp. 19–20)

We can now see the story of the social self becoming fraught with peril. Too much of the social leaves the individual with little beyond the conformist reflec-tion of the surroundings. Certainly, this can be socially, interactionally useful in the proper circumstances, among polite company, so to speak. But when "soci-ety" turns against the individual, when social reflections are disparaging, if not damning, the implications for identity can be disastrous. From valued social com-modity to embattled social casualty, the unfinished story of the social self in the latter half of the twentieth century leaves its fate in doubt.[7] The onslaught of post-modernity soon turns this into an outright narrative crisis as the very possibility of a discernible social self comes into question.

CHAPTER FOUR

Two Options for the Postmodern Self

J ust when it looked like things couldn't get much worse, some very audible voices at century's end announced that the story of the self was over. These "post-modernists" claimed that the modern notion of a reality that can be distinguished from its representation was a mirage. Of course this included the reality of the empirical self, whether positive or negative. While the early pragmatists, the later symbolic interactionists, and other sociological observers viewed the empirical self as socially formed, reformed, or deformed, as the case might have been, it nonetheless was a self that was a concrete element of society, not a mere image of itself. As effective or defective as the empirical self was conceived to be, it was still located in experience—a socially shaped, interpersonally responsive, yet constant agent of everyday life. At the end of the twentieth century, however, this was seriously questioned, as postmodern critics referred to one of modernity's key social structures as not "amounting to much" anymore (Lyotard 1984).

While some view postmodernism as an intellectual fad, it is broadly consequential because, according to feminist Patti Lather (1994), the term has become "the code-name for the crisis of confidence in Western conceptual systems" (p. 102). Lather's definition points us well beyond the empirical or social self, to even include the world according to the transcendental self. Postmodernism, she suggests, jars overarching Western sensibilities concerning the way we understand ourselves:

> Postmodernism is born out of the uprising of the marginalized, the evolution in communication technology, the fissures of a global multinational hypercapitalism, and our sense of the limits of Enlightenment rationality, all creating a conjunction that shifts our sense of who we are and what is possible. (P. 102)

This crisis of confidence extends to the question of how we can continue to view ourselves as self-conscious agents who have direction and a semblance of control over our lives. What can we say of the self as we confront the looming possibility that the modern world, in which rationality is valorized and prudent decision-making and action are touted, has been more a living myth than our primary existential reality?

Postmodernists differ in how radically they articulate this crisis of confidence and in their responses to the question of the continued existence of the self. Pauline Rosenau (1992) distinguishes between "affirmative" and "skeptical" (radical) postmodernists. Affirmatives maintain the view of a socially constructed, yet evidentiary reality, which would include an experiencing, if constructed, self. For affirmatives, the word *postmodern* signals a world that multiplies and hybridizes our identities. This is the diverse and complex, if not frenzied, world of the polysemic self, a self refracted, but not displaced, by all manner of signification. These postmodern commentators, including Kenneth Gergen and Norman Denzin, continue to affirm the self of everyday life, but consider our world to be exploding with images and representations of who we are, knocking our sense of self off center, but not totally eliminating identity as a primary category of experience. (Some prefer the term *late modern* for this viewpoint, since the fundamental reality of experience is not put into doubt.)

Skeptical or radical postmodernists, in contrast, doubt modern reality altogether, including the reality of the self. For skeptical postmodernists, the real world is one more myth of Western rationality. Such postmodernists take us away from the real into what Jean Baudrillard (1983) calls "hyperreality," where the self is an image, among myriad others, for conveying identity. In this "reality," the self is altogether removed from its traditional moorings as the central agent of experience to become the mere shadow of what it was. For skepticals, *postmodern* connotes a world in which there is nothing—no things at all in the traditional sense of a universe of objects separate and distinct from their representation.

The story of the social self ends differently, depending upon which path one chooses and how one responds to the crisis of confidence. One option has been to *react* to it. Such reactions parallel the affirmative/skeptical distinction. Some commentators reaffirm familiar renditions of identity, retrenching in "tried and true" versions of the social self formulated by the early pragmatists. They offer a plot showing how the social self might withstand the current siege, adapting to postmodern (or late modern) times, to be sure, but remaining essentially intact as it has been known for decades. Others skeptically dismiss the self as an empirical reality, effectively putting an end to its narrative by catapulting into an altogether different universe.

A second option for extending the story of the self *transforms* the crisis of confidence rather than deflecting or capitulating to it. Acknowledging the hard, complex times that confront the social self, this transformation reconceptualizes the self as a form of working subjectivity. Drawing upon its own cast of radical commentators, including Jean-François Lyotard, Ludwig Wittgenstein, and Michel Foucault, this option formulates a self that not only is a polysemic product of experience, but is also a byproduct of practices that diversely construct it in response to varied senses of what it could, or need, be.

We explore the first option in the following section, initially considering affirmative and then more skeptical endings. We finish the chapter by introducing the second option, showing the possibilities it holds for a new conclusion.

One Option: Reacting to the Crisis of Confidence

Affirmative postmodernists might react to the emergent crisis of confidence with hopeful, if not altogether optimistic, conclusions. While the examples we present can't characterize all affirmative reactions, they do suggest ways in which the social self might be salvaged from the postmodern onslaught.

The Saturated Self

Psychologist Kenneth Gergen is deeply troubled about the condition of the self in a postmodern world.[1] His 1991 book *The Saturated Self* provides a view of contemporary life that shakes his confidence in experience, but not to the extent that he radically denies the continuing significance of the self. He won't give up on it. Gergen affirms the self's reality, but worries over the way postmodernity makes it increasingly difficult to sustain a sense of unity and constancy in our lives. It's evident that this comes in crisis proportions when he writes, "Like the concepts of truth, objectivity, and knowledge, the very idea of individual selves—in possession of mental qualities—is now threatened with eradication" (p. x).

The postmodern threat is immediately apparent in the title of Gergen's book. According to Gergen, the postmodern world is so full of meanings that it risks saturating the self. Filled to overflowing, the self loses any distinct identity. It can no longer distinguish itself from all that it could be. This is alarming indeed, especially for a psychologist, who operates in a disciplinary context that traditionally has firmly centered the empirical self, if not prized an individualized subjectivity.

The postmodern world and its crisis are not just "out there" for Gergen; they affect him personally. For example, the first chapter of his book is titled "The Self Under Siege," and it's quickly apparent that it is the author himself who is being inundated. Deservedly an academic celebrity, he feels himself pulled in myriad directions at the same time. He wants experiential unity and mastery over his affairs, but these elude him. He can barely manage a life that seems to spin out of control at great speed in all directions. Returning to his office from a trip out of town, Gergen recounts what awaited him:

> An urgent fax from Spain lay on the desk, asking about a paper I was months late in contributing to a conference in Barcelona. Before I could think about answering, the office hours I had postponed began. One of my favorite students arrived and began to quiz me about the ethnic biases in my course syllabus. My secretary came in holding a sheaf of telephone messages, and some accumulated mail. . . . My conversations with my students were later interrupted by phone calls from a London publisher, a colleague in Connecticut on her way to Oslo for the weekend, and an old California friend wondering if we might meet during his summer travels to Holland. By the morning's end I was drained. The hours had been wholly consumed by the process of relating—face to face, electronically, and by letter. The relations were scattered across Europe and America, and scattered points in my personal past. And so keen was the competition for "relational time" that virtually none of the interchanges seemed effective in the ways I wished. (P. 1)

Gergen is clearly on the academic fast-track. He has contacts across the globe and demands come at him with lightning speed. Yet he's troubled. As honorific as the recognition is, something is missing, something that would signify a coherent sense of satisfaction with himself. As he begins the very next paragraph, we learn what that is: "I turned my attention optimistically to the afternoon. Perhaps here I would find moments of seclusion, restoration, and recentering"—three defining empirical characteristics of the modern self. Did the afternoon fulfill its promise? "No such luck," he laments.

From the very start, Gergen conveys the personal contours of the self he desires, which he is apparently losing to the increasingly frenzied pace of life. This is a self that regains its composure away from the daily rat race. While there is no doubt that such a self knows itself from social experience, ironically, it is most likely to really "find itself" *away* from the social. In seclusion, it can take stock of who it is and what life is all about, and perhaps restore itself. It requires a measure of separation from others, distance from the world, in order to function properly. In a word, it needs to be periodically "recentered" to be experientially secured.

Gergen continues, describing the afternoon during which he drifts farther off center:

> There were not only two afternoon classes, one rescheduled from the time spent in D.C., but more calls, an electronic-mail dispatch, more students, and a colleague visiting the campus from Chicago. At day's end, should I by chance feel understimulated, my car radio and the cassette deck awaited the homeward drive. Arriving at home I noticed that the grass was overgrown and the house trim badly needed painting. No time for such matters, as there was also the day's mail, newspapers, and my family eagerly waiting to talk about what they had been doing. There would be messages on the answering machine, additional calls from friends, and television beckoning with twenty-six channels of escape. . . . In effect, I was immersed in and consumed by social connection, and the results were numbing. (Pp. 1–2)

Gergen cringes from both the source and the consequences of the numbness. The anesthetizing source is a postmodern world where the global is becoming the local (and vice versa), and whose diverse and competing messages are very fast outpacing a self whose modern bearings seem no longer capable of reasonably managing input. Gergen explains that "the process of social saturation is producing a profound change in our ways of understanding the self" (p. 6), displacing both rationalist Enlightenment (which he calls "modern") and romanticist skills. We are no longer coherently thinking or deeply feeling entities as we increasingly become a "multiplicity of incoherent and unrelated languages of the self" (p. 6). The consequences are fragmenting.

> For everything we "know to be true" about ourselves, other voices within respond with doubt and even derision. This fragmentation of self-conceptions corresponds to a multiplicity of incoherent and disconnected relationships. These relationships pull us in myriad directions, inviting us to play such a variety of roles that the very concept of an "authentic self" with knowable characteristics recedes from view. The fully saturated self becomes no self at all. To contrast with the modern and romantic approaches to the self, I shall equate the saturating of self with the condition of *postmodernism*. (Pp. 6–7)

This saturating postmodern condition is, first of all, a life situation in which "all previous beliefs about the self are placed in jeopardy." From the foregoing extract, we take it that these featured a self that was integrated and coherently related to others. It had reasonable direction and was normally authentic. As Gergen explains, with postmodernism, "the very concept of personal essences is thrown into doubt" (p. 7). There is no essential, foundational understanding, only a plethora of possibilities for what we can be. As such, selves are in continuous construction, never completed, never fully coherent, never completely centered securely in experience. In a postmodern world where, according to Gergen, "anything goes," "each reality of self gives way to reflexive questioning, irony, and ultimately the playful probing of yet another reality. The center fails to hold" (p. 7).

We are not only numbed by the postmodern world's social saturation, but have become its major victims. Rapid technological change, especially what Gergen calls the proliferation of "technologies of social saturation"—including the print and broadcast media, rapid transit, computers, electronic mail, and diverse languages of identity—pull us every which way. This is not change per se, which we've always had to cope with. Rather, it's a fast, frenetic, and diversely articulated change whose informational consequences are rapidly eclipsing our capacities as human beings to digest and make coherent sense of. There are simply too many messages about who we are; informational overload inundates the real self. Gergen calls the resulting personal saturation and fragmentation the condition of "multiphrenia." This is not the experience of a split mind or of any other disease entity. Rather, it is a life condition characterized by the consumption of myriad self signifiers, none of which is privileged over the other, but all of which are allegedly genuine, each competing for the self we can be.

While Gergen refers to the intriguing irony of postmodern narrative with its myriad authenticities and the playful probing of basic understandings about the self, his general tone is foreboding. This is a sure sign of an affirmative postmodernism. Gergen's self is numb with social saturation and he nostalgically longs for some form of personal beacon, for a self that is centered in an experiencing agent. Even as Gergen suggests many negative outcomes from technologies of social saturation, he doesn't think all is lost. He figures that a certain degree of optimism is warranted for the self-liberating possibilities of postmodern pluralism. His final chapter provides a way out from the despair of total saturation. Looking back, Gergen figures that the modern world wasn't all that good anyway. If the empirical self triumphed through progress, the social horrors that resulted from modernism and the personal pain produced in the name of individual freedom were abominable. We can only "look back" weakly, he decides. Gergen writes that we might reappropriate limited selves for experience, as more dimly lit, yet certainly illuminated, beacons. These would have to be selves reckoned in relation to the newly emerging human possibilities of postmodernity, multiply centered, writ small, but nonetheless centered.

The Cinematic Self

Like Gergen, Norman Denzin is not radically skeptical about social reality, but he is deeply concerned about the fundamental challenges of knowing ourselves through the increasingly pervasive mediating images of cinema and television.

Unlike Gergen, Denzin is not overwhelmed by the technologies of saturation, perhaps because he is a sociologist by trade and presumes a socially formulated self in the first place. Instead, he examines new postmodern dimensions of the social as he critically orients to a world of media images that vie with reality for defining the empirical self.

Denzin (1991) contemplates a decentered self in his book *Images of Postmodern Society*; his symbolic interactionist roots still inform him that the social self draws from diverse sources for identity, even while there may now be significantly more of these sources. The idea of a self relatively free from social connection doesn't make much sense, especially in contemporary society, where social connection through both face-to-face and media encounters conveys a plethora of views of who and what we are, and can be. The issue is not so much decenteredness, but rather a crisis born of images that convey selves unrelated to the complex realities of everyday life. For Denzin the word *postmodern* is the code name for an "astral" or star-studded Hollywood image industry whose formulaic renditions of who we are divert attention from the concrete experiences of individuals. Hollywood is far too glib in representing—or misrepresenting—the complexities of the experience, most notably those relating to gender, class, race, and ethnicity.

There clearly is a semblance of reality at stake in Denzin's analysis, especially the "basic existential experiences of self, other, gender, race, nationality, family, love, intimacy, violence, death, and freedom" (p. xi). Inspired by C. Wright Mills (1963) and Stuart Hall (1985), Denzin (1997a) aims to point the way— analytically and methodologically—for a critical examination of how a mass-mediated, cinematic, and televisual world tortuously blurs the boundaries between images and "the so-called real world." Following Mills and Hall, he advocates new kinds of ethnography and analysis that might uncover the public myths that gloss over the many dimensions of our lives, to trace how public culture broadly infiltrates local narratives to produce one-dimensional identities.

> C. Wright Mills (1963) and Stuart Hall (1985) remind us that humans live in a secondhand world of meanings. They have no direct access to reality. Reality as it is known is mediated by symbolic representation, by narrative texts, and by cinematic and televisual structures that stand between the person and the so-called real world. In critically reading these texts, the new ethnographers radically subvert the realist agenda because the real world is no longer the referent for analysis. Ethnographies of group life are now directed to this world of televisual and cinematic narrativity and its place in the dreams, fantasies, and interactions of everyday people. (P. xvi)

This isn't the writing of someone with a radically skeptical, amorally playful attitude to the world, nor is it a multiphrenic numbness from being saturated by it. Rather, Denzin's position is a solid yet interpretively complex foundation for ideology critique (see Simons and Billig 1994). He argues that we are currently adrift in a sea of simplistic images, with the existential contours of the postmodern condition providing a basis for outrage and critical revelation. Orienting to a postmodern cinematic field, Denzin (1991) conducts what he calls "cinematic ethnography." He describes his method this way:

I offer, then, a critical ethnographic reading of this world and its meanings, as given in [social theory and in cinematic representations of life in contemporary America], [which] means that I am neither a custodian of nor a defender of post-modern culture, and the theories generated about it. I seek instead to write a post-modernist theory of cultural resistance, which acknowledges and explores my place in the creation of this culture and its meanings. I seek not a theory of cul-tural indifference (Connor 1989, p. 181), but a theory of resistance (Fields 1988). Such a theory examines how the basic existential experiences with self, other, gen-der, race, nationality, family, love, intimacy, violence, death, and freedom are pro-duced and given mythical meaning in everyday life. (P. xi)

Denzin proceeds to analyze critically six award-winning films from the 1980s: *Blue Velvet*; *Wall Street*; *Crimes and Misdemeanors*; *When Harry Met Sally*; *sex, lies and videotape*; and *Do the Right Thing*. He takes the films to be "readings of life in contemporary America" and examines them to "find postmodern contradictions . . . that mirror the everyday in this society and its popular culture" (p. ix). His leading question is: "How are the crucial identities grounded in class, gender, and race defined in the postmodern moment?"

Denzin locates postmodern motifs in each film, discerns their emphases, and compares them for how imaged or "realistic" they are. Again, this is not a play-ful analysis of signs of identity and experience in relation to mere signs of their real counterparts. Rather, the films are a postmodern field within which Den-zin does a kind of modernist fieldwork. His cinematic ethnography is highly evaluative, as he compares and judges the cinematic fields in relation to the everyday realities they depict, especially with respect to race, ethnicity, class, and gender.

Denzin's discussion of Spike Lee's 1989 film *Do the Right Thing* is most telling. He refers to the film as "an ethnography of the lived experiences of ordinary, everyday black and white, Italian, Korean, Puerto Rican, and Spanish-American men, women, and children in Brooklyn" (p. 126). The film provides us with a field of images of the lives it documents. Denzin assesses it for how well it conveys the multiperspectival meanings of everyday life for these Brooklyn men, women, and children, and concludes that it comes the closest of the six films to repre-senting lived reality. It can thus serve as a critical benchmark for evaluating other images of postmodern society.

According to Denzin, *Do the Right Thing* presents contemporary lived reality better than the other films because its gaze is self-reflective and offers the viewer choices. It doesn't present clear conclusions; issues are neither black nor white, so to speak.

Do the Right Thing provides an apt contrast to the films thus far considered. It takes its problems seriously, critiques its own solutions, and offers no easy an-swers to the conditions that it sees. It forces the viewer (black and white) to con-front hard, moral choices concerning the racial order in America today. . . .

In asking us to do the right thing, Spike Lee asks that we reconsider the mean-ings we have thus far brought, unthinkingly, to the ordinary signifiers that we wear on our backs. In opening our eyes in this way Lee has created a way to see past semiotics to a political economy of signs that does more than set the postmodern world adrift in a sea of unattached signifiers without meaning. Race is the unraveled sign of the contemporary age. (Pp. 126, 135)

Images of Postmodern Society concludes where it began. The book opens with a quotation from Maurice Merleau-Ponty (1964) that questions totalized portrayals of the real (sounding much like the transcendental philosopher who would turn the tables on the likes of James, Cooley, and Mead).

> "You believe you can think for all times and all men," the sociologist says to the philosopher, "and by that very belief you only express the preconceptions or pretensions of your culture." That is true . . . but where does he [she] speak from, the sociologist who speaks this way? The sociologist can only form his idea . . . by placing him[her]self outside history . . . and claiming the privileged position of absolute spectator. (P. 109)

With this, Merleau-Ponty transforms all totalities into particular stories, located in existential time and lived spaces.

Denzin ends his book on a similar note, pointing out that "theorists of postmodernism are storytellers," who don't dismiss the self, but communicate its complex identities in diverse ways. Again there's a quotation, this time from novelist and poet Robert Penn Warren (1959).

> By the time we understand the pattern we are in, the definition we are making for ourselves, it is too late to break out of the box. We can only live in terms of our definition, like the prisoner in the cage. . . . Yet the definition we have made of ourselves is ourselves. To break out of it, we must make a new self. But how can the self make a new self when the selfness which it is, is the only substance from which the new self can be made? (P. 351)

Penn Warren doesn't question the reality of the self, only the view that it comes with clear and distinct definition. For Denzin, the postmodern moment requires us to reveal the selves we are, not just the selves we imagine ourselves to be. That is what it means to "do the right thing." Denzin is not nostalgic for a centered self, but hopes for a self that "will itself be a tangled web of all that has come before."

The Self in Hyperreality

While affirmative postmodernists don't necessarily give up on the self, skeptical reactions to the crisis of confidence abandon the self to postmodern imagery. Perhaps the most radical example of this is Jean Baudrillard's full-throttle journey beyond modernity and reality.[2] This isn't a world that increasingly saturates a self in need of restoration and recentering, nor is it a world simplified beyond recognition by an image industry. Instead, it's a world in which there really isn't a paramount self—or any other paramount social form, for that matter. In the skeptical version of postmodernism, self references, self concerns, and definitions of self-worth are no more authentic than the ostensible realities of television commercials or Super Bowl half-time shows. For skeptical postmodernists, there is no "real" or "authentic"—or even substantial—self to compare. As a result, their commentaries on the real don't have moral force and can only be playful. Skeptical postmodern commentary is fancifully and ironically oriented to a sea of self-images, mere signs of other signs.

What sense of the real could possibly lead to such radical conclusions? Baudrillard (1983) describes the postmodern world as "hyperreal." Hyperreality doesn't rest on a metaphysics centered on a reality fundamentally independent of representation. That is a modernist metaphysics, classically concerned with the nature of the real, its relation to the representational, and the conditions of truthfulness. As far as human experience is concerned, the traditional modern questions would be what is the nature of conduct, how is it related to its signs such as speech and writing, and under what conditions are we to take what is said or written as truthful representations of people's lives? Indeed, the various human sciences have been devoted to answering just such questions.

Hyperreality, in contrast, obviates metaphysics, since the state of the universe is no longer a consideration. Skeptical postmodern commentary doesn't begin with the real and then consider its relationship to the representational. Rather, it conceptualizes an originary world of images, of signs of signs and signs of those signs. Ontological beginnings and endings are conflated and thus implode into a black hole of mere signposts of the real. Baudrillard (1995), for example, writes about the 1991 Persian Gulf War as an event that didn't "actually" happen. Rather, he suggests that it was more a continuous barrage of television images resembling a commercial advertising campaign, an MTV music video, or a Nintendo video game. Physically and emotionally distant, with virtually no American casualties, the war for the viewing public could just as well have been the artillery, missiles, radar, and antiaircraft fire of a video arcade.[3]

Notwithstanding distinctly modern sensibilities about the realities of the war in their own right, Baudrillard contends that monumental events have become absorbing visual experiences; as hyperreality, it doesn't matter whether or not they really happened. The distinction between the actual and what's seen to happen is blurred. Ironically, the Iraqi public itself experienced "the" war in similar visual terms, as they turned to CNN for its images of events, even while (modern) destruction and casualties brought home another reality. In this kind of world, what is real and what is image or representational can hardly be sorted out, let alone ultimately determined.

Baudrillard (1995) argues that the Iraqis were an enemy conjured up, and that the Gulf War was won in advance. The American war machine not only made that a certainty, but, more importantly, its hyperreal image apparatus deterred us from any contact with actual events and the "other." Stephen Pfohl (1997) puts this nicely in a review of Baudrillard's essays on the war:

> So as to deter an actual confrontation with such reality, a stereotypical image of total war was conjured up on screens worldwide and then artfully defeated by the flip of a switch, the press of a button, the turn of a dial. This was no "real" war but its simulation—a deceptively staged, one-sided, sign-driven, and premodeled promotional campaign. (P. 139)

Baudrillard is not concerned with whether the media may have misrepresented the realities of the war, since there is no distinction between the real and its signs in hyperreality. He makes this abundantly clear from the beginning of his book *Simulations* (1983), which he opens with a quote from Ecclesiastes. "The simulacrum is never that which conceals the truth—it is the truth which conceals that there is none. The simulacrum is true." Baudrillard then turns to an allegory from Borges, as a way of discussing just what the simulacrum might be:

> If we were able to take as the finest allegory of simulation the Borges tale where the cartographers of the Empire draw up a map so detailed that it ends up exactly covering the territory (but where the decline of the Empire sees this map become frayed and finally ruined, a few shreds still discernible in the deserts— the metaphysical beauty of this ruined abstraction, bearing witness to an Imperial pride and rotting like a carcass, returning to the substance of the soil, rather as an aging double ends up being confused with the real thing)—then this fable has come full circle for us, and now has nothing but the discrete charm of a second-order simulacra. (P. 1)

Baudrillard's point is that the map is not a simple representation of the territory, but becomes the territory. Like Marshall McLuhan (1967), Baudrillard insists that the medium itself is the message.

> Abstraction today is no longer that of the map, the double, the mirror or the concept. Simulation is no longer that of a territory, a referential being or a substance. It is the generation by models of a real without origin or reality: a hyperreal. The territory no longer precedes the map, nor survives it. Henceforth, it is the map that precedes the territory—PRECESSION OF SIMULACRA—it is the map that engenders the territory and if we were to revive the fable today, it would be the territory whose shreds are slowly rotting across the map. (P. 2)

Baudrillard is arguing that we have entered a new age; we can no longer view maps and territories, representations and realities, in the same way. Indeed, we can't even sustain a discussion in such oppositional terms. Metaphysics itself, as a philosophical enterprise centered on the nature of being, is no longer of any significance, since being is always already something other than what it is. It's a designation or vocabulary—if not an image—for itself. Returning once again to Borges's fable, Baudrillard elaborates the world of the hyperreal and the precession (coming before), not the procession (following), of simulacra. It is worth quoting him at length to capture the striking breadth and characteristic breathlessness of his argument.

> In fact, even inverted, the fable is useless. Perhaps only the allegory of the Empire remains. For it is with the same Imperialism that present-day simulators try to make the real, all the real, coincide with their simulation models. But it is no longer a question of either maps or territory. Something has disappeared: the sovereign difference between them that was the abstraction's charm. For it is the difference which forms the poetry of the map and the charm of the territory, the magic of the concept and the charm of the real. This representational imaginary, which both culminates in and is engulfed by the cartographer's mad project of an ideal coextensivity between the map and the territory, disappears with simulation—whose operation is nuclear and genetic, and no longer specular and discursive. With it goes all of metaphysics. No more mirror of being and appear-

ances, of the real and its concept. No more imaginary coextensivity: rather, genetic miniaturization is the dimension of simulation. . . . It no longer has to be rational, since it is no longer measured against some ideal or negative instance. It
is nothing more than operational. In fact, since it is no longer enveloped by an
imaginary, it is no longer real at all. It is a hyperreal, the product of an irradiat-
ing synthesis of combinatory models in a hyperspace without atmosphere. (Pp.
2–3)

With this, Baudrillard sweeps his readers into an entirely different universe,
a world awash in images. Yet, as radical as it is, it is presumably *our* postmodern
world nonetheless. It's different from Gergen's pseudo-postmodern milieu because it isn't organized within time and space; instead, it organizes them. There
are no privileged rules, no standard order, no clear experiential boundaries, no
centered or otherwise coherent selves. Hyperreality differs from Denzin's cinematic society in that it has no crucial social encounters against which to evaluate
received images. If, for Denzin and others, the image industry insidiously dis-
guises the real, for Baudrillard it produces consumers of the only "reality" available. In hyperreality, class, gender, and race are no more real than Mickey Mouse
or Donald Duck, except as their images might be conveyed as such. If anything,
hyperreality is like a carnival, according to Douglas Kellner (1989), without standard forms or moral order. Indeed, as Kellner explains, "For Baudrillard, the hyperreal is not the unreal, but the more than real, as when models of the United
States in Disneyland appear more real than their instantiations in the social world,
as the United States becomes more and more like Disneyland" (p. 82).

The electronic media, especially television, are largely responsible for this state
of affairs (see Baudrillard 1983, Kellner 1989). Images displace words; the visual
is paramount. Through television, we are taken instantly to distant and disparate
places. Space in terms of distance doesn't seem to matter. In seconds, contrasting
images of, say, the self, are juxtaposed, jarring a modern sensibility that usually
keeps them apart. An advertisement for cotton fabric (the "fabric of our lives"),
cloyingly warbled in the mood and phrases of existential longing, flashes into the
fantastic glitz and dizzying pastiche of the Academy Awards presentation, or the
sex and violence of a James Bond movie, which soon whizzes into an ad for the
coolness and masculinity of light beer and fast cars. It's never clear where one
ends and another takes off. And, if that weren't enough, the viewer can increase
the speed and further collapse space by channel surfing via remote control. As
Kellner (1992, p. 147) explains, television is a site of "pure noise," "a black hole
where all meaning and messages are absorbed in the whirlpool and kaleidoscope
of radical semiurgy, of the incessant dissemination of images and information to
the point of total saturation."[4]

A central presence in experience hardly matters in this world. Self is nowhere
and everywhere at the same time, totally abstracted, rapidly flitting before us in
myriad versions unanchored to concrete experiences. It's strutted about on news
programs, in sound bites from talking heads. We hear its authentic secrets from
the pained, troubled, and morally triumphant, who speak on television of their
inner sorrows, feelings, and private desires. They easily, plastically, and publicly
convey the profoundly personal. In a hyperreal environment, the self is totally on

display, multiply commodified for mass consumption. We receive the sights and sounds of a thousand inner spaces. A mere flick of the switch or flip of the channel selector offers an array of "we's" and "them's," of what we were, are, and can be. It's impossible to harbor or protect secrecy. Indeed, in postmodernity, privacy is tantamount to pathology, if not just another feature of hyperreality. The intimate is open to public view, the private totally exposed, with no personal spaces or needed experiential reckoning.[5]

Hyperreality puts an end to the story of the social self. The crisis of an embattled self is over, because any sense of a central point or fulcrum for being or from which to evaluate experience has disappeared. The metaphysics of presence, which oriented us to experiential time and space, is no longer meaningful; the self has no location as such, no witnessable presence to which we can coherently respond. Indeed, if we even try to speak of the self in the context of hyperreality, which Baudrillard does not, we can at best refer to it as a field of images for itself. The self appears in myriad locations, untamed by criteria of authenticity.

Perhaps we are actually glimpsing this in the explosion of self presentation in America at the turn of the twenty-first century, where nothing holds selves in place for any length of time and all manner of self definitions collide with each other. The mass media ply us with myriad accounts and images of possible selves, especially of our inner worlds. Radio call-in programs and Internet chatrooms present individuals with almost every conceivable triumph, trouble, and disorder, all embedded in telling personal stories. Television talk shows are virtually in the "self communication business." From Oprah Winfrey, Geraldo Rivera, and Jerry Springer to Ricki Lake, Montel Williams, Sally Jessy Raphael, and back again, we're informed of what we were, what we are, and what we could be by way of the "real" experiences and "true" confessions of endlessly "intriguing" or otherwise "interesting" people. Complicating the mix are the many identity experts who teach us the theoretical and clinical foundations for these lives, providing orienting narratives for the individual stories conveyed.[6]

"Who is this?" we ask. "Could it be me? Am I one of them?" Questions abound as we listen and compare personal accounts and explanatory narratives with our own experiences. And what exactly are our "own" experiences? How can we compare these mediated images with what lies within us when our own inner selves are themselves constructed from the same outer (social) world we view in front of us? Isn't the self that is "me" itself drawn from these mass-mediated communications, as Penn Warren suggested earlier? Are we simply doubles, mutually simulated forms of a common hyperreality? Is what I imagine myself to be, compared with what is being imagined for me, a mere succession of images, my own and others? We can easily extend such questions to the proliferation of the helping professions, to those whose business it is to define selves as healthy, dysfunctional, or recovering. Can we distinguish what is actual from the variety of selves others hope or direct us to be? Entering the extended field of selves that we peruse in the hundreds of advice and self-help books that we find in every supermarket, let alone bookstores, which images do we use to redesign ourselves, or help others to remake themselves?

But these are modern questions, raised at the cusp of postmodernity. They are questions whose inspiration relies on the division between the real and the representational, between actual selves and their possible identities. In hyperreality, where such divisions are obliterated, the questions are merely part of fanciful parlor games, delighting us even as they incite our misery. "The real is no longer what it used to be," Baudrillard (1983, p. 12) teases us. Neither is the self.

And, with that, the story of the social self stops in its tracks. While not all versions of this ending are as flamboyant as Baudrillard's,[7] the skeptical reaction chronicles the demise of a self that can no longer stand as a grounded source or object of experience. No longer an embattled or inundated survivor of the crisis, the self, like other modern social forms, is utterly swept away as a distinct entity in its own right. Skeptical postmodern commentary offers no role for a willful agent, for a socially established beacon of experience, for any other form of presence. It simply writes this out of the plot—or into it as one more image of itself.

A Second Option: Transforming the Crisis of Confidence

Hyperreality prompts us to ponder several issues. Does skeptical postmodernism mean that the empirical self vanishes from everyday life? Is the self merely an evanescent shadow of itself located in another universe? Has its serious narrative fallen forever silent? Does the challenge to modern conceptual systems obliterate the social self as a commanding presence, erase it as a social structure? Or is there another option for responding to this crisis? Is there any reason to believe that we continue to live by an empirical self of some sort? Is there a way in which an empirical self can be grounded in everyday life, yet retain the postmodern characteristics of decenteredness and diversity of meaning? Can the self's location in lived experience be conceptualized to coincide in some fashion with postmodern sensibilities?[8] Answers to these questions demand a different response to the crisis of confidence, one that resists total capitulation to skepticism and hyperreality. We believe we can tether the rampant and ubiquitous "playfulness" of the hyperreal by turning to the interpretive practices of everyday life, in particular the ordinary work of constructing and reflexively managing who and what we are. Let's begin to piece together that option for continuing the story of the social self toward a new ending.

Language Games and Pragmatics

Lyotard, a postmodern critic of the self in his own right, has stated flatly that the paramount self doesn't amount to much. Still, we think he does offer a way of conceptualizing the empirical so as to provide space for a self that we live by. Lyotard's position isn't as philosophically radical as Baudrillard's; for example, he isn't ontologically skeptical about the existence of objects and events in the world, including the self. But he is concerned with the question of how objects, events, and our identities are represented to us in contemporary life. His book *The Postmodern Condition* (1984) discusses the form that knowledge about such matters might take in a postmodern world. Notably, it provides a basis for considering the issue of self-knowledge, by ourselves and others, without altogether giving up on the self's reality.

Lyotard describes postmodernity as a condition of knowledge in highly developed societies. It's a condition in which we can no longer simply speak, write, and refer to things in the way we had before the late nineteenth century. We can infer from this that before then, words were taken to refer to things separate from the words themselves. Things were assumed, in principle, to have a constancy distinct from their diverse representations. Of course, words could incorrectly represent things, and in that sense transmute knowledge, but in that context the "thingness" of things was not so much in question as was their accurate representation. For example, one could misrepresent one's intentions or incorrectly read others', but the discrepancy between representation and reality would be taken as a matter categorically separate from the continuing existence or presence of intentions in the world.

Lyotard considers the hallmark of the postmodern condition to be the demise of this understanding, the "breaking up" of the grand bases or metanarratives of knowledge. "Simplifying to the extreme," Lyotard writes (p. xxiv), "I define postmodern as incredulity toward metanarratives." This, we would assume, includes the breakup or delegitimation of the grand narrative of self constancy. Unlike Baudrillard, who simply dismisses the self as passé, Lyotard provides for a continuing narrative of a more local kind centered on an empirically grounded postmodern self. This points the way toward a new ending for the social self's story (see Gubrium and Holstein 1994).

If the self is far removed from "the" self of yesteryear, Lyotard conceives of something far less evanescent than mere images in hyperreality. It is a self grounded in the concrete discursive locations of self construction, in the various places in everyday life where subjectivity is addressed and its meaning assembled and assigned. He hearkens a familiar vocabulary by calling his approach a "pragmatics" of knowledge. Borrowing from Wittgenstein (1953), Lyotard likens the current dizzying array of meanings and articulations to socially organized "language games." He locates these language games at "the crossroads of pragmatic relationships," centering them in practical activities.

The self, Lyotard explains, is increasingly constructed at the intersections, or institutional "nodal points," of specific communication circuits, whose language games serve to differentiate the modern centered *self* into the postmodern condition of communicated *selves*. Echoing pragmatism, Lyotard writes:

> A [modern] *self* does not amount to much, but no self is an island; each exists in a fabric of relations that is now more complex and mobile than ever before. Young or old, man or woman, rich or poor, a person is always located at "nodal points" of specific communication circuits, however tiny these may be. Or better: one is always located at a post through which various kinds of messages pass. No one, not even the least privileged among us, is ever entirely powerless over the messages that traverse and position him at the post of sender, addressee, or referent. One's mobility in relation to these language game effects (language games, of course, are what this is all about) is tolerable, at least within certain limits (and the limits are vague); it is even solicited by regulatory mechanisms, and in par-

ticular by the self-adjustments the system undertakes in order to improve its performance. (P. 15, emphasis in the original)

Lyotard is aware that locating self knowledge at "nodal points" of communication risks the possibility that the self might be viewed as overly determined.
In response to this, he argues that while the self can be thought of as "moves" in
language games located in particular institutional contexts, "the limits the institution imposes on potential language 'moves' are never established once and for
all (even if they have been formally defined)" (p. 17). What Lyotard apparently
has in mind is the idea of language games linked to institutions as the location of
rationalized and routinized, but not determinant, discursive offerings for self
definition. "No self is an island" because the language games of specific communication circuits, such as psychiatric clinics or marriage counseling, mediate
who and what we are. Yet these circuits do not have unlimited power "over the
messages that traverse and position" us as selves, but respond to our mobility
and our action in relation to them.

The self, then, is a particular set of sited language games whose rules discursively construct the semblance of a more or less unified subjectivity centered
in experience. This is not merely playful exercise. In certain societies, our own included, the self is a widely recognized, if not deadly serious, set of language
games. Not only do we speak of the self when we apply personal pronouns to individual action, thought, and sentiment, but the activity of doing so readily signifies a shared understanding that an experiential entity called the self is under
consideration, with its internal and external features in tow. Such language games
constitutively link representation (the subjectivity collectively referenced by the
self) with the reality represented (the self referenced). As a matter of practice,
self's representations construct the self as part of communicating it.

Where does such a self stand in relation to truth and authenticity? Certainly, postmodern narratives of self cannot be evaluated in terms of their universal truth value; they can only be truths in relation to "interpretive communities," as Stanley Fish (1980) might put it. Along similar lines, we can say that
a self can claim authenticity only within a particular language game or "form
of life," to again borrow from Wittgenstein. The emphasis is clearly on the locally produced character of the real and the genuine. Truth and authenticity
are placed squarely within and spread between language games, not in the relation between a grand narrative and the objects or matters it references. In Lyotard's form of postmodernism, the truths of objects like the self are matters
of local discursive recognition.

In this context, the self is not an arbitrary, "anything goes" (Gergen 1991, p.
7), "hyperreal" (Baudrillard 1983) "sea of images" (Denzin 1991). It is first and
foremost a *practical project* of everyday life. It is a self not necessarily referenced
in quotation marks, because our experience of it is not cosmically evanescent; it's
as real as its ordinary production and by-products. Its authenticities are situated
and plural—locally articulated, locally recognized, and locally accountable. Self
no longer references an experientially constant entity, a central presence or pres-
ences, but, rather, stands as a practical discursive accomplishment. (Which, of

course, could include the accomplishment of a sense of central presence in our lives.)

This positive framing of the postmodern condition of the self restores and restories our confidence in self's reality, but in new terms. It is now as much narratively constituted as actually lived. This transforms the either/or division between skeptical and affirmative postmodernisms, making the division itself, as well as other divisions, a matter of practical usage. In this transformed option, both the affirmative and the skeptical, both the modern and the postmodern, become interpretive resources; they are working frameworks and divisions we use in practice to derive a sense of the varied truths and authenticities we are. For example, we might take Gergen to have been playing a language game of postmodernity with his self at work on the very busy day described earlier, yet also find him hoping to play a modern game with his self in the near future.

The word *self* thus becomes a representational horizon for presence and personal agency. It exists in experience to the degree that it can be accountably communicated within an interpretive community. It is a "floating" signifier that is nonetheless socially organized, flexibly yet systematically constituting presence and agency through practical usage. To speak of the postmodern self is to mark a discursive framework within which further references, exchanges, accounts, desires, and resistances might be articulated. The "fabric of relations" and institutional "nodal points" in a postmodern world are so complex and mobile as to keep self construction a constant undertaking.

Alternative Subjectivities

This stance shifts the broad focus of interest to the practice of subjectivity and to the varied language games used in practice. By subjectivity, we are referring to the putative agent that is held practically and morally responsible for our actions. Most of us are so familiar with the contemporary Western vision of the self as this agent that we find it difficult to comprehend alternative subjectivities. In other societies and historical periods, however, agency and responsibility have been articulated in relation to a variety of other social structures, such as the tribe, the clan, the lineage, the family, the community, or the "crown." These forms of agency, of course, aren't completely unfamiliar, as we often assert the larger sources of our motives, reasoning, and passions. But, typically, these sources are taken to bear upon agency, not to be our final moral arbiters in their own right.

Nevertheless, for some time now, anthropologists and historians have been documenting alternative ways of constructing subjectivity (see, for example, Ariès 1962, Carrithers et al. 1985, Foucault 1977, Geertz 1984, Laslett 1965, Rosen 1995, Shore 1996, Shorter 1975, Tufte and Myerhoff 1979). Various cultures can figure subjectivity quite differently from our own. Recall from Chapter 1 that the Peruvian Akaramas barely distinguished the individual, formulating subjectivity instead in terms of the collectivity. Clifford Geertz (1984) offers additional illustrations of how subjectivity is conceived in other cultures. As a point of contrast and departure, he describes the Western conception of the person and the self as a bounded, unique, more or less integrated motivational and cognitive universe, a dynamic center of awareness, emotion, judgment, and action organized into a distinctive whole and set contrastively both against other such wholes and against its social and natural background. (P. 126)

As familiar as this sounds. Geertz points out that it is "a rather peculiar idea within the context of the world's cultures" (p. 126). He turns to his studies in Java, Bali, and Morocco for alternatives.

The Javanese conception of self, Geertz writes, is bifurcated, half comprising "ungestured feeling," the other half "unfelt gesture" (p. 128). By this he means that the Javanese conceive of the self in terms of contrasts, between "inside" and "outside," "refined" and "vulgar," between feelings and actions. In indigenous terms, the distinctions designate two sets of phenomena—inward feelings and outward actions—that stand as independent realms of being to be put into proper order independently of one another. According to Geertz,

An inner world of stilted emotion and an outer world of shaped behavior confront one another as sharply distinguished realms unto themselves, any person being the momentary locus . . . of that confrontation, a passing expression of their permanent existence, their permanent separation, and their permanent need to be kept in their own order. (P. 128)

For the Javanese, these are far from theoretical distinctions; they amount to the "empirical" subjectivity that the Javanese attribute to themselves. The separation of emotion and action seems to violate the powerful Western expectation for an integrated whole; it's the basis for our notions about phoniness and inauthenticity, for example (see the discussion of Hochschild's managed self in Chapter 3). Nevertheless, this is the preeminent subjectivity in the Javanese experience, one that is firmly incorrigible from their perspective; its discourse is indeed a form of life for them, as Wittgenstein would put it.

Subjectivity for the Balinese is constructed differently from both the Javanese self and familiar versions of the Western self. According to Geertz, an "intricate, obsessive ritual life" flourishes in Bali, where ceremony and performance form the basis of everyday interaction. While Goffman uses metaphors of the stage and theater to describe his version of the presented Western self, Geertz writes that the Balinese are "a much more dramaturgic people, with a self to match" (p. 128). If Goffman suggests that life is like theater in the West, it "*is* theater in Bali" (Geertz, p. 128, emphasis added).

As a result, there is in Bali a persistent and systematic attempt to stylize all aspects of personal expression to the point where anything idiosyncratic, anything characteristic of the individual merely because he is who he is physically, psychologically, or biographically, is muted in favor of his assigned place in the continuing and, so it is thought, never-changing pageant that is Balinese life. It is dramatis personae, not actors, that endure; indeed it is dramatis personae, not actors, that in the proper sense really exist. Physically, men come and go, mere incidents in a happenstance history, of no genuine importance even to themselves. But the masks they wear, the stage they occupy, the parts they play, and most important, the spectacle they mount remain and comprise not the façade but the

substance of things, not the least the self. Shakespeare's old trouper view . . . —
all the world's a stage and we but poor players, content to strut our hour, and so
on—makes no sense here. There is no make-believe; of course players perish, but
the play doesn't, and it is the latter, the performed rather than the performer, that
really matters. (P. 128)

Clearly, there are no unique selves for the Balinese. Instead, their paramount subjectivity takes the form of enduring roles or generic types. There's no backstage
or offstage where roles are momentarily abandoned or masks doffed to reveal
more authentic inner selves. Far from ineffable, the Balinese sense of *being* their
roles or masks (and not playing or wearing them) is the tangible source of practical and moral agency.[9]

If the Balinese *are* their roles or masks, self is something borrowed from social context and setting in Morocco, as the following account from Geertz indicates.

> The selves that bump and jostle each other in the alleys of Sefrou [the small Mo-
> roccan city Geertz studied] gain their definition from associative relations they
> are imputed to have with the society that surrounds them. They are contextual-
> ized persons. . . . Men do not float as bounded psychic entities, detached from
> their backgrounds and singularly named. As individualistic, even willful, as the
> Moroccans in fact are, their identity is an attribute they borrow from their setting.
> (P. 132)

While this sounds like Mead's version of the social self, according to Geertz
the Moroccan concept of selfhood is much more dynamically individualistic. Social encounters provide merely the parameters of self—a "vacant sketch" or an
empty "framework." These spare structures or skeletal outlines need to be filled
in, and this is forcefully accomplished within the flow of social interaction. This
idea of self and system of categorization, Geertz argues, leads to a sort of "hy-
perindividualism" in public relations:

> . . . by providing only a vacant sketch, and that shifting, of who the actors are . . .
> it leaves the rest, that is, almost everything, to be filled in by the process of in-
> teraction itself. What makes the mosaic work is the confidence that one can be as
> totally pragmatic, adaptive, opportunistic, and generally ad hoc in one's relations
> with others—a fox among foxes, a crocodile among crocodiles—as one wants
> without any risk of losing one's sense of who one is. Selfhood is never in danger
> because, outside the immediacies of procreation and prayer, only its coordinates
> are asserted. (Pp. 133–34)

If subjectivity varies across cultures, the familiar individualized self we
know also has a history. Its subjectivity was not always paramount in the Western experience. Family historian John Demos (1970, 1979) provides the glimpse
of an alternative. If Demos isn't concerned with the self per se, his interest in
the changing image of the family from American colonial times to the present
shows us that the everyday linkages of experience in colonial America were constructed in ways that differ markedly from the present. To use familiar phrasing, experience was embedded in a different set of language games than it is
now.

Demos (1979) argues that the social form we refer to as *the* family was "rather thinly sketched" in colonial America, casting doubt on the idea of a distinct and separate traditional family. Demos suggests that the language we use today to refer to *the* family is of recent vintage. In other words, the so-called traditional family we constantly refer to is a different language game from the one engaged in by our colonial forebears.

> When we seek to approach the colonial American family, one thing we notice immediately is that the "image" itself is rather thinly sketched. In short, people of this rather distant time and culture did not have a particularly self-conscious orientation to family life; their ideas, their attitudes in this connection, were far simpler than would ever be the case for later generations of Americans. Family life was something they took largely for granted. It was no doubt a central part of their experience, but not in such a way as to require special attention. This does not mean that they lacked ideas of what a "good family" should be and do—or, for that matter, a "bad" one—just that such notions carried a rather low charge in comparison with other areas of social concern. (Pp. 45–46)

From the documentary record of the colonial period, Demos shows that the term *family* did not stand alone in written material to reference a separate and distinct entity, but rather was a term of reference linked with broader social identities. In other words, the family was not a collective representation sui generis, in a category by itself, as we now commonly refer to it (cf. Durkheim 1961). Demos makes his point from many sources, among them a Puritan preacher's essay (Gouge 1622), from which Demos quotes the following.

> A family is a little church, and a little commonwealth, at least a lively representation thereof, whereby trial may be made of such as are fit for any place of authority, or of subjection, in church or commonwealth. Or rather, it is as a school wherein the first principles and grounds of government are learned; whereby men are fitted to greater matters in church and commonwealth. (P. 46)

Demos explains that the family and the community in the colonial period were connected in a relation of mutual reciprocity. They were part of a seamless set of concerns. Demos adds that this seamlessness was a general premodern pattern. While individuals, of course, moved back and forth between families, churches, governments, and other social enterprises, these were not conceived as distinct spheres of life. Rather, as the preacher writes, the family was a "lively representation" of the community. Demos comments in detail:

> [The family's and the community's] structure, their guiding values, their inner purposes, were essentially the same. Indeed the family was a community in its own right, a unit of shared experience for all its individual members. It was, first and foremost, a community of work—in ways hard for us even to imagine today. Young and old, male and female, labored together to produce the subsistence on which the whole group depended. For long periods they worked literally in each other's presence—if not at the same tasks. In other ways as well the family lived and functioned as a unit. Most leisure-time activities (which consisted largely of visiting with friends, relatives, and neighbors) were framed in a family context, as were education, health care and some elements of religious worship. (P. 47)

Putting it in Wittgensteinian terms, the colonial American family was a different "form of life" than it is today. As terms of reference for family life started to change in the early decades of the nineteenth century, a sharp new image for the family developed, according to Demos. No longer was the family "thinly sketched," but rather became categorically distinguished, profusely written about, and vociferously discussed as an entity unto itself. One might venture to say that the family as a distinct and separate collective representation, separate from the community, the church, and other social forms, began to appear for the first time in America as family discourse proliferated (see Gubrium and Holstein 1990).

The family's rise to prominence partially rested on the way it was being differentiated from, and compared with, other social forms. No longer "seamlessly" interwoven with other aspects of everyday life, the emergence of family as a distinctive entity virtually required the articulation of contrasting social forms if it was to be recognized as an entity in its own right. It needed discursive counterparts—for example, the exterior worlds of "society" or "work" or the interior world of self—if it was to be separately distinguished. Demos continues:

> Within this matrix of ideas the family was sharply defined. Henceforth the life of the individual home, on the one hand, and the wider society, on the other, represented for many Americans entirely different spheres ("spheres" was indeed the customary term they used in conceptualizing their varied experiences). The two were separated by a sharply delineated frontier; different strategies and values were looked for on either side. . . . Home—and the word itself became highly sentimentalized—was pictured as a bastion of peace, of repose, of orderliness, of unwavering devotion to people and principles beyond the self. Here the woman of the family, and the children, would pass most of their hours and days—safe from the grinding pressures and dark temptations of the world at large; here, too, the man of the family would retreat periodically for refreshment, renewal, and inner fortification against the dangers he encountered elsewhere. (P. 51)

This separation of spheres gave rise to a framework for thinking about, and worrying over, the relation between public and private experience; it created an awareness of the entire range of desires, thoughts, feelings, and actions as they played out in the competing realms. The individual was in authentic repose in the private sphere, suffering from impersonal artifices and insults in the public sphere, if it wasn't being overwhelmed by it.[10] This prompted further discussion of the place of the individual in the social mix, especially in terms of what Demos refers to as the cult of the "self-made man." One result was the advent of the image and discourse of the experiencing, responsible, morally accountable individual, with his or her *own* personal needs, interests, thoughts, feelings, and life-space. In effect, the emergence of the public/private distinction also provided a "logical geography" (Ryle 1949) for the formation, as well as for the spoilage, of the distinctly experiencing individual.

Alternative Discourses

It's important to underscore the broader argument upon which our new option for the postmodern self rests, especially as it relates to existing and newly emerging language games, their social practices, and the issue of subjectivity. For this, we turn to what Michel Foucault (1977) calls the "history of the present" or genealogical analysis. Summing up his project in *Discipline and Punish*, a book on the "birth of the prison" in the French penal system, Foucault states clearly what he is and isn't aiming to do:

> I would like to write the history of this prison, with all the political investments of the body that it gathers together in its closed architecture. Why? Simply because I am interested in the past? No, if one means by that writing a history of the past in terms of the present. Yes, if one means writing the history of the present. (P. 31)

By writing a history of the present, Foucault is avoiding what Demos implicitly warns us against. Demos, of course, isn't engaged in the same type of analysis as Foucault's, but he is concerned that his reader not figure that he is comparing, pure and simple, family life in colonial America with the twentieth century American family, with their respective implications for self definition. When Demos states that the colonial family is "thinly sketched," we can take him to mean that it hasn't emerged as a distinct "discourse," to use Foucault's term (see Gubrium and Holstein 1990). In the thought, action, and vocabulary of the times, family is not yet a separate entity of its own, constituting a categorically distinct set of related social practices. Nor has the related discourse of the ordinary, "self-made" individual developed.

Foucault's own project centers on the political technology of the body and the formulation of the subject. His leading goal is to account for the place of the subject in social life, how that subject is conceived, its vocabulary of agency, and, in particular, how the subject is constituted through the force of its bodily relations with others. Foucault is not especially concerned with the self as such, but, rather, with what it is that prompts us to view the body as possessing, say, a self with interests of its own and that rationally orients to itself and to the world.

In *Discipline and Punish*, Foucault focuses on the social and political processes that constitute the modern prison as a form of social (and self) control. He asks what underlying practical sense of the relation between social control and subjectivity—what "discourse"—led us away from bodily torture toward more humane incarceration and a correctional orientation for the modern prison? What language games for the subject, in other words, made for a break from the political torture of the body? Centering his analysis on the relation between the power of the state, the body, and conceptualizations of subjectivity, called "bio-power," Foucault first presents us the residue of a pre-Enlightenment discourse of that relationship in the opening scene of *Discipline and Punish*. We are shocked by the horrid portrayal of the torture of a man condemned for attempting to assassinate King Louis XV. We cringe as his body is flayed, burned, drawn, and quartered in public view.

> On 2 March 1757 Damiens the regicide was condemned "to make the *amende honorable* before the main door of the Church of Paris," where he was to be "taken and conveyed in a cart wearing nothing but a shirt, holding a torch of burning wax weighing two pounds;" then, "in the said cart, to the Place de Grève, where,

on a scaffold that will be erected there, the flesh will be torn from his breasts, arms, thighs and calves with red-hot pincers, his right hand, holding the knife with which he committed the said parricide, burnt with sulphur, and, on those places where the flesh will be torn away, poured molten lead, boiling oil, burning resin, wax and sulphur melted together and then his body drawn and quartered by four horses and his limbs and body consumed by fire, reduced to ashes and his ashes thrown to the winds." (P. 3)

Foucault asks why criminals were subjected to such horrible bodily torture. Why were they made to beg for forgiveness in a public spectacle? The answer is that the spectacle was a political event that was informed by a sense of the seamless relation between the body of the king (the crown), social control, and subjectivity. As all people were, Damiens was conceived literally as a subject of the king, his body and soul an inseparable extension of the crown. An attack on the body of the king had to be attacked in turn, as a red hot iron might be used to cauterize an open wound. The spectacle was not a scene whose central character was an independent subject, with a self of his own, being tortured. This might have caused one to consider it cruel and unusual punishment. (Only now, given our current sense of individualized subjectivity, can we feel sorry for what Damiens "must have gone through" or how "he must have felt," implicating both our own and his inner self.) Rather, the spectacle rested on a discourse of knowledge and power with the crown in command of a certain scenic truth. As Hubert Dreyfus and Paul Rabinow (1982, p. 146) summarize it, "the figure of torture brings together a complex of power, truth, and bodies. The atrocity of torture was an enactment of power that also revealed truth. Its application on the body of the criminal was an act of revenge and an art."

What was the "subjectivity" at stake? Foucault suggests that Damiens was not so much an individual, agentic self as he was an offending appendage to the crown that had to be publicly excised. Within the prevailing discourse of subjectivity, Damiens was something like a cancer on the sovereign. As such, he was simply inconceivable as an object of sympathy or compassion.

Further into the book, Foucault introduces the reader to the subjective byproduct of an alternative discourse, one that is immediately less spectacular in its consequential bodily practices. As Foucault illustrates from the rules "for the House of young prisoners in Paris," the criminal's body is now, eighty years later, strictly regulated, not publicly and brutally assaulted. Articles 17, 18, and 28 provide a glimpse of a contrasting regimen of power, which, as we will see, belies a different truth regarding subjectivity and the body.

Art. 17. The prisoners' day will begin at six in the morning in winter and at five in summer. They will work for nine hours a day throughout the year. Two hours a day will be devoted to instruction. Work and the day will end at nine o'clock in winter and at eight in summer.

Art. 18. *Rising.* At the first drum-roll, the prisoners must rise and dress in silence, as the supervisor opens the cell doors. At the second drum-roll, they must be dressed and make their beds. At the third, they must line up and proceed to the chapel for morning prayer. There is a five-minute interval between each drum-roll.

Art. 28. At half-past seven in summer, half-past eight in winter, the prisoners must be back in their cells after the washing of hands and the inspection of clothes in the courtyard; at the first drum-roll, they must undress, and at the second get into bed. The cell doors are closed and the supervisors go the rounds in the corridors, to ensure order and silence. (Pp. 6–7)

Torture as a public spectacle has gradually disappeared. The "gloomy festival of punishment" is dying out, along with the accused's agonizing plea for pardon. It is replaced by a humanizing regimen, informed by a discourse of the independent, thinking subject whose criminality is correctable. Scientific methods of scrutiny and courses of instruction are viewed as the means for returning the criminal to right reason, back to the proper folds of society. The subject is no longer a mere appendage of the crown; rather, he is considered to precede categorically the power and regime to which he is now being rationally subjected. This is a new kind of subject, one conceptualized as independent and separate from the state. This subject's distinct self-interests lead him to freely agree with others in acknowledging the broader social entity—society—of which he will contractually be a part. It is a subject with a mind or self of his own, at least in principle, who can be incited to self-scrutiny and who responds to corrective action. Foucault characterizes this as a new discourse (regime and regimen) of power/knowledge:

> This discourse provided, in effect, by means of a theory of interests, representations and signs, by the series and geneses that it reconstituted, a sort of general recipe for the exercise of power over men: the "mind" as a surface of inscription for power, with semiology as its tool; the submission of bodies through the control of ideas; the analysis of representations as a principle in a politics of bodies that was much more effective than the ritual anatomy of torture and executions. (P. 102)

Under this regime, it became much more efficient to effect control through the minds of subjects than through "mindless" appendages of the sovereign. The new discourse of subjectivity constituted a self that could control itself from within, making the brutal, now ostensibly inhumane, assault of the body an unnecessary redundancy.

For Foucault, Jeremy Bentham's plan for the Panopticon prison actualizes as well as symbolizes this form of governance, combining a new concept of power with concrete application. The Panopticon consists of a tower located at the center of a large courtyard, facing a set of surrounding buildings. The cells of the buildings, and the inmates within, are completely visible from the tower, but the inmates, who are sequestered from each other, cannot see if the guard is in the tower. So, the inmates must act as if surveillance is ever-present, in effect causing them to rule themselves because they take surveillance for granted. This epitomizes a new disciplinary technology, where power does not operate like a force from the outside, but works through inner self-scrutiny, the subject disciplining (and thus ruling) himself according to what he takes to be a hidden guardian. The political technology of the body in the new discourse operates as a language of the self within the body, not just on the body as such, even while the body still serves as a surface of signs of what lies within. Quoting from Servan, Foucault conveys the political utility of the new discourse: "When you have thus formed the chain of ideas in the heads of your citizens, you will then be able to pride yourselves on guiding them and being their masters. A stupid despot may constrain his slaves with iron chains; but a true politician binds them even more strongly by the chain of their own ideas" (p. 103).

A discourse, then, is a kind of constructive history of the present; in practice, its vocabulary, real objects of reference, and system of representation work to constitute their own subjectivities, along with the latter's respective pasts, presents, and futures. As Foucault would have put it, discourse virtually speaks the subject (Schneider 1991). Foucault also has traced how the bio-power of discourse constituted new subjectivities in medicine (1975) and in the history of insanity (1973) and sexuality (1978a). Across the various institutional realms, newly emergent discourses formed subjectivities of their own. Rather than the individual self being the center of experience through time immemorial, Foucault argues that the idea of a centered presence is itself a discursive formation, part of a historical set of language games, if you will, that articulate the discourse of a present subjectivity on several fronts. "Knowable man (soul, individuality, consciousness, conduct, whatever it is called)," writes Foucault (1977, p. 305), "is the object-effect of this analytical investment," the product of a distinctive discourse of power/knowledge.

Our second option for extending the story of the self into postmodern context relies upon this notion of variable discourses and their subjectivities. When we can entertain multiple possibilities for how subjectivity is constructed—in line with the pragmatics of different sets of language games—it's possible to spin a new ending that implicates diversely representational yet grounded selves. Nikolas Rose (1990) provides a view of where this story can take us in his description of how the "soul" or self became increasingly "governed," that is, discursively constructed, by emerging institutional discourses during and following World War II.

> Our intimate lives, our feelings, desires and aspirations, seem quintessentially personal. Living at a time when we are surrounded by messages of public troubles that appear overwhelming—war, family, injustice, poverty, disease, terrorism—our mental states, subjective experiences and intimate relationships offer themselves as perhaps the only place where we can locate our real private selves. There is, no doubt, much comfort to be afforded by such a belief. But it is profoundly misleading.
>
> Our personalities, subjectivities, and "relationships" are not private matters, if this implies that they are not the objects of power. On the contrary, they are intensively governed. Perhaps they always have been. Social conventions, community scrutiny, legal norms, familial obligations and religious injunctions have exercised an intense power over the human soul in past times and other cultures. . . . Thoughts, feelings and actions may appear as the very fabric and constitution of the intimate self, but they are socially organized and managed in minute particulars. (P. 1)

Locating the self in discourses, not in itself, Rose decenters it from experience. He shows how the technologies of self construction applied by psychologists and other mental health professionals during World War II, in particular, worked to give concrete, especially textual, shape to the private, inner self now so familiar to us. More to the point, Rose indicates that these technologies of self construction simultaneously constituted and fleshed out a subject they otherwise were only meant to assess. The technical discourse of a private self emerged across the self-constituting professions, reflexively motivating its practitioners to produce the objective "facts" of inner experience to substantiate the self. As these professions gained popular acceptance, an informing discourse was embellished into a fine-tuned "therapeutic culture." This did not produce an inner self that was a mere fleeting image of itself or an entity that didn't amount to much. Rather, it gave rise to the core subjectivity of one of the major industries of our times, whose business is the exacting construction, concise interpretation, and therapeutic reformation of the empirical self.

Rose's storyline jibes with postmodern claims of self construction, if not with hyperreality or evanescence. It shows how the business of self construction has now spread well beyond the psychological sciences. Selves are now paraded and bandied about in diverse institutional sites, from pastoral counseling, self-help groups, and mental commitment hearings, to romance novels, television talk shows, and advice books. Much like Bentham's Panopticon, we have taken on board—within ourselves—the language games and associated subjectivities of Foucauldian "guardians" of all kinds, inciting ourselves to display and communicate the selves expected of us and that we assume others, in turn, share with us.

This contemporary panopticism is a massive set of language games we engage in virtually every day. Their various terms locate and discursively ground the construction of the empirical self. This ending for the story of the self directs us to the local incitements of seemingly endless personal narratives. These are not grand narratives of the self, to be sure; instead, they are accounts that borrow from diversely situated and formulated language games to convey who and what we are in our private spheres and very "own" inner lives.

CHAPTER FIVE

Ending the Story in Interpretive Practice

The revised plot of our story of the self takes us immediately to the myriad sites where subjectivity is constructed in today's world. These sites, as Lyotard (1984, p. 15) informs us, present the self with "a fabric of relations that is now more complex and mobile than ever before." Our leading concern in this chapter is how to conceptualize that complexity and mobility—how to think about the processes by which the questions of who and what we are can be interpreted and their answers applied to experience. In other words, we want to know how the intricate social apparatus of everyday life articulates the language games for the selves that we take each other to be, which, in turn, we assume to be the identities underlying our actions.

We embark on this new ending with the reminder that self interpretation is more prevalent in today's world than ever before. Now, more than ever, self conceptualization and related technologies of self construction have moved from the grand theoretical halls of academe to become virtually everyone's business. The self has become a cottage industry. From formulating psychological profiles and developing "social" legal defenses (such as the argument that perpetrators are products of irresistible social circumstances) to publicly authenticating our feelings in pop psychology's vernacular, ubiquitous language games of the self continually incite us to formulate who we are, articulating ourselves and each other in terms of the categories we employ. We all participate in the varied practices that construct the selves we live by, giving voice to the beacon of experience some consider the self to be.

The Self at Work

If we can no longer view the self as experientially centered, nor straightforwardly study it using positivist research techniques, how do we bring its diverse language games and their associated practices into view? Conceptualizing a method is, first and foremost, a matter of formulating a way of thinking about a phenomenon. Certainly, specific research techniques come into play as one gathers empirical material and then applies various analytic strategies. But the prior concern, the one of conceptualization, prompts us to ask how to orient to the subject matter in the first place. The postmodern denigration of the empirical self also prods us to wonder what, after all, is now called the self? Does the self, indeed,

amount to nothing (no thing) and thus warrant only passing attention as a cu-
riosity of our social psychological past? Or, if the self is now in more places than
ever—as much a commonplace figure of speech as the now constructed beacon
of action—how do we conceptualize a method for documenting the way this
works in contemporary life?

Language On and Off Holiday

Such analytic questions are close to the heart of Ludwig Wittgenstein's (1953,
1958) later writing on the philosophy of language. His formulation of the relation
between terms, objects, and meanings provides a point of departure for conceptualizing a method for studying the pragmatics of the postmodern self. Wittgenstein leads us to ask, how are we to orient to the relationship between the terms
we use to describe ourselves and the selves we are?

Early in his book *Philosophical Investigations* (1953), Wittgenstein introduces us
to the concept of *language games*, which we discussed briefly in the last chapter in
relation to Lyotard's pragmatics. When Wittgenstein first mentions the term, he
is considering the question of how to think about the meaning of words. To start,
he offers the following commonplace view of "the essence of human language":
"Every word has a meaning. This meaning is correlated with the word. It is the
object for which the word stands" (p. 2). He then introduces his well-known argument against this view. In the course of the discussion, Wittgenstein makes case
after case for the varied meanings that a word can have in the diverse contexts
of its use.

Consider, for example, the word *state*. The word takes a particular meaning
in the context of governmental or political jurisdiction, as in, say, the state of Wis-
consin. It means something distinctly different in the context of "a state of confusion," where it represents a mental or emotional condition or disposition. And
of course there are "Secretary of State," "state of disarray," "lying in state," "state
of equilibrium," or "state your piece!" Examples of other terms abound: "leather
belt," "seat belt," "Bible Belt," "belt a home run," "belt down a shot of whiskey,"
"belt out a song." Wittgenstein's point is that the meaning of a word derives from
the connections made within the contexts of its use.

While Wittgenstein doesn't speak directly about the actual written form that
terms can take, we might envision the meaning of terms as implicit hyphenations.
The term *state* connotes one thing when it is used as "state-as-a-territorial-
designation," and quite another as "state-as-a-psychological-disposition." It may
be any number of other things, depending on how it might be hyphenated. In
any case, Wittgenstein's point is that a word's meaning depends on how it is actually *used*. If it weren't so awkward, we could take him seriously in how we write
and necessarily hyphenate all terms of reference the way we did for the term *state*
(see Sandywell et al. 1975).

Focusing on the meaning of words-in-use, Wittgenstein then refers to different configurations of usage as language games. He doesn't use the term *game*
lightly. In his view, usage is more or less wittingly guided by the rules of language games, so to speak. In practice, these rules specify how terms, meanings,

and things are to be connected. These are working rules in the sense that they are not necessarily formally specified, but provide a working sense of direction for "what goes with what." For example, working rules provide a sense for how to respond to *state* when it is hyphenated "lying-in-state" as opposed to hyphenated "state-of-disarray." Being rule-like, a language game is also a course of action; in practice, these rules inform participants how to make proper moves in the game, as it were.

For Wittgenstein, then, language is far from being neatly ordered, where every word has a meaning that correlates with its object in the world. Instead, he views language (games) as working systems of usage or "forms of life," as he also often calls them, in which speakers and other participants articulate more or less recognizable linkages between words and things, drawing from well-established connections, adding their own, and coming upon new ones as communication unfolds. Old rules, new rules, and unforeseen rules guide usage *in practice*. Language is always both old and new in that regard, never fixed into some highly structured configuration of meaningful terms of reference. In other words, language is always *at work*, specifying new meanings, rearticulating old objects, assigning both old and new connotations to terms of reference.[1] Wittgenstein likens this to an ancient city: "Our language can be seen as an ancient city: a maze of little streets and squares, of old and new houses, and of houses with additions from various periods; and this surrounded by a multitude of new boroughs with straight regular streets and uniform houses" (p. 8).

What happens when the philosopher lets language go "on holiday," Wittgenstein asks. What happens when we ignore the work that language does in everyday life? According to Wittgenstein, that is when unyielding philosophical problems arise. When we don't take the time to consider how language works in practice, we run into vexing complications, if not contradictions, concerning the relation between terms, meanings, and objects. For example, aiming to define things precisely, we might seek to discern the essential or precisely correlated set of meanings for the term *state*, in order to specify to what the term and meaning actually apply. But what would we do with the diverse, multilayered, and emergent meanings of the term that continue to develop and that criss-cross everyday life? Would we treat most of them as somehow in error, figuring that they incorrectly, irregularly, or even arbitrarily reflect what we, as proper philosophers, have discerned on our own? Does this lead us, at the end of the day, to conclude that proper meaning can only be philosophically specified?

It's evident that Wittgenstein has designs to alter this face of philosophy altogether. He argues that by traditionally approaching language as if it were on holiday and not doing the work of constructing meaning (off holiday), philosophy has created the very problems that plague it. It isn't so much language that's the problem, but how philosophers have treated it. As a form of life, language use has problems enough of its own. Why add to them by squeezing the life out of it? Thus Wittgenstein leads us to seriously consider language at work, and to describe how it reflexively articulates and constructs the terms, meanings, and objects it ostensibly specifies.

Inspired by Wittgenstein, Lyotard (1984) advances the notion of the self at work as part of his "pragmatics" of self knowledge. Lyotard views the self as a set of language games, less centered in experience than actively put to work in various ways, at specific times and places, to interpret, designate, and guide our actions and related senses of our inner lives. While a grand philosophical self is diminished, but not eliminated, in usage, a practical self emerges. Still empirical, it is a kind of subjectivity that is *used* to reflexively specify who and what we were, are, and will be. It's a self whose subjectivity is now interactionally at stake rather than philosophically taken for granted. If it can no longer be viewed as the leading beacon of experience, its diverse forms discursively anchor who we are in virtually every quarter of daily life. If it is no longer some essential structure located behind or within our actions, the self nonetheless "comes up" continually in contemporary life.

Who are you? Who am I? What kind of persons are we? What have we personally done? Who will we become? What do we really think? How do we actually feel? We *use* the self to answer these questions, to locate our selves and formulate borders between them. In the process, we construct identity and difference. In practice, the self and its associated vocabulary are a living language game, applied to locate and define who we are as individual members of society.

Socially Situated Language Games

Years ago, but well ahead of his time, Mills (1940) first suggested that we consider motives as a kind of language game. He argued that spoken references to motives can be used to account for our actions; they are not something that determines them. Mills doesn't actually describe the accounting process as a language game, but he does recognize how accounts are put to work to explain why people act as they do. Mills refers to this family of explanations for action as "vocabularies of motive" and goes on to argue that distinctive vocabularies might emerge in response to the needs of particular social settings.[2] He takes seriously the fact that "human actors do vocalize and impute motives to themselves and to others" and chooses to "analyze the observable lingual mechanisms of motive imputation and avowal as they function in conduct" (p. 439). His analysis of motives-in-use shows how individuals account for their actions as they construct their subjectivities.

Mills draws upon the early pragmatists to make his point, anecdotally illustrating the properties of motives at work. In the following scenario involving a "businessman," he suggests that vocabularies of motive are not just rhetorical, but, in the long term, become actual components of the self, serving to designate our identities in practice.

> One of the components of a "generalized other," as a mechanism of societal control, is vocabularies of acceptable motives. For example, a businessman joins the Rotary Club and proclaims its public-spirited vocabulary. If this man cannot act out business conduct without so doing, it follows that this vocabulary of motives is an important factor in his behavior. The long acting out of a role, with its appropriate motives, will often induce a man to become what at first he merely

sought to appear. Shifts in the vocabularies of motive that are utilized later by an individual disclose an important aspect of various integrations of his actions with concomitantly various groups. (Pp. 444–45).

If Mills conceives of vocabularies of motive as a kind of language game, it's also clear from this extract that usage is influenced by the speaker's social location. The businessman proclaims a public-spirited vocabulary appropriate to a particular way of conducting business. Subsequent participation in other groups—changes in social location—provoke shifts in vocabulary. Motives and social location are interdependent. If vocabularies of motive are language-in-use, they are also socially distributed. Particular situations influence their participants to speak locally relevant vocabularies of motive, turning such vocabularies into situationally accountable language games.

Mills thus directs us to "situated" actions and language use, and, in the process, urges us to take note of the broader social structures of which language games are a part. The self (including its motives) may be diversely and spontaneously articulated in talk and interaction, but this isn't the whole story. Self constructions are also conditioned by factors lying outside of talk, by the social arrangements in which talk is embedded.[3] Wittgenstein only adumbrates this in his references to "language games" and "forms of life." While the self, especially in postmodern times, might be usefully viewed as a set of language games at work and not on holiday, these language games are nonetheless variably located across the social landscape. They are neither free-floating systems of signs within hyperreality nor isolated, unaccountable speech acts and conversational exchanges. To move beyond Wittgenstein's philosophical (or, more precisely, antiphilosophical) point of departure, we must follow Mills's lead in developing an analytic procedure that takes the social distribution and localization of language games more fully into account.

The Self in Everyday Life

Lyotard's obituary for the metanarrative and the paramount self doesn't obviate an empirical self so much as it redeploys it into the varied contexts of the practice of everyday life. In Lyotard's view, the self's story must attend to both the processes by which, and circumstances in which, the self is put to work. How does one orient to such a self? What does it mean to view the construction of self in this way? How, analytically, do we prevent language from going on holiday?

Phenomenological Sources

Phenomenological sociology and ethnomethodology provide a set of guiding principles for viewing reality and, by implication, the self as a social accomplishment. Alfred Schutz (1962, 1964, 1967, 1970) draws from Edmund Husserl's (1970) phenomenological philosophy to build a conceptual bridge to sociology. Husserl was concerned with the subjective underpinnings of knowledge and insisted that the relation between perception and its objects, such as the self, was not passive.

Husserl explained that human consciousness is not a mere receptor, but actively constitutes objects of experience. Focusing on everyday life, Schutz took up Husserl's interest in the ways in which ordinary members of society constitute their worlds, which we presume would include themselves.

Stressing the constitutive or reflexively constructive nature of consciousness and social interaction, Schutz (1964) argues that, in the first instance, the social sciences should focus on the ways that the life world—that is, the lived world that every person takes for granted—is produced and experienced. To view this world in production requires that we temporarily set aside the experiential assumptions of the "natural attitude" (Schutz 1970), which is the everyday cognitive stance that takes the world and its objects to be principally "out there" or "in here," separate and distinct from acts of perception or interpretation. In the natural attitude, language is indeed put on holiday. It is assumed that the life world exists before members are present and will be there after they depart. It is "objective" in the sense that meanings are in their place, separate from us in space and time, being only indirectly affected by usage.

Schutz recommends that we study social reality by eschewing the natural attitude, by in effect "bracketing" the life world. By this, he meant temporarily setting aside one's taken-for-granted orientation to a world of essential objects. Bracketing requires us to put ourselves in a constructive frame of mind in order to see the *process* by which social reality becomes real for its adherents, in order to view, among other things, the language of the self being put to work to provide identity with substance and form. As far as the self is concerned, the point would be not to take it for granted as simply "out there" in others' lives or "in here" within our persons. Rather, we must ask ourselves how it is that we come to view it as "out there" or "in here."

This amounts to temporarily suspending ontological judgments about the nature and essence of things. The researcher can then focus on the ways in which members of the life world themselves constitute its recognizable social structures such as the self, which they treat as real. It provides a basis for examining the commonsense knowledge and everyday reasoning members use to objectify social reality, that is, to confer objectivity on its social structures. In other words, bracketing offers a method for viewing *how* figures of speech, such as the self, come to take on a life of their own that appears to exist outside of language, how they become objects of experience.

Schutz also indicates that individuals orient to their life worlds by way of diverse stocks of knowledge. These are composed of commonsense constructs and categories that are social in origin and location. Images, theories, ideas, values, beliefs, and attitudes, among other forms of knowledge, are reflexively embedded in social constructions, making them meaningful. We use our stocks of knowledge to meaningfully frame who we are, to typify our intentions and motivations, to derive intersubjective understandings, and to coordinate interaction. Paralleling what Wittgenstein teaches us about language use, stocks of knowledge are part and parcel of everyday life, not separate and distinct from it; they are always incomplete and open-ended, sensitive to, and yet informing, the ongoing practice of reality construction. As such they are ever-emergent resources that can be brought to bear on the self-construction process.

Ethnomethodological Foundations

If ethnomethodology shares social phenomenology's orientation to everyday life, it is not a mere extension of the latter's analytic program. The self in ethnomethodological practice would be a self located directly in the everyday *hows* of real-time talk and social interaction. The philosophical tenets for a socially constituted self are extended into a fully empirical yet philosophically informed pragmatics of knowledge. As Douglas Maynard and Steven Clayman (1991) explain, ethnomethodology addresses the problem of order in everyday life by combining a "phenomenological sensibility" with a paramount concern for constitutive social practice. From an ethnomethodological standpoint, the world of everyday objects, which would include the self as an object, is accomplished through members' social practices.

Harold Garfinkel (1967) pioneered ethnomethodological analysis, responding as much to his teacher Talcott Parsons's theory of action as to phenomenological principles (Heritage 1984). For Parsons, social order was made possible through institutionalized systems of norms, rules, and values. In this context and following its formation out of social experience, the self becomes a distinct structure of society, whose internalized yet socially reflexive content and organization serve to guide individuals' actions. Parsons's self is a working, even central, structure of social order, a thoroughly reified social fact.

Garfinkel sought an alternative approach, one in which actors were not portrayed as socialized "judgmental dopes" responding to external social forces and motivated by internalized moral directives. Instead, he developed a model of social order built on the contingent, embodied, ongoing interpretive work of ordinary members of society, similar in certain respects to that envisioned by Wittgenstein. Garfinkel viewed members as possessing practical linguistic and interactional skills, through which the observable, accountable, and orderly features of everyday life were meaningfully produced. Ethnomethodology's actual topic of study became members' practical everyday procedures ("ethnomethods") for creating, sustaining, and managing their sense of objective reality. While Garfinkel did not focus on the self as such, the approach could have readily led to a consideration of the practical production of selves along the lines we are suggesting here.

Ethnomethodology employs its own version of phenomenological bracketing. Adopting a policy of "ethnomethodological indifference" (Garfinkel and Sacks 1970), ethnomethodologists temporarily suspend ontological commitment to a priori or privileged versions of social structures, focusing instead on how members accomplish, manage, and sustain their sense of these structures. Analysis centers on the properties of practical reasoning and the constitutive interactional work that produces an unchallenged appearance of a stable reality, such as the reality of the self. At the same time, it assiduously resists judgments about the "correctness" of members' activities. Applied to the self, this would entail a decided indifference to whether or not selves are actually viable, healthy or sick, thriving or under siege, relatively fluid or fixed. Rather, the goal of ethnomethodological analysis would be to document how members use categories such as these to structure their personal experience.

Ethnomethodology's emphasis on the practical production of a sense of the real forms its analytic horizons. Rather than assuming that members share meanings and definitions of themselves and their situations, ethnomethodologists take account of how members continuously rely on the interpretive capacities of co-participants in interaction to assemble and reveal a locally evident sense of who they are and what they are engaged in doing. Attention centers on how everyday language-in-use serves to construct answers to such questions. Indeed, the notion of a single, objective reality, such as the reality of a centered self, can itself be made into a topic, turning an erstwhile grand narrative into a matter of local storytelling. This is a more radically empirical approach than the one envisioned by the early pragmatists and the later symbolic interactionists. An ethnomethodological examination of the self, for example, would seek to document "just how" this self is actually constructed, conducted, managed, and sustained in ongoing talk and interaction.

From an ethnomethodological perspective, social structures such as the self are self-generating, practical accomplishments. This implicates two important properties of language in everyday use. First, meanings are "indexical," that is, they depend on their context, as Wittgenstein convincingly informs us. Objects and events have equivocal or indeterminate meanings without an evident context. This of course would apply to the self; its meaning is necessarily generated from its particular context. This brings us to the second important property of language-in-use. The contexts that provide meaning are themselves self-generating; language and its contexts are "reflexive." Practical reasoning is simultaneously in and about the circumstances to which it orients. For example, to speak about a group of people being in a collective state of confusion does more than simply describe the perplexity that confounds members. It simultaneously—reflexively—constructs a context for the meaning of what group members say and do. Collective confusion signals a social, not individualized, subjectivity. In turn, what emanates from members is seen as an index, or the product, of interpersonal befuddlement, not the result of personal ignorance, malice, or premeditation. Acknowledging a state of collective confusion specifies a range of possible meanings associated with that state, while ruling out alternate meanings, such as individual responsibility for the confusion. Individual actions understood in this fashion then reconfirm the collective confusion that characterizes the situation (see Garfinkel 1967). Indexicality and reflexivity are thus opposite sides of the same linguistic coin, documenting each other as they figure circularly into the constitution of everyday life.

Ethnomethodological studies have necessarily paid close attention to the fine details of talk and interaction. The direction this takes, however, has varied. Although always concerned with how everyday conversation proceeds, ethnographically oriented studies emphasize the situated content of talk as constitutive of local meaning (e.g., Wieder 1974). As we consider the everyday technology of self construction in the following chapters, we will examine how the locally formulated meaning or content of talk works to produce individuals' senses of who and what they are. We will explore, for example, how individuals in particular situations use binary distinctions such as them/us, normal/abnormal, stable/unstable, spiritual/secular, adjusted/maladjusted, and sick/well to locate themselves in relation to each other and construct their inner lives for the purposes at hand.[4]

Other ethnomethodologically oriented studies emphasize the conversational machinery of everyday interaction (see Heritage 1984; Sacks, Schegloff, and Jefferson 1974; Zimmerman 1988). Conversation analysis (CA), which we address in greater detail in Chapter 7, attempts to describe and explicate the socially constructive and collaborative practices within sequences of talk that speakers use and rely upon when they engage in social interaction. Both the production of conduct and its interpretation are viewed as accountable products of conversation's turn-taking apparatus. Through this machinery, members accomplish the intelligibility of their social worlds, including varied senses of themselves.[5]

This focus on the real-time, sequential details of ordinary conversation requires a precise method of inquiry. Naturally occurring talk is usually taperecorded, although increasingly videotaping is encouraged (see Heath 1997).[6] Analysis then centers on the collaborative, constantly emerging structure of the conversational machinery, such as the local management of turn-taking; practices related to opening, sustaining, and closing orderly sequences; how interactional troubles are managed; how extended turns at talk for storytelling are established; and how perspectives are displayed (see Psathas 1995, Sacks 1992a, 1992b, Silverman 1998).

Although some contend that CA's connection to ethnomethodology is tenuous (Atkinson 1988; Lynch and Bogen 1994), conversation analysis and ethnomethodology undeniably share a common interest in the local production of social forms (see Maynard and Clayman 1991; ten Have 1990). In CA, the emphasis is on the sequential structuring of talk and the ways that builds up context and meaning, including, we would assume, the social construction of self. Still, its focus on conversational machinery—sometimes to the exclusion of the scenic presence of interaction's ethnographic details—limits it to a particular level of explication. In the following chapters, we will discuss the everyday technology of self construction through sequential analyses of turns at talk, but also attend to talk and interaction's contents and external contexts.

Discursive Practice

Lyotard, Wittgenstein, and ethnomethodology inspire a new story line for the social self, introducing the conception of a practical, interactionally crafted identity. This narrative highlights *discursive practice* as the means through which the self is constructed.

An Analytics of Discursive Practice

Ethnomethodologists maintain that adopting a policy of analytic indifference elucidates the ways that members of society "do" social order. Our particular concern focuses on *how* members "do" the self. To examine how anything is "done" is to describe the processes and procedures through which it is accomplished, not what that thing is, what its dimensions are, or the way it relates to other things or why. These *what* and *why* questions are the stock-in-trade of methodologies concerned with the existing realities of social life. Such methodologies are geared to unveil existing self attitudes, for example, not the social constitution of such attitudes in the first place. They focus on the ways, say, that self attitudes influence behavior, which, we recall, was of special interest to the Iowa school of symbolic interactionists. In a word, such methodologies use the self as a *resource* for explaining action. Ethnomethodology reverses this, bringing the self as an everyday project into view, making its construction itself *topical* (see Zimmerman and Pollner 1970).

The field of study for ethnomethodology is the domain of interaction; it is scrutinized for the ways talk and other modes of interaction are employed to construct, manage, and secure social structures. It's not everyday conduct *in* the world that comes under examination. Instead, the analyst concentrates on the practices of what Melvin Pollner (1987) calls "worlding" (Pollner 1987), the linguistic actions that constitute the social world. Adapting Geertz's (1973) colorful phrasing, we might say that ethnomethodology looks at how members of society work at "*spinning* the webs of significance in which they themselves are suspended" (p. 5, emphasis added). The phenomenon of interest is the process of the self being spun, not the whole cloth or the featured design in the fabric per se. It's the "spinning" that commands analytic interest, not the finished product as such.

This is a theoretically minimalist perspective on social structures in that there is, as a consequence of bracketing, no a priori social order available to theorize or correlate. Propositions and hypotheses concerning the relationship between social structures, specified as variables, cannot be formulated because these have been set aside in order to make their construction visible. Indeed, such propositions and hypotheses *must not* be formulated, lest ethnomethodological indifference or phenomenological bracketing be compromised. If ethnomethodology is concerned with theory at all, it is interested in members' own indigenous theorizing, especially ways in which they apply their theoretical skills to the business of everyday life. The aim is to document how members themselves use theory (or philosophy, or methodology, for that matter). As such, ethnomethodology is an *analytics*, not a theory, of discursive practice, specifically an analytics of social interaction. Applied to the self, this becomes an analytics of the everyday interactional processes of self construction.

Language Games in Everyday Use

As the practice of social construction is set in motion, we still need to discern *what* will be built up in the process. Will it be a centered self? Will it be multiple selves? Will it be a self largely designed in early life, a kind of Freudian self? Will it be a calculating self, whose attention is focused more on rational choices than on moral imperatives? Will it be a behaving self that searches out rewards and avoids punishment? Will it be a postmodern self, which builds itself up time and again in response to diverse moral orders? Indeed, will it be a self at all? The new ending for the story of the self takes these questions to heart.

A way of directly incorporating concerns with content into the analysis of talk and interaction was initiated by ethnomethodologist Harvey Sacks, the founder of conversation analysis. Sacks (1974, 1992a, 1992b) figured that terms such as *mother, child, self,* and *family* could be viewed as "membership categorization devices" or MCDs (also see Baker 1997, Silverman 1998). References to them in the give-and-take of everyday conversation provide specific ways of categorizing actions or persons. They present users with working rules, in effect, for making connections between them and other terms, thus articulating culturally recognized configurations of meaning. Sacks was keenly interested in culture and centered the operating logic of MCDs in the natural cultural linkages of each device. To Sacks, culture was an "inference-making machine" in practice (1992a, p. 119), which he took to operate through members' categorizing activity. In actual operation, this put diverse sets of categories to nuanced application, introducing a local element to the configurations that the categories brought with them, again paralleling Wittgenstein's sense of language use.

Following Sacks, we might, for instance, find that there is a language game that applies a vocabulary of volume to the self. Cultural expectations could reasonably lead users to think about themselves as having depth and, from that, prompt them to consider that some of them were more deeply self-conscious or personally insightful than others. The construction of a related personality type, with specific social characteristics such as being thoughtful or easily embarrassed, might be a short step away. Or the vocabulary of volume and depth might be used sarcastically in another type of language game to degrade selves, as in the following exchange between "jiving" adolescents.

1. BOY A: [To B, but referring to and heard by Boy C] Get that dude!
2. BOY B: He be hot shit, man.
3. BOY A: Yeah, real deep.
4. BOY B: Deep shit.
5. BOY A: He really full o' shit.
6. BOY B: He so full o' shit his mind's floatin'.
7. BOY A: [To Boy C] Hey shithead! Where your head, boy?
8. BOY B: His head in the toilet, where it should be.

In this exchange, MCD analysis would trace the scatological linkages that the boys recognizably put to use in relation to volume, toilet, and the location of mind, with the resulting "evident" degradations of self. *What* is being made of a self is as important as *how* it is being constructed. When a link is established in line 2 between "hot" and "shit," with Boy C as the object in question ("He be hot shit, man."), the collection of categories implicated is large and could be positive or negative. We know that the category "hot" can be diversely referenced in the context of American adolescent culture. "Hot shit" might refer to something like a "big deal," an important person, or a "cool dude"—a positive association—or fresh feces, which is less immediately recognizable as positive. Boy A and B's statements at lines 3 and 4 are equivocal, the adjective "deep" again possibly implicating something positive or negative. Boy A's statement at line 5 begins to sort this out, suggesting a set of negative linkages of categories, which "full o' shit" often flags in American culture. Line 6 elaborates this, the exchange in lines 6 through 8 playing out the negative linkages as they possibly relate to toileting. Finally, at lines 7 and 8, as an emerging collection of recognizably negative linkages is articulated, they are directed at Boy C, to whom they are ostensibly meant to apply.

Of the large number of categories that could potentially be linked with the terms used early in the exchange, the developing collection of linkages retrospectively (and only retrospectively) suggests that the early usages were categorization devices for a degrading collection of linkages. As far as the social logic of MCDs is concerned, the operating principle is that when several terms, characteristics, or categories, such as "shit" and "deep," can be heard as coming from the same collection or family, they are heard and responded to in that way. For all practical purposes, usage becomes less and less equivocal as the exchange unfolds. Concurrently, the meaning of the terms describing those concerned is built up over time; it is not fully discernible in any particular term.

MCD analysis provides an apparatus for viewing culture-in-use, for analytically bridging *how* with *what* concerns. It gives us local insight into the cultural reproduction, as well as the artful generation of new collections of categories, showing how culture is asserted, articulated, and modified in social interaction. Yet, as important as this contribution is, it does not solve the *what* problem beyond serving as a way of understanding how configurations of external meaning, including their subjectivities, are locally built up, skillfully elaborated, or reconfigured for the purposes at hand. It tells us very little about available configurations, their varied institutionalization, or their potential application or lack of application in particular circumstances.

MCD analysis depends on our knowledge of these *what* matters, such as the knowledge that jiving adolescent boys make use of certain collections of categories and elaborate them in particular ways in everyday talk and interaction, for recognizable ends. But it doesn't tell us much about what, if anything, is likely to compete with scatological jiving for degrading selves, who is likely to use particular configurations, or where and when these will probably apply, if they apply at all. Consequently, we will not employ this form of analysis wholesale as we turn to the technology of self construction in the following chapters. Instead, we will borrow from Sacks's insights but also look at the constructed categories themselves to see how they are configured and distributed in society at large.

Discourses-in-Practice

Foucault's historical studies of systems of thought suggest a method for discerning the interpretive possibilities that might be available for self construction at any particular time or place. Broad configurations of meaningful action—which Foucault called "discourses"—set the conditions of possibility for usage and supply a way of more fully responding to the *what* questions we have raised. For example, the different discourses of subjectivity distinguished in *Discipline and Punish*, which we discussed in Chapter 4, inform us that the "self" as we know it was not in common usage before the rise of panopticism. The language game we now call the individualized self would literally have been "incredible" at a time when the discourse of the individual body did not so much articulate a vessel for the self as specify an appendage of the sovereign. Since there was only a general, sovereign will to seriously take into account in adjudicating action, there was no individual self to speak of. Used in this context, the term "self" must necessarily be placed in quotation marks since terms of personal reference marked the body in a different way than they do now. (Foucault used the general term *subjectivity* for this very reason.)

An Analytics of Discourse-in-Practice

Foucault's approach complements ethnomethodology's analytics of discursive practice, but it focuses more on the historical or cultural *whats* than on the present-time *hows* of social practice. As an analytics, its aim is not to formulate a priori definitions of subjectivity or to theorize its social conditioning or effects. Rather, it traces the variable social constructions of the subject historically. Foucault proceeds in relation to the institutional contexts of medicine, madness, crime, corrections, and sexuality. In each instance, he documents shifting systems of understanding and usage (discourses) through time, drawing sharp distinctions between juxtaposed discourses, such as the one drawn between the prepanoptic and the panoptic deployment of subjectivity, with their respective regimens of surveillance. The juxtaposition of discourses, while historical, is meant to be read paradigmatically, not developmentally. Foucault does *not* argue that the discourse put into practice for Damiens and his contemporaries, for example, led to a self that was permitted to express itself later in time. Rather, Foucault contends that what discourse put into practice for Damiens as a subject cannot be understood in the context of the discursive regime/regimen that succeeded it. Each regime constructed its own subjectivity, separate and distinct from the one that came before.

Ethnomethodology's emphasis on the indexical and reflexive features of language use bears a striking resemblance to what Foucault (1980) refers to as "power/knowledge."[7] For Foucault, power operates in discourse as the other face of knowledge. Discourse puts words into action, constructs perceptions, and formulates understanding. Simultaneously, it reflexively constitutes the realities that words are taken otherwise to reference and specify. Deploying a discourse of subjectivity is not simply a matter of representing the subject, but of simultaneously constituting the subjects that are meaningfully embedded in the discourse itself. Discourse is not more or less correlated with what it represents, but is "always already" a form of life, which further links Wittgenstein with Foucault.

Ethnomethodologists attend to the everyday methods members use to articulate social structures, which we've called "discursive practice." Foucault makes us aware of the conditions of possibility for these practices as they are embedded in historically or institutionally available discourses. We can label these "discourses-in-practice." Their complementary analytics center their projects on social practice or the practice of everyday life, as the case might be.[8] Because Foucault's project operates in a historical register, real-time talk and interaction are understandably missing from his empirical material. Conversely, ethnomethodology's commitment to documenting the real-time interactional construction of reality understandably distracts it from a broader consideration of discursive possibilities. But clearly there is a parallel, as both analytics aim to reveal the way language works in relation to what is taken to be real, evident, and significant in social life. It's this parallel that we exploit as we elaborate an approach for describing the technology of self construction implicated in our new ending to the story of the self.

Interpretive Practice

Moving a step ahead, we view the respective analytics of discursive practice and discourses-in-practice as converging on the local construction of social structures. As far as subjectivity is concerned, an analytics of discursive practice highlights the interactional articulation of meaning with experience, centering on the artful procedures through which selves are constituted. The analytics of discourses-in-practice accentuates the discursive possibilities for, and resources of, self construction at particular times and places. Taken together, they elucidate what we call "interpretive practice"—the constellation of procedures, conditions, and resources through which reality (in this particular case, subjectivity) is apprehended, understood, organized, and represented in the course of everyday life (Gubrium and Holstein 1997, Holstein 1993, Holstein and Gubrium 1994).

Interpretive practice consists of both social processes and meaningful possibilities; it occupies the space where ethnomethodology and Foucauldian discourse studies overlap. Metaphorically speaking, the term encompasses both the labor involved in reality-building projects (the construction work) and the more substantive aspects of the project (possible designs, blueprints, building materials, and conditions under which the work is done). Applying terminology introduced earlier, interpretive practice comprises both the *hows* and the *whats* of reality construction (see Gubrium and Holstein 1997). It is a way of conceptualizing the entire technology of self construction, from the conversational machinery involved in interactionally storying the self, to the sorts of subjectivity that might possibly be conferred, to the settings and institutions within which selves are crafted.

Going Concerns

Years ago, Everett Hughes (1984 [1942], p. 21) referred to institutions as "going concerns," expressing a view of social organization that resonates with our working sense of interpretive practice. Going concerns could be as large as corporations or as small as families, as unseemly as brothels and gangs, or as loosely organized as developing friendship groups. While Hughes was interested in socially organized activity, he was careful not to reify the patterns he took to comprise institutions. Patterns were established through concerted activity, and were subject to variable contingencies. For Hughes, there was as much "going" in going concerns as there were "concerns."

The postmodern condition is replete with transitory images, diverse and variegated patterns of social life, protean characterizations of who and what we are. The self is all over the place, yet it's not randomly placed across this landscape. Its construction evolves in a multitude of institutions, unfolding in a thousand social spaces. Using Hughes's and Foucault's terminology, as going concerns, these sites more or less incite participants to speak their subjectivities, as participants play out their respective roles within them. Selves are themselves institutional projects in the sense that institutional discourses provide the conditions of possibility and institutionalized discursive practice supplies the mode of production for putting into effect our identities as part of accomplishing matters of ongoing local interest. Indeed, subjectivity often figures as a going concern in its own right, as participants actively talk over, review, debate, discover, grow distressed by, or celebrate the agents they are, were, or will be in the process.

The activity that skillfully puts institutional discourses to work to construct selves and their worlds is the heart of interpretive practice. Focused on the ubiquitous going concerns of contemporary living, the analysis of interpretive practice reveals the local ways that subjectivity is constituted in our times. While a paramount self may be on the ropes, so to speak, the individual self is still of significant interest to ordinary members of society; their lives continue to depend on it. Echoing what Foucault (1978a) argued in relation to sex in his book *The History of Sexuality* (Volume 1), and contrary to current opinions that the self is trivial or even dead, the self is now more topical than ever; it's discussed and constituted virtually everywhere.

Conditions of Interpretation

Interpretive practice places self construction in the context of going concerns, balancing interactional with institutional analysis. It focuses on the kinds of critical questions we raised earlier: What are the cultural codes available for defining who we are? How are they locally applied? What regulates usage? These questions are somewhat old-fashioned (modern) in that they direct us to the meaningful conditions of everyday life, conditions that are "there" in the sense that members take them for granted, at least temporarily. But they are important in siting what otherwise would be too discursive a form of analysis.[9]

Conditions of interpretation include such things as the "fact" that in ongoing talk and interaction, a particular language game is likely to be played out, excluding other possibilities. This may extend to the "fact" that this language game is one out of many more or less related types. The institutionalization of these types—where they get played out in everyday life—informs us of the possible language games that could be locally applied in figuring the self. Institutional-ization indicates the possible selves we could be at various times and places.

This orientation to language use takes us into newer territory. As Foucault points out time and again, discourse is not owned by anyone in particular, nor is it centered in formal authority. Rather, as power/knowledge, it is played out through language at work, put into effect by all concerned wherever and when-ever usage is in order. But, equally significantly, discourse also works locally and contingently. Applied here as opposed to there, it is articulated in relation to what is locally accountable. Still, discourses don't operate like templates. They aren't rubber stamps in the hands, and mouths, of those who use them. The categories of available discourses are articulated in practice, realizing available selves ac-cording to the ongoing work of self construction.

Those discourses and language games that are applied—those that are avail-able from the range of locally possible discourses—are selected and applied in the immediate scheme of things. As going concerns, institutions virtually "think" by articulating their discourses according to participants' working understand-ings (see Douglas 1986). And, reflexively enough, those needs can themselves be topicalized to further designate, from the ground up, what going concerns dom-inate the immediate circumstances. This is a view of members actively *using* in-stitutions to build up, account for, or otherwise justify what they are concerned with, in the very process of advancing their going concerns. It extends the con-cept of regulation well beyond notions of sovereign power or formal authority. To ask how usage is regulated is to look through sovereignty and authority to the interpretive practices through which members articulate regulation.

Interplay and the Analytics of Interpretive Practice

As we conceive it, an analytics of interpretive practice centers on the *interplay*, not the synthesis, of discursive practice and discourses-in-practice (cf. Schrag 1997). It assiduously avoids theorizing social forms, lest the discursive practices associ-ated with the construction of these forms be taken for granted and practice overde-termined. It concertedly keeps discourses in view, lest discourse be dissolved into empty language games. By focusing on interpretive practice, an analytics of self construction takes us, in real time, to the going concerns of society's members, who artfully put discourses to work to constitute their subjectivities. It's an ana-lytics that orients to the different subjectivizing discourses at play in everyday life, whose institutionalization offers up, but does not fully determine, our iden-tities for all practical purposes in the local scheme of things.

If Foucault works in a historical register, and ethnomethodology in an inter-actional one, we tell the story of the self at the crossroads of narrative, social in-teraction, culture, and institutional life. Working historically, Foucault had little access to the everyday operation of discourses, of discursive practice. We are more attuned to everyday interaction as it bears on self construction. At the same time, taking direction from Foucault, we are more deeply concerned with the resources and conditions of self construction than is typical of ethnomethodology. While certainly appreciating the *hows* of self construction, we are equally interested in the various *whats* that bear on the process—*whats* that extend to discourse and surrounding institutional environments of talk and social interaction.

Analytic Bracketing

Access to the interplay of discursive practice and discourses-in-practice comes by way of a new form of "indifference" to the realities of everyday life we call "analytic bracketing" (Gubrium and Holstein 1997). Recall that ethnomethodology's interest in the *hows* by which realities are constructed requires a studied, temporary indifference to those realities. Ethnomethodologists (and phenomenologists) suspend belief in the real in order to bring into view the everyday practices by which events, objects, and subjects come to have a sense of being real for members of society. The ethnomethodological project moves forward from there, documenting how discursive practice constitutes social structures such as the self. The bracketing process makes sure language is not "on holiday"; analytic attention focuses on language use in order to show how it works to meaningfully construct matters that we commonsensically presume words merely describe.

Such a priori bracketing and an orientation to language at work reveal an amazing panorama of constitutive activity. But, at the same time, they tend to neglect the related *whats* that potentially stand for the real *for those involved*. While the discourses and language games members use to build up, manage, and regulate members' sense of the real are the point of departure for ethnomethodological studies, they are set aside in order to capture the details of the active work of reality construction. Interpretive practice, however, involves more than just this work; practice connotes activity in relation to constructive materials and institutional context. In order to move beyond the sheer mechanics of constructing social order, we also need to take account of constitutive materials and circumstances.

This is where analytic bracketing comes in. The procedure amounts to alternately bracketing the *whats* and the *hows* of reality construction. This means alternately holding *both* lived realities *and* their constitutive activities temporarily in abeyance in order to describe both the artful and substantive sides of interpretive practice. While we don't aim to resurrect a real and given world (or self) in the process, we want our analytics to attend to the *putatively* real—that is, that which members know and treat as real—because it's a stock of meaning-making possibilities, resources, and constraints to which members orient as they conduct the interpretive work of everyday life.

Unlike a priori bracketing, analytic bracketing works throughout analysis, not just at the start. In ethnomethodological parlance, analytic bracketing alternately orients to the activities of producing everyday realities, then to those realities as substantive resources that members use in these activities. Initially indifferent to the realities of everyday life in order to document discursive practice, it then brackets discursive practice in order to assess the availability and regulation of resources for doing the work of everyday interpretation. In Wittgensteinian terms, this translates into considering both language "at work" and "on holiday," in order to trace and document how language games operate in everyday life and what language games are likely to come into play in particular circumstances. In Foucauldian terms, it leads to alternate considerations of discourses-in-practice (typical of Foucauldian or continental discourse analysis) on the one hand, and the local documentation of related discursive practices (typical of ethnomethodology and Anglo-American discourse analysis) on the other.[10]

Analytic bracketing thus amounts to deliberately and purposefully bracketing the *whats*, then the *hows*, of interpretive practice in order to assemble a more complete picture of language use. The objective is to move back and forth between discursive practice and discourses-in-practice, in turn documenting each, making informative references to the other in the process. Either the narrative machinery of social interaction, on the one hand, or the available discourses, descriptive resources, and institutional constraints, on the other, become the provisional phenomenon. Interest in one or the other is temporarily deferred but not forgotten.

The movement back and forth is not arbitrary; it is keyed to emergent analytic needs. As the analyst documents constructive activities, questions regarding what is being constructed, what resources are used, and what conditions shape the process provoke a shift in analytic stance—a change in analytic brackets that is necessary to address such questions. Subsequently, the analyst's attention to the *whats* under consideration will, in turn, prompt him or her to ask *how* these features of lived experience came to be regarded as real, inducing yet another shift in brackets.

The constant interplay between the analysis of these two sides of interpretive practice mirrors the lived interplay between the artfulness and the substantive resources that reflexively effect, and simultaneously enter into, the production of everyday realities, including selves.[11] Questions related to discursive possibilities, conditions, and resources constantly arise throughout the study of self construction; these are questions pertaining to the experientially grounded meanings and contours of the self. Their answers provide us with a working sense of the shapes that social structures like the self are likely to assume on the varied occasions of their production. Within the artful bounds of discursive practice, answers to such *what* questions can provide a basis for developing cautious explanations for *why* certain selves and not others are constructed and nuanced as they are (see Gubrium and Holstein 1997, Silverman 1993).

Because the self-construction process and the selves that are eventually constructed are mutually constitutive, one cannot argue that analysis must begin or end with either of these. As a practical matter, we typically begin "where people are," as Dorothy Smith (1987) puts it, in the actual places or going concerns where they address and figure their identities. But neither the experientially real nor its construction has priority over the other. If we set aside the need for an indisputable resolution to the question of which comes first, we can designate a point of departure based on the compelling issue immediately at hand, then proceed with our analysis, so long as we keep firmly in mind that the interplay within interpretive practice requires that we move back and forth between these leading components of the process.

Analytic bracketing requires both procedural pluralism and caution. Like ethnomethodology, it employs a variety of techniques for closely examining inter-action. Real-time talk-in-interaction is a principal object of study, and in some in-stances, conversation analysis becomes the method of choice for capturing it (see Psathas 1995; Sacks, Schegloff, and Jefferson 1974). But other parts of a study may demand a more content-oriented form of discourse analysis (see Potter 1996; Pot-ter and Wetherell 1987). Still other aspects, especially more scenically institutional ones, benefit from methods of "constitutive ethnography" (Mehan 1979), the "ethnography of practice" (Gubrium 1988), or other circumstantially sensitive con-structionist approaches (see Holstein 1993; Miller 1991, 1994). These focus as much on the contextual features of social interaction as on its discursive machinery.

Still, while the analysis of interpretive practice is informed by a continual awareness of substantive conditions—such as the preferred discourses of partic-ular going concerns—we must take care not to appropriate these naively into our analysis. We share ethnomethodology's desire to distinguish between members' resources and our own. As a result, as we consider substantive matters, we at-tempt to understand and document their operation as they relate to members' constitutive activities. Our interest is not in their substantive reality per se, but in the reality of their existence for, and use by, members themselves.

We must also remember that analytic bracketing is always substantively tem-porary. It resists full-blown attention to discourses as systems of knowledge, sep-arate from how discourses operate in practice. It is enduringly empirical in that it does not take discourses and substantive conditions for granted, but treats them as the operating truths of a setting. Systematic observation centers on the local mediations of discourses, on what Foucault (1988) calls "truth games." Analytic bracketing does not let us concentrate exclusively on the discourses employed in interpretive practice, nor does it emphasize the artfulness and differentiating nu-ances of local articulation. Rather, the *interplay* of discursive practice and dis-courses-in-practice is the heart of the matter. It is here that we might discover the grounded, yet discursively diverse, self of contemporary life.

Invariably, there's a certain amount of interpretive "slippage" in the interplay of discursive practice and discourses-in-practice (a topic to which we will turn in Chapter 6). This means that the analysis of interpretive practice requires a toler-ance for the "messiness" of explanatory indeterminacy. Then again, social life is messy in practice. Varied discourses of the self mediate interpretive practice; they do not predictably cause us or others to become who or what we are. Members of particular settings selectively call upon, and make use of, the language games available to them to produce their subjectivities, but in the process they specify meanings locally and contingently. At the same time, the identities that members use, apply, and produce in the course of constructing who they are, are not con-jured out of thin air. Culturally recognizable discourses come into play. We se-lect from what's available and tailor it to the interpretive task at hand. The self we live by is not fully determined, but discernibly slips about in the interplay of discursive practice and discourse-in-practice.

Conceived as a hallmark structure of contemporary interpretive practice, the self clearly remains a prominent feature of everyday life. It continues to be part of the story of Western subjectivity. But, in practice, the story is open-ended, varying in its details from one going concern to another. As contemporary life grows increasingly diverse, with meanings realized in an ever-expanding landscape of institutions, self is ubiquitously accomplished.

If the story of the paramount self is over, the narratives of an empirically grounded, institutionally diverse postmodern self are still unfolding. In Part II of the book we examine just how this self is constructed in the manifold circumstances of our daily lives. Our story turns to the everyday technology of self construction. Initially emphasizing the *hows* of the process, but progressively highlighting more of the *whats*, we illustrate the elasticity as well as the narrative conditioning of identity in today's world. The result remains a distinctly social self, but one more complex than its pragmatist originators could have ever imagined.

2

The Everyday Technology of Self Construction

> *I am interested in the way in which the subject consti-*
> *tutes himself in an active fashion, by the practices of*
> *self. . . . [These practices] are patterns that he finds in his*
> *culture and which are proposed, suggested, and imposed*
> *upon him by his culture, his society and his social group.*
>
> —Michel Foucault, 1988

> *Such practices consist of an endless, ongoing, contingent*
> *accomplishment . . . carried on under the auspices of,*
> *and made to happen as events in, the same ordinary*
> *affairs . . . they describe.*
>
> —Harold Garfinkel, 1967

CHAPTER SIX

Narrating the Self

The everyday technology of self construction stands at the junction of discursive practice and discourses-in-practice. Speaking figuratively, it's an intersection where Garfinkel and Foucault might have crossed analytic paths, even as they worked with different empirical materials. One source of convergence would surely be the recognition of the artful yet locally structured stories that comprise the contemporary self in practice.

Social commentary and research are increasingly pointing to the narrative quality of lives, showing how the storying of the self is actively rendered and locally conditioned. The personal story, especially, is being resuscitated as an important source of experiential data.[1] Early texts are being revisited for their heuristic value (Allport 1942; Dollard 1935; Murray 1938; Shaw 1930, 1931; Thomas and Znaniecki 1927[1918–1920]), while narrative analysis has ascended as a significant procedural genre (see Alasuutari 1997; Cortazzi 1993; Dégh 1995; Denzin 1989; Hinchman and Hinchman 1997; Linde 1993; Richardson 1990, 1991; Riessman 1990, 1993). Over and over, we are relearning that selves are constructed through storytelling (Ezzy 1998, Randall 1995).

The collection and analysis of personal stories are becoming more methodologically self-conscious than ever (Rosenwald and Ochberg 1992, Shotter and Gergen 1989). Leading work in the area rarely takes stories simply to more-or-less represent individual experience through time. Narrative analysts no longer view storytellers and their accomplices as having unmediated access to experience, nor do they hold that experience can be conveyed in some pristine or authentic form separate from the institutions and events of the day (see Atkinson 1997, Scott 1995). On the contrary, stories—especially those of the self—are now analyzed as much for the ways in which storytellers and the conditions of storytelling shape what is conveyed, as for what their contents tell us about the selves in question.

This is a broad and complex landscape, to be sure. The self's stories are definitely at work, not on holiday. Narrators artfully pick and choose from what is experientially available to articulate their lives and experiences. Yet, as they actively craft and inventively construct their narratives, they also draw from what is culturally available, storying their lives in recognizable ways. Narratives of the self don't simply rest within us to motivate and guide our actions, nor do they lurk behind our backs as social templates to stamp us into selves according to the leading stories of the day. The narrative landscape of self construction is clearly also a busy one.

What discursive practices effect the process by which available images and understandings are assembled into accountable identities? Our answer will show that storytellers are not the mere narrative puppets of their actions. Personal accounts are built up from experience, differentially combined, and actively cast in preferred vocabularies, even while this is sensitive to the circumstances. If Foucault (1975, 1977, 1978a, 1978b, 1980) has shown that the discourses of particular sites and institutions establish conceptual limits for storytelling, the local and the particular continually insinuate themselves to construct diversity and difference in the stories that emerge. In practice, the technology of self construction extends beyond the institutional apparatuses that designate subjectivities into the integral everyday interpretive work done to locally construct who and what we are (see Garfinkel 1967).

Investigating Narrative Practice

Narrative practice lies at the heart of self construction. It is a form of *interpretive practice*, a term we use to simultaneously characterize the activities of storytelling, the resources used to tell stories, and the auspices under which stories are told (Gubrium and Holstein 1998). Considering the self in terms of narrative practice allows us to analyze the relation between the *hows* and *whats* of storytelling; analysis centers on storytellers engaged in the work of constructing identities and on the circumstances of narration, respectively. We can view the storytelling process as both actively constructive and locally constrained. Put differently, our approach is concerned with the activeness and spontaneity of performativity (Bauman 1986), on the one hand, and attending to the narrative resources and auspices implicated in storytelling (Mills 1940[1963]), on the other.

Resources are broadly construed. They might include any and all experiences that can be accountably incorporated into personal stories, ranging from brief recollections of an event to blow-by-blow renderings of a virtual lifetime of experience. "Coherence structures" (Linde 1993) provide another kind of resource. They work like language games that are locally available for casting selves in preferred ways, with particular themes and plot lines. Professional or institutional models of treatment, such as behavior modification systems or twelve-step programs, are prime examples. Institutional settings of all sorts provide the narrative auspices under which selves come to be articulated in distinctive ways, deploying the storytelling mandates and constraints that characterize a particular going concern. Whether they are "experience-near," as in a household, or "experience-distant," as in a drug rehabilitation clinic, the locally available discourses of subjectivity mediate and condition personal storytelling (Geertz 1983).

People-processing and -regulating institutions elicit, screen, fashion, and variously highlight personal identity and are increasingly prevalent in today's world (Ahrne 1990, Czarniawska 1997, Drucker 1993, Foucault 1978a, Giddens 1992, Presthus 1978). Their diverse and now seemingly ubiquitous narrative practices work to constitute subjectivities in accordance with local relevancies that link broadly with familiar experiential themes. Schools, clinics, counseling centers, correctional facilities, hospitals, nursing homes, support groups, and self-help organizations, among other expanding sites for storying experience, provide occasions for conveying selves—for what is taken to be relevant in our lives, and why the lives or experiences in question developed the way they did. In some sense, these settings incite participants to construct the stories they need to do their work. But they don't do so completely on their own terms. Our aim is to make visible the way the narrative activities of such going concerns play out in everyday practice to both produce coherent selves and construct diversity and difference.

While we tend to focus on the formal organizational or professional auspices of storytelling (for example, Gubrium and Holstein 1993, 1997), self construction also orients broadly to the interpretive mandates, controls, and constraints of group membership more generally. For example, in the right circumstances, membership in racial, ethnic, or gendered groups carries with it distinctive auspices that some call "standpoints," which significantly shape storytelling (see Andersen and Collins 1998; Anzaldúa 1987; Collins 1990; Denzin 1997a, 1997b; Quiroz and Ragland 1998; Seidman 1996; Smith 1974; Trinh 1991). Along with membership in such social categories come the identity implications of being embedded in particular relationships for which the categories are practically consequential. Rephrasing what Denzin (1991) and others suggested in Chapter 4, race, class, and gender are deep reservoirs of self-construction resources comprising influential conditions for self-narration.

As significant as these "standpoints" are for the storying of selves, however, it is still important, analytically, to allow for the standpoints' circumstantial realization and not to essentialize the narratives that result from them. As penetrating as racial or gendered identity might be, it still shares experiential space with myriad other sources of the self; self construction isn't one-dimensional. As Judith Butler (1990) points out in relation to gendered identity, for example, it is problematic to discuss women in general because

> gender intersects with racial, class, ethnic, sexual and regional modalities of discursively constituted identities. As a result it becomes impossible to separate out "gender" from the political and cultural intersections in which it is invariably produced and maintained. (P. 3)

To this we should add the myriad going concerns of everyday life which also shape women's selves, from their intimate relationships, marriages, and families to their professional, occupational, and recreational affiliations. As Trinh Minh-ha (1992) suggests, the question of identity is moving away from traditional queries into *who* am I to progressively become questions of *when, where,* and *how* am I. Noting that "There is no real me to return to, no whole self that synthesizes the woman, the woman of color, and the writer" (p. 157), she underscores the need to view the various incarnations of a gendered or racial self in relation to an individual's full round of everyday going concerns.

While the various standpoint theories have certainly enriched our understanding of sources of the self, their propensity to essentialize and homogenize the realities of race, class, ethnicity, gender, and sexuality has both oversimplified and overly specified the more general technology of self construction. Writing about this penchant for totalizing identity in relation to race or ethnicity, Pablo Vila (1997, p. 148) suggests that people articulate the self "in any number of social relations whose meaning—however fragmented, contradictory, or partial—is narratively constructed" and "mediated" by myriad possible "anchors" of the identity construction process. Taking issue with some standpoint theorists, Vila argues against the homogenization of racially grounded experiences and identities, suggesting instead that the experiential "borderlands" that implicate race are also the complex intersections of myriad other related concerns. Calling upon the later work of Renato Rosaldo (1994), Vila argues for a sensitivity to the differentiation of racially grounded experiences, and, by implication, for an awareness of variegated racial identities within racial communities. Race, class, and gender, like other going concerns, always compete for their roles in the self's stories; they never exclusively determine their plots.[2]

Stories thus reflect their sources and circumstances, but they also take shape through their active narration. Years ago, Dell Hymes (Cazden and Hymes 1978) underscored the importance of not setting the internal organization of stories against the study of storytelling. Commenting on the then "current movement to go beyond [the] collection and analysis of text, to [the] observation and analysis of performance," Hymes argued for a "[third moment] continuous with the others, this third [being] the process in which performance and text live." He referred to this as practice, viewed it as grounded in everyday life, and considered it to be ethnographically accessible. Our approach derives in part from Hymes' third moment, which neither dissolves stories into a self-referential performance, nor overshadows the artfulness of storytelling with the structure and themes of stories in their own right.

Norman Denzin (1989) and Matti Hyvärinen (1996) have recently reiterated this sentiment. Criticizing Pierre Bourdieu's (1986) diatribe against biographical coherence, Denzin writes:

> The point to make is not whether biographical coherence is an illusion or reality. Rather, what must be established is how individuals give coherence to their lives when they write or talk self-autobiographies. The sources of this coherence, the narratives that lie behind them, and the larger ideologies that structure them must be uncovered. Bourdieu's general position glosses [over] the complexities of this process. (P. 62)

Dispelling the polarities of coherence and diversity, which relate respectively to modern and postmodern sensibilities, Hyvärinen succinctly poses the pertinent question: "How do individuals give both coherence and diversity to their lives when they write or speak self-autobiographies?" (p. 3).

As texts of experience, personal stories are not complete before their telling, but are assembled in relation to interpretive needs. There are discernible circumstances for narratively conveying our identities. There are audiences with stories of their own who listen to what we communicate, and these audiences may have quite definite preferences for particular plots and themes (see Gubrium and Buckholdt 1982). In other words, narratives are occasioned, put together in the context of particular times and places; these circumstances influence how the self might be storied by presenting local relevancies. Storytelling thus wends its way between the substantive task at hand, which is the composition of a story, and these interpretive considerations within the circumstances of storytelling.

The coherence of a personal story is not a simple matter of internal consistency. A life or self described and heard as coherently relating who or what we are on one occasion may not come off in the same way on a different occasion. How a story is put together is sensitive to local understandings about how a story is composed. What may be a humorous tale about a "bad boy" in one situation and heard as one of those "boys will be boys" stories, might better be narrated more diagnostically in a different situation under the auspices of a more clinical concern, for example. Such occasioned differences suggest that anyone's personal story may have multiple coherences, linked to the circumstances of its telling. As a result, the diverse circumstances and shifting narrative auspices of contemporary life present remarkable diversity in who and what we are taken to be.

Still, the occasioned nature of stories and the selves they convey are not separate and distinct from the process of storytelling. Storytelling itself contributes to the circumstances of its own narration; the active storyteller shapes the occasion in the process of conveying his or her account. For example, on the occasion of a medical review, clinical staff may earnestly elaborate a patient's identity in keeping with their appraisals of a sick body or disturbed mind. But a clinician may also sarcastically signal, with a prefatory remark such as "I ran into another one of those nut cases today," that subsequent discussion of the condition and the identity of the patient in question should be taken with levity. This could very well be expanded into joking narratives of, say, the "[psychiatric] gems you run across in this kind of work." In practice, circumstances are always the circumstance-at-hand. It's important to remember that narrative practice does not simply unfold within the interpretive boundaries of going concerns, but contributes to the definition of those boundaries in its own right.

Narrative Composition

If experience provides an endless supply of potentially reportable, storyable items, it is the incorporation of particular items into a coherent account that gives them meaning. Individuals *compose* their accounts; these do not come fully formed or organized on their own. While local and broader narrative formats offer familiar or conventional guidelines for how stories might unfold, they do not determine individual storylines. Who and what we are is not frozen in available discourses of subjectivity, even while the technical resources of those discourses—such as the use of police profiles of the so-called criminal mind—can have an established narrative momentum of their own in certain settings. Rather, the integral work of putting discourses into narrative play stretches the boundaries of the self on its own, supplying substance and organization.

There's a persistent interplay between what is available for conveying a story and how a particular narrative unfolds in practice; it's from this interplay that both self coherence and diversity develop. Telling one's story in the context, say, of a group that shares a relatively fixed repertoire of storylines presents one with a set of discernible plots, offering distinct ways of giving shape and substance to who we are. But even in this context, individual stories become differentiated as biographical particulars enter into what is told.

Narrative Linkage

The meaning and coherence of a story, and of the self it conveys, are drawn from the linkages built between what is available to construct personal accounts, the biographical particulars at hand, and the related work of contextualizing who and what we are. (Recall our discussion of MCD analysis in Chapter 5.) Susan Chase's (1995) book *Ambiguous Empowerment*—a study of career narratives—provides an interesting case in point. The study highlights the variable linkages and narrative slippages that exist between received cultural categories like race and gender and the way those categories are referenced (or ignored) to convey identity. Looking at contrasting stories, Chase captures the indeterminate yet skillfully organized interaction between race, culture, biography, and storytelling. There is considerable narrative play at work in the way shared understandings about power, success, and discrimination are brought to bear on matters of self definition. It's evident that cultural categories—which might be used as membership categorization devices—are not invoked in any automatic fashion, but, instead, provide narrative resources for constructing each story, so it's distinguishable from the stories told by others in similar circumstances.

Analyzing in-depth interviews with women from various racial and ethnic backgrounds who work as superintendents in rural and urban school systems, Chase documents the diverse ways a successful professional career can be narratively assembled by those located in what for them amounts to an occupational borderland. The women all speak of professional power and success, on the one hand, and discrimination in a white and male-dominated occupation, on the other. Their stories, however, wind up being quite different. Chase asks how is it that a common standpoint in relation to work experience results in such diverse accounts? How do the women produce difference out of a shared institutional reality?

Chase presents four case studies and we briefly compare two of them for the way the respondents assemble their stories and, in turn, communicate their identities as career women of color. Anna Martinez, a Hispanic woman, excludes talk of discrimination and highlights competence in her narrative. She is asked about both the successes and the elements of inequality that shaped her career, topics which Martinez acknowledges as relevant to the lives of women superintendents, but she doesn't talk in terms of discrimination. Chase notes that, like the other women, Martinez has trouble combining the contradictory themes of success, inequality, and discrimination into the same story.

Chase wonders, "How can she [Martinez] connect this story about subjection [to discriminatory practices] to her broader story about professional competence and commitment?" For Martinez, the solution is to construct an account whose success is built on a clear narrative separation of applicable themes. According to Chase, Martinez's way of resolving the narrative tension is to exclude themes of discrimination from her account. Tellingly, in response to a question about whether ethnicity figured in her career, Martinez offers a "metastatement" or comment about what she is communicating: "Uh because [pause] although I recognize the inequities that exist I don't dwell on them. [Chase: hm hmm] I don't talk a lot about them" (p. 82). The ensuing story articulates the discourse of achievement.

Another respondent, Margaret Parker, an African-American woman, combines elements of various themes, putting her own artful gloss on the woman superintendent's story. Parker doesn't suppress themes of inequality and discrimination, but rather links them together with success into the story of a strong and resilient self. Her narrative uncovers layers of vulnerability and strength. As a woman and an African American seeking success in what is largely a white man's world, Parker is admittedly vulnerable to discrimination throughout her career. She tells the story of job discrimination several times. But she also relates sources of inner strength. While Parker speaks of being discriminated against, her ability to work through the consequences adds to a tale of fortitude in the face of adversity, which narratively enhances both her career achievements and her self. The following comments refer to her way of handling her relations with a man who was hired for a job that should have been hers. Note how Parker uses these particular linkages to story her identity in the context of a particular career, and how she concludes with the self-defining point, "That's just who I am." The resulting story articulates the discourse of fortitude.

> And my people who were working with me were saying [whispering], "Boy how is she doing this? How is she taking it?" [Return to normal voice] Especially when the guy came on board [pause] and he was introduced to the cabinet as the assistant superintendent and everybody's eyes sort of propped on me and I'm sitting there holding back all my feelings 'cause I'm *very* pained, *no* question about that. [Chase: hm hmm] Um [pause], but I went right ahead doing my job and people'd see him and me standing talking together. They'd see us eating lunch together you know [Chase: hm hmm] and uh that's just who I am. [Chase: hm hmm] That's just who I am. (Pp. 136–37)

Narrative Slippage

Both Martinez and Parker tell good stories, if that means displaying sequentiality and making a point (see Gergen and Gergen 1986; Labov 1972, 1982; Polanyi 1979; van Dijk 1993). The stories are narrated in terms of how the women superintendents succeeded over time, despite the odds, to become leaders in their respective school systems. Their points are made in the context of the competing themes of success and discrimination. But, while competently made, the points are quite different, due to the discourses they invoke, the categorization devices they deploy, and the ways they establish narrative linkages. Martinez builds links between self and success that skirt issues of race and discrimination, while Parker links encounters with racial discrimination to her acquisition and demonstration of strength and character.

The differences between these stories highlight considerable narrative slippage. Recognizable cultural images of race and discrimination, as well as standard themes of success, are certainly apparent in the women's narratives, but they are applied partially, contingently, judiciously, and variably. Discourses are selectively tailored to the lives under consideration, yielding stories that are understandable in broad terms, but that still differ in their particulars. This also highlights the slippage between discursive practice and discourses-in-practice, between actually storying the self and the prototypic storylines—for example, those of discrimination or success—available for conveying who these women are. The women superintendents are active storytellers, playing an actual part in how their work narratives are put together, skillfully constructing who they are as career women in relation to individual preferences, narrative resources, and local interpretive demands.

Would these women have narrated their career stories the same way on a different occasion, at a time and place other than in an open interview? Would there be similar differences in the sense of self conveyed, as women with minority backgrounds working in a white man's world? The questions, of course, can't be answered from the material Chase provides. We can only speculate that alternate contexts might make for differences of their own. How the women present their stories, and their respective identities, in the exclusive company of colleagues might result in a different set of linkages, perhaps coalescing around sameness, such as the collective story of the personal costs to oneself of being successful in his environment. Regardless of the outcomes, the narratives would still have to be assembled with an eye toward the context in play. A comparison of contexts would shed light on the sorts of options context makes available for storying the self.

Narrative Options

Options for composing an account can be evident within the storytelling process. References to potential linkages may be used reflexively to signal possible plots and themes. In the process, the possible stories adumbrate alternative selves, serving to present the potential subject in question in distinctive ways. For example, in parent effectiveness classes observed as part of the study of a residential treatment center for emotionally disturbed children, it wasn't uncommon for mothers and fathers to frame comments about their children as a set of alternative stories. Some stood in considerable contrast to the center's therapeutic philosophy, which privileged narratives of rational, behaviorally oriented parenting (Buckholdt and Gubrium 1979).

At one class meeting, for instance, a mother, Connie, responded in the following way to another mother, Barb, who had just told a brief story about how much progress her daughter, Kim, had made recently in controlling her temper. Connie commented on the way Barb's story was put together, contrasting it with how she, in turn, might have to assemble the story of her own daughter, Celeste.

> I like the way you said that, Barb. You know, the kinda things ya don't really think about [in behavioral programming]. It made me think about what I'd say if someone asked me how Celeste was doing. I guess if I tried hard enough Celeste would come out smelling like a rose, just like Kim maybe? But, sad to say,

that's not the whole story. There's more to it. Celeste is Kim up to a point, just like you said Barb, but then the story changes. [Discusses Celeste's own treatment program for temper control.] I don't know. When Celeste starts in on her brother, it's just not the same story.

As Connie elaborates Celeste's story, she weaves elements of Barb's account of Kim's progress into her own narrative, assembling the story both in relation to the linkages Barb admirably constructed, and in terms of what "more [there is] to it." Later in her account, Connie arranges her story to expressly reveal both similar and contrasting sets of linkages, highlighting behavioral programming and progress, on the one hand, and elaborating on what "more [there is] to it," on the other. At one point, as if to inform us that her daughter Celeste's identity draws from more than one language game, Connie explains, "Here's another one of those places the story changes." As she continues, it's evident that she constructs her story explicitly with Barb's narrative in mind, as indeed Connie signaled she might do at the start of the preceding extract. Yet, like Chase's women superintendents, Connie also weaves common themes into a distinguishing story of her own, creating alternative identities for her daughter out of both shared and distinctly individualized linkages. At times, Celeste's subjectivity is linked to Kim's; at other times, it is constructed in contrasting terms.

From start to finish, Connie's narrative works both for and against a particular self for Celeste. Narrative options await Connie's and others' active involvement to sort biographical particulars in relation to the self in question into a coherent account. The institutional context within which Connie's and others' stories are conveyed privileges narratives of attention deficits, emotional turmoil, lack of behavioral control, and the like. Institutional assessment transforms these themes into kinds and degrees of learning dysfunction, affective self-control tallies, and accumulated points in a token economy. Behaviors such as eye contact, temper control, and being on- or off-task are locally significant. Yet, as Connie states in the extract and several other times in the meeting, there are other "things you don't really think about [in behavioral programming]." She accordingly hints at difference, giving notice that what is forthcoming will not be a simple matter of reproducing a shared story, but articulating related options for storylines.[3]

Optional linkages can be explicitly indicated in the prefatory specifications of perspective, where storytellers articulate possible points of view or the positions from which they can construct their accounts.[4] This also provides listeners a sense of the kinds of stories that could be told and various themes that might be emphasized. The following extract from another parent-effectiveness class is illustrative. Child-rearing practices are the topic of discussion and Tanya, a mother of three, has been asked whether she models herself after her parents in disciplining her own children, leading to the following response:

It depends. When my kids are really bad, I mean really bad, that's when I think how my mother used to do with us. You know, don't spare the rod or something like that in those days? But, usually, I feel that Mother was too harsh with us and I think that that kind of punishment isn't good for kids today. Better to talk about it and iron things out that way. Still, like I say, it depends on how you want to think about it, doesn't it?

By the end of the extract, we learn that the prefatory statement "it depends" marks two possible sets of linkages, both forming potentially good stories, but representing contrasting disciplinary identities, with different plots and morals. We can interpret Tanya's account as initially pointing her listener to a story about her parenting concerns "when [her] kids are really bad." In this story, Tanya comments that she thinks about discipline in terms of how her own mother acted, paraphrasing the maxim "spare the rod and spoil the child" to highlight related sentiments, which are contrary to center policy. If she had continued with that story—developing its plots, themes, and identities—she might have reasonably made linkages with, say, the rampant breakdown of discipline in today's younger generation. In that narrative context, her own mother would have served as a positive model for parenting, pointing to the need to be strict, lest children go out of control, as they now do. In that account, Tanya and her children's identities reproduce those in her mother's family.

Mid-response, however, Tanya begins to reveal another option for composing her narrative and its identities. While her initial, inchoate story foregrounded the excessive misbehavior of children, mid-course the account becomes a tale focused on the impropriety of corporal punishment, a familiar theme to the group. The prefatory phrase, "but, usually" sets off a shift to a different set of linkages, in which punishment rather than misbehavior is narratively highlighted. These linkages present a language game that orients more to consequences than causes. The story still relates to her mother's disciplinary practices but produces a model of someone prone to exacting excess punishment, this time presenting the mother's negative identity. Tanya states that, currently, "ironing things out" is more effective, now narratively reproducing one of the residential treatment center's guiding principles, along with an institutionally preferred disciplinary identity.

Taken as a whole, the extract indicates that Tanya is aware she has two options for composing the story, extending the possibilities for defining who she and her mother are as parents and how her children will turn out as a result. At the end of the extract, it isn't clear which set of linkages will form her story, which MCDs will predominate, or, indeed, whether she won't combine them in some distinctive way, as Chase's respondents did. Repeating "it depends," Tanya offers a kind of metanarrative, in effect broaching a story about narrative options in its own right. She explains that what one makes of her own and her mother's child-rearing experiences depends upon "how you want to think about it." This not only signals the equally compelling narrative force of two quite different stories, with distinct implications for plot development and contrasting points about domestic discipline, but also evokes the narrative reflexivity that always lurks about the storytelling process to complicate narrative identity. Tanya effectively instructs her listeners that she is not just a narrator propelled by the stories she is prepared to tell, but that she also is aware that she is actively involved in deciding which story—which self—to convey, and how to formulate it.[5]

Narrative Editing

Other things being equal, we find that storytellers like Tanya are not locked into particular narrative positions, but regularly and openly decide what direction to take in telling a story. They needn't reproduce particular coherences, even if there are local imperatives suggesting that they do so, although storytellers are accountable for veering off locally preferred courses. They display their reflexive agency when, for example, they state that they have to think things over before answering, or that they recognize diverse contexts for interpretation, or need to take certain matters into account in deciding how to put something, what to say, or what point to make. They also tell their listeners how they can or should be heard, thus shaping others' narrative identities in the process.

The storyteller, in effect, is an editor who constantly monitors, modifies, and revises themes and storylines. Invoking shifts in perspective, such as referring to the position from which a storyteller offers an account, is one prominent type of narrative editing. As Catherine Riessman (1990) puts it, storytellers "step out of their stories" to attend to perspective and to the ways they expect their accounts to be heard. The selves that stories convey, as well as the identities of storytellers and listeners, are thus shaped and edited as storytelling proceeds.

Consider the progressive editing done by Betty, the elderly caregiving wife of an Alzheimer's disease sufferer, as she recounts home care experiences at a caregiver support group meeting. The following extended extract from the proceedings is reconstructed from ethnographic fieldnotes, with the paragraphs numbered for easy reference.

> **[1]** I'd say that as a wife of fifty years, it's been up and down, mostly up, probably, like most "happily" [*signals quotation marks*] married couples. Actually, as far as husbands go, George's been a pretty good husband. [*Other participants recount episodes from their own "good" marriages, which encourages Betty to elaborate on George's "good" qualities and, as a result, what she "owes" him.*] He's the kinda guy who'd give you the shirt off his back and joke about it. [*Describes George's generosity and relates to participants' "stories" that wind up like hers, "after all those years."*] We had good times and he was always right there when I needed him. [*Mentions how good it makes her feel to be able to take care of him "after all those years."*] Like they say, you can't forget that, can ya? I guess what I'm saying is that I owe the big lunk in a real big way. Gotta keep him with me [*in home care*] as long as possible. [*Betty stares out the window.*]
>
> **[2]** But, you know, I have to ask myself, even after all those years, what's he now? You know, like they say we need to ask ourselves at Chapter [*local chapter meetings of the Alzheimer's Association*]. Who is this big lug I'm living with? Who am I supposed to be? A saint? Most of the time, he doesn't know me. He's like a shell. You all know how terrible that is. Lord, he weighs over 200 pounds and you know what a burden *that* is. [*Elaborates and recounts her relations with George from that viewpoint, this time drawing from the familiar stories of local caregiver exemplars, including the so-called caring martyrs she's known.*] When I think back over the years, maybe I was just "dreaming," like Sally [*a former participant*] said one time. Remember that? Geez, what an eye-opener that was! I ask myself that sometimes, now that he can't patch things up all the time. [*Others describe similar feelings.*] Did

I spend all those years living *for* George, to make *him* happy? I don't know. He was pretty darned cross and demanding sometimes, that I have to say. [*Another participant details life with her "demanding," "vegetative" husband, which Betty then partially integrates into her own narrative.*]

[3] Now don't get me wrong, but what about that? What about me? You know what I mean. What about this here "maturing" [*again signals quotation marks*] woman? [*Laughter.*] You know, this here woman with her own needs? [*Recounts details of her current "lonely" married life.*] I've got my own life to live. We all have, at least that's what we keep hearing and telling each other. Sometimes I ask myself if I ever did [have my own life]. [*Betty's emotional recollections develop into a story of unnecessary sacrifice, self-effacement, and the need to be more realistic.*]

[4] I wish I had the words to tell all of you how I feel sometimes, like I just wanna bust free and be who I am, Betty, not just George's wife. But not really, I guess. [*Chuckling, another participant suggests that Betty is sounding "like one of those feminists."*] Well maybe I am! [*Laughter.*] It was *my* life, too, you know.

[5] I'm just blabbing away here. I have to admit, though, that we were a pretty happy couple. Lots of close years. [*Recounts aspects of that story.*] Fifty years of being a wife. That's a lotta years. [*Embellishes her "happy" years of marriage story.*]

Beginning with the prefatory remark, "as a wife of fifty years," Betty informs her listeners of how they should hear her forthcoming story. Responding to several shared recollections of married life, Betty tells others she feels obligated to take care of her spouse George, "the big lunk," at home for as long as possible. From the outset, her caregiving sentiments support her related story, adding to its particular narrative flavor. Sentiments are not the whole story, but support or distract from the authenticity of particular accounts, as we will soon see. In the first paragraph, properly hyphenated, Betty's narrative identity is the story-of-a-wife-of-fifty-years. It's not just a woman's, nor just a caregiver's story, but the account of someone who is positioned to communicate her thoughts and feelings in a particular way. Betty is communicating the self of a wife-of-fifty-years.

As she continues in the succeeding paragraphs, it is evident that Betty has alternative stories to tell and selves to present. She can draw upon distinct perspectives to link together her experience into different narratives. Note that, in paragraphs three and four, she begins to retell "her" story from what we will eventually learn is the point of view of a woman-with-her-own-life-to-live, thus engendering her narrative in a distinctive way. At the end of paragraph three, she displays other sentiments; this time they signal remorse, the emotional underbelly of a life lived more for someone else than for one's self, a life perhaps wasted because of that. Feelings, too, are parts of language games. As Betty continues with that account in paragraph four, she somewhat uncertainly banters with the other participants about just who her story might have been about, "Betty" or "George's wife," blurring the self under consideration.

Later, in paragraph five, she again switches perspective, communicating her story from the point of view of a participant in a close, long-term relationship with her husband, once more foregrounding the wife-of-fifty-years. At this point, we have no idea which story she prefers, which self she promotes, or even if she conceives of the difference in such terms. She may, indeed, eventually inform her listeners—or her listeners inform her, as sometimes happens—that she is "of two minds" and let it go at that, momentarily multiplying her subjectivity. It's not evident either what her "true" feelings are, even while they are variously expressed throughout her account. One thing is clear in that regard: if we are to take feelings as a warrant for the authenticity of accounts and the genuineness of the self in question, their expression must be appraised in relation to the editing that sorts narrative options and their accompanying identities. Feelings don't stand on their own in stories of any kind.

Betty is in even greater communicative control of what she conveys than the specification of perspective would suggest. She not only edits her account, but positions her listeners as well. For example, later in the meeting, the conversation reverts to the familiar topic of caregiving responsibilities. At one point, Betty urges members to "think of this from a woman's point of view" and goes on to recount the story of what she felt the first time her husband failed to recognize her as his wife. As Betty tells that story, she again steps out of the account and marks her comments with reminders to her listeners that she is assuming they are hearing what is being conveyed as women. She asks rhetorically, "You know what I mean? Woman to woman?" She then proceeds to communicate what she feels, as a woman, not just as a spouse, and seeks confirmation with "You know the feeling." At yet another juncture, she expressly positions herself as a woman by "putting her woman's hat on," which she admonishes two listeners to likewise do, continuing with that story. She tells her listeners to put themselves in her place and try to understand from that point of view, among other familiar ways of varying storylines and their associated selves.

Throughout, Betty adroitly builds contexts for her identity. She not only actively constructs perspective, but manages her listeners' viewpoints in the process, simultaneously editing the contents of her story as it might relate to her listeners' responses. Not wanting to sound too harsh in speaking as a "woman with her own life to live," she prefaces her various comments with "now don't get me wrong," as in extracted paragraph 3 above, and later in the meeting with "don't take this personally, but . . . ." Following that comment, Betty relates what now goes through her mind when George doesn't recognize her or fails to show any appreciation for what she's doing for him. Adding "you have to admit you'd feel exactly the same," she suggests that what she has said is not gratuitously harsh, but part of the shared sentiments of a particular account of the caregiving experience, conveying who they are in common. Several listeners confirm the editorial remarks. When she subsequently accounts for her descriptive "indiscretions" and seemingly "exaggerated claims" with the ostensible need to put harsh realities "in plain English" and "not gussy them up" because, among other things, "it's not a pretty picture," she further shapes the intended storyline and the selves in question.[6]

As proceedings unfold in meeting after meeting like the one Betty attended, varied discourses of the caregiving experience come into play, drawn from widely shared stories proffered by the public culture of the Alzheimer's disease experience (see Gubrium 1986a). At one extreme, these stories center on the caregiver as martyr, expressed in narratives of the "extent some people will go" to care for a family member who is cognitively impaired. At the other extreme, we hear accounts linking together the experiences of "realistic" caregivers, who realize "before it is too late" or "for their own good" that they have their own lives to live and, in any event, "owe something" to other family members, if not to themselves. These further divide according to gender and intergenerational expectations (see Abel and Nelson 1990). Storytellers are more or less aware of these alternative subjectivities, formulating personal accounts in relation to what they know, or are apprised of, as the case might be. Who and what they are for all practical purposes wends its way through related narrative activity, which undergoes constant editing along the way.

Narrative Elasticity

Some storytellers and listeners show a keen awareness of what is locally applicable, sometimes offering reminders to that effect by informing errant storytellers that a particular account is, say, "not the way this [or that] happens," that a story is "strange," or "not the way we normally think about" an aspect of experience, among other ways of signaling the local accountability of narrative. Other storytellers seem to be continually learning what to say about, and how to story, themselves. Circumstances themselves vary in the extent to which the use of diverse resources is acceptable. Some provide working templates for the iteration of particular narratives, while others tolerate considerable exploration and experimentation. Overall, the narrative interplay between discursive practice and discourse-in-practice makes for considerable elasticity in what is accountable in the course of social interaction. What is or is not properly tellable in a particular locale is never completely distinct from the ongoing construction of narratives. New narrative resources develop and are reflexively employed both to story selves and to revise expectations about the acceptability of accounts. All of this serves to diversify the resources available for constructing identity.

The stories we can be don't stand over and above narrative practice, even while we can, to a limited degree, discern possibilities by temporarily bracketing attention to everyday usage. Stories take shape on the occasions of their use, as parts of the very identity projects for which they serve as resources. The recognizable stories of one going concern, such as those commonly told in a parent effectiveness class, are not necessarily the recognizable stories of another, such as a twelve-step group focused on recovery from drug addiction. These varied groups may story the self quite differently, or available narratives may overlap in remarkable detail. Yet none of their stories enters into everyday use as a narrative template. Rather, the stories are continuously shaped and reshaped as participants variously borrow from, keep separate, combine, individually formulate, or even suppress stories to construct difference and sameness.

A Diversely Storied Collective Identity

The Mirror Dance (1983), a study of a lesbian community, is intriguing in this regard. Author Susan Krieger's empirical material shows just how diversely con-

structed a narrative resource "the community" can be, for example. As we wr
show, a community with a strong collective identity becomes, in narrative practice, a varied set of language games for articulating the self.

While working at a Midwestern university, Krieger became involved in the local lesbian community. She actively participated in its social life and eventually
chose to conduct sociological research on issues of lesbian identity. A year of
participation-observation combined with two months of intensive interviewing with
seventy-eight women produced rich narrative material on the construction of identity. The research shows that even if self narratives derive from a shared stock of
narrative resources, individual accounts of what "we're all about" can be the source
of considerable difference, indeed differentiating what is ostensibly shared.

What began as a project focused on the theme of privacy seemed to put the
cart before the horse, according to Krieger.[7] The theme presumed that the issue
of the identity in question was settled. But were these women simply lesbians,
from whom answers to questions about privacy could be elicited, coded, and so-
ciologically analyzed? Was community identity itself in need of examination? Indeed, was the women's sense of their relationships to the lesbian community problematic in its own right, to be analyzed itself before the matter of privacy could
be considered? What, in effect, was this narrative resource variously called "the
community," and how did it relate to stories ostensibly communicating individual identity? Krieger recounts her early concerns in this way:

> In time . . . I came to understand that my inquiries into privacy required me to
> explore dilemmas of identity. I moved from thinking of privacy as an ability to
> close the door of a house in order to protect oneself from view, to thinking that,
> more accurately, it was an ability to both open and close the door to affect how
> one might be known. I came, in other words, to be concerned with control over
> definition of the self. I also came to realize that my study was destined to be about
> something even more compelling to me: the problem of loss of self—how it oc-
> curs and how it may be dealt with in a social setting. (Pp. xi–xii)

"The" lesbian community became the key to understanding the issue in question. Viewed in the context of self construction, Krieger interprets the stories these
women told about themselves and the resulting meanings of privacy in complex
relationship to the stories they conveyed about the community as a whole. The
broader story of the community as collectively representative of each of their own
identities was continuously mediated by a related narrative of personal engrossment and isolation, according to Krieger. The community could be so engrossing
as to leave the women feeling bereft of identities of their own. Narratively speaking, they risked having few or no individual stories to tell about themselves. On
the other hand, guarding against this form of engrossment risked narrative isolation; it could mean the loss of a story that mirrored a valued self and a useful
resource for dealing with confrontations outside the community. A shared discourse of identity, it seemed, could work as much to threaten the self as to positively define it. Krieger explains:

> This, I came to feel, was true in large part because the community was a com-
> munity of likeness, one in which individuals were encouraged to value a com-

mon identity as women. It was also a community of intimacy in which members were given support for experiences of closeness and union, including those which might reach their peak in shared sexuality. It was a community of ideology and, in particular, of an ideology that stressed the oneness of women working together for a better life, an ideology that dealt minimally, if at all, with possibilities for conflict latent in the differences between members. It was a stigmatized or deviant community, a condition that also emphasized the need for oneness and solidarity. It was a relatively new community and so lacked many predetermined rules and roles that might give its members established ways of exercising their differences. Finally, and not of the least consequence, it was a community of women: individuals with life experiences that tended to encourage, indeed to view as virtuous, the giving up of the self to others. (P. xii)

According to Krieger, the lesbian community, for better or worse, both defines and secures members' identities. Through their own interpersonal relations, their search for a sense of self-worth among women like themselves, and the stories they repeatedly relate to each other, these women collectively represent who and what they are, and in the process variably construct themselves. They form a virtual society of surveillance whose collective narrative ostensibly disciplines and defines them as individuals, which, for those aware of the subjective risks involved, can be distressful.

Yet the women's accounts leave us wondering about the constancy of "the community" as a narrative resource, despite its varied individual engrossments. Attempting to avoid the distant third-person voice of the dispassionate sociologist, Krieger formulates each woman's own story. One after another, each of them is given to talk about herself in relation to what we initially figure to be "the community." Story after story specifies who and what they are collectively, which ostensibly constructs their individual identities as lesbian women, consuming or isolating them in the process. The community is clearly being addressed, but it is far from interpretively fixed. While a socially shared and recognizable entity referred to as "the community" is present in the women's narratives, it is constructed in relation to the individual identity in question. We are gradually apprised of the highly varied linkages each woman makes to assemble the very resource whose discourse ostensibly centers their individual differences. We become witness to the narrative elasticity of collective identity as one woman after another modifies "the community's" story as she puts it to individual use. If the women's identities dynamically dance before a community mirror, the mirror itself also dances to some degree.

Listen to articulations of "the community" as each of the following women assembles the entity that serves as the source of her identity. The first speaker, Ruth, talks forthrightly about the community of which she and the other women are a part, but notice how she constructs it. Ruth differentiates it from other lesbian communities by thematizing it as "definitely the most out" and the most important to members because in it "they found a sense of being, belonging, fellowship, and sharing." For Ruth, "the community" marks what brings members together into a coherent whole.

RUTH

She saw several different lesbian communities in town, said Ruth, though she understood what people meant when they said "the community." It was definitely the most out, the most woman-identified. It was a group of women who were almost exclusively lesbians, who had been out or around for just about as long as she had been here, which was about five years, or longer than that. These were women who were the lesbian community almost because it was important to them and because they found a sense of being, belonging, fellowship, and sharing that way. . . . As a claim to being "the community" they probably had it, she thought, because they named themselves in such a way and wanted it. (P. 7)

Compare this with other narratives, which make different linkages to designate the community. Irene, for example, discerns the community in terms similar to how one might define a formal organization, highlighting membership qualifications and organizational missions. Membership especially rests on the criterion of sexual involvement with other women. "The community" is exclusive, because Irene's narrative restricts it to women who are sexually involved with women. While Irene doesn't say it, the implication is that heterosexual women need not apply.

IRENE

They were basically a social network, felt Irene. The common denominator was people who defined themselves as lesbians. The community was a social entity that had its own rules, its own membership, its own qualifications. It was primarily devoted to itself rather than a proselytizing organization (like a church or Rape Crisis). It had functions: it gave its members a group identity; it gave them support for their life style and a sense of security and affirmation; for some people who didn't have a strong identity other than the fact of their lesbianism, it was crucial. It was also exclusive. The membership qualifications were pretty narrowly defined: a woman had to be either sexually involved with another woman, or planned to be, or had a good strong history of having been. (P. 8)

From Madeleine, we learn that sexuality is a code word for other facets of attachment. Madeleine constructs the community by way of its social and emotional bonds, differentiating collective identity in terms above and beyond sexuality, centered on the "shared vision" that make the women who they are as sexually whole beings.

MADELEINE

It was basically women who chose to relate to other women sexually, felt Madeleine, who generally were in relationships with other women, although some were not. But it was the idea of community as opposed to single women relating sexually. There was a whole culture, a camaraderie, a support system, a network, shared understanding, shared vision. Then within that there were strong friendships and people who met each other in cluster arrangements. (P. 9)

For Hollis, "the community" was something altogether less sanguine. She constructs the community in terms of her social network, which she differentiates from what a proper community should be. We might presume that a proper community stands for the opposite of what Hollis states her "social network" repreats; a proper community should not be hedonistic, self-interested, or inward-looking.

HOLLIS

They were an anti-intellectual group, said Hollis, very hedonistic, self-interested in that sense of being self-maintained, very inward-looking. If she wasn't one of them, she didn't think she would find their community admirable. If she didn't need these people socially, she would not have had anything to do with them. What was the community exactly? It was everybody in town she knew, the ones she saw regularly, whose faces were on it. It rested on face-to-face knowledge of one another. She didn't see it as a community really. It was mainly a social network. She thought it was much more a reference group than a community. (P. 11)

Even something as concrete as the size of "the community" is fluid. Compare four representations in these terms, illustrating the folk demography of collective identity.

PAT

There were fifteen to twenty women in it, said Pat. These were the most active, the core. They represented no cross section of anything really, which was a problem she had with the whole thing.

STEPHANIE

There were thirty to forty, she would guess, said Stephanie, an estimate which came from the fact that you usually didn't see more than thirty to forty of the women in one place at one time.

ELLEN

There were a hundred or more, thought Ellen, a number which came from the number of names on the newsletter mailing list. The list had about 140 names on it the last time she mailed it and about a third of them didn't have local addresses.

MARIA

The number varied, said Maria, depending on how you defined it. (P. 12)

From these accounts, we can see that the discourse of "the community" is anything but stable and uniform. While the women all have a sense of being part of a collective identity, in practice they construct its meaning and significance in relation to biographical particulars. The community, in other words, isn't strictly defined, nor does it strictly define who and what these women are as lesbians. As we so clearly hear in these accounts, discursive practice complicates discourse-in-practice.

The Narrative Elasticity of "Hitting Bottom"

Formally organized settings present similarly pliant resources for storying selves, even while the storylines they promote are often quite formulaic. Consider, for example, recovery groups sponsored by Alcoholics Anonymous (AA). As a going concern, AA virtually disperses minipanopticons throughout the identity landscape, with techniques of self construction including the ubiquitous personal testaments of one's sobriety before a group (sometimes called "drunkalogues" AA), a formula for recovery but never being fully recovered (the Twelve Steps, and sponsors who help to support and manage sobriety. Carole Cain (1991) explains that AA is a cultural system "that no one is born into," but whose technology of self construction is part of a widely recognized discourse for contemporary identity, depicting alcoholism and other substance abuses as addictions, diseases over which the afflicted are powerless (see Denzin 1987b).

Drunkalogues are self-stories. AA relies heavily on these round-robin accounts of sobriety that follow the recitation of the so-called serenity prayer at the start of each group meeting. Accounts typically begin with declarations of how long it's been since one had the last drink, often down to the exact hours and minutes, followed by applause. There are recollections of progress through the Twelve Steps, especially when and how people finally "surrendered" to the fact that they were alcoholics, admitted they were "powerless over alcohol—that [their] lives had become unmanageable," and "came to believe that a Power greater than [themselves] could restore [them] to sanity."

There's no doubt that in the context of AA, the self becomes alcoholic. Denzin (1987a) portrays the process as a series of dramatic realizations, with discernible acts and scenes. His observational study of the presentation of "the alcoholic self" in AA meetings provides diverse narratives of related experiences, whose repeated and widespread communication makes it clear that AA is definitely in the identity business. The drama's accounts tell two kinds of story, within the overall script of a redemption narrative. These stories overlap considerably, and are endlessly reiterated and reassembled. One kind is the before-story, conveying what it was like before one realized and "surrendered" to the fact that he or she was alcoholic. This is a diverse and multifaceted collection, including colorful but depressing stories of the various ways one "hits bottom," becoming so emotionally distraught and physically and cognitively degraded that there is nowhere to go but up. Old-timers recount tales of woe and despair, publicly revealing to newcomers who they were at their worst. Time and again, they remind their audience how to frame and communicate their own experiences of surrendering to the Twelve Steps of the recovering alcoholic.

The other kind of account is the after-story—a narrative of recovery experiences following one's surrender to being powerless over the disease. While these are usually less embellished than before-stories, they are more hopeful, even while there are tales of returning to drinking following a period of sobriety. Some after-stories are humbly heroic, prefaced by exact counts of the large number of days that have passed since the last drink. Sober old-timers take center stage in conveying these narratives; their alcoholic selves play a starring role in their accounts.[8]

The key event dividing these stories is hitting bottom, said to be the experiential impetus for taking AA's so-called first step. An early AA publication (1953) portrays the significance of the event in this way:

> Why all this insistence that every AA must hit bottom first? The answer is that few people will sincerely try to practice the AA program unless they have hit bot-

tom. For practicing AA's remaining Eleven Steps means the adoption of attitudes that almost no alcoholic who is still drinking can dream of taking. Who wishes to be rigorously honest and tolerant? Who wants to confess his faults to another and make restitution for harm done? Who cares anything about a Higher Power, let alone meditation and prayer? Who wants to sacrifice time and energy in trying to carry AA's message to the next sufferer? No, the average alcoholic, self-centered in the extreme, doesn't care for this prospect—unless he has to do these things in order to stay alive himself. (P. 24)

Despite its formulaic pattern, there can be considerable narrative play in the discourse of the alcoholic experience. The "AA template," as Melvin Pollner and Jill Stein (1996) describe it, is made to stretch in many directions as it is applied in practice. For example, "hitting bottom" and "surrendering" to one's alcoholism are widely shared and recognized as key experiences, but what it means to hit bottom or surrender is far from uniform. Like Krieger's women's representations of "the community," hitting bottom is as much a part of the unfolding stories of the drunk experience as it is a central and discernible feature of the discourse that formulates selves in AA. Group members construct and reconstruct "bottom" according to their narrative needs. Each experiential location of bottom is part of a living language game that develops and takes shape within, not separate from, storytelling. Members, in other words, work at specifying bottom as a narrative resource. This accomplished, hitting bottom provides a basis for recognizably conveying one's present identity.

The narrative elasticity of hitting bottom is conveyed in the following account, where we can see how "bottom" comes in multiples (Denzin 1987a, p. 158).

In order for the alcoholic to surrender he or she must "hit bottom." Two "bottoms" are distinguished by AA: "high bottom" and "low bottom." In AA's early days its cofounder Bill Wilson stated:

Those of us who sobered up in AA had been grim and utterly hopeless cases. But then we began to have some success with milder alcoholics. Younger folks appeared. Lots of people turned up who still had jobs, homes, health, and even good social standing. Of course, it was necessary for these newcomers to hit bottom emotionally. But they did not have to hit every possible bottom in order to admit that they were licked. [AA 1967, p. 209]

Denzin's observations at AA meetings show how "bottom" is a continuously adaptable narrative resource, as much constructed in the process of storying an alcoholic self as it is the actual bottom of the self represented in the voice of experience. An AA member with fifteen years of experience and a veteran of the Twelve Steps, describes bottom in fluid, even cosmic terms, as he explains that hitting bottom can't be predicted in advance and, indeed, knowing it may be an incommensurable "gift."

You never know when it will happen. I've taken one man to detox 14 times. He's still drinking. Someday he'll get it. You never know. It's a gift. You never give up on anybody. (P. 158)

In another account, a recovering alcoholic, a 37-year-old graduate stude. uses an elevator metaphor to describe what it means to hit bottom, again con veying its elasticity.

> It is like an elevator that keeps going down to lower levels and lower floors un- til it hits bottom. I have stopped drinking, surrendered, come to AA and worked the Steps, but each time before it was at a level that still allowed me to drop lower. I started at too high a level. It took me a long time to hit the lowest level. I have finally hit what I hope is the bottom floor for me. But I don't know. I thought this before, too. There's always a new bottom for me to hit. Last time it was a DUI ["driving under the influence" of alcohol]. But I've had those before too. It has taken me a long time, a long time, to learn this program. I just pray that I have it today. (P. 171)

If the discourse of the alcoholic self is pervasive in AA meetings, providing a shared and recognizable template for locally centering experience, it nonethe- less enters into narrative practice as a variable form of life. This discourse-in- practice shifts about in discursive practice, as those concerned enter into the lo- cal narrativity of surveillance, which in talk and interaction convey their iden- tity as alcoholics. The resulting storytelling constructs as much difference as same- ness in who and what they were and are now becoming.

Demarcating Space
for Self Narration

C learly, the self is actively narrated, dynamically accomplished as narrative practice provides the ever-developing stories that constitute our selves. Mead,
James, and others, of course, told us that we could have as many selves as there are
social relationships. But as much as they realized the self-generating powers of the
social, they had neither the foresight nor the empirical technology to fully comprehend and appreciate the complexity of the self-construction process. As astute as
they were, the early pragmatists were never keenly aware of, nor interested in, the
communicative practices by which the self was accomplished. The simple yet profound recognition of the self's social origins was their major breakthrough.

But the self doesn't just burst forth from its social encounters. As we showed
in the last chapter, stories of the self don't simply happen, they are actively composed in relationship to others. Unlike measles or chicken pox, we don't break
out into the stories of who or what we are. Nor do we come to conclusions by
just as suddenly getting over them. Still, if we can modify this tortured analogy
a bit, we do find that some selves and their stories can be contagious, at least in
terms of the prevalence of their communication. Some have even become epi-
demic in the contemporary identity landscape, as, from start to finish, we work
in conventional or institutionally sensitive ways to bring off particular identities,
such as that of the recovering alcoholic.

If we want to understand comprehensively *how* the self is produced, we need
to examine further the complex interactional frameworks within which stories of
the self are told, to listen very closely to how selves are "talked into being" (Heritage 1984). The structure of ordinary conversation, as we shall see, provides the
scaffolding that supports the discursive practice which constitutes selves. In this
chapter, we consider the sometimes minute, yet significant, communicative details by which space for self narration is demarcated, showing how artful, yet collaboratively methodical, the process is in practice. We begin by looking at some
very generic features of ordinary conversation, then consider how these mundane
activities are deeply implicated in storying the self.

The Machinery of Everyday Conversation

Social structures such as the self are "methodically produced by the members of
society for one another" through social interaction (Schegloff and Sacks 1973,

p. 290). Harvey Sacks, Emanuel Schegloff, Gail Jefferson, and a cadre of other conversation analysts have highlighted the vast "seen but unnoticed" structures and contingencies of competent conversation that are the bedrock of our social worlds, including storied selves (see Atkinson and Heritage 1984; Boden and Zimmerman 1991; Drew and Heritage 1992; Heritage 1984, 1997; Silverman 1998). Their work demonstrates that ordinary conversation is a highly coordinated activity requiring participants' keen attention and competence.

Sacks (1992a, 1992b) has used the metaphor of machinery to convey the systematic way that conversation is self-organized so as to produce orderly communication. While the metaphor risks making conversation appear mechanical, it's useful because it emphasizes the way that talk proceeds in an orderly fashion, one person speaking at a time, in sequences of exchanges. As Jack Whalen (1992) summarizes,

> Turns at talk do not simply happen to occur one after another but rather "belong together" as a socio-organizational unit and where there is thus a methodic relationship between the various turns or parts . . . a set of mutual obligations is established by the structural relations between these sequence parts, with each action projecting some "next." (P. 306)

We see this in ordinary, smoothly flowing conversations, the most obvious example of this sequential organization being question-answer pairs in which the asking of a question "demands" an answer or some accountable substitute. Changes between speakers occur at recognizable speakership transition points, preserving single-person speakership, with orderly mechanisms for designating who will speak next. While speakership exchange does not occur mechanistically, conversational participants are always aware of, and accountable to, this set of normative expectancies.

A more detailed look at this simple but basic phenomenon reveals some of the myriad systematic activities that transpire in what are generally taken to be the unimportant conversational actions within which narratives of the self develop. The organization of single-speaker turns, for example, is not an interactional given. Speakers usually take their turns at talk, with one party speaking at a time. A conversation may involve several speakers, however, so transitions from one speaker to the next must be orderly or conversational chaos ensues. The trick is to transfer speakership from one person to a single next speaker, without having speakers overlap one another's talk, and without an extended pause or gap between adjacent turns. As Sacks, Schegloff, and Jefferson (1974) explain, coordinated single-speaker turns are achieved with remarkable regularity, regardless of substantive variations in the conversation, such as participants' identities, topic of conversation, setting, and the objective of the conversation. This is also the case when the task is complicated by the participation of multiple potential speakers.

Sacks and colleagues (1974) have outlined the machinery through which this regularity is achieved. One mechanism they identify is the practice of the current speaker allocating the next turn by virtue of the design of the initial turn and its completion. Alternatively, another party may select himself or herself to speak at the completion of a turn if the current speaker's utterance doesn't allocate the next ırn. There are "rules" or normative expectancies for this process. First, a current speaker may construct his or her turn so as to select the next speaker by a variety of direct and indirect techniques (e.g., explicitly asking a designated person for a response). The person so designated then has the right and obligation to speak next. If the current speaker doesn't allocate the next turn at the first possible speaker transition point—a place in the conversation at which the possible completion of the original turn might be detected—another person may select herself or himself to speak. Finally, if the first speaker fails to designate the next speaker, and if no one self-selects at the first transition relevance point, the current speaker may (but does not have to) continue, until one of the above transfer mechanisms results in a change in speakers, thus sustaining the interaction.

These "rules" coordinate turn-taking, organizing the transition from one speaker to another, minimizing gaps and overlaps (Sacks et al. 1974). Whether someone has been selected to speak next, or the next speaker selects himself or herself, speakership transfer is determined turn-by-turn. That is, speaker selection is *locally managed* within the series of exchanges. The obligation to listen to the conversation—to monitor the possibilities it may hold for the next turn—is thus built into the conversation, since any participant may be selected to participate at any time. The production of some current conversational action proposes a local, here-and-now definition of the situation to which subsequent talk will orient. One turn projects a relevant next activity or response that must be fashioned to meet the demands of the immediate occasion. Thus, each utterance is "sequentially implicative" (Schegloff and Sacks 1973).

Schegloff and Sacks (1973) have observed a variety of generic features of conversational sequences centered around what they call the "adjacency pair" structure. As summarized by Heritage (1984), an adjacency pair is (1) a sequence of two utterances that are (2) adjacent, (3) produced by different speakers, (4) ordered as a first part and a second part, and (5) typed so that a first part calls for a second part (or range of second parts). Schegloff and Sacks offer a simple rule of adjacency pair operation: "Given the recognizable production of a first pair part, on its first possible completion, its speaker should stop and a next speaker should start and produce a second pair part from the pair type the first pair part is recognizably a member of" (p. 206). These sequences are normatively invariant:

> The adjacency pair structure is a *normative* framework for actions which is *accountably* implemented . . . the first speaker's production of a first pair part proposes that a second speaker should relevantly produce a second pair part which is accountably "due" immediately upon completion of the first. (Heritage 1984, p. 247, emphasis in the original)

Even when the second pair part is not forthcoming, this format requires the second speaker to show that he or she is oriented to the normative framework, regardless of its substance, and that the action taken is accountable in some other fashion. When turn-taking "errors" or adjacency pair "violations" occur, participants exhibit accountability by invoking "repair mechanisms." For example, when more than one speaker talks at a time, one of them may stop before a normally

anticipated completion point, recognizing the basic "rule" of one speaker a
time. Or if speakership transfer fails to occur at an appropriate place, the speak
may repair the sequence by speaking again, respecting the ongoing sequence-in
progress. Or, in still other instances, if repairs by someone other than the current
speaker are in order, the next speaker waits until the next possible completion
point before speaking again. Thus, the turn-taking system is respected, even when
violations and repairs occur.

To understand what is happening in the course of ongoing talk—from exchanging simple greetings to narrating life stories—one must view conversation
as *sequences of action*. These sequences, and the exchange of turns within sequences,
rather than individual utterances or sentences, are paramount conversational
components, the units most responsible for the production of interactional order.
Because the turn-taking sequence also compels potential participants to pay attention to the ongoing conversation, and to be prepared to display an understanding of what is going on, it virtually binds them into a joint, collaborative enterprise. This is the communicative scaffolding of social interaction—action that,
through the sheer sequential mechanics of exchange, takes account of others.

Taking account of others conversationally means that what one says must orient to both what has gone before and what is anticipated to follow—another way
of saying that talk is both retrospective and prospective in its orientation. This
also means that interactional accountability is achieved through the "recipient design" of one's contributions to the conversation (Sacks 1992a, 1992b; Sacks et al.
1974; Sacks and Schegloff 1979). What one says and does within the ongoing conversational sequence displays an awareness of prior talk, and respects the variety of contingencies comprising and shaping talk yet to come. Any particular turn
at talk must be designed so that recipients are likely to understand what's being
said and what's going on interactionally. As we shall see, all of this has immediate bearing on how stories of the self are conversationally designated.

Stories in Conversation

Narrating the self engenders special interactional complications. Typically, transitions between speakers occur at any point where a next possible speaker may
nondisruptively claim a turn at talk. Commonly, the first possible application of
this rule will come at the first possible completion point, which generally will be
at the hearable completion of the first sentence (Sacks et al. 1974). However, since
stories involve extended turns at talk, usually more than a single sentence,
prospective storytellers are immediately challenged to secure the right to extend
their turn at talk (Schegloff 1984). As Sacks (1992b, p. 18) puts it, a story is "an
attempt to control the floor over an extended series of utterances."

For a story to emerge, the teller must be able to string together multiple sentences while retaining the attention of listeners without having them intrude into
the conversation with anything more than signals that they are being attentive.
A space for narrating the self, in other words, must be established in the give-
and-take of social interaction. Sacks (1992b) notes that, technically, this amounts

an attempt to control a "third slot" in conversational sequence from a "first ot." This involves getting potential next speakers, who may use the first possible completion point as an opportunity to speak themselves, to forego the opportunity to enter the conversation. There are many ways to accomplish this, all having to do with depriving the initial utterance of its relevance as a springboard for speaker transition (Schegloff 1984). To understand how the self gets told in this context, then, we must look at the conversational techniques that storytelling might entail.

Sequentiality

First of all, stories arise out of the ongoing flow of talk, taking account of both what has gone before and what will follow in the flow of conversation (Jefferson 1978). In the language of conversation analysis, they are both "locally occasioned" and "sequentially implicative." Sequentiality, explains Gail Jefferson (1978), is crucial in that stories must jibe with the conversational context of their telling; they must fit with what has preceded them and merge back into the ongoing flow of talk that will follow.

Any number of things may trigger a story in the course of conversation. Someone may say something at a particular moment that reminds another participant of a particular story, which subsequently may or may not be told. Often incipient stories relate to the line of conversation already under way, but it's also possible that they may not be "topically coherent" with the talk in progress (Jefferson 1978). In either case, if the teller wants to produce the story, it must be done methodically, folded into the turn-by-turn talk that is under way. Jefferson (1978) suggests a variety of techniques that are used to introduce or initiate a story, all of which display a relationship between the story and prior talk. This both creates a sequential environment that allows the story to emerge and establishes the appropriateness of the story's telling.

Thus, the emergence, placement, meaning, and relevance of a story of the self are not pregiven, to be analytically assumed or determined by inspection of the story alone. Rather, such a story is best conceived as a complex social activity that is interactionally negotiated and managed as conversation proceeds (Schenkein 1978). In perhaps its simplest form, Jefferson (1978, p. 219) notes, "storytelling can involve a story preface with which a teller projects a forthcoming story, a next turn in which a co-participant aligns him- or herself as a story recipient, a next in which teller produces the story, and a final turn in which the story recipient again speaks, this time with reference to the now-complete story." But if this is the archetypal form, there are countless variations. Let's elaborate on some of the ways in which stories get told, how they are initiated, extended, and completed, with a continuing eye (and ear) to the storying of the self.

Incitement

Perhaps the simplest way to introduce a story—or a self—into a conversation is by way of a direct invitation or a question. This virtually solicits storytelling, invit-

ing an extended response. We can see this most clearly in situations where or
party formally requests information from another. Interviews are just this type o.
situation. Whether it's in a research interview, on a TV talk show, in a clinic,
speaking with a school guidance counselor, or in a social service eligibility office,
stories of selves are formally solicited all the time. Interviewers intentionally "ac-
tivate" or "incite" (Holstein and Gubrium 1995a) narratives of self, showing us
one basic pattern of how stories and their selves might be induced and emerge.
More and more, interviews are eliciting narratives of the self as we attempt to
find out just who we are and what we are "up to." Indeed, as Paul Atkinson and
David Silverman (1997) argue, we have become an "interview society" whose subjectivity comes to us in the form of stories elicited through interviewing. Inasmuch as the interview has become a ubiquitous method of inquiry, so far flung
that it is virtually everybody's way of acquiring personal information, the self is
becoming a widespread artifact of this form of narrative incitement. What was
once almost exclusively a social scientific tool is now a natural part of the identity landscape.

Consider the following examples taken from an interview project conducted
in nursing homes where informants were asked to tell the researchers their life
stories. In the first example, Jay, the interviewer, asks Rebecca Bourdeau, a 76-
year-old nursing home resident, to tell her life story in an open-ended interview
format. Among many similar exchanges, the following question elicits part of that
story.[1]

JAY: How would you describe yourself as a person?
REBECCA: I don't know. Right now I'm very discouraged and I'm not a bit up-
          beat. Maybe I should be. I get really upset about my life when I think
          about all the things that I could do and what happened to me [she had
          a stroke] and here I am. [The story continues.] (Gubrium 1993, p. 29)

Note that the question directly and explicitly solicits a story of the self, which is
produced at length without evidence of concern for establishing the right to extend a turn at talk. The question, especially in the context of the interview situation, gives permission for the story to emerge without interruption.

Of course requests for information come in many forms, as in another interview Jay conducted with nursing home resident Julia McCall:

JAY: Ms. McCall? Why don't you tell me a little about your life?
JULIA: About my life?
JAY: Yeah. Tell me about it.
JULIA: Well, you done asked, bless your heart. I was raised in a little place in
        Georgia called Damen and my granddaddy, my mother's daddy, was
        from England. [The story continues.] (Gubrium 1993, p. 70)

Here McCall is asked to "tell me a little about your life," which initially causes
some hesitancy. The interviewer's subsequent encouragement, however, provokes
an extended story of Julia's background, family history, and many experiences

lat eventually lead her to remark that she had a "pretty good life," despite her pains and sicknesses." Once again self narration is formally prompted and encouraged.

Nearly all social science interviewers are cautioned against asking "leading" questions (see Holstein and Gubrium 1995a); it's a methodological stricture. But interviews are conversations like any other conversation in many respects, and talk-in-interaction like this demands a certain topical continuity, an attentiveness to what has come before, and to what might follow, in order for the conversation to proceed smoothly. Interviewers simply cannot ignore this and carry on the desired conversation. And, like other conversational participants, we see the necessity for them to "encourage" stories if they are to satisfy their information-gathering agenda.

Take the storytelling implications of the following exchange between the interviewer and Peter, a 77-year-old nursing home resident.

JAY: Why don't we talk about your life a bit now? Tell me a bit more about it, Pete.
PETER: Well, Jay, I was born in Connecticut. . . . Then I went into sales. . . . My wife and I traveled all over the country, in a travel trailer that we
JAY: You had a travel trailer?
PETER: Um hm. And we hauled that with a Ford van. . . . And I was in that until I fell. It was 1971, I think, that I fell but I'm not sure.
JAY: How did that happen?
PETER: [Peter continues with the story of how he fell off the roof while putting up a TV antenna, which left him with a severe spinal injury and chronic pain.] (Gubrium 1993, pp. 110–11)

In this case, what is interesting about the interactional development of the story is the way in which the interviewer/story recipient shapes the story by suggesting what amount to items of interest in the storyteller's life. While the stories that might be triggered over the course of a conversation are always uncertain, the recipient of the story presented above pointedly invites the construction of select aspects of the storyteller's life and self by virtue of how he prompts and encourages elaborations in particular lines of talk. These prompts and encouragements, however, are necessary if conversation is to flow smoothly, and if topical continuity is to be maintained. Both speaker and recipient, as Sacks and others (1974) remind us, must always display their attentiveness to what the other is doing conversationally if the talk is to proceed smoothly and meaningfully. If the interviewer were to remain completely silent or uninvolved, the speaker would likely seek some sort of signal that what he or she was saying was being understood or was of interest to the listener. If this were not forthcoming, we would likely hear the conversation end, or, as we will see later in this chapter, the storyteller might initiate new conversational moves in the interest of sustaining the conversation.

So, the demands of ongoing conversation require at least minimal participation by story recipients. Even simple tokens of understanding (e.g., "Uh huh") have implications for the story line that will emerge, and the demand for co-participation often leads to more substantial influence over the storytelling process. As we see in the instance above, the interviewer provided what might be seen as the "narrative horizons" of the storytelling project (Gubrium 1993, Gubrium and Holstein 1997). While this might appear to be bad interviewing procedure in terms of standardized methodology, the demands of ongoing interaction make the "ideal" interview a practical impossibility, because the interview itself always remains accountable to the normative expectancies of competent conversation as well as to the demand for a good story to satisfy the needs of the researcher (Holstein and Gubrium 1995a).

Indeed, some stories of the self may be more conversational than narrative in the sense that they emerge across a number of turns of talk (see Sacks 1992a, 1992b). Courtroom interrogation is a prime example, but we can see similar conversational stories emerge in all sorts of everyday talk as well. The following example is another excerpt from a nursing home interview.

JAY: What does life look like from where you're at now, Mrs. R?
LILY: Well, I say it's hopeless, to me. I'm just in other peoples' way here. I'm no good.
JAY: Being in someone's way, that makes a difference?
LILY: Yes, it do.
JAY: Would you explain that a little more?
LILY: Well, when you can't do anything for yourself, I think you're in other folks' way. If I was up and doing for myself and others, I would enjoy living, but I don't enjoy it.
JAY: So would you say it's the place you're at or you?
LILY: [Continues with story of the place she lives and how she can't do anything for herself.] (Gubrium 1993, p. 127)

Note that the story emerges in the give and take of question-answer sequences, not in any single utterance. Once again we see the interview's collaborative character, underscoring the sense in which conversation itself is always collaborative.

Of course conversational encouragement, incitement, or other moves to elicit or shape stories are not confined to research interviews where the information-gathering agenda is highly developed. It also takes place in the myriad informal settings of everyday conversation. Consider this exchange during a spate of "small talk" between an insurance salesman (Alan) who has just been invited into the living room of a potential client (Pete).

1. ALAN: . . . Whatiyou teach?
2. PETE: At-tuh Crayton.
3. ALAN: O:h. Whattiyou teach?
4. PETE: Well, I really don't teach I I'm a graduate student there, I taught =
                                                              //
5. ALAN: // O:h

6. PETE: = A couple of quarters lass quarter but I'm not really a teacher I'm working on my degree.

7. ALAN: *Oh.* Okay. (2.0) (Schenkein 1978, p. 58)

Alan initially triggers Pete's story with a direct question. Pete's initial response, however, does not answer the question, so Alan repeats it (line 3). This time, as Pete replies, Alan signals his particular attention to Pete's revelation that he didn't really teach (line 5, "O:h"). This prompts Pete's subsequent elaboration, which clarifies the situation in which Pete found himself to be a graduate student who taught classes, but was not an actual faculty member. Once again, it's the *recipient's* contribution, as minimal as it might be, that leads to a particular elaboration of the story and its contribution to self construction, underscoring in conversational detail Mead's insistence that the empirical self is a *social* structure. We shall have more to say later in the chapter about the role of such "response tokens" in the production of extended stories, and, by implication, narratives of the self.

Prefaces

Stories, of course, are not always directly or explicitly invited. When they are not, they must be methodically introduced by the storyteller. Sacks (1974, 1992a, 1992b) has noted that stories take more than a sentence to tell and that the initial challenge to storytelling is extending a story beyond that first sentence. Recall Sacks's argument that, as a story begins, the completion of its first sentence provides an opportunity for someone else to claim a turn at talk, which would effectively short-circuit a nascent story (Sacks et al. 1974). The storyteller, however, may turn to a number of devices in an attempt to secure the conversational "right" and "space" to extend his or her turn at talk, building it into a full-blown account. Story prefaces serve just this function. By offering a preface, which, in effect, says that the speaker has a story he or she wants to tell, the speaker establishes the reasonable expectation that the next speaker will reselect the prospective teller to speak again, thus providing the opportunity to launch a more extended turn at talk (to produce the intended story). From that point onward, the storyteller may expect that others will refrain from treating each sentence ending as a possible turn-completion point at which they would vie for speakership.

    We have already considered a form of prefacing in discussing how storytellers "edit" their stories. For example, in Chapter 6 we described practices whereby a storyteller would indicate a narrative position from which a story was going to be told, and the terms in which it was meant to be heard. This sort of prefacing was used to set up a preferred way of understanding the *content* of the emerging narrative. Here we will address prefacing in terms of the way it serves to facilitate the production of a particular *form* of conversation, namely, the extended story.

    The most recognizable kind of story preface comes in statements like "Did you hear what happened to me last night?" and "I heard something interesting today," which virtually announce that there is a story pending and that other po-

tential speakers should remain silent (or minimally involved) until it is hearabr̃
complete (Sacks 1992b). Direct requests for the opportunity to tell a story are als̀c
common in ordinary conversation. In the following example, an animated conversation is in progress, with mother and daughter discussing what the teenager
will take for her school lunch. In the midst of the exchange, the daughter uses a
type of story preface to demarcate the conversational space for elaborating and
explaining her position and, by implication, her self.[2]

1. MOTHER: Whatter you takin' for lunch?
2. DAUGHTER: Peanut butter, there's nothin' else.
3. MOTHER: What about yogurt?
4. DAUGHTER: I don't like yogurt.
5. MOTHER: Wait a minute. You don't like yogurt?
6. DAUGHTER: Not // for lunch.
7. MOTHER: // You won't eat yogurt? I ASKED you Tuesday what you'd
   eat and you specifically said yogurt. // Why do you think we
   bought it?
8. DAUGHTER: // No:::oo it's not that. I
   just I just I don't // want it.
9. MOTHER: // That's it! You change your mind about what
   you'll eat twice a week. That's it. I'm makin' your lunch // from
   now on.
10. DAUGHTER: // No
    no::oo just lemme tell you // I wanna say something
11. MOTHER: // What
12. DAUGHTER: I like yogurt, I know I said to buy it but I did NOT change my
    mind, I always eat it. I have always liked yogurt, but not for
    lunch. Not for lunch at school. I eat it at home. I am NOT chang-
    ing my mind.
13. MOTHER: Well how can I tell.
14. DAUGHTER: All right I'll EAT it.

In the exchange, both parties move quickly to claim turns at talk. Their interaction is marked by frequent interruptions or overlaps. There is considerable
disagreement. Finally, at utterance 10, the daughter objects ("No no::oo") to her
mother's prior declaration ("I'm makin' your lunch // from now on") and offers
a prefacing move that strongly indicates that she has something to say that may
involve an extended turn at talk ("just lemme tell you // I wanna say something"), securing a space for the self-revealing story that emerges at utterance 12.
First it elicits an expression of interest and invitation to proceed from the mother
("What"), which then leads to the extended utterance in which the daughter offers an elaborate story/explanation. The prefacing move actively works to create
an opportunity to extend an utterance in a conversational environment previously
marked by the rapid seizure of next turns at talk. Clearly, offering a story of one's
self in this environment was an interactional challenge that required considerable
conversational dexterity and cooperation. If the storytelling space had not been

ooperatively established and the daughter had just "broken out" into utterance 2, what had been a rapid-fire and heated exchange might have become a brawl.

Demanding the opportunity to speak or declaring that a story is in the offing, however, is not always enough to get the story told. A prospective storyteller must also ensure that somebody is listening, paying attention. Recall that Betty did something like this in Chapter 6 when she rhetorically asked her listeners if they remembered something she was describing. As Sacks (1992b, p. 226) explains, saying something like "I'm going to talk for more than one sentence," requires a caveat, something like "and what I'm going to say may oblige you, if you are going to talk after me, to have listened." Thus, a story preface has two jobs: it announces a bid for an extended turn at talk, and requests the attention of potential recipients. How is this accomplished? Sacks argues that story prefaces must be designed so as to arouse interest from potential recipients—informing them that a story is forthcoming and it may be interesting—while at the same time allowing recipients the opportunity to indicate that this proposal is acceptable to them and that they will pay attention to the story.

We can see this work being done in the following extract from Sacks's lectures, which is a segment of a radio call-in program, where B is a female caller and A is the show's host, the recipient of the telephone call.

1. B: I hev a gurripe. Hhhnh!
2. A: What's the gr//ipe dear?
3. B: And oh boy hhhnhh heh heh heh hhh! Well, eh-eh the trains, Yuh know, theh-the-the- people . . . uh-why . . . do not. They hh respec'. The so called white cane. In other words, if they see me with the cane, trav'ling the city essetra, why do they not give me, the so called right of way. Etcetra. (Sacks 1992b, p. 263, transcription slightly simplified for readability)

In this instance, B offers a preface, signaling that she has a story to tell. By using the term "gripe," B intimates that something noteworthy or interesting (especially in the context of a call-in radio show) is forthcoming. A explicitly acknowledges this, repeating that he wants to hear B's "gripe," thus inviting the story, which is forthcoming in detail in the subsequent turn at talk. Note that the preface and its acknowledgment allow the storyteller to proceed with the extended story in the third utterance, and to extend beyond several places at which speakership transfer might be possible, even expected. The preface thus serves to clear the conversational space for the story to emerge without interruption, its acknowledgment indicating to the prospective teller that the recipient will attend to what she is saying.

Any response to a story preface or announcement—even a negative or indifferent one—can nonetheless serve as a story's point of departure as its narrativity cooperatively develops. We see this in the following example, again from Sacks's lectures.

A: I was at the po<u>lice</u> station this morning.
B: Big deal.

A: "Big deal" yeah. Somebody stole all my radio equipment outta my car. (Sacks
     1992a, p. 681)

This extract illustrates how the newsworthiness of an incipient story—as announced in its preface—can become an important factor in how the story emerges.
Here, A offers a story preface that implies the story's newsworthiness, empha-
sising "police," but B replies in a way that denies this claim ("Big deal."). Nevertheless, A continues, ironically reiterating the denial of newsworthiness and immediately following it with an announcement of the real news of the forthcoming
story—that somebody had stolen radio equipment from the storyteller's car. Adjusting the preface to the local demand for newsworthiness thus allowed the
telling of a story initially rejected as unworthy of further telling.

Story prefacing may be quite straightforward, where the recipient can clearly
hear that an extended spate of talk is being requested, or it may be less direct. In
some instances, prefacing even requires its own preface. Schegloff (1980) has observed that prospective storytellers often initiate potential extended turns at talk
by asking questions themselves. "You know what?" or "Guess what?" are commonplace examples. At first glance, such moves appear to ensure that potential
next speakers will take a turn at talk, seemingly truncating the extended turn
needed by the first speaker to produce a story. But, paradoxically, such moves
may also limit and contain the next speaker's utterance because it gives the next
speaker something quite specific to do in that turn, that is, merely answer the first
speaker's initial question with a simple "What?," which works to extend the first
speaker's turn at talk. This promotes continuation of the line of talk that the
prospective storyteller is trying to develop (Schegloff 1980).

Schegloff (1980) has identified another paradoxical feature of conversational
story prefacing where questions are involved. The paradox emerges when a
speaker asks something like this: "Can I ask you a question?" This may be daunt-
ing, of course, because if permission were required to ask a question, it must be
granted *prior* to asking "Can I ask you a question?" Schegloff specifies another
interesting feature of this sort of utterance: the next thing said by the speaker of
the question *is not a question* (Schegloff 1980, p. 106). What possible function, Schegloff asks, can this serve?

He finds an answer in what he terms "preliminaries" and "preliminaries to
preliminaries." Such devices can play a facilitating role in the storying of the self
by themselves serving as "story prefaces" of sorts (Sacks 1992b). One simple function performed by asking if one can ask a question is that it typically results in
an invitation to ask the question, permitting an extended turn at talk while the
recipient waits for the question to emerge. This conversational space may then be
filled with a story, as we can see in the following instance from a late-night television show, where host David Letterman is bantering with his musical director
and sidekick Paul Schaefer[3]:

DAVE: I've got a question for you Paul.
PAUL: Okay.
DAVE: My real hair is starting to look like a toupee. A damn foreign toupee.

That's not politically correct, a foreign toupee. [Dave elaborates on the appearance of his hair and the implications for his self-esteem.] (CBS-TV, 10/2/97)

Here Dave used Paul's agreement to entertain a question as a sort of license to tell a self-revealing story, while never actually asking the question.

Schegloff (1984) suggests that requests or questions about asking questions may be viewed as types of "action projections." When such utterances are not followed by the projected action, they are typically treated by recipients as preliminaries to the projected action—things needing to be done before, or leading up to, the projected action. They are taken to be preliminary to something that is yet to come. For example, "Can I ask you a question?" leads the recipient to both expect a question and withhold further response until the question emerges. If the projected question is not immediately forthcoming, several things may happen. By virtue of having yielded the turn at talk back to the original speaker, the recipient has tacitly permitted the speaker to proceed with the telling until the projected question has been completed. In effect, this provides conversational license for an extended turn at talk.

Of course the recipient might break in, demanding the delivery of the promised question, but Schegloff suggests an alternate possibility, one that helps explain frequent failures to deliver promised speech actions. He notes that "reference preparation" is common following preliminaries, as a way of setting up, clarifying, or otherwise preparing the recipient for the still forthcoming action (in the example we are considering, a question). Given that the speaker has been allotted the opportunity for an extended utterance, the reference preparation is allowed to emerge, and as it does, it can be heard, not as a topic in its own right, but as another preliminary. As Schegloff (1984, p. 116) argues, "The initial action projection [preface or preliminary] gets the projected action's relevance into the conversation before the action itself and before the action is adequately prepared. It motivates what directly follows by reference to what will follow *that*" (emphasis in the original). The initial question, then, might be considered a preliminary to a preliminary (Schegloff 1980).

For our purposes here, however, the technical design of the conversational machinery of action projections is not as important as how preliminaries work more generally to provide conversational opportunities for storying the self. We can see in the following extract from an exchange during an involuntary mental commitment hearing how a preliminary to a preliminary sequence unfolds so as to create an opportunity for a brief presentation of self in the midst of a courtroom interrogation. In this instance, a representative of the District Attorney's office (DA) is cross-examining candidate patient Camilio Pasqual (CP).[4]

1. DA: Can you tell me where you plan to stay?
2. CP: I'll stay with my cousin, he's in Orange County, by Disneyland.
3. DA: How are you going to get there?
4. CP: I'm gonna take the damn bus.
5. DA: Do you know where to get a bus schedule?

6. CP: No, but I figure to just wait at one of them benches. You think I'm too crazy to figure that out?

7. DA: That's fine, Mr. Pasqual, just answer the questions.

8. CP: Whatever you say, man.

9. DA: Now, how do you plan to pay for the bus?

10. CP: I got an SSI check, I can pay for myself. That check's good for over five hundred bucks.

11. DA: That's good, Mr. Pasqual, I just want to know if you have the money for the trip.

12. CP: Sure do, course I do. Can I ask you somethin'?

13. DA: I suppose.

14. CP: I get this check and I ain't no kid, and I ain't no stranger to the street. I been gettin' around all my life, you know what I'm sayin'. Once I get outa here I'm goin' straight and gonna get my mind clear and I'm gonna go to Disneyland and just do some relaxin'. Now, don't you think I can figure how to catch a bus?

15. DA: Let's just stick to business here, Mr. Pasqual. . . .

As the sequence of questions and answers proceeds, the question Pasqual asks in utterance 12 turns out to be a preliminary to a preliminary—a preface to an extended story that Pasqual tells as a lead-in to the eventual question he asked permission to ask. The first question negotiates the conversational space for a telling that subsequently provides the basis for the almost rhetorical question that terminates Pasqual's turn at talk at the end of utterance 14. This preliminary to a preliminary thus provides the opportunity for the story to emerge, and sets up what turns out to be something of a "squelch" at the end of the story. Aspects of Pascal's self were projected in order to confront the hearer (and the overhearers, including the judge) with the practical irony that a demonstrably "competent member"—one who can claim he is clear of mind and can get around town—should be questioned about such trivial and obvious matters as catching a city bus.

We can see a similar maneuver in the following example of conversation in a household setting. This time the exchange involves a father and daughter negotiating the issue of getting a family pet.[5]

1. FATHER: No, we're not getting a dog.

2. DAUGHTER: That's not fair. You had pets.

3. FATHER: We had a yard.

4. DAUGHTER: We have a yard and I'd take a dog for a walk.

5. FATHER: Right. Just like you let the hamster out for a run.

6. DAUGHTER: It's not the same. // A dog is more of a pet.

7. FATHER: // Yeah, yeah, it is, and more of a responsibility. Who's gonna take care of that?

8. DAUGHTER: I would. (2 second silence) I would. // Really.

9. FATHER: // Sure. We have to nag you about your chores as it is. A dog is a big responsibility. Who's gonna be responsible? I'll tell you who. Me, that's who.

10. DAUGHTER: Well lemme ask you something. I'm old enough to have chores,
                  cleaning, that sort of responsibility. You make me take care of
                  Jenna [a younger sister], make sure she doesn't run off up the
                  street. You don't think I'm irresponsible then, when you ask me
                  to do that? I take care of the neighbors' dogs, walk them, feed
                  them. I'm responsible enough for that but not for a pet. Is that
                  fair?
11. FATHER: Maybe it isn't, but since when is fairness the issue?

Here, once again, a preliminary at the beginning of utterance 10 ("lemme ask
you something") does not immediately lead to the question it announced. Rather,
the daughter engages in an extended story full of claims about herself, which
serves as a kind of reference preparation—a way of laying the groundwork, so to
speak—for the rhetorical question she eventually asks. The story initially emerges
in the place where the question might be expected, substituted for the question
that is not yet asked. The preliminary request to ask the question appears to hold
the father at bay, awaiting the question he expects to hear. Only at its appearance
does the father assume a turn at talk. In effect, the daughter has used this prefacing maneuver to create a storytelling opportunity and to move the line of talk
toward a spate of self construction.

Another kind of prefacing move that both creates an opportunity for extended
utterances and directs the line of talk involves what Douglas Maynard (1989b,
1991a, 1991b) calls a "perspective display sequence." This interactional sequence
includes the initial speaker's question or query, the recipient's response, and the
asker's subsequent follow-up in which the asker displays a sensitivity to the
other's opinions while advancing his or her own conversational interests. The following hypothetical scenario is prototypic. Here, an elementary-school teacher
has arranged for a conference with a parent of a student who has proved troublesome in the classroom. The conversation began like this:

TEACHER: How do you think Sally is doing in school this year?
PARENT: Well, she seems to be having a little trouble adjusting.
TEACHER: I'd have to agree with you. She's had trouble focusing her attention
            and at times she's been a bit of a problem.

Such sequences, according to Maynard (1989b, p. 91) are designed "to solicit another party's opinion and to then produce one's own report or assessment in a
way that takes the other's perspective into account." In effect, by demonstrating
some degree of agreement or affiliation with the recipient, the speaker can "co-
implicate" the recipient in his or her ongoing conversational project. Where stories of the self are concerned, we can see this conversational maneuver as a means
of getting a sort of advance confirmation of the claims about identity that the storyteller might intend to make.

Consider, for example, the following exchange between two university pro-
fessors concerning the announcement of a job opening at another university. If
the parties have any interest in pursuing the job opportunity, the conversation is

likely to get around to some sort of self-assessment in relation to what are taken to be the requirements for the position. In the following extract, the speakers are discussing the job and its attractions. Talk then turns to whether the position might be suitable for either of the participants.[6]

1. PROF. A: I'm not nearly as motivated [to apply for another academic position] as I used to be and I don't see anybody bustin' down our doors lookin'.
2. PROF. B: Me either. I don't have a problem with what I'm doing now. I'll look but things could be a lot worse.
3. PROF. A: Yeah, but, well, whatta you think? Whatter they lookin' for?
4. PROF. B: Hard to know. It says a track record in health research.
5. PROF. A: Yeah, I suppose, I guess I'm a mental health guy, sorta. Done the book and they know about that. I been doin' all these methods workshops for doctors and nurses, health care. Writing all that stuff about aging might count as health. I suppose I could fit, be their kinda guy if they take it broadly.
6. PROF. B: As much as the next guy.

   This exchange exhibits many of the features of the typical perspective display sequence. At utterance 3, A solicits B's opinion as to what sort of candidate the advertisement is describing. B responds at utterance 4 with an opinion that echoes one line of the ad, and A picks up on this statement by offering an agreement, but one that is qualified ("Yeah, I suppose."). This may serve as a mark of mild disjuncture as well, preparing the listener for something not totally congruent with what has already been said. A then picks up on the agreement about the position being health related, but offers a qualification ("I'm a *mental* health guy," emphasis added here), a slight departure from what B initially said, but still incorporating part of B's language. Note how A moves tentatively into the incipient self-description by playing off of his apparent agreement with B's initial assessment but introduces modifications along the way. Maynard (1989b, p. 93) suggests that the use of a perspective display sequence is an inherently cautious maneuver that is handy in circumstances where the possibility for conflict or embarrassment might be a concern. By using such a sequence to launch a story of the self, the teller moves delicately into self construction, minimizing the risk of contradiction by his or her listeners, thus increasing the likelihood that the self being storied will be acceptable to the audience at hand, at least for the time being. On occasion, such sequences can also be used to implicate the intended story recipient in the storytelling itself, virtually incorporating the recipient's own words into the teller's narrative.

Continuations

If prefacing gets stories under way, the interactional demands on storytelling don't cease once the storyteller has the floor. For an extended utterance to continue across possible speakership transition points, the storyteller must both secure permission to continue at possible turn completion points and detect signs that the ongoing story is being understood and appreciated. Obvious examples of such "response tokens" (Sacks 1992b) are often sprinkled across a story's telling; statements like "Go on" or "You don't say" indicate that the recipient is following the story, signaling the storyteller to continue. Most encouragements to continue and displays of attentiveness or understanding, however, are not as direct or explicit. Indeed, many are parsimonious utterances like "Mm hm" or "Uh huh" that are dropped into the conversation at the ends of the storyteller's sentences or at other speakership transition points, as we saw in Chase's responses to two of her interviewees' stories in Chapter 6. While such conversational contributions are minimal, they are by no means trivial; they serve as communicative "lubricants" for the storytelling machine.

"Mm hm" and other such devices (e.g., Chase's "hm hmm") indicate that their speaker recognizes that a story is in progress and that he or she will decline possible turns at talk that might interrupt the story (Sacks 1992b). According to Sacks (1992b), they provide a way for the recipient to say something like "The story is not yet over. I know that" (p. 9), which also informs the storyteller that he or she can continue speaking. Indeed, response tokens almost require the storyteller to continue, even if he or she is not bidding to extend the turn at talk. This is, of course, a familiar technique used in psychotherapy to elicit extended and elaborated "self talk."[7]

While both minimal response tokens and stronger claims of understanding ("Oh really") can further a story, an even stronger signal of appreciation is offered when recipients incorporate the actual vocabulary, topic, characters, or other aspects of the emerging story into their own turns at talk. This "co-selection" (Sacks 1992b) sustains topicality and may even be built into a subsequent and related story. The apparent relatedness of such "second stories" not only shows that the recipient understood the first story but also allows the story recipient to then tell his or her own story, as often occurs in the round-robin drunkalogues discussed in the last chapter.

So second stories may spin off of first stories, in effect making first stories occasions for additional storytelling; one story provides an opportunity—almost an invitation—for a second (or subsequent) speaker to depict his or her experience in relation to the first story (Sacks 1992b). This, of course, suggests that the storied self is not merely a reflection of individual lived experience or its recollection, but also relies upon, and implicates, others' experience, both triggering and interpersonally contextualizing the telling.[8] Again, Mead's socially constructed self resonates in the background.

Endings

Once under way and continued beyond possible speaker transition points, a story may proceed relatively unimpeded, but for it to be recognized as a viable story, it also must be brought to completion. There are at least two functions that may be performed at possible story endings. First, for a story to have come off successfully, hearers must display an appreciation for the story's completion. If this doesn't happen, the storyteller's utterance sequence may be prolonged, with the story as yet having no point or conclusion. Second, and relatedly, over the course of an extended utterance, hearers are essentially limited in terms of opportunities to display their ongoing understanding of the story. As we discussed above, there are a number of ways this may be done along the way to a story's completion. One way to demonstrate comprehension emphatically is to show appreciation at an obvious possible completion point. Thus, showing appreciation of a story's completion and displaying understanding of the story are linked tasks that mark the end of a story (Sacks 1992b).

This implies, of course, that a story cannot end until it is acknowledged as complete by its hearer, underscoring once again storytelling's (and the self's) collaborative character. As Schegloff (1984, p. 45) points out, "In conversation, little if anything can be done assuredly unilaterally." As we explained earlier, even the completion of single utterances within storytelling requires collaboration. That is, at the first *possible* completion point, someone else does not automatically take a turn at talk. Hearers may defer, the speaker may continue, or another speaker may build something onto what might have been a hearably complete utterance. A story, then, is complete when a storyteller allows for or proposes its possible completion, and its completion is accepted by the hearer through some form of recognition of completion and display of understanding. In the absence of such finalizing gestures, the story remains open-ended, awaiting clarification, elaboration, or closure. Clearly, the initiator of an utterance is not fully in command of what the utterance might turn out to be. In the case of stories—even self-implicating stories—this means that the storyteller is not the story's (and the related self's) sole proprietor, since he or she can't unilaterally control when the story is over.

Storytellers and recipients can both indicate that they are attentive to the progression of the story and are sensitive to the point at which the story might be hearably complete. Of course storytellers can simply announce that they have finished their stories: "And that's the end of that story" or simply "The end" serve this purpose directly, if recipients acknowledge that they hear that the story is adequately complete. Concluding a story, however, is typically more interactionally complex than this, calling upon both teller and recipient to achieve the story's completion.

In a sense, the end of a story starts at the beginning. Story prefaces, Sacks (1992b, p. 11) argues, often provide information about "what it will take for (a) story to be over . . . right at the beginning" so that recipients can attend from the start to when the story might possibly conclude. Sacks illustrates such prefacing, using the example of the preface "I have something terrible to tell you." The expected response would be something like "What's that?" or "Oh really?," utterances that would signal both permission to continue and attentiveness to what is about to be said. By virtue of this preface, recipients can then monitor the emerging story for mention of anything that might pass for "something terrible," at which point they might then respond with something like "Oh how terrible." Such a move reasserts the recipient's attentiveness, but, more importantly, says something to the effect that "I see the story is now over," marking its possible completion. This work of signaling completion can be done in the very terms initially provided by the storyteller. That is, if the story is prefaced by "I have something terrible to tell you," the recipient may signal the story's completion by saying something like "Gosh that's terrible" when something hearably terrible has been spoken. Of course, the length of the story is also partially controlled by the preface, as recipients conversationally obligate themselves to wait for the "terrible" news to be conveyed before acknowledging completion. Taken together, the storyteller's prefacing work and the recipient's related attentiveness both launch and close successful stories of various lengths, with both teller and recipients agreeing about what was conversationally transpiring.

Both storyteller and recipient, then, constantly monitor the emerging story and keep each other apprised of their attentions and intentions. Their interactional partnership never ceases. Therefore, if we want to understand how the self is storied, we need to carefully attend to and appreciate storytelling for its artful *and* methodical practices, as well as for its content. *What* stories come to mean involves the myriad integral "seen but unnoticed" features of *how* they are interactionally introduced, developed, and completed. While we have discussed but a few aspects of the conversational machinery of storytelling, it should be evident that stories, of the self or otherwise, emerge from elaborate and complex interactional processes and maneuvers.

Working Together on Narrative Particulars

When we speak of the social with regard to the self, we are referring to persons acting together to articulate who they are. So far, we've seen how interactional partners work together by operating the machinery of ordinary conversation to demarcate space for self narration. We've also noted how cooperation extends through the telling of selves to the completion of their stories. We now turn to a different aspect of the partnership in which the *hows* of storytelling collaboratively implicate narrative particulars—the *whats*—that the storied self might come to look (and sound) like, specifying emplotment.

Collaboration

On occasion, complicity in actions that "keep the story going" also contributes to *where* the story is going. As we saw earlier in examples from research interviews, "prompts" can serve as narrative incitements for particular story lines. Similarly, listeners to informal stories of the self can virtually induce the elaboration of particular dimensions of the self through their own story-facilitating actions. Consider the following instance taken from another nursing home interview. Grace Wheeler is a 70-year-old nursing home resident, confined to a wheelchair due to a form of cerebral palsy with which she's been afflicted since birth. She shares a room with her 93-year-old mother, Lucy. While Grace is the designated interviewee, in the following extract we can see how her self story is guided, if not directed, by Lucy's contributions to the conversation, as

Lucy conscientiously attends to Grace's telling of a life story. Again, Jay is the interviewer.

1. JAY: Why don't we start by your telling me about your life?
2. GRACE: Well that was quite a many years ago. I was born in Brinton Station, Ohio.
3. LUCY: She was a seven-month baby.
4. GRACE: I was a seven-month baby. That's what I was. [Elaborates story of growing up with her sisters and brother.] They've all been wonderful.
5. LUCY: They taught her . . .
6. GRACE: And they taught me as well as my mom and dad. And then when radio and television came to the farm, why I learned from them. I love the quiz shows.
7. LUCY: She types with a stick in her mouth.
8. GRACE: I type with a stick in my mouth. I paint with a brush in my mouth. [Grace elaborates a story of travelling with her sisters and the exchange between Jay and Grace continues.]
9. JAY: So you're a real sports fan.
10. GRACE: Yes.
11. LUCY: Yes, she is. That television's on . . .
12. GRACE: I love it!
13. LUCY: That television's all sports to her.
14. GRACE: Well, sports and shows. [Giggling] I love animal shows, too. I love animals.
15. LUCY: Game shows.
16. GRACE: Game shows, animal shows, detective stories. I like to read detective stories. My favorite author is John D. McDonald. (Gubrium 1993, pp. 152–53)

It's clear that Lucy points the way for Grace's life story. It's not uncommon for story recipients to display appreciation and understanding by co-selecting words used by the storyteller to build and sustain topical continuity (Sacks 1992b). We see something like that here, but with a new twist. Lucy, a listener to the story, begins in utterance 3 to encourage a line of talk by picking up on Grace's mention of where she was born (utterance 2), and elaborating in terms of what kind of a "baby" Grace was. In her next turn at talk (utterance 4), Grace, the ostensible storyteller, appropriates Lucy's term "seven-month baby" to her story and elaborates the story of her (Grace's) childhood. At a possible completion of this utterance, Lucy again offers her own elaboration on how the siblings related to one another, and in the next utterance (utterance 6), Grace once again commandeers Lucy's phrase ("They taught her . . .") to begin a new storyline. As the discussion progresses, we continue to hear Grace using Lucy's words to tell her (Grace's) own story.

While it may be tempting to say that Lucy was speaking for Grace in this instance, this is not precisely the case. Note that Grace is rather concise in her responses to the initial story solicitation and subsequent prompting by the interviewer. Lucy, however, does not let the story lag at the possible turn completion points that Grace's succinct storytelling creates. At each point, where a next speaker may take a turn at talk, Lucy speaks. One might expect this slot in the conversation to be filled by the interviewer, since ostensibly this is a conversation between Jay and Grace, but in the absence of a specific designation of the next speaker, Lucy seizes the turn, and, in effect, extends Grace's story by providing an appropriately topical extension of Grace's prior utterance. For her part, Grace latches her elaborations to Lucy's utterances, her repetition of Lucy's phrasing virtually establishing the topical continuity of the story. While not telling Grace's story, Lucy provides both topical content and conversational momentum by collaborating in the story's continuation at possible speaker transition points where Grace's story might otherwise terminate. And while Lucy definitely contributes to what Grace is saying, it is the machinery of storytelling as well as Lucy's prompting that brings about the life and self that Grace stories.

While Lucy assists in constructing Grace's account of herself, there are occasions when second parties assertively redirect another's story, relatedly aiming to redesign the other's narrative identity. Consider the collaborative life story—including selves—that was produced in an interview with nursing home resident Don Hughes (Gubrium 1993). Don shares a room with his wife, Sue, at the Westside Care Center. Don was formally designated as the interview respondent, but the life story requested of him quickly becomes something quite different, a narrative collaboration deeply implicating Sue, who re-enters the room as Don is being interviewed. Wheelchair-bound, Sue had wheeled herself out of the room before the interviewing actually started. The interviewer (I) begins by asking Don to describe his life:

I: [To Don] I was hoping you'd tell me about your life.
DON: I was a hobo!
I: You were a hobo.
SUE: [To Don] Why don't you tell her where you were born?
DON: I was born in Minnesota and I left when I was 16 years old.
SUE: Go on. So why did you leave?
DON: Just to bum, see the country. So we went, another boy and myself. We went out west on the Northern Pacific Railroad. . . . [Don tells a story of his exploits working out west with a buddy, and how he came to return to Florida.] So I came to this part of Florida here and we both were working. That's where I met my wife and that's the end of my life story.
SUE: [Sarcastically] Why don't you tell her that we got married in the meantime? I'm part of it, too, you know.

As Don proceeds, Sue continues to add to the story, including more of their life together. While the initial version of the story dealt with Don's work experiences and "bummin' around," at Sue's insistence the story begins to include marriage and family. We return to the interview as Don concludes a lengthy description of his many years working as a masonry contractor.

I: Was this after the depression?

DON: The depression was [pause]

SUE: It was just over.

DON: I walked ten miles to work for ten cents an hour. [Story continues about Don's work life.] When I retired, I thought we had money to last.

SUE: You forgot to tell her one thing, that we built our own home stick-by-stick and every nail.

DON: Yeah. Anyway, our money didn't last. I got so's I couldn't work too much anymore and she got sick two or three more times.

SUE: [Chuckling] Just listen to him. In the meantime we had three more children. [Sarcastically] Remember that?

DON: Yeah, in the meantime we had three more children. That's all. That's it.

SUE: [Laughing] That's it? You're joking.

Following this, Don's story narratively shifts from being his story to being Sue and Don's together. It suddenly becomes retroactively clear that they did everything "together." The story ostensibly is now firmly *theirs*, not just an intermittently redesigned narrative of Don's individual experiences, as we see in the following extract.

DON: [Chuckling] This much I can tell ya. We've been married 63 years and enjoyed every bit of it. We worked together and never left. For instance, she had a bunch of girlfriends and she never went out at night. And I had boyfriends and I wouldn't go out at night. If we went to any place, we went together.

SUE: We traveled together. We went all over the country together. We didn't have such a bad life. We loved to camp. We loved to fish. We loved to do all kinds of outdoor sports. We like baseball, football. Name it. And we did all the things together. We never went to one place and let the other fella go another place.

As the interview winds down, Don's life-with-Sue is further elaborated against the "sassiness" they bring out in each other. Don's story becomes the story of a couple, two selves completely dependent on one another under the circumstances. The narrative linkages of togetherness, currently established jointly in their story, become the central feature of what initially was Don's life.

DON: [Chuckling] I was a no-good bum.

SUE: He's no bum. We're just as close as we were before and I love him. He's the only thing that makes this place tolerable. But he gets sassy sometimes and I have to knock him down a peg or two, but other than that, we still have fun together. He plays cribbage and cheats, but we still manage to get by. We gab and blab, about the old days, you know. That keeps us goin'.

DON: But this isn't the place for us. That's all I can say. It's too much like prison. If I didn't have her, I'd go crazy and so would she. [Elaborates] At least we have each other.

SUE: I know dear. We've had a good life, but now we're bitching like the devil. [Chuckling] I hope that isn't on the tape.
I: Well, it is.
DON: [To Sue, sarcastically] You mean to say you're not "itching" now?
SUE: [Chuckling] I didn't say "itching." I said "bitching." We still manage to giggle.

Given conversation's collaborative nature, a storyteller's control of narrative particulars can be markedly diffuse. We can see this in the following example of how the details of self are conversationally claimed and challenged. Donna Eder (1995, pp. 65–66) reports hearing a story in a school setting, the particulars of which quickly shift from jovial banter to serious challenges to masculine self and toughness among adolescent boys. One of the boys, Sam, begins the story, presenting himself as stoic and tough in the face of a football injury. The others, however, add details and nuance to Sam's self-presentation, leaving his toughness more equivocal than it might have been portrayed on its own.

1. SAM: Hey Joe, remember when I told ya, I go, "my finger hurt so bad I can't even feel it?" He goes, "Good, you won't feel 'em hit it." [Laughter] He didn't know I'd broke it, man. You remember in the Edgewood game, I broke my finger? //
2. HANK: // I called him a big pussy when he told me that. "Hey, you big pussy, get out there 'n' play."
3. SAM: He [referring to the coach] goes, "Don't worry, you won't feel it when they hit it."
4. HANK: Sam goes, Sam goes, "Look at my finger." [In a high voice] I said, "Oh you pussy cat, you can't play."
5. SAM: *You liar.*
6. HANK: I did too //
7. SAM: // Well I did, I played the whole game.
8. TOM: [To Sam] You was cryin' too.
9. SAM: Yes I did man.

Sam's story, and Hank's own subsequent story, are built up through many of the conversational moves we have previously discussed. Responding to the conversational machinery, the explicitly competitive stories provide an additional complexity to how selves may be storied—and who might be their authors—in interaction.

The designation of narrative particulars can be manipulated even more subtly in relation to the expectancies of the turn-taking machinery in which it's embedded. While conversational assistance and assertiveness operate actively to shape stories, conversational inaction or silence also can be worked to manifest particulars of special interest to a party in social interaction. The following spate of conversation is illustrative. It occurs in an involuntary commitment hearing in which the state is seeking psychiatric hospitalization for a woman who denies its necessity (Holstein 1988, 1993). At first passively incited and later actively encouraged, a story of sorts emerges from the interrogation of the candidate patient, even as its teller appears to have no apparent design on producing such a story from the start. In the following extract, a representative of the District Attorney's office (DA2) is questioning Lisa Sellers (LS), whose bizarre talk and behavior had precipitated efforts to have her committed. The DA begins by asking Sellers a series of questions about the routine circumstances of her life. After initiating fourteen question-answer pairs (one immediately following the other) regarding Sellers's intended residence and whom she plans to live with, the DA enters into the following exchange.[9]

1. DA2: How do you like summer out here, Lisa?
2. LS: It's OK.
3. DA2: How long have you lived here?
4. LS: Since I moved from Houston.
5.   ((SILENCE)) [Note: If unspecified, length of silence is one to three seconds.]
6. LS: About three years ago.
7. DA2: Tell me about why you came here.
8. LS: I just came.
9.   ((Silence))
10. LS: You know, I wanted to see the stars, Hollywood.
11.   ((Silence))
12. DA2: Uh huh.
13. LS: I didn't have no money.
14.   ((Silence))
15. LS: I'd like to get a good place to live.
16.   ((Silence 5 seconds))
17. DA2: Go on. ((spoken simultaneously with onset of next utterance))
18. LS: There was some nice things I brought.
19.   ((Silence))
20. DA2: Uh huh.
21. LS: Brought them from the rocketship.
22. DA2: Oh really?
23. LS: They was just some things I had.
24. DA2: From the rocketship?
25. LS: Right.
26. DA2: Were you on it?
27. LS: Yeah.
28. DA2: Tell me about this rocketship, Lisa. (Holstein 1993, pp. 104–5)

In this extract, the questioning and answering proceeds rather directly through line 4. At this point, however, Sellers offers an answer that is hearably complete, but the DA refuses to resume his questioning, declining his turn at talk. The result is that silence emerges at the completion of Sellers' answer. Silences are conversationally disruptive, and typically implicate the prior speaker (Maynard 1980). One way of terminating the silence is to extend the previous line of talk, which, in this case, Sellers does at line 6, elaborating on her previous answer, creating a nascent story. The DA thus passively prompts an extended turn at talk—a brief spate of storytelling—that departs from the prior question-answer format. We see this practice continue in the subsequent exchanges.

At line 7, the DA resumes his interrogation, but this time, instead of asking a question, he makes a more general request for information. Sellers responds briefly, but receives neither response nor acknowledgment from the DA. By declining possible speakership, the DA again encourages Sellers to elaborate particulars, which she does at line 10, expanding on the story. At line 11, the DA once more refuses to take a turn at talk, but encourages Sellers to continue ("uh huh") at line 12 (see Schegloff 1982). With a combination of silences and minimal encouragements, the DA passively collaborates with Sellers to string together an extended, if somewhat conversationally discontinuous, story of Sellers' recent activities, culminating with the mention of the rocketship at line 21. At this point, the DA's response ("Oh, really?") is a strong indication of apparent interest (Schegloff 1982), which elicits an elaboration of Sellers' prior utterance. The DA is now eagerly responsive to what Sellers is saying, and by line 28, he is virtually inviting a full-blown story, which Sellers subsequently provides. In the process, Sellers is passively incited to tell a story that, in the context of the commitment hearing, provides palpable evidence of her mental incompetence.

Let us briefly consider a second example from another commitment hearing where passive collaboration extends into another storied self—one narrated in a somewhat different fashion. In this case, another DA (DA4) is cross-examining candidate patient Henry Johnson (HJ). After several questions and answers, the DA initiates the following dialogue[10]:

  1. DA4:   How you been feeling lately?
  2. HJ: OK
  3.   ((Silence))
  4. HJ: I been feeling pretty good.
  5.   ((Silence))
  6. DA4:   Uh huh
  7.   ((Silence))
  8. HJ: Pretty good, ummm all right
  9.   ((Silence))
 10. HJ: Got a job with (several words inaudible)
 11.   ((Silence))
 12. HJ: Pays OK, not bad.
 13.   ((Silence 4 seconds))
 14. HJ: My car got hit, an accident, really messed it up
 15.   ((Silence))
 16. HJ: Got to get it on the street
 17.   ((Silence 5 seconds))
 18. HJ: They gonna let us go to the truck out front?
 19. DA4:   When you're all done here they might. (Holstein 1993, p. 108)

The spate of talk that emerges is hearable as Johnson's story of what has been happening in his life lately. While not directly responsive to the initial question by the DA, it is a commonsensically coherent account of the recent events that Johnson terminates at line 18, when he initiates a new line of talk with a question of his own.

How this story is accomplished, however, is another interesting illustration of a multiple-utterance storytelling that emerges out of passive conversational partnership. Having asked the initial question, the DA places himself in the conversational position of signaling at possible utterance completion points whether the question has been adequately answered. The first of these occurs at the end of Johnson's response at line 2. Here, Johnson has ostensibly completed his turn at talk by providing an answer to the initial question. At this point, where the DA might be expected to take another turn in the question-answer sequence, the DA remains silent, refusing his turn, signaling that the preceding utterance did not suffice as an answer to his question. Johnson responds in a conversationally accountable fashion, terminating the emerging silence with an elaboration of his utterance, offering a more complete answer to the initial question. Once again, at the end of the utterance, a speaker transition point emerges, but, rather than taking this opportunity, at line 6 the DA offers a minimal response (Uh huh) that serves to demonstrate his attentiveness as well as to invite continuation (Maynard 1980). Johnson continues to elaborate, but when he tries to end his next utterance (line 8), he again encounters the DA's silence.

Such silences may be heard as conversational difficulties that implicate the prior speaker, in this case, Johnson. One common solution to emerging silence is for the speaker to resume talking and to attempt remedial action, as Johnson does in this instance. Maynard (1980) suggests that participants encountering silences like this usually try to restore continuous talk by pursuing the ongoing line of talk. Only when this fails will they attempt to alter the line of talk, disrupting topical continuity. In this instance, Johnson's attempt to hold the conversation together in the face of his partner's reluctance to take a turn at talk results in a series of utterances broken up by silences but that nonetheless constitute a story of sorts. The DA passively contributes to the construction of this story; his refusal to talk at points where his speakership might be anticipated provokes Johnson's elaborations and continuations, resulting in the story we eventually hear. The emergence of Johnson's story of himself thus depends on both participants, even though Johnson does all the talking.

Speaking the Other's Self Story

As we consider the collaborative aspects of storytelling, it becomes increasingly evident that stories of the self reflect the contingencies of interactional storytelling as much as they convey storytellers' personal experiences, implicating the *social* self. Indeed, if we listen carefully, we may even hear one person literally speak for another as self stories are told. We probably all have heard exchanges like the following, this case being that of an elderly couple, Hank and Millie, who run into their friend Marge at the grocery store[11]:

MARGE: So how have you been feeling Henry?
MILLIE: Oh he's been perkin' right along.
MARGE: Think winter's about through huh Hank?
MILLIE: He sure does. He's really happy to be able to get out. (Gubrium, Holstein, and Buckholdt 1994, p. 136)

Virtually putting words into Henry's mouth, Millie in fact speaks at junctures where we would expect Henry to talk. Still, this comes off as a relatively uneventful spate of conversation. Despite the fact that the "wrong" person seems to be answering the questions that Marge asks, why can we hear this as a reasonably nonproblematic exchange about Hank's condition?

The answer lies in part in the ways in which the emerging conversation remains at least partially accountable to the normative expectations of casual conversation. In most ways, this is a very typical question-answer sequence, but with significant variations. The first speaker, Marge, asks a question, and by directing it explicitly at Henry, selects Henry as the next speaker. Millie, however, responds in Henry's place. According to Sacks et al. (1974), third actions in conversational sequences are often pivotal in establishing how conversations proceed and are understood. It's at this point in question-answer sequences, for example, that repairs may be occasioned or further questions raised about the second speaker's understanding of what is being said. In this way, third slots serve to project the subsequent direction of the conversation. Third-slot utterances that implement some sort of normal, onward development or trajectory for a sequence, however, tacitly confirm the displayed understanding of the sequence so far.

In this example, Millie violates what might be seen as Marge's right to select the next speaker, or Henry's right to speak. Note, however, that Marge does not treat Millie's utterance in this fashion. Instead, she asks another question, indicating that, for the practical purpose at hand, the original question has been adequately understood and answered. This, in turn, confirms the trajectory of the conversation. Rather than hearing Henry's silence as an instance of Millie inappropriately usurping Henry's turn at talk, we can view the silence as a tacit endorsement of what's going on in this sequence. As long as no attention is drawn to the unconventional speakership transfer, the sequence can proceed. With no objection, call for repair, or other signal of disruption emanating from the third slot in the sequence, talk proceeds normally. That Millie has, in fact, spoken for Henry, takes place within a more or less conventional sequential environment, and thus passes without disruption.

Actual collaborators are not even necessary for such storied selves to emerge. Consider another sort of conversation in which we hear the inner lives of pets spoken by others.[12]

KATE: What's wrong Mouser? [Kate's cat]
MOUSER: Mweow.
KATE: You're lonesome. Don't like to be alone do you? Poor boy we're not
         going

MOUSER: Mweoeow.
KATE: Don't be silly boy. We're staying home.

In this exchange the initial question invites a reply, and the second slot in the anticipated question-answer adjacency pair is filled by the cat's vocalization. Kate's response in the third conversational slot provides a kind of clarification and confirmation that the second-slot utterance is adequate to the conversational task at hand. Kate then offers another question, Mouser fills the reply slot, and another formulation follows.

"Formulations" are utterances that characterize what was done in a prior turn at talk; they are interpretive devices for offering the sense of a conversation so far (Heritage and Watson 1980, Sacks 1992a, 1992b). For example, in the preceding extract, Kate's third-slot formulation of what Mouser might have "said" about himself articulates Kate's understanding of the ongoing "dialog." While sometimes found in environments of challenge or disagreement, formulations are not particularly associated with explaining problematic matters. They are routine indications of what the conversation is being taken to mean, and where it is likely to go. Formulations thus serve to demonstrate understanding, to signal the course of the conversation. Since the preceding extract's third-slot formulation goes unchallenged, it can stand as a benchmark of what has been said to this point, a virtual endorsement in this case of Mouser's self and state of mind as Kate formulates it out of Mouser's "reply" to her question. The narrative particulars of the self under consideration (i.e., Mouser's self) are collaboratively constructed as Kate develops the story that specifies the cat's inner life. Of course, Kate is speaking Mouser's self for him, but she does so within the normative conventions of everyday conversation. It is precisely this interactional scaffolding that must be respected and utilized if such talk is to proceed into a coherent narrative.

Now consider a human example of the use of formulations, in which the self of one person is seemingly articulated by others, with the appearance that the individual in question had contributed to the project. Melvin Pollner and Lynn McDonald-Wikler (1985) have studied interactions between members of a family in which one of the members, 5-year-old Mary, has been diagnosed as severely retarded, having virtually no cognitive or linguistic capabilities. When family members described their interactions with Mary, however, they insisted that she often acted quite normally. Pollner and McDonald-Wikler report some of these interactions, showing how family members literally "put words in Mary's mouth" as they now formulate and then respond to an emerging sense of the child's attitudes.

[1. Mary is wearing a newly bought robe:]

MOTHER: You don't like the robe? It fits you
MARY: (gurgling)
MOTHER: What did you say about Daddy?
MARY: Mmmmmmm, gurgle.
FATHER: She thinks it's too cheap.

[2. Encouraging Mary to talk into the recorder:]

FATHER: OK, you tell me your name and age into that thing [tape recorder], and I'll give you $5 to go out and buy a present that you want to buy yourself.
MARY: (gurgling)
FATHER: Your name and age—
MARY: Goo ga gurgle.
FATHER: She's bargaining with me for more money!

[3. Later:]

MOTHER: Time for your pills.
MARY: (gurgling)
MOTHER: You don't think you need them.
MARY: Mmmmmm, ga.
MOTHER: I think you need them. (Pp. 248–50)

Each instance reveals a family member responding to Mary's vocalizations as if they were comprehensible utterances. In repeated formulations of what Mary ostensibly has said, each family member manages the "conversation" so as to conform to normative turn-taking expectancies. The formulations give meaning to Mary's vocalizations by reiterating what they might have meant, while the questions imply that a meaningful utterance has been conveyed. In either case, family members supply the meaningful responses that are necessary for Mary to be seen as an active conversationalist.

Robert Bogdan and Steven Taylor (1989) write of similar usages when they analyze the social constructions whereby sympathetic nondisabled persons interpret the humanness of severely disabled individuals. Even more poignantly, Jaber Gubrium (1986b) shows how caregivers of Alzheimer's disease sufferers can persist in articulating the latter's minds and selves long after they have evidently lost their capacity for self-expression. Interactionally complicating Mead's view that selves derive from interaction with others, this study suggests that others literally "do" the minds and selves of dementia sufferers as a way of preserving their identities. Speaking the sufferer's self story, caregivers sustain his or her lived presence in their everyday lives.

Taken together, these illustrations reveal the complex interactional scaffolding for narrating the self. As we saw, stories of the self are locally managed to respect and respond to immediate interactional contingencies. But storytelling also responds to more wide-ranging self presentational goals. This means that, as methodically and artfully as stories of our working identities are told in conversational practice, the skill entailed is always accountable to the circumstances of storytelling, to which we turn in the next chapter.

CHAPTER EIGHT

The Circumstances of Self Construction

T he discursive practices of self construction furnish a postmodern environment with a remarkable variety of adroitly crafted stories. As impromptu as it might sometimes appear, however, self construction isn't merely extemporaneous; as we've seen, it's methodically articulated through talk and social interaction. In addition, it's also profoundly conditioned by its circumstances and available resources. Erving Goffman alerted us to this by highlighting the situatedness of self presentation.[1] And, long before Goffman, Marx reminded us that while people construct their lives, it's never done completely according to their own desires. This, of course, also reverberates in Foucault's discussions of the everyday regimens of discourses of subjectivity. If self stories are built up through the machinery of communication, it's always done somewhere, in response to some practical demand, using some stock of knowledge, some discourse-in-practice. Stories of the self are continually mediated by the increasingly disciplined, institutionalized circumstances of contemporary life.

We certainly don't mean that separate and distinct social forces determine what selves are storied, but we don't want to overstate the extent to which the self is extemporaneously constructed, either. Instead, our sense of self construction resonates with the metaphor of the "bricoleur" discussed by Claude Levi-Strauss (1966). As a bricoleur, the self constructor is involved in something like an interpretive salvage operation, crafting selves from the vast array of available resources, making do with what he or she has to work with in the circumstances at hand, all the while constrained, but not completely controlled, by the working conditions of the moment. In this metaphor, self construction is "always ineluctably local" (Geertz 1983), a practical and artful response to prevailing circumstances, an application of what is available in relation to the narrative tasks at hand.

Deprivatization and Institutional Talk

In a postmodern world, the everyday circumstances of self construction are more multisited than ever. The vast majority of American adults are employed outside the home, participating daily in the institutional life of organizations large and small. Despite laments of the declining family, many of us live in some form of stable domestic relationship for most of our lives. With life more and more intertwined with the discourses of organizations and institutions, people are likely to call upon, or be called upon by, professionals and agencies to interpret, define, and respond to personal questions, dilemmas, and troubles. Human service agencies abound, offering help and advice at every turn. Schools, day care centers, and churches socialize the young, while recovery programs and support groups see us through mid-life and the later years. These are but a small fraction of the settings in which we live our lives. On any given Sunday, for example, one can scan the local newspaper and find literally dozens of self-help groups listed for parents of the troubled or gifted, alcoholics, codependents of substance abusers, cancer sufferers, survivors of cancer, Bible study, spiritual fellowship, Gulf War veterans, victims of sexual assault, perpetrators of domestic violence, AIDS victims, the friends and significant others of AIDS sufferers, right-to-lifers, and transvestites and their spouses, among countless others. Robert Wuthnow (1994) has estimated that 40 percent of the U.S. population participates in such groups, seeking personal meaning and community.

As greater portions of our lives are spent in such social settings, these going concerns—from informal groupings to formal organizations—facilitate or inform talk of personal experience. They touch nearly all aspects of daily living, from domestic relations and job stress to sexuality, substance abuse, eating disorders, and spirituality. Organizations and their agents make it their business to describe our lives and experiences so that they can address, assess, and ameliorate the challenges of daily living. In the process, they become sources of experiential definition—purveyors of identity, so to speak. Borrowing Norbert Wiley's (1985) apt term, we can say that everyday life and the interpretation of experience have become *deprivatized* (see Gubrium and Holstein 1995a, 1995b, 1995c; Holstein and Gubrium 1995b).

To the extent that self presentation is ubiquitous in organizational life, we can also argue that the self, itself, is becoming more and more deprivatized. By this we mean that the self as our primary subjectivity is increasingly constructed within, and from, distinctive public circumstances; identity accordingly takes myriad hyphenated forms: "the-self-according-to-this-agency," "pathological-self-from-that-professional standpoint," "personality-as-viewed-by-this-expert," and so on. The diversity of selves is limited only by the availability of representational categories.

One way in which organized social settings shape self construction is through "institutional talk" (Drew and Heritage 1992), forms of talk that articulate particular discourses-in-practice. Chapter 7 presented self construction in terms of the conversational machinery of everyday interaction. The process is further complicated by the discernible modifications of everyday conversation mediated by institutional discourses. These settings provide a distinctive conversational environment—a set of methods and constraints—that circumstantially shape storytelling and self constructions.

Institutional talk is manifested in systematic variations from ordinary conversation. According to John Heritage and David Greatbatch (1991), these modifications comprise the very essence of "institution," even while specific variations might not distinguish particular settings. They argue that variations in how interaction is manifested—in its preferred shapes and normative constraints—provide for the recognizability of institutional settings and events (p. 94).[2] Paul Drew and Heritage (1992) summarize the fundamental character of institutional talk in three propositions: (1) Institutional interaction involves an orientation by at least one of the participants to some core goal, task, or identity conventionally associated with the institutional setting. That is, institutional talk is normally informed by orientations to the execution of institutional tasks and functions (going concerns). (2) Institutional interaction often involves special constraints on what participants treat as allowable contributions to the business at hand. Put simply, this amounts to restrictions on the kinds of talk that are permitted. (3) Institutional talk is associated with the inferential frameworks and procedures of a specific institutional context (Drew and Heritage 1992, pp. 23–25).

We see these features of institutional talk most clearly in formal settings like classrooms, courtrooms, and broadcast news interviews, where the institution and its forms of talk are ostensibly synonymous (Drew and Heritage 1992). That is, institutions like courts of law are identifiable as operating courts by virtue of the distinctive forms of talk comprising them, and the normative and/or statutory rules that support these modifications of everyday conversation. These modifications typically address ordinary turn-taking conventions as a means of allocating or controlling access to speakership. Courtrooms, for example, formally restrict the presentation of evidence to question-answer adjacency pairs; an attorney asks the questions and the witness answers. Variation from this expected sequence typically draws immediate sanctions (see Atkinson and Drew 1979, Holstein 1993). Hugh Mehan (1979) shows us similar, if less formal, patterning in classroom talk, where he observed "lessons" routinely proceeding within a "(teacher) initiation-(student) reply-(teacher) evaluation" format. While there are no explicit rules constraining classroom talk, normative expectations about just what constitutes a "classroom lesson" keep participants accountable to this pattern.

Institutional talk amounts to more than restrictions on turn-taking, however. It may also be embodied in preferences for, or restrictions on, how something may be put, when it might be appropriately said, and to whom talk might be addressed. John Conley and William O'Barr (1990), for example, offer an extensive list of constraints that legal settings impose on ordinary conversation, including the following:

1. A witness may not ordinarily repeat what other persons have said about the events being reported;
2. A witness may not speculate about how the situations or events being reported may have appeared to other people or from other perspectives;
3. A witness may not ordinarily comment on his or her reactions to, or feelings and beliefs about, events being reported;
4. In responding to a question, a witness ordinarily may not digress from the subject of the question to introduce information that he or she believes critical as a preface or qualification;
5. A witness may not normally incorporate into his or her account any sup-

positions about the state of mind of the persons involved in the events being reported;
6. Value judgments and opinions by lay persons are generally disfavored;
7. Emphasis through repetition of information is restricted;
8. Substantive information should not be conveyed through gestures alone; and
9. A witness is generally forbidden to make observations about the questions asked or to comment on the process of testifying itself. (Pp. 13–14)

For the most part, these restrictions are supported by statutes or common law, or unwritten legal custom, even while the forbidden narrative practices are common in everyday conversation (Conley and O'Barr 1990). Conley and O'Barr go on to argue that such restrictions often lead "the voices of lay people to go unheard in the formal legal process" (p. 34). Our interest here is not so much in the possible injustices deriving from institutional restrictions as it is in the ways that institutional conventions constrain, promote, and otherwise shape the conversations, stories, and related selves that emerge under institutional auspices.

The form that self presentation may take, for example, is institutionally constrained in legal settings. The rules of courtroom procedure mandate that witnesses respond only within the conventional interrogatory format. If they don't, they meet with something like the following. In this instance the attorney conducting the questioning had initially asked the witness what had happened at the scene of an accident:

WITNESS: Well, I went, uh, Mr. N told me to go outside.
LAWYER: Object.
WITNESS: Well, I
JUDGE: Just describe the physical act of what was done. Not what was said, but what actually transpired.
WITNESS: Well, I wasn't really doing anything in relation to the patient. Mr. N was doing all that.
LAWYER: Did you go, did you go back, did you return to the emergency vehicle?
WITNESS: I returned to the emergency vehicle. (Conley and O'Barr 1990, p. 15).

Here, the witness begins to present himself in what Conley and O'Barr (1990, p. 15) call "everyday discourse." The response initially includes reference to what Mr. N told the witness to do. This, of course, is outside the purview of the original question, and draws an immediate (and accountable) objection from the opposing attorney. The judge intervenes and instructs the witness in how the question and the self under consideration should be properly addressed *in the courtroom*. Evidentiary conventions are thus brought to bear by the "objection," which incites the assertion of the rule as it pertains to this particular situation.

Now consider how the imposition of legal conventions exerts institutional influence over opportunities to narrate the self more fully. During a formal appeals hearing held before a state-appointed hearings officer, a former welfare recipient was contesting the state's termination of his welfare benefits (Miller and Holstein 1996). In the following extract, the hearings officer (HO) was questioning Samuel Natt (SN) about his failure to contact his welfare worker after missing compulsory meetings:

HO: So you didn't contact employers because you didn't feel [the welfare agency worker] was giving you adequate assistance?
SN: I was looking out for my own.
HO: Wait, just a moment. Just answer my question. (P. 219)

In response to the hearings officer's question, Natt embarked on a story possibly leading to an explanation of why he had failed to contact prospective employers, one which was likely to include significant self construction. While Natt's response in the extract only hints at what self that might be, his subsequent testimony suggests that he might have constructed a story implicating his sense of personal responsibility and independence (see Miller and Holstein 1996, pp. 218–20). The story, however, was short-circuited by the hearings officer, who insisted the question be answered directly, without embellishment. In such circumstances, the rules governing the proceedings explicitly permit the hearings officer to impose narrative control, which in turn shapes both the *whats* and the *hows* of communicating the self.

Legal proceedings of all types generally constrain presentation in similar fashion. Typically, stories of the self emerge utterance by utterance, within the context of interrogation and response, but extended self narratives are rare (Miller and Holstein 1996). If stories do emerge, they must be pieced together at the virtual request of the interrogating attorney. We can see this in direct examinations conducted by representatives of a public defender's office (PDs) as they try to elicit information about their clients from the clients as they testify in involuntary commitment hearings (see Holstein 1993). The following extract from James Gold's hearing is illustrative:

1. PD2:   Do you think you are ready to go home today?
2. JG: Yep, I'm much better.
3. PD2:   Are you taking care of yourself?
4. JG: I'm doing very well, keeping my mind straight with my program.
5. PD2:   Where do you plan to live?
6. JG: I live with my family and that's what I'll do.
7. PD2:   They will let you stay there.
8. JG: Always have. I'm a family man.

Note that Gold's account of feeling better, sticking to his program, and returning home to his life as a family man is not instantaneously constructed so much as it emerges one discrete, succinct item at a time, in response to specific questioning by the PD. The courtroom environment prescribes this format, and allows the PD to claim another turn at talk immediately upon the hearable completion of an answer to the prior question. When he does this, the questioner closes down the possibility of the client embellishing any particular utterance into an extended story or self presentation.

As we can see in the next extract, attorneys are allowed to claim speakership at any point where their prior question has been hearably answered, even if they violate expectations of ordinary conversation. The interactional upshot is that attorneys often interrupt witnesses at points in the conversational exchange where speakership transfer is not normatively expected. We see this in the following illustration where the PD is questioning Katie Maxwell (KM) about what she will do if her temporary commitment is terminated.

1. PD4: If they let you go today, Katie, do you have a place to live?
2. KM: Uh huh my mother's (place)
3. PD4: Where is your mother's place?
4. KM: In Bellwood.
5. PD4: What's the address?
6. KM: One twenty Acton Street.* I can come // and go as I please.
7. PD4: ((breaking in))   // That's fine Katie.
8.   Does your mother say you can live with her?
9. KM: Yeah it's OK with her.
10. PD4: Can you eat your meals there?
11. KM: Yeah* there's no one there // always watching me.
12. PD4: ((breaking in))   // You can just answer yes or no. Okay?
13. KM: Okay.
14. PD4: Do you have clothes at your mother's house?
15. KM: Yes.
16. PD4: Can you dress yourself?
17. KM: Of course I can.
18. PD4: Do you get an (SSI) check in the mail?
19. KM: Yes.
20. PD4: Will you give it to your mother?
21. KM: Yes.
22. PD4: And will you let her give you your medication?
23. KM: Yeah,* whenever I // need it.
24. PD4: ((breaking in))   // That's good Katie. (Holstein 1993, p. 97)

Note how the PD's questions were formulated to elicit brief, direct answers, most of them answerable in a single word. Clearly, this works against the narrative presentation of Maxwell's own sense of herself and her situation. The PD established the adequacy of each answer to her questions by accepting brief responses as complete, moving directly to the next question without hesitation. Speaker transition was immediate as the PD claimed her preallocated turn; extended utterances were foreclosed in the process. Indeed, when Maxwell's testimony extended beyond what might be heard as a first possible completion point (marked with *), the PD repeatedly broke into Maxwell's talk. In three instances (lines 6, 11, and 23), Maxwell tried to embellish or qualify her minimal answer to the PD's question, and each time the embellishments met with intrusions of simultaneous speech. The content of each overlapping utterance indicated that the client's answer was adequately completed (e.g., line 7: "That's fine Katie"), but, just as significantly, the incursions into the client's turns discouraged further talk—virtually preventing the narrative extension of any emerging and damaging story line.[3]

All institutional talk, however, does not necessarily curtail the storied self in this fashion. To the contrary, myriad contemporary settings are specifically designed to facilitate self narration, both as an end in itself and in service to other goals. As we mentioned in Chapter 7, we live in an "interview society" where our personal, private selves are pervasively disclosed by way of the face-to-face interview. Interviews of all sorts—those conducted by social researchers, mass media reporters, therapists, counselors, eligibility workers in social service agencies, law enforcement officers, to name just a few—provide increasingly prominent and prevalent institutionalized venues for self construction. Interviews do not merely reveal selves; they are also occasions that shape selves for local usage and consumption (Atkinson and Silverman 1997, Holstein and Gubrium 1995a).

Many interviews strive for just the opposite of the constraints that legal settings place on self construction. The point is to prod respondents to speak about themselves in their "own" words, a goal being an elaborate personal account. Any social research methods textbook is sure to offer a detailed technology for extracting both structured and unfettered narratives of respondents' lives and experience.[4] Psychotherapists, especially those with psychoanalytic predilections, are taught interview skills that encourage uninterrupted narratives, with therapists removing themselves to the interactional background as much as possible. The classic example of this is the therapist whose interviewing technique consists only of minimal incitements and nondirectional requests for continuation (e.g., "Uh huh," "Why don't you go with that").[5]

Broadcast news interviews owe their commonsense credibility to their ability to display neutrality in eliciting narratives from their subjects (Clayman 1988, 1992). It is the subject's, not the interviewer's, story that is newsworthy in this form of discourse, and thus the interviewers' own stories are kept to a minimum. News interviews constitute a distinctive institutional environment in which conventions of turn-taking and conversational management depart from ordinary conversation in several consequential ways so as to bring off extended and, especially, publicly fascinating tellings of experience by the interviewee. Take the following extract from a British television interview conducted by IR with a man (IE) who claims he had been jailed for a crime he did not commit. Note that this format permits an extended report on experience, allowing IE to reveal a surprisingly upstanding self.[6]

IR: Have you any sort of criminal connections or anything, uh // hh
IE: // Not at all.* I
      was working for the Gas Board at the time as a salesman.* I had no (0.2) emphatically no er associates that (would) had criminal records,* or I did not associate with people with criminal records.* hhhh I- I- I- was living a life o-

o- of a family man in Stockton-on-Tess,* hhh where I was a representative for the Gas Board,* hhh and it was out of the blue to me.

IR: hh Were you surprised when you w- went to court, and- and indeed went down? (Heritage and Greatbach 1991, P. 98)

Generally, news interviews involve the interviewer asking questions so as to elicit rich answers from the interviewee. As we saw in Chapter 7, one way of eliciting extended turns at talk is for the first speaker—in this instance, the interviewer—to pass up possible opportunities to talk, thereby prompting the interviewee to continue. In the extract above, we see that after IR asks the original question, he encounters several possible turn transition places in IE's response (marked with *). In each instance, however, IR refuses the turn at talk, so IE continues. The result is an extended narrative by IE in which he portrays and embellishes both his (innocent) self and the (unjust) circumstances, without interruption.

While the interview participants trade on the normative expectations of ordinary conversation, they are also cognizant of—indeed, they are the interactional authors of—an institutionalized way of interacting that is recognizable as a news interview (Heritage and Greatbatch 1991). And, as a routinized way of interacting, normative expectancies provide for other modifications of ordinary interaction, with further implications for self construction. The following British television interview conducted with a politician (AS) is illustrative.[7] IR is the interviewer.

IR: What's the difference between your Marxism and Mr. McGahey's Communism?

AS: The difference is that it's the press that constantly call me a Marxist when I do not, and never have er er given that description of myself. hh I-//

IR: // I've heard you'd be happy to to er hhh er describe yourself as a Marxist.* Could it be that with an election in the offing, you're anxious to play down that you're a Marx // ist?

AS: // er Not at all, Mr. Day. And I'm sorry to say that I must disagree with you, you have never heard me describe myself hhh er as a Marxist. ((Continues)) (Heritage and Greatbatch 1991, p. 100)

In this interview, the interviewer solicits the distinction between AS and an avowed communist, Mr. McGahey, affording AS the opportunity both to reject what he believes are false claims propagated by the press and to clarify how AS describes himself. The interviewer responds by directly contradicting AS, asserting that he has all but heard AS call himself a Marxist. Ordinarily at the end of the sentence launching a contradiction (at the point marked with *), a speaker put in the position AS finds himself might take advantage of this first possible turn transition point to reclaim speakership in order to refute or rebut the claim. However, Heritage and Greatbatch explain that the normative expectation that the news interviewer's turn at talk will end in a question delays AS's response until the question is, in fact, forthcoming. By withholding responses until recognizable questions are asked, interviewees both orient to, and help to produce, the interview character of the interaction (Heritage and Greatbatch 1991).

(Re)Sources of Self Construction

The self is always built up out of something; its assembly depends on the narrative resources available for self construction. What plots, themes, and characterization do storytellers call upon in conveying who and what they are? How are these resources used to do the work of storytelling? The answers we find may seem familiar, but in discursive practice they have a locally contingent flavor.

Local Culture

One way to conceive of the circumstantial resources for self construction is in terms of "local culture," situated discourses that specify locally accountable selves (Gubrium and Holstein 1997). Borrowing from Durkheim (1961), we can think of locally delimited cultural categories as collective representations that are diversely and artfully articulated with, and attached to, lived experience in order to produce locally comprehensible meanings. Culture, from this perspective, is not a set of prescriptions or rules for interpretation and action; rather, it's a constellation of more or less regularized, localized ways of understanding and representing things and actions, of assigning meaning to lives. It provides familiar standards of accountability to which cultural members orient as they formulate their actions. Some of these amount to highly formalized, official vocabularies for depicting experience. Regarding selves, we find psychiatric and psychological treatment programs, therapy facilities, and support groups that offer specific professionally developed resources for self characterization. These may differ vastly from the resources available in circumstances that might also be concerned with self, but in less formal, less focused ways—such as in households where family members express interest and concern for one another's everyday experience, well being, and development.

The matter of local availability is always somewhat indeterminate; those engaged in acts of interpretation must elaborate locally serviceable discourses in relation to the circumstances at hand. Discourse does not simply stand as a circumscribed collection of interpretive building blocks, to be selected for application based on some standard of correspondence or appropriateness. Local culture is not so much a museum-like repository of meanings as it is a dynamic yet delimited assemblage of interpretive possibilities. That which is locally "available" is something of a reflexive matter, as the "current" stock of resources is assembled at the same time it is referenced. Simultaneously, however, local accountability structures (which are themselves reflexively recognizable) have a way of reigning in what might otherwise be seen as the completely arbitrary, swirling attachments of ungrounded interpretation. By characterizing culture as local, we are emphasizing that it comprises the proximate, ordinary, circumstantial particulars that are taken into account in ongoing social interaction.

Above all, local culture is not a monolithic set of injunctions or absolute directives. Like Foucault's (1973, 1975, 1977) notion of the institutional gaze, local culture may incite particular interpretations and supply the vocabulary for their articulation, but, as a matter of practice, it neither dictates nor determines what is interpretively constructed. Local culture is always in the making, as members reflexively refer ongoing experience to their stocks of cultural knowledge and categories, both making sense of experience and reinforming the cultural parameters called upon in the process.

Culture is also always a resource for local *use*; it's not automatically invoked. Because persons are not "judgmental or cultural dopes" (Garfinkel 1967), the ways that culture is used—the fashion in which cultural categories are applied—is always variable and contingent. For example, while distinct models of the self may be situationally available for self presentation, the interpretations of self that emerge will be shaped by concern for what, under the circumstances, is arguably appropriate or otherwise accountable. Culturally circumscribed self construction is never automatic in practice. Instead, it yields variable images that reflect the artful combination of diversely available interpretive resources.

Configurations of interpretive resources, orientations, and concerns may coalesce in and around any enduring group, setting, or institution from the most formally organized—such as prisons or the army—to the most casual going concerns, like children's play groups. Formal or not, these configurations offer ways of thinking, seeing, and talking—virtual paradigms of experience—to which participants continually turn and, in turn, shape to make sense of their lives and selves.

Consider, for example, the local culture that Elliot Liebow (1967) reports in his classic ethnography of an urban neighborhood, *Tally's Corner*. Liebow's observations reveal how a group of men who "hung out" in and around the New Deal carry-out shop in downtown Washington, D.C., developed and used a set of locally crafted understandings of everyday life in the vicinity to make sense of themselves and others who might venture into their midst. Grounded in the geographical and experiential space shared by participants in this "life world" (Schutz 1970), a distinct form of life is evident in the myriad interactions comprising Tally's Corner.

One feature of local culture is apparent in the accounts provided for the various trials, tribulations, and failures of marriage and other relations between men and women. Liebow calls this a "theory of manly flaws" (p. 116). It's a local understanding of subjectivity that informs nearly all stories of intergender relations and carries with it strong implications for locally gendered selves. The fact that this is an "indigenous" theory makes it no less compelling or useful to the local inhabitants, especially as a resource for presenting and explaining themselves to each other. As a guide to self construction, Liebow first notes that the theory of manly flaws is judiciously invoked to excuse men's failures as husbands or to account for sexual infidelities while fending off moral outrage and condemnation:

In each instance, the man is always careful to attribute his inadequacies as a husband to his inability to slough off one or another attribute of manliness, such as independence of spirit, a like for whiskey, or an appetite for a variety of women. They trace their failures as husbands directly to their weaknesses as men, to their manly flaws. . . . One of the most widespread and strongly supported views the men have of themselves and others is that men are, by nature, not monogamous; that no man can be satisfied with only one woman at a time. (Pp. 118, 120)

The theory of manly flaws is a discourse that corner habitués employ to represent themselves as men, and especially to account for why men are as they are, and act as they do. It also informs their courses of action, as those who apply the discourse to their lives come to actually gaze upon each other in these terms. Liebow shows us the manner in which the theory is put into practice as he recounts how the corner men call upon images of men's baser instincts—their uncontrollable "animal" nature—to present themselves as flawed yet largely blameless for their shortcomings. One of the men of Tally's Corner puts it vividly as he constructs a self at the mercy of his manly nature:

Men are just dogs! We shouldn't call ourselves human, we're just dogs, dogs, dogs! They call me a dog, 'cause that's what I am, but so is everybody else—hopping around from woman to woman, just like a dog. (Pp. 120–21)

Another man, narrating aspects of self in relation to his marital woes, embellishes the picture: "I'm a sport. I'll always be a sport. I was born that way. I got a lot of dog in me" (Liebow 1967, p. 126).[8]

Local culture offers ways of constructing self that are reflexively both productive of and responsive to everyday interpretive circumstances. It doesn't force particular self definitions upon participants; rather, it makes them accountable in the local scheme of things. It does not dictate how persons see or convey themselves, but provides shared-in-common resources to a community that, in turn, comes to identify itself in terms that the culture provides. Always crafted to the circumstances at hand, the stock of salient, accountable resources provided by settings, communities, organizations, or institutions comprises self-defining images and vocabularies that are realized in locally storied selves.

What is especially significant about local culture is that it is multidimensional in use. It may simultaneously reflect any number of going concerns, providing a complex yet versatile set of interpretive resources. Carol Stack (1974) illustrates the interpretive use of the intricate "fictive" kinship patterns to which members of a Midwestern African-American community orient as they construct the subjectivity of their interpersonal relations. Social organization in terms of kinship, Stack argues, plays a large role in how members arrange their lives and conceive of themselves and others. In this black community (and, as Stack implies, in other African-American communities in the United States), kinship is not solely a matter of birth. Rather, kinship terms are used to identify the practical relations, emotional ties, and long-standing linkages between individuals, who may or may not be related by blood. One earns "family status" in this community by demonstrating caring, sharing, enduring commitment to others, and this status is conveyed and reflected by the application of kinship terms (e.g., "mama," "daddy," "sister").

Close relationships are crafted out of local culture more than formal kinship. Stack suggests, for instance, that a woman could not think of, let alone present, herself as a "mama" if she was not the person primarily responsible for raising and nurturing a child, even if she were the child's biological mother. Conversely, a woman would surely consider herself a "mama" if she had responsibility for a child's upbringing or welfare, even if the child was not biologically (or adoptively) her own. Stack writes of a young mother who gives her newborn child over to the care of her own mother, "While she may share the same room and household with her baby, her mother . . . will care for the child and become the child's 'mama,' both in the eyes of the community and in her own view" (p. 47). Locally, then, one can consider one's self to be a "mama" only under particular relational circumstances, regardless of what biological ties might indicate.

Self constructions in relation to family ties observe similar conventions where being a father, sister, or other family member might be concerned. Consider how Billie, a young woman living in the community Stack studied, identified herself in relation to others who occupied salient roles in her "kinship" network:

> Most people kin to me are in this neighborhood . . . but I got people in the South, in Chicago, and in Ohio too. I couldn't tell most of their names and most of them aren't really kinfolk to me . . . . Take my father, he's no father to me. I ain't got but one daddy and that's Jason. The one who raised me. My kids' daddies, that's something else, all their daddies' people really take to them—they always doing things and making a fuss about them. We help each other out and that's what kinfolks are all about. (Stack 1974, p. 45)

The local status of kinship claims and related identities is clear in Billie's description of many of the significant others in her life.

Still, as in other culturally circumscribed settings, the local conventions and resources for self construction condition, but do not determine, the way individuals think about and present who they are. The ongoing contingencies of social interaction can always alter the applicability of an identity, as we pointed out earlier in discussing Chase's (1995) school superintendents' self constructions. For example, we can imagine that even in the community Stack studied, claims to being "mama" to a child are not automatic, even while that category locally signifies caring upbringing. We would assume that the category might be contested and redefined in stricter terms if and when others convincingly claimed that someone who considered herself "mama" to someone and lovingly cared for him, was, say, "doin' it for the money and nothin' else."

The point is that in discursive practice, the discourses that comprise local culture need to be articulated with the developing relevancies of daily living. While local culture and its operating discourses are discernible and, to that extent, predictive of certain patterns of subjectivization, that alone does not automatically determine what selves are constructed, or how it's done. It should be evident in the examples from Tally's Corner and the community Stack studied that members *use* culture to designate their identities. Culture doesn't automatically assign particular selves.[9]

Organizational Embeddedness

Formal organizations significantly concretize self construction. Their service mandates, such as specialized institutional missions or professional, therapeutic outlooks and orientations, provide publicly designated resources for producing selves. To the extent that localized configurations of meaning are mediated by organizational conditions, we consider the self-construction process to be "organizationally embedded" (Gubrium and Holstein 1997).

It can be most striking how organizational or professional circumstances and outlooks influence self construction when persons move between different organizational venues or when organizational discourses change. In involuntary mental hospitalization hearings, for instance, the judicial concern for the "manageability" of mental patients released into the community leads the patients (and their advocates) to present selves in terms that relate to self care. As a practical matter, patients may portray themselves in terms of how well they can control their own lives and how little trouble they may be for others, utilizing the court's preferred discourse of community manageability. This self depiction can stand in stark contrast to self presentations patients offer when relating to the more "psychiatric" concerns and agendas that they confront during psychotherapy or counseling. Under these circumstances, a discourse acknowledging frailties and stressing affective rather than custodial matters may lead to considerably different (but not inauthentic) claims about the self (Holstein 1993).

Markedly different treatment philosophies may structure subjectivity well beyond what simple notions of personal identity might suggest. Consider, for example, the local cultures of two family therapy agencies that held similar goals but drew from distinctly different models of troubled lives and families (see Gubrium 1992). Westside House viewed the family as an authority structure; this supplied its staff and clients with interpretive resources and standards for evaluating individual and family troubles in the context of properly hierarchical relations. The view was decidedly different from the one held at nearby Fairview Hospital, which emphasized affective linkages between family members as the common source of individual and family dysfunctionality.

When participants in the two organizations were asked to indicate signs of trouble, distinct discourses of subjectivity provided them with different ways of specifying the selves and circumstances involved. For example, physical comportment during therapy sessions was taken to be an important indicator of personal and domestic order and disorder in both agencies, but local culture presented quite different frameworks for interpreting related bodily signs. In observing a videotaped family therapy session, for instance, therapists at Westside might note that the father had taken a central seating position, surrounded by various family members. At Westside, this would be interpreted as an empirical indication that the father was responsibly assuming his rightful, authoritative position as the head of the household. It was a provisionally significant statement about the father's fundamentally healthy sense of familial responsibility, suggesting that this family was well on the way to becoming functional again.

The very same choice of seating position, read through the interpretive culture of Fairview's understanding of the functional family as a democracy of emotions, however, was likely to engender a different view, especially if the father used his position to dominate social interaction. Staff members (and the father himself, upon being encouraged to reflect on the matter) typically would conclude that the father was distorting the family circle, drawing it out of emotional balance by inappropriately asserting an overbearing presence; he would likely be portrayed as imposing himself in ways that prevented free and equal communication and the open display of feelings, implicating both personal and domestic dysfunctionality.

Changes in organizational discourses also serve to alter self constructions. For example, in still another therapy agency, staff and clients' sense of their troubles and the solutions for them were dramatically reconstrued when an existing therapeutic philosophy changed. Gale Miller's (1997a) twelve-year ethnographic study of Northland Clinic, an internationally prominent center of "brief therapy," describes a marked shift in client subjectivity that accompanied a conscious alteration of treatment philosophy. When Miller began his fieldwork, Northland employed an "ecosystemic brief therapy," which emphasized the social contexts of clients' lives and problems. In this therapeutic environment, clients' subjectivity was linked with the actual systems of social relationships that formed and fueled their problems. The approach required the staff to discern the state of these systems and to intervene so as to alter their dynamics and thereby effect change. Miller notes that this approach was informed by a "modern" sense of the reality of the problems in question.

Several years into the fieldwork, Northland shifted to a more "postmodern" approach, embedding intervention in a linguistic and constructivist framework. Therapists began to apply what was called "solution-focused brief therapy," which meant viewing troubles as ways of talking about everyday life, prompting the staff to orient to the therapy process as a set of language games, expressly akin to Wittgenstein's sense of the term. The idea here was that troubles were constructions—ways of talking and related "forms of life"—as much as they posed real difficulties for the clients in question. This transformed clients' organizational subjectivities from being relatively passive agents of systems of relationships, personal troubles, and negative stories, to being active solution-seekers with a potential to formulate positive stories about themselves and design helpful views of their situations. As the language of solutions, not of problems, became the basis of intervention, the narrative identity of clients was transformed to reveal entirely different selves.[10]

In comparing these differences in organizational embeddedness, our point is not that one agency or treatment philosophy provides a more plausible discourse for subjectivity than another one. Nor are we saying that signs of the self would always be read this predictably in these organizations. Rather, we are suggesting that organizations are vested with relatively stable orientations and resources—"conditions of possibility" (Foucault 1975, p. xix)—for interpreting the self. These establish the going parameters and expectations for the kinds of self interpretations that readily "make sense" in the existing institutional scheme of things; they routinely construct subjectivity according to distinctive organizational discourses. Being official, these relatively stable resources have a cultural mandate over and above what we would expect in less formal settings, but, needless to say, their variety in a postmodern world also offers a greater number of opportunities for self construction than ever before.

Three Caveats

At this point, let us reiterate three caveats. First, while organized settings provide accountable modes of interpretation, we must emphasize that settings do not determine how selves are constructed. Local cultures or formal organizations supply *resources* for interpretation, not injunctions or absolute directives. Selves constituted in a particular site or organization may take on the general qualities that the setting or organization promotes, but practitioners of everyday life are not "cultural or organizational dopes," mere extensions of organizational thinking (Douglas 1986). They exercise interpretive discretion, mediated by the complex combinations of meaning that competing professional and institutional affiliations might offer (e.g., such as differences in points of view between hospital nurses and social workers as they interpret and apply organizationally preferred discourses). Locally prevailing discourses of self thus emerge as continuing adaptations of discourses-in-practice.

Second, it's important to emphasize that organizational embeddedness refers to the circumstances in which interpretation takes place, not to the integration of actual selves into the workings of groups or organizations. It is interpretive practice and, in particular, self construction, that is embedded in, and shaped by, the organizational meaning making apparatus.

Finally, we must keep in mind that self construction is a complex process that responds to multiple "layers" of interpretive constraint and narrative resources. While discursive practice is always local, those contingencies that are brought to bear at any particular place and time coalesce from a vast array of possibilities, including those taken from broader cultural understandings such as might be drawn from race, gender, class, and myriad other configurations of meaning. This, of course, invites narrative slippage and innovation, as stories are locally crafted from a variegated range of standpoints and resources.

Featuring the Ordinary

Self construction is part and parcel of the ubiquitous and mundane work we do to constitute and navigate our lives. Following the early pragmatists, we must remember that subjectivity is fundamentally crafted out of everyday representational resources and ordinary interpretive practices. Indeed, Sacks (1992b) has argued that one of our most prevalent preoccupations is "doing being ordinary."[11] By this, he meant something that we have taken for granted throughout our discussion, namely, that we are continuously engaged in the ordinary work of con-stituting ourselves so that we appear to be nonexceptional members of the groups in which we participate (which of course would include nonexceptional mem-bership in extraordinary groups). This is not to say that we don't present ourselves as distinctive but, rather, that we work hard to keep our essential mem-bership from being called into question by presenting ourselves in commonsen-sically understandable terms. One means we employ for constituting these ac-ceptable, familiar selves is to craft them out of the mundane resources proximately available to us.

Using Ordinary Resources

The process of social construction can be all but invisible to those engaged in it, while interpretive resources appear similarly insubstantial because they are taken to be identical to those things they represent. It's precisely their ordinary charac-ter that renders them practically imperceptible. Consider, for example, the way that ordinary images of what is normal and what is deviant are used to establish a sense of self in settings where mental health problems and treatment are going concerns (see Holstein 1993). When the attorney representing David Rudy dur-ing an involuntary commitment hearing asked Rudy about his condition, Rudy responded with the following:

> I'm okay. I have my ups and downs, but I'm doing as well as the next guy. I know
> I have problems, but I'm not like most of these characters [referring to other men-tal patients]. I'm compliant. I know I need the meds or I'll get off track. I take
> them. Not like the rest of these guys on the ward.

We can identify several ordinary resources at work here, beginning with the colloquial language utilized to convey the ordinary quality of personal lives. "I'm okay," "I have my ups and downs," and "I'm doing as well as the next guy" draw upon commonplace expressions to convey the benign, if somewhat variable, state of Rudy's mental health. As Garfinkel (1967) has shown in his breaching demon-strations, characterizations such as these depend upon taken-for-granted mean-ings that appear both obvious and ordinary until further specification is de-manded. It is their sheer mundanity that precludes such demand, allowing the expressions to stand as something "everyone knows" under the circumstances.

Rudy's comparisons with "these other characters" draws upon ordinary im-ages of "mental patients" in order to establish what Rudy is not, by way of con-trast. On one level, this implicates everyday commonsense knowledge of mental patients and their ilk, but Rudy also invokes the language of surveillance to sup-port his contrasting narrative. In stating "I'm compliant," he invokes vocabulary from a locally relevant psychiatric culture, applying a technical term to reference those patients who voluntarily and consistently abide by their medication regi-mens. In doing so, Rudy presents himself as distinct from the known type "guys on the ward," that is, mental patients. In so doing, he seamlessly commandeers the psychiatric terminology to convey in locally preferred terms that he is doing well and is fit to leave the hospital.

Biographical Particulars

As ordinary as it might be, familiar personal experience is a featured building block for self construction. Biographical particulars are something we always have with us; they're perhaps our most readily available resource for self construction. Experiences as mundane as an adult's recollections of unexceptional childhood events might be assembled into an account for a presently salient trait or behavior. Empirically, we see the appropriation of past experience all the time, as persons construct present selves out of what they choose to notice from their immediate and distant pasts.

We are not arguing, of course, that biographical particulars themselves structure the self. Rather, they are used circumstantially, identified and descriptively mobilized to become part of local selves-in-the-making. Biography does not determine identity any more than organizational location or institutional discourses dictate selves. Albeit sometimes highly salient locally, biography is simply one further resource for assembling who and what we are. Indeed, in practice, one's past—one's life history or biography—is itself constructed in the process of self construction. A more or less fixed repository of past experiences is not simply sifted for relevant materials to bring to bear on identity. Rather, we engage in ordinary "biographical work" to assemble aspects of personal history that can be used to bolster present claims of and about ourselves (Gubrium and Holstein 1995a, 1998; Gubrium, Holstein, and Buckholdt 1994). Our view of this process is not one of miners excavating personal histories for telling artifacts of the self. Rather, it's more the aforementioned image of the bricoleur who artfully, yet accountably, assembles an interpretively useful past for the practical purposes at hand.

This is more than a matter of recall or memory, because it involves the active construction of what one claims to remember. It's not an unfettered process of simply conjuring up the past, since commonsense reasoning suggests that claims about the past are always subject to substantiation by arguably independent evidence of their actual occurrence. One cannot arbitrarily "make things up," since one may always be asked to "prove" one's claims, which is itself subject to the same process of substantiation. The construction process is thus thoroughly accountable. Indeed, the use of biographical particulars is regressively accountable to what might reasonably be shown to have actually happened all the way down the line, so to speak.

Consider the reflexive complexity, yet ordinary development, of this process in the following discussion that took place during a parenting effectiveness class (Gubrium and Holstein 1995a). Over the course of the discussion, note how various parents make telling identity claims as they virtually manufacture a stock of biographical particulars upon which they subsequently rely to describe themselves. Kitty begins the discussion by recounting some of her family problems. In locally familiar terms, she explains that she had a lot of trouble with her son because she failed to "actively listen" to him when he interacted with her, but that things are improving because she's learned to listen better. We enter the discussion as it turns to Liz's son, Ned, whom Liz has called "my troublemaker."

LIZ: It's good to know that someone is getting somewhere with these kids, because I was really, really worried that nothing could be done. As you
know, Ned is not just your plain old mischievous kid. He's a handful.
Lying, stealing, swearing, running all hours of the day and night, God
knows where. It makes my blood boil. Really stresses me out. [Pause] But
like Kitty says, maybe there's light at the end of the tunnel, huh?

KITTY: I don't want to give you the impression that it was easy, Liz. [Elaborates on
her troubles with her son.] I know I've got to get help for myself, get real
serious and listen before things go whacko again. I'm hopeful, but I need

LIZ: [Interrupting] No, that's good to hear. I'm not going to hold my breath,
but I am going to think about that, that we [Liz and her husband] might
be part of this, maybe how we've dealt with Ned could be part of the
problem, you know, the inconsistency and stuff, not listening like you
said, Kitty. (Pp. 561–62)

In the exchange, Liz offers the self revelation that she and her husband might
be "part of the problem," based on what she presently suggests were their past
inconsistencies and failures to listen actively. But note that these biographical particulars did not just leap out of her past experience, but were prompted by Kitty's
story. Liz casts her own emerging story in light of particular aspects of Kitty's
narrative. She constructs her own past as an instance of a more general biography, one she ostensibly shares with Kitty. It is only now, in the present, that Liz
comes to see what her contributions to her son's troublemaking might have been,
and what that means for her identity as a parent. Unwittingly, at Kitty's behest,
Liz presently figures that she might have been as much a troubling parent as a
parent with family troubles.

A long discussion of parental inconsistency and failure to listen follows this
exchange. In time, another consideration of biographical relevance emerges when
it is suggested that peer pressure and other hazards of growing up in today's
world can adversely affect children's moral development. Parents, they agree, are
not completely at fault for their children's misbehavior. In the following extract,
we pick up the discussion as the parents are about to generalize their individual
troubles into the common difficulties of contemporary parenting. In the process,
biographical particulars begin to be shadowed by another identity—being parents of "kids these days"—an identity they all share, but that doesn't wholly implicate their pasts.

LIZ: I can see how Ned might have never learned how to be respectful, like
you said, Kitty. That's a real thought. But I guess I never saw how much
we could be involved in this, like what we did or should have done. [Elab-
orates]

JUDY: Gary, how does a dad think about this? What do you make of what Kitty
said? Do you think we're at fault just as much as the kids?

GARY: I think she has a point. I'm not sure I'd go as far as sayin' that it's my
fault that Fred [Gary's son] is off the wall half the time, but you know
what they say, it takes two to tango. Anyway, it does make you think.

BETH: It does, really. Remember how we got into this sort of thing a couple of months ago? Remember, Gary, how much you thought Fred might be reacting to you being too hard on him, that you—how'd you put it?

GARY: I think I said that times have changed and maybe I can't boss Fred around like my old man used to do me. Kids want to be independent nowadays. [Elaborates] So I had to learn to listen, to give him a little rope and [laughing] hope that he doesn't hang himself.

LIZ: I'm glad you mentioned that, Gary, because that makes sense, [turning to Kitty] like what's going on with Steve [Kitty's son] and kids these days and how you began to deal with it. [Elaborates] I think, myself, maybe that's part of it. [Pause] Hey, I'm willing to try anything, right? [Talking to herself] So girl, wake up and smell the coffee!

KITTY: I'm not saying we should take all the blame. For Christ's sake, he's a big kid and has a mind of his own. But we gotta figure that we're part of their lives. I figure it's good to remember that.

JANET: Well, ladies and gentlemen, it keeps happening, doesn't it? You're all depressed and bingo, someone like Kitty tells us to wake up to the caffeine—the wake-up gang. How do you like that?

LIZ: We've got a case of "Kitty troubles."

GARY: Is that what we have? I'd say we're learnin'.

LIZ: Seriously, though, I can see how I—maybe all of us?—I can see how I might be able to deal more effectively as a parent, like Kitty and, well, like Gary too, if I think a bit more about how involved I am in what Ned is doing to himself and what these kids are like nowadays. (Pp. 562–63)

As this discussion unfolds, we hear the speakers linking their own experiences to the theme of parental contributions to their children's troubles, but also resisting full blame, because of the times they live in. They inform each other that both parents and children are part of the problem, which Kitty suggests they keep in mind and Janet features by providing the group a momentarily telling identity—"the wake-up gang." Yet their past indiscretions as parents are relevant only up to a point "nowadays." Each of their stories as troubled parents becomes an account of who they are together, which, in turn, serves as a common narrative for drawing from, but also placing limits on, their individual biographies as the sources of their children's problems.

Narrative Control

The availability of distinctive discourses of the self delimits self construction, mediating if not dictating how individual selves are assembled, more or less specifying just what sorts of selves individuals are in the local scheme of things. In the preceding extract, Kitty, Liz, and the other parents rather unwittingly constructed their identities in relation both to their separate experiences and to their common identity as parents in today's world. This set the local conditions of storytelling, providing both the means and materials for self construction. In some settings, we can actually discern the social processes through which institutionally preferred discourses are mobilized or resisted as those concerned actively erect and enact particular contexts for the matters in question. We can witness narrative control being put into practice as competing going concerns directly come into play.

A degree of narrative control was of course visible in many of our previous illustrations, where circumstantially preferred themes and terms of reference were either adopted or contested. Recall, for example, the self stories that Betty presented in Chapter 6. If we revisited some of the storytelling practices surrounding her narrative, we might have found that while Betty edits her story in relation to standpoints she prefers or figures others favor, participants occasionally remind each other very explicitly to attend to the kinds of stories that are generally told in the group. It is, after all, a support group for the caregivers of Alzheimer's disease sufferers, as might be noted when the discussion veers off course. This serves to control the substantive parameters for storytelling. Stories told in such support groups typically relate to the experiences, trials, and successes of home care for dementia sufferers. When participants get sidetracked from discussions of caregiving, we are soon apt to hear reminders to that effect, admonitions to stick to what is locally relevant or perhaps urgently needs attention. Actively monitoring the local relevance of their accounts, participants simultaneously monitor their identities, reminding each other that, as far as the group is concerned, there are limits to the kinds of self narrative that are relevant under the circumstances.

While forms of institutional talk are in themselves a kind of narrative control, the use of institutional discourse is subject to direct management with respect to prevailing vocabularies of subjectivity. The means of control may be less formally asserted than in, say, a courtroom, but they nevertheless openly condition discursive practice, suggesting if not imposing locally preferred narratives of the self in the process.

Consider, for example, the way direct narrative control is asserted during interactions in the psychiatric unit of a Veteran's Administration center providing inpatient treatment for victims of post-traumatic stress disorder or PTSD (Young 1995). This service is available to combat veterans suffering from the long-term repercussions of traumatic battlefield experiences, generally having occurred during the Vietnam War of the 1960s and early 1970s. Intensive individual and group psychotherapy is aimed at addressing the etiology and symptoms of psychic distress. While the center ostensibly offers an eclectic approach, the psychotherapeutic philosophy guiding the PTSD program is fundamentally psychoanalytic. The keys to recovery are said to be located in the victim's past; problems must first be uncovered before they can be therapeutically addressed. The approach relies upon two assumptions about PTSD: (1) the psychodynamic core of PTSD is a repetitive compulsion; the victim is psychologically compelled to reenact the behavior that precipitated the disorder in a futile attempt to gain mastery over the circumstances that were originally overwhelming, and (2) to recover, the patient must recall the traumatic memory, disclose it to the therapist and fellow patients during group psychotherapy, and subject the memory and its narrative to therapeutic scrutiny (Young 1995, p. 183).

The therapeutic discourse-in-practice is most visibly embodied in the clinical description of PTSD and the language used to characterize the disorder and its cure. Conveyed by the staff and in memoranda, a well-articulated model of the disease provides staff and patients with a way of conceptualizing and characterizing PTSD; "the model," as it is locally known, comprises a set of propositions that serves to define PTSD and its treatment, and is presented as the official therapeutic orientation to the disease. Briefly summarized, the model holds that mental life is dominated by two instinctual drives: aggression and libido. Normally, the drives are fused so that they tend to neutralize one another; the aggressive urge to assault and destroy is counterbalanced by the libidinal drive with its urge for tenderness and longing for attachment. The traumatic experiences of PTSD victims mobilize both drives simultaneously, so that neither can be adequately satisfied. For these vets, the result is often a violent and conscious act of commission that the perpetrator at least partially regrets. Battlefield "atrocities" are the prototypic acts of this type: the marine who shoots and kills a fellow marine whose erratic behavior under fire is endangering the entire squad; the GI who indiscriminately kills villagers who have sheltered enemy soldiers responsible for slaughtering U.S. troops.

As a result of such traumatic acts, the self dysfunctionally splits into two part-selves, an aggressor-self organized around feelings of anger and destructive impulses, and a victim-self organized around pathological feelings of tenderness for victims of aggression. The splitting of the self leads to the reproduction rather than the resolution of the traumatic conflict that precipitated the condition. "Splitting" is a classic symptom of PTSD as well as an obstacle to recovery. Each part of the self is imprisoned within its own emotions—one part anger, the other pity and guilt. The split self, consumed by anger, pathological tenderness, and guilt, repeatedly "reenacts" and "reexperiences" the precipitating events, never being able to come to emotional grips with them or itself. "Stress responses" emerge as victims attempt to manage the anxiety associated with the reexperienced trauma; these responses are held to be intrinsically pathological. The pathological responses, in turn, feed off of the reexperienced trauma, compounding the anxiety in a form of "contagion" (pp. 200–03).

Recovery, in the model's terms, means restoring the integral self, fusing the aggressive and libidinal drives and "making the past dead." To achieve this, the victim must be brought back to the traumatic memory, back to the willful aggression at the moment just prior to the time of committing the traumatic action. Authentic knowledge of the event, it is felt, demystifies the source of the symptomatic behavior, demonstrating that the victim is responding to internal psychic distress rooted in the past and not to the here-and-now provocations that victims generally cite as causes for their psychological and social troubles. To recover, the victim must willfully acknowledge that he is responsible for the traumatic act, that he chose to hurt and to destroy when the choice could have been otherwise. Only then can the victim begin to reintegrate the split self (p. 201).

The model is more elaborate and complex than this in practice, but the preceding sketch offers a sense for the mediating discourse of PTSD that shapes clinical interpretations and motivates therapeutic interventions at the center. Staff, of course, constantly articulate the model, bringing it repeatedly—often explicitly—to bear on interpretations related to PTSD. Patients are taught to accept the model as their narrative framework as well; they become proficient in the use of its language and vocabulary and come to communicate what they do, and what they have done, accordingly. Patients learn to "govern" themselves to present biographical particulars in terms of the model, enacting what Nikolas Rose (1990, 1997) describes as the subjectivizing consequences of psychotherapeutic discourses.

Take, for example, how experiences are interpreted during segments of a group psychotherapy session involving patients Marion, Roger, and Alvin, who are meeting with Carol, a psychological counselor. During a session on February 19, Marion tells the following story:

> Our squad was cut off. NVA [North Vietnamese Army] was close enough to lob grenades into our position. Perimeter fire kept them back, but when we stopped firing, they lobbed grenades in. The grunt [marine] next to me was on the ground, curled into a ball and crying. Whenever I attended to him, more grenades were lobbed in. I returned to firing, and this guy jumped up and ran away from our position. I shot him in the back. For years I felt justified. Now I feel guilty. He was only eighteen. It was his first fire fight, and he couldn't handle it. (Young 1995, p. 238)

Five days later, on February 24, the group therapy discussion returns to Marion's feelings, as Carol and the others frame Marion's emerging account in terms of the model.

MARION: I feel real aggression towards Alvin now. He's been here two weeks longer than me, but there's still nothing about his trauma complex [traumatic memory] and nothing about his reenactment. He gives back just enough of the program to be left alone. I want to help Alvin. I don't want to feel aggression toward him. I see a lot of myself in Alvin.

CAROL: What aspect of *your* reenactment is being triggered by Alvin?

MARION: Withdrawal—it's the withdrawal that I see. It's the same pattern I see in my relation with Sheryl [his current companion]. I have it because it's the way my father was to me, completely nonresponsive whenever he was confronted. . . . Alvin here is putting me right back home.

CAROL: Also back to Vietnam?

MARION: Well, there weren't many times when I felt I was being cut out there—except possibly in my event, when I saw the grunt wasn't firing, and then I saw him run. I felt frustration and anger. It's funny, because Alvin even looks like the guy, now. The way he's hugging himself, the way he's curled over in his seat.

ROGER: It's the same reason why the guy got shot. Isn't it? I mean because he was a "nonparticipant."

CAROL: In Vietnam you felt as if you had been abandoned. You felt you were
           helpless. The enemy were pushing in on you, and you couldn't rely on
           the people you thought you could. You felt anger and you—
MARION: I'll tell you, I felt lots of anger against officers. They were supposed to
           be our leaders, and they put our squad out in front. It was obvious to
           anyone, from the beginning, that they were putting us where it would
           take nothing for the NVA to cut us off.
CAROL: How does this feeling get personalized here, at the center? In your feel-
           ings towards Alvin?
MARION: You know, we've all tried to help him in group. We tried to help him
           process, but his response is aggressive. He doesn't give anything.
           (Young 1995, pp. 238–39, emphasis in the original)

Throughout the session, the language of the model is apparent as Marion repeatedly articulates his feeling in the model's terms. A living language game, its
references to aggression, anger, and guilt emerge throughout the exchange, casting Marion's problems accordingly. The model's conceptualization of PTSD as
"reenactment" is noted and is thoroughly explored, in relation to both Marion's
and Alvin's problems. The psychoanalytic focus on past experience as it relates
to present feelings is clearly evident as Marion likens his current relationship with
Alvin to the one he had long ago experienced with his own father.

The use of the center's prevailing clinical discourse is obvious to participants
and develops quite "naturally" as each displays his command of the language
and its application. But we can also hear traces of interpretive control, both subtle and overt, throughout the session. Perhaps most obviously, the entire group
appears quite coercive in attempting to have Alvin (who is present but silent) articulate his problem in, and on, the model's terms. While pertinent to Marion's
PTSD condition, most of the discussion is directed toward his relations with, and
feelings about, Alvin. The message is clear that Alvin is not conforming to the
center's expectations for how patients should talk, think, and behave.

We also see narrative control in the way that Carol questions and prompts
group members. Her first response to Marion's concern about Alvin is to ask Marion about *Marion's* "reenactment," which serves to focus the discussion firmly on
a matter of central importance in the model's scheme of things. Each of Carol's
subsequent remarks or queries in some way directs participants to articulate their
own problems and questions in relation to some aspect of the model—its concern
with retelling, then refiguring the past, its sensitivity to misplaced anger, its focus on linking past trauma to present affect and actions. The give-and-take of the
therapy session subtly yet persistently imposes the model on the way selves and
experience are articulated, the emphasis being on speaking the self.

Narrative control can become quite explicit in relation to the local priority of
the model. When talk of selves, lives, and troubles emerges in ways that do not
resonate with the model, group participants may be directly instructed to "use
the model," to rethink or restory experience more precisely in terms of the center's therapeutic discourse. In such instances, we literally hear discourse-in-
practice, with its distinct subjectivity evinced in the process. Consider the fol-

lowing exchange in a group psychotherapy session involving Carol and a different set of patients.

CAROL: Say to yourself, I've been punishing myself and people around me for twenty years. Say Jack, you *can* choose to stop.
JACK: Listen, Carol. On some nights, I feel anxiety going through my body like electricity. It started in Vietnam. It wasn't just a feeling. It was anxiety together with terrible chest pains and difficulty breathing. . . . And I'm still getting them.
CAROL: What would you call it?
JACK: Well, I know that it's called a "panic attack." But I didn't know it then.
CAROL: No, I mean what would you call it using the terms of the model—the model that you learned about during orientation phase?
JACK: I don't really know, Carol. My mind is confused right now.
CAROL: The model says that we're dominated by two drives, aggression and sex, and that—
JACK: Listen, Carol. When I got these attacks, I sure didn't want to get fucked, and I can't believe it was my aggression.
CAROL: We've got to think of these events, your difficulty breathing, we've got to think of them in terms of *guilt*, of your wanting to *punish* yourself. We need to get in touch with your conflict . . . (Young 1995, p. 245, emphasis in the original)

Jack's initial story calls upon a commonplace clinical vocabulary for describing the psychic distress that started in Vietnam. His use of "panic attack" to portray his experience is neither clinically incorrect, nor commonsensically unfamiliar. Nonetheless, Carol moves to bring the articulation of the problem under the discursive purview of the model, asking Jack to think back to how he had originally been taught to conceptualize his problem "using the terms of the model." She continues to specify just what the model might say in relation to Jack's problems, only to be interrupted by Jack's assertion that the model didn't seem to apply in this case. Insisting that he felt that neither his libidinal drives ("I sure didn't want to get fucked") nor his instinct toward aggression ("I can't believe it was my aggression") was behind his condition, Jack resists the application of the model. Carol, however, perseveres, insisting that "we've got to think of them" in terms specified by the model. While resistance is always possible and often succeeds, the model—as a narrative resource—is a constant presence, a source of interpretive control asserted as the reigning institutional discourse.

The Complex Interplay of Self Construction

The intersection of discursive practice and discourses-in-practice is the operating space within which self construction takes place. How the self can be storied, the means by which self construction is interactionally accomplished, what types of stories are locally preferred or most accountable, the dimensions of self that are locally salient, and what language of the self is situationally employed simultaneously converge in interpretive practice to articulate and form our identities.

Let us now put these together by illustrating the complex interplay of these discursive components. We turn to case studies of identity in an institutional environment, Alcoholics Anonymous, that distinctively embodies the self of the alcoholic. We've already mentioned AA in our earlier discussion of narrative practice and now return to it to explicate more fully the complexities of self construction at its practical crossroads.

AA's Local Culture

We first return to Norman Denzin's (1986, 1987a, 1987b) studies of self construction in AA. Denzin observed three treatment centers that utilized AA principles, documenting the biographical workings of AA groups in over two thousand open and closed meetings. By immersing himself in this environment, Denzin was able to describe an array of interpretive resources that participants use in making sense of their lives, experiences, and, most central to our interests, themselves. The most salient and significant resource was the language of treatment and recovery that he found permeating—and constituting—the AA environment, forming a discourse of considerable local reckoning.

Denzin explains that the language of AA emanates from AA's "Big Book" (Alcoholics Anonymous 1976)—the most important statement of the AA program and philosophy. This language suffuses the AA literature as well as the formal and informal talk of AA leaders, lecturers, and members. The now familiar "Twelve Steps"—found on the first page of AA texts—set the tone:

THE TWELVE STEPS
1. We admitted we were powerless over alcohol—that our lives had become unmanageable.
2. Came to Believe that a Power greater than ourselves could restore us to Sanity.
3. Made a decision to turn our will and our lives over to the care of God *as we understood Him.*
4. Made a searching and fearless moral inventory of ourselves.
5. Admitted to God, to ourselves, and to another human being the exact nature of our wrongs.
6. Were entirely ready to have God remove all these defects of character.
7. Humbly asked Him to remove all our shortcomings.
8. Made a list of all persons we had harmed, and became willing to make amends to them all.
9. Made direct amends to such people whenever possible, except when to do so would injure them or others.
10. Continued to take personal inventory and when we were wrong, promptly admitted it.
11. Sought through prayer and meditation to improve our conscious contact with God *as we understood Him,* praying only for knowledge of His will for us and the power to carry that out.
12. Having had a spiritual awakening as the result of these steps, we tried to carry

this message to alcoholics, and to practice these principles in all our affairs. (Alcoholics Anonymous 1953, p. 2, emphasis in the original)

Denzin (1987a) argues that AA's fundamental lexicon of subjectivity—its institutional language of self construction—emanates from this text. It consists of a distinctive vocabulary that gives shape to persons constituted within this discourse:

These Twelve Steps contain the following problematic terms and phrases: admitted, powerless, "lives had become unmanageable," restore, sanity, will, "lives," "care of God," "as we understood him," searching, fearless, "moral inventory," "admitted to God," "exact nature," "wrongs," "entirely ready," remove, "defects of character," humbly," shortcomings, "persons we had harmed," "make amends," (direct amends), "injure," personal inventory, wrong, prayer, meditation, conscious contact, pray, "knowledge of his will for us," "power to carry that out," "spiritual awakening," carry this message, "practice these principles in all our affairs." (Denzin 1987a, p. 45, punctuation as in the original)

Denzin (1987a, p. 46) contends that this language and the meanings it conveys "permeates as a threatening presence, every interaction that occurs between patients and their counselors" during treatment at the centers he observed. It carries over into the discourse found in other AA settings, including the myriad meetings AA participants typically attend.

Denzin's catalog of terms encapsulates AA's interpretive vocabulary. The terminology offers familiar and available narrative resources that stand ready for accountable use in the countless circumstances where AA—its principles, practices, or participants—might be made salient. While the language may not be formally imposed, its use is so pervasive that persons and their experiences typically come to be storied in its terms.

Narrative Maps

According to AA, alcoholism manifests itself in physical deterioration, emotional illness, and moral or spiritual emptiness. Physically, alcoholics have an obsessive craving for alcohol that produces an allergy-like reaction in their bodies. Among other things, this causes them to lose control of their drinking. As obvious as the symptoms may become, self-delusion and denial prevent the alcoholic from realizing that a problem exists. Recovery requires complete abstinence from alcohol and an admission that one is powerless to resist it. At the same time, one must admit a power greater than one's self into one's life. The "alcoholic ego" must be renounced as the recovering alcoholic surrenders to a "spiritual" way of life (Denzin 1987b). In other words, the AA philosophy, culture, and vocabulary offer what Pollner and Stein (1996) call "narrative maps" for navigating and recounting the experiential and psychological terrain of alcoholism. These maps point the way for stories of the AA self.

The self, of course, is central to AA treatment and recovery and is foregrounded in most of AA's narrative maps. Indeed, AA traces excessive, addictive alcohol consumption to an illness of the self, an "emotional illness" that involves unsound thinking structures, difficulties with letting go of the past, and obsession with drinking (Denzin 1987b). The "Big Book" calls for the circulation of AA stories that describe AA participants and their experiences. It explicitly recognizes the importance of narrating the AA self in "personal stories" told in AA terms: "only by fully disclosing ourselves and our problems will others in need be persuaded to say, 'Yes, I am one of them too; I must have this thing'" (Alcoholics Anonymous 1976, p. 29). It's not surprising, then, that talk of the self is prominent in AA lectures and meetings. Denzin argues that AA treatment and participation are largely about narratively reformulating the alcoholic self into an AA self.

That reformulation is expressly linked to the AA philosophy as embodied in the Twelve Steps. The going concern here is a self articulated "step by step" with the program's formal principles mapping out how the self might be reconstructed. This is evident, for example, in the following self inventory offered by Jack, a member of an AA recovery group. Asked to share the meaning of his AA experiences with the entire group of recovering alcoholics, Jack frames his story this way:

> Step One. I know I'm powerless over alcohol. I take one drink and I can't stop. My life must be unmanageable. I have bills up to the ceiling and the family is about to leave and I've been put on notice at work. Step Two. I want to believe in God. I used to but I got away from the Church. But this isn't the God of my church. It's different. I want a God of love and caring. I know I was crazy when I drank. The last time I went out, I ended up in a motel room across town under a different name. Now that's not sane!

> Step Three. I want somebody else to run my life. A.A. and treatment seem to be doing a pretty good job right now, I hope I can stay with it. (Denzin 1987a, p. 70)

This brief self narrative is sequentially structured by the Twelve Steps. The AA principles virtually dictate the way the self is storied in this instance; they are a veritable set of rules for self characterization. Just as a topographical map shows users how to locate one's self within a geographical domain, AA's narrative map locates self presentation precisely and specifically in relation to AA's experiential landmarks.

Resources-in-Use

While not always so clearly delineated step-wise, testimonials to the emergence of an AA self abound in AA circles. They embellish AA literature and pervade nearly all AA-related discussions. Regardless of venue, the selves that emerge under AA's auspices draw upon a shared stock of interpretive resources from which selves may be crafted. If self construction is always artful, it invariably reflects the organizational materials from which selves are produced. This combination of common resources, artfully articulated, gives us the possibility of individualized selves that nonetheless bear a striking resemblance in the way they are structured. We can see this across the AA experience, in written and spoken narratives of the AA self. For example, consider the following portion of a classic story told by a recovered AA "luminary" in the Big Book. Known only as "Number Three," he reconstructs his experience of being hospitalized for intoxication for the eighth time in six months.

> ... I lay there on that hospital bed and went back over and reviewed my life. I thought of what liquor had done to me, the opportunities that I had discarded, the abilities that had been given me and how I had wasted them.... I was willing to admit to myself that I had hit bottom, that I had gotten hold of something that I didn't know how to handle by myself. So, after reviewing these things and realizing what liquor had cost me, I went to this Higher Power which to me, was God, without any reservation, and admitted that I was completely powerless over alcohol, and that I was willing to do anything in the world to get rid of the problem. In fact, I admitted that from now on I was willing to let God take over, instead of me. Each day I would try to find out what His will was, and try to follow that, rather than trying to get Him to always agree that the things I thought of myself were the things best for me. (Alcoholics Anonymous 1976, pp. 186–87)

Compare this with a housewife's account of her self-image and her fight to quit drinking:

> I had problems. We all have them, and I thought a little brandy or a little wine now and then could certainly hurt no one.... But from one or two drinks of an afternoon or evening, my intake mounted and mounted fast. It wasn't long before I was drinking all day.... I should have realized that alcohol was getting hold of me when I started to become secretive in my drinking.... I had to hide.... I needed it and I knew I was drinking too much, but I wasn't conscious of the fact that I should stop.... I needed that alcohol. I couldn't live without it. I couldn't do anything without it. I couldn't do it [quit drinking] among my relatives, I couldn't do it among my friends. No one likes to admit they're a drunk, that they can't control this thing.... [After beginning to attend AA meetings] It was at that point that I reached surrender. I heard one very ill woman say that she didn't believe in the surrender part of the AA program. My heavens! Surrender to me has meant the ability to run my home, to face my responsibilities as they should be faced, to take life as it comes to me day by day.... Since I gave my will over to AA, whatever AA has wanted of me I've tried to do to the best of my ability ... life for me is lived one day at a time, letting the problems of the future rest with the future. When the time comes to solve them, God will give me strength for that day. (Alcoholics Anonymous 1976, pp. 336–41)

While not identical, these self-presentational stories draw upon similar themes, idioms, and vocabularies; in other words, they employ the same narrative maps. The first story is a virtual recitation—in the language of AA—of the prototype alcoholic's story.[12] The language of the Twelve Steps and the terminology Denzin catalogs above are apparent at every narrative turn, serving as the discursive building blocks of the story depicting the descending alcoholic, his or her self-realization, and eventual recovery. While the second story draws less explicitly upon the language of AA, it, too, is assembled out of the primary interpretive resources AA makes available to its participants for understanding their lives. Available resources clearly do not determine how selves are storied; individual circumstances, biographical particulars, experiential variability, and interpretive inventiveness and discretion are at play at every turn. Still, it is equally clear that AA self stories are adroitly crafted from a common stock of interpretive building blocks.

The narrative mediation of local cultural resources is most visible when viewed comparatively. Consider, for example, how AA selves are distinctively constructed in contrast with the way members of a Secular Sobriety Group (SSG) narrate themselves (see Christopher 1988). The following extract recounts a conversation between an SSG member and some friends. Note how the narrator expressly assembles aspects of self out of the particular set of resources, and in relation to the specific organizational orientations, that his SSG membership provides for him:

"What exactly is it you do to stay sober? I mean is it a state of mind, or what?" My two friends were interested in a new Secular Sobriety Group I'd recently started. . . . I explained as best I could that our priority is staying sober and that we met once a week in a friendly, informal candlelit atmosphere to share our thoughts and feelings as alcoholics living sober.

"As you know," I said, "I've never kept my alcoholism a secret. I'm proud of my sobriety. Some other things in my life I'm not so pleased with, but sobriety is my most precious asset, my priority, my life-and-death necessity. . . . Now, from a factual perspective, I am just as alcoholic as I was prior to achieving sobriety; that is, I must reaffirm my priority of staying sober *no matter what!* I go to the market, work, see movies, make love, eat, sleep—all as a sober alcoholic. I'm a person with an arrested but lifelong disease. I place my sobriety and the necessity of staying sober before anything else in my life. . . . Alcoholism results in the inability to control one's drinking. Sobriety requires the acknowledgment of one's alcoholism on a daily basis, and it is never to be taken for granted. I must endure all my feelings and experiences, including injustices, failures, and whatever this uncertain life doles out. . . .

"So," I continued, "in answer to your questions: I have my alcohol problem licked only on a daily basis and I continue to stay alive by protecting my conscious mind, by staying sober and avoiding the muddy waters of religion. I can't deal with reality by way of fantasy.

"A.A. and other groups fight demons with dogma or gods or the 'powers' of belief and faith. That's too scary for me. The more I stay in reality, in rationality, the better my chances. So, yes, my sobriety is a state of mind rather than mindlessness." (Christopher 1988, pp. 87–88, emphasis in the original)

Clearly the SSG has a different view of personal control than that offered by AA. Most prominently, of course, are differences with respect to spirituality. The SSG, however, also offers a distinct set of resources for conceptualizing and expressing the "alcoholic self." These resources comprise a vocabulary of self-reliance, individual responsibility, and rationality—the discourse of secular humanism. In practice, this translates into self constructions different from those assembled under the auspices of AA. As we can see in the preceding extract, the self is conceived in terms of personal responsibility, unlike the AA self, which comes into its own only by surrendering to a higher power. In SSG terms, the self is the locus of human will, which stands in stark, binary opposition to the resignation of will that the AA self embraces. The "conscious mind" is the center of self-control, in contrast with the AA self, which abandons control in favor of divine guidance. In SSG culture, the self is firmly grounded in secular reality as opposed to the AA self, which centers itself in spirituality. Indeed, the two recovery organizations provide SSG adherents with sharply contrasting interpretive resources and descriptive vocabularies, whose binary opposition itself contributes to the production of distinctly different selves.

Conventions and Constraints

The discourse of AA virtually "speaks" the selves interpretively constituted under AA auspices, providing the resources and directions for narrating their lives. Persons in AA groups progress through several structured "stages" of treatment and recovery. This progression expressly requires participants to learn to confront and define the alcoholism experience in AA terms. Not only does this involve the formulation of experiences in relation to the AA model of alcoholism and recovery, but it also requires a conventionalized self-presentational style. AA group meetings, according to Denzin, typically involve over a dozen discrete elements, from opening salutations to prayers, announcements, discussions of pressing topics and issues, and closing remarks. Not only must group members become familiar with the meeting format, but they must learn how and when they may speak, what they may speak about, and how they might present their thoughts, concerns, and beliefs in relation to the business at hand.

The institutional preferences for particular forms of talk are evident from the initial introductions at an AA meeting. Denzin takes us inside the first meeting of a therapy group, where the counselor introduces herself, then invites other participants to do the same:

> "My name is Alice and I'm an alcoholic. Welcome to First Step Group. Let's go around the room and introduce ourselves. Mary, you go first."

> "My name's Mary Jones." Alice cuts in. "No, your name is Mary and you are an alcoholic. We don't want to know your last name." . . . Mary corrects herself. "My name's Mary and I'm an alcoholic." Mary starts to cry, turning away from the group, trembling. The group looks away. Alice turns to Mary and says: "That's O.K. We all had to say it for the first time." (Denzin 1987a, p. 64)

From the very start, we witness overt narrative control as the self is storied. Persons are told that they will be known by first names only. Their identities are limited to this, and to the admission that each member is an "alcoholic." This convention for self presentation persists throughout AA meetings; the now widely familiar AA mantra of "My name is X and I'm an alcoholic" sets the stage for subsequent constructions of the self.

Storytelling is continually reinforced and reasserted through the myriad institutionalized ways in which AA culture and narrative maps are conveyed to new members. As we've seen, newcomers are explicitly trained in the traditions of AA through lessons, literature, and direct instruction. Experienced members informally draw narrative maps for neophytes as they convey "cartographic pre-

presentations" of the ways and workings of the as-yet-unknown world of AA (Pollner and Stein 1996). The basis for asserting a way of viewing the world, argue Pollner and Stein (1996), derives from a variety of different practices for accumulating knowledge. The essence of "expert" mappings, they suggest, is found in the trained and credentialed mastery of texts and techniques. The psychoanalytic therapist, for example, would qualify as an expert in mapping thought and affect in psychodynamic terms. AA's "cartography," however, does not derive so much from expert sources as it does from "experiential" authority (Pollner and Stein 1996). Put simply, the "voice of experience" is credible because it appeals to having "been around."

According to Pollner and Stein, AA culture emphasizes that the program is sustained by how others have gone down the alcoholic path. Meaningful experience and its significance are reflexively established in the course of personal narratives offered in AA interactions. Such narratives establish experiential credentials for the teller, and work rhetorically to draw newcomers into exemplified cultural understandings. For example, in the following extract, an AA veteran suggests why his vision of the alcoholic experience is trustworthy.

> See I don't believe in counselors. And I don't believe in programs. Because uh, some counselors I've talked to didn't have my feelings. You see. You can't get my feelings out of reading a book. You can't get the hurt that I went through by reading a book. If I burned my finger with this cigarette lighter, and I say "aw damn that hurt," you don't really know that really hurt 'til you've burned your finger. . . . Some of you have never felt the cold, go down to that Q-Street park tonight and lay down under that hedgerow. With nothin'. And then you'll have the feeling. Then you can talk about the feeling. But you can't talk about somethin' you know nothin' about. And I'm a firm believer that you have to, you've got to have been there. . . . If you haven't been there, you can't tell me about it. (Pollner and Stein 1996, pp. 207–8)

Personal experience, we hear from this speaker, is the sole source of authenticity, the only way one can truly know and understand the AA experience. Pollner and Stein contend that the voice of experience is *the* credentialed voice of AA. Qualifications to speak in these terms may be claimed in several different ways, but the "bottom line" is that AA's narrative maps are to be conveyed by and learned from those who have traversed the territory. Narrative auspices are thus asserted in the name of "having been there."

"Being there" at AA meetings invites further institutional constraints on how self construction may proceed. As we've already noted, meetings have a pre-specified format and develop through a variety of interactional conventions. As multiparty, task-oriented interactions, group meetings require some adjustments of the turn-taking "rules" of everyday conversation if the business at hand is to be efficiently completed. Without modification, speakership transfer would be quite complicated and distinct lines of talk might fail to emerge efficiently. Group sessions rely upon special devices for managing these problems so that the activities that come to be seen as a "meeting" emerge in recognizable form (see Atkinson and Drew 1979, Dingwall 1980, Holstein 1993). Some of these are explicitly set out in formal rules that supplant typical expectations for turn-taking. For example, Denzin (1987b) notes that in open-discussion segments of meetings where self revelations often emerge, speakership typically is designated by the group leader, at least at the outset. As each speaker is designated, the familiar personal introduction format launches each story in a similar fashion. Consider the following discussion that "Cl," the chair, begins by asking for a topic for discussion.

CL: Does anyone have any problems or topics for discussion?

TN: I do. Twelve Stepping [Proceeding through the twelfth step of the AA process—"Having had a spiritual awakening as the result of these steps, we tried to carry this message to alcoholics, and to practice these principles in all our affairs."]. I have a problem. I got a neighbor who is fighting this thing. I've talked to him several times. . . . [Discusses the neighbor's situation] I'd like to hear your thoughts on this.

WS: I'm Ws. I'm an alcoholic. I wasn't going to speak today. Eight years ago today they took me to the fifth floor. Not the second, not the third, but straight to the fifth. The floor for the crazies. I was Twelve Stepped while I was there. You had a successful Twelve Step, Tn. You came back sober. You carried the message. . .

KHY: I'm Khy. I'm an alcoholic. I don't know what got me sober. It was many different things. It had to be the sum that was greater than its parts. It was 10% this part, 20% this part. It was things I did and didn't do. I know that it finally worked and it worked when I was ready. I don't know how it worked. I don't think it is any specific thing.

CL: I'm Cl. I'm an alcoholic. Two-and-a-half months ago my father killed himself. The day of the night before he killed himself I felt that something was wrong. I was at the club (city) and I called the man who got me into A.A. I said, do you need a meeting tonight? He said that he did. He came over and he told me, "I don't know if I should tell you this, but 10 years ago I took your father to some A.A. meetings." That made me feel good because I knew there was nothing I could do for my Dad.

DV: I'm Dv. I'm an alcoholic. I don't know. I'm working with someone right now. He's sober, sober then drunk, drunk, then sober, then drunk. I don't know what works. I know I was successfully Twelve Stepped. I hope to be able to do that someday. Thank you, I'm glad to be here today. . . .

JN: I'm Jn. I'm an alcoholic. My only advice to Tn is to be patient. It takes time. It may take several days for everything you said to sink in. Thank you.

DT: I'm Dt. I'm an alcoholic. I'm just glad to be sober and to be here today. Thank you Cl. (Denzin 1987b, pp. 111–12)

There are some notable patterns to this interactional sequence. Once under way with the personal introduction, each speaker continues uninterrupted until his or her brief story is completed. "Speaking out of turn" is expressly prohibited, and according to Denzin, everyone is expected to offer at least a brief story to the discussion. Each speaker talks for approximately one to three minutes (truncated in the extract), before bringing the story to a close.

The normative expectations for these discussions minimize the interactional work of managing speakership transfer, thus reducing the turn-by-turn effort required to narrate the self. The leader or chair is authorized to select next speakers if no one volunteers to speak at possible transition points. And the prohibition of interruption minimizes intrusions into an ongoing turn at talk. As we might recall from Chapter 7, however, speakership transfer is accountably possible at the end of each sentence unless the right to extend a turn at talk is claimed or signaled. The AA understanding that a speaker will continue until his or her story is complete provides this warrant. But the end of each turn must still somehow be signaled. As Denzin notes, in the AA groups, the end of a turn is often marked when the speaker explicitly thanks the group for letting him or her be present and speak. We can see this at the end of some of the stories in the extract above. Other turns simply end as the speaker falls silent, clearly inviting another speaker. If no one volunteers, the chair will select a next speaker.

These group discussions superficially take the form of dialogs relating to the topic at hand, but they are hardly ordinary conversations (as conversation analysts view it). Rather, they are a series of invited monologues ("drunkalogues") that allow each speaker the conversational space to offer an extended account. Conventional devices open and close each turn, and "protect" the middle of each turn—the emergent story—from intrusion or interruption. Denzin indicates, however, that the monologues are always addressed to the group, are of short duration, and move from one speaker to another until all members of the group have spoken. A full-blown monologue, then, is unlikely to emerge; instead we hear what Denzin calls "one-way dialog" with individuals sequentially addressing the group, which does not directly respond to any particular speaker. In this way, space for storytelling is created, a space that tolerates only particular kinds of stories and storytelling.

Denzin also identifies several conventions relating to the typical *content* of AA discussions that he calls "The Prose" of the group. Among other things, Denzin notes that each speaker stays on topic, taking up the issue introduced by the initial speaker and relating it to his own experience. Each individual personalizes the issue, bringing his or her own biographical particulars to bear on the discussion. The stories that emerge all express gratitude for being sober as well as thanks to the group for being present. Pollner and Stein (1996) make similar observations about the content of the drunkalogues they observed in AA meetings. They add that AA stories frequently convey information about the social world of AA, and often do so in chronological order, building stories from the past into the present. Pollner and Stein explain that the stories suggest that general patterns should be inferred from the particular experiences recalled. They observe that AA stories often center on the difficult paths to sobriety and the pitfalls that must always be navigated. Using their analytic imagery of narrative mapping, they summarize that stories of alcoholic selves and experiences are guided by AA's interpretive culture, call upon AA's descriptive resources, and utilize AA's narrative maps as guides for reality construction.

Taken together, these observations reveal the complex interplay of self construction in the going concern that is AA. The institutional discourse, Denzin suggests, "is an individual and collective production that speaks the language of ordinary people woven through the understandings of A.A." (1987a, p. 113). The AA self is told through AA's discursive format, following AA's narrative maps.

> These are not the utterances of the workplace, the home, the telephone, the letter, the hospital emergency room, the psychiatrist's office, or group therapy. . . . [AA stories are] embedded in the sequential talk of A.A. members doing an A.A. meeting. The sequentiality, the biographical detail, the hovering presence of alcohol as an organizing "Third Party," and the shared constraints of A.A. tradition and ritual serve to produce a structure of "understanding" discourse that is perhaps unique to A.A. meetings. (Denzin 1987a, pp. 113–14)

The self is thus deprivatized, embodying an identity made apparent through the complex, socially conditioned work of putting a discourse into practice.

CHAPTER NINE

Material Mediations

A ccording to Erving Goffman (1959), ordinary actors bring selves into view by taking account of, managing, and developing their performances in relation to fellow actors, audiences, and the settings in which the performances unfold. The presentation of self is practical in that it's not fully scripted as a stage production might be, but, rather, performatively wends its way through the everyday interactive contingencies of being who and what we are. Changes in one's working identity that come with sudden shifts of audience or the unexpected physical rearrangement of a social setting are exemplary. Goffman's view is that people manage their identities, and he repeatedly reminds us that this doesn't settle upon any final form, which we have taken to heart in formulating our story.

For Goffman, some of the most important performative contingencies are the material features of a social setting, such as stigmatized bodies, posture, demeanor, closed doors and similar barriers to perception, furniture arrangements, lighting, and other corporeal or environmental props that might be used to communicate a particular narrative. These, Goffman argues, play as much a role in the work of self presentation as do talk, interaction, emotional expression, or the frames that mediate them. Subjectivity, in other words, is embedded in the material features of a performance, sometimes quite firmly so. It is part and parcel of how we scenically signal who we are to others and, in turn, how they similarly interpret who we are being for the purposes at hand (see Goffman 1959, Chapter 3).

Following Goffman's suggestions, we turn to this material world to see how its related circumstantial *whats* mediate self construction.[1] The physical context of interaction is our point of departure, but records and texts of various kinds, such as patient charts, school reports, advice books, glamour magazines, behavior assessments, and test results, are an increasingly important part of the material scene, well beyond what Goffman envisioned just a few decades ago. So are auditory and visual paraphernalia, such as tape recordings of counseling sessions and video cassette reenactments of domestic situations, and websites of every conceivable variety, as we noted earlier. All of these, in one way or another, add to today's self narratives. The material conditions that Goffman himself focused upon remain with us and are now just as likely to be encountered in the many institutional records, texts, and visual images we listen to, read, or watch as we story the selves we are or could be.

What Goffman discerned from the perspective of the 1950s, Dorothy Smith (1990) describes as ubiquitous in the current identity landscape; varied and sundry inscriptions of selves often quite unwittingly specify particular personas for us.

It is now difficult even to describe social organization separate from what Smith calls "textual mediation." Sociologists who focus on what, for them, are broader social forces typically ignore these mediations because they are so local and ordinary. Echoing Foucault and implicating her own text, Smith writes:

> The phenomenon with which [I] am concerned is one to which sociology has been extraordinarily blind. It is also ubiquitous—at least in contemporary society. We [our selves] are constantly implicated in and active in it—indeed this chapter, this book you're reading, are among its manifestations. It is the phenomenon of textually mediated communication, action, and social relations. As intellectuals we take it for granted much as we take for granted the ground we walk on or the air we breathe. Yet it not only constitutes both the arena and the means of our professional work, but permeates our everyday world in other ways. We get passports, birth certificates, parking tickets; we fill in forms to apply for jobs, for insurance, for dental benefits; we are given grades, diplomas, degrees; we pay bills and taxes; we read and answer advertisements; we order from menus in restaurants, take a doctor's prescription to the drugstore, write letters to newspapers; we watch television, go to the movies, and so on and so on. Our lives are, to a more extensive degree than we care to think, infused with a process of inscription, producing printed or written traces or working from them. (P. 209)

The panopticon of contemporary identity is not just figurative, but takes discernible material form. This textually laden material world, of course, doesn't stand on its own; it doesn't determine our identities in some independent fashion, as if it were separate and distinct from the practical work that is done to read, listen to, observe, and "silently" narrate what its paraphernalia present to us. But it nonetheless is there and mediates the construction of selves in its own terms. It's a topic worth pursuing, lest we disembody and dislodge the self from its everyday physical moorings, putting it on material holiday.

The Material-in-Use

As many of our illustrations will show, material resources are ubiquitously available for narrative application (cf. Hodder 1994). An ordinary object like a ticking clock, for example, can be used to represent one's self in relation to pressing decisions that loom ahead in one's life. We find just such an instance in a study of Alzheimer's disease sufferers and their caregivers (Gubrium 1986a). In the middle of a support group discussion of the burdens of home care, the wife of a dementia sufferer describes the difficulty of deciding whether to place her husband in a nursing home. Pointing to a ticking clock, she remarks, "That there clock's me. It'll keep ticking away until it's time [to decide] and won't stop for a minute, until it winds down, I guess." As we listen, we learn that for the wife and others, "winding down" signifies the gradual decline of the increasingly burdened caregiving wife who doesn't keep an eye on the proverbial clock. She needlessly wastes away, martyring herself for someone who has become the "mere shell" of his former self.

The clock and the empty shell are culturally recognizable symbols conscripted for self description. Their familiar characteristics metaphorically yet concretely convey to the wife and those with whom she is communicating what the experience of dementia care is like, on the one hand, and what the dementia sufferer becomes, on the other. The clock visibly represents a self whose incessant temporal progression into ill health might not be readily communicated on its own. The empty shell of the dementia sufferer signifies a different subjectivity—an emptiness within. But usage isn't idiosyncratic. Both objects referenced in this instance—the ticking clock and the empty shell—are virtual cultural clichés, presumably recognizable to other competent members of society, and certainly familiar to those who have participated in the growing public culture of the Alzheimer's disease movement (Gubrium 1986a).

Appropriated to storytelling, material objects are used much like literary metaphors, as devices for understanding and experiencing one thing in terms of another (Lakoff and Johnson 1980). Using ordinary material objects metaphorically allows us to borrow or transfer meaning between interpretive realms. We import the everyday in order to interpret the equally ordinary, especially when the latter is ineffable because, as it's sometimes explained, "You just can't put it in words." Consider the way a common metaphor is developed from a weed that happens to catch someone's eye during a discussion in another caregiver support group meeting (Gubrium 1986a). One of the authors had been observing this group for several months and this was the first time the metaphor of the "hardy weed" was applied to the caregiving experience. Eventually, this material object was widely inferred to be the self in question. The following extract starts in the midst of a discussion of the personal energy it takes to be a responsible caregiver. Coincidentally, one of the participants, Maude, notices a plant growing vigorously into the room from under a door to the outside. Other members of the group—Henry, Vera, Sam, and Anne—respond.

MAUDE: Would you look over there at that!
SAM: What? What're you looking at? The door?
MAUDE: Sam, the weed. That little weed over there. See it. It's growing under the door from the outside.
HENRY: It's coming into the room for shelter. It's getting nippy out there and wants to come in.
MAUDE: That weed's got it rough out there by that busy street. [Elaborates] But it's makin' it. All that dust, grime, and traffic. It's hard on a weed. Kinda like us, I guess I was thinkin'. All the energy it takes. If we didn't have that kind of energy, we'd be dead by now.
VERA: All shriveled and dried up. No good to no one.
SAM: Ya got to give it to the weed. It's a survivor.
ANNE: Well, I ain't a weed. But if that's what it takes, ya keep right on agrowin' and gettin' to where you can survive and keep going. [Elaborates] Gosh, sometimes I think I won't be able to make it. He's [her demented spouse] gettin' awful heavy and he really can't help me any more. I'm going to

need all the strength of that there old dandelion plant or I ain't goin' to make it.

MAUDE: If that weed can make it, so can we. That's what I'm thinking. You've gotta get up all your strength and just do it! [Getting up from her chair] I think I'll give that little old weed some water. We all need a boost and a bit of kindness, right? (Gubrium and Holstein 1995b, p. 564)

As the discussion turns to other matters, the group doesn't forget the weed; members refer back to this material reminder of their challenges as caregivers. Whenever the topic of persistence or endurance comes up, they use the weed to describe the kind of person it takes to deal with the trials and tribulations of dementia care on a daily basis. In subsequent meetings, as the weather quickly changes and the weed withers, the group methodically alters its metaphorical usage, establishing new meanings that apply to different aspects of the individuals involved. Members use the weed's withered condition to warn of possible things to come, of the rigors and stress of caregiving. They now see the weed in the context of the progressive outcome of becoming physically and emotionally overwhelmed, poignantly conveying the weed's embodiment of the gradual but inevitable exhaustion of the caregiver.

Whether the weed is used in simile-like fashion ("Kinda like us") to fashion the self, or serves as a concrete object of negative comparison ("Well, I ain't a weed"), it is a very ordinary resource for understanding the identity referenced by those gathered together in the group. Calling upon common cultural understandings of the material object, they use the *hardy* weed to represent, even glorify, dimensions of self, conferring stamina and persistence upon themselves, individually and collectively. They summon another ordinary image, of a *withered* weed, to convey something decidedly less sanguine in relation to the burdens of care that seem to mount in caregivers' lives. Contrasting narrative projects demand artfully variable usage, the results of which show how a material object can be brought to bear on self construction in extraordinary ways.

Scenic Presence

The sheer scenic presence of social interaction shapes the way identity is conveyed. The self is not just sensitive to the interactions in which it unfolds, but it also is mediated by the settings in which it finds itself. As Goffman (1959, p. 252) reminds us, "[The self] derives from the whole scene of [its] action." Television soap operas, for example, make a fine art of this as they manage the scenic presence of their characters' actions to make meaning and, in the process, cast the identities of the characters in one way or another. It makes considerable narrative difference for the identities in question, for example, whether an embrace is situated in a dimly lit motel room or on the sunny steps of a wedding chapel.

Goffman (1959) is masterful at portraying the self's scenic presence. Of course, he's careful not to suggest that the material mediations of time, space, and physical objects determine identities, but he nonetheless finds it insufficient to presume that identity can be constructed solely out of talk and interaction. Indeed, in practice, natural mediations can cause us to act as if the premises themselves were telling us something. The scenes of everyday life are as much present in defining who and what we are, as we ostensibly are in our own spoken rights. The intensity, certainty, and verisimilitude of our conduct and of the selves we take for granted can be virtually bound up in their scenic presence.

A simple doorway, for example, can prompt as much satisfaction as consternation, as it mediates the identities of work life in an ordinary setting. Goffman describes the mediating presence of the doors leading from the Shetland Hotel kitchen to its public areas as this enlightens the identities of the maids and managers who go back and forth between them. In the following extract, he explains in particular how much the open status of the doors marks the scene's working selves.

> Given, then, the various ways in which activity in the kitchen contradicted the impression fostered in the guests' region of the hotel, one can appreciate why the doors leading from the kitchen to the other parts of the hotel were a constant sore spot in the organization of work. The maids wanted to keep the doors open to make it easier to carry food trays back and forth, to gather information about whether guests were ready or not for the service which was to be performed for them, and to retain as much contact as possible with the persons they had come to work to learn about. Since the maids played a servant role before the guests, they felt they did not have too much to lose by being observed in their own milieu by guests who glanced into the kitchen when passing the open doors. The managers, on the other hand, wanted to keep the doors closed so that the middle-class role imputed to them by the guests would not be discredited by a disclosure of their kitchen habits. Hardly a day passed when these doors were not angrily banged shut and angrily pushed open. (P. 118)

The Scenic Presence of Troubled Selves

What Goffman describes for the Shetland Hotel is commonplace and probably has been as long as there have been hotels, work life, and an associated discourse of status and identity. The lesson, of course, is that who we are is more bound to the scenic presence of our everyday lives than we might otherwise imagine. But there also is a historical element of contemporary relevance in this, which Smith, Foucault, and Lyotard, among others, point to in their discussions of the proliferating self-defining practices of institutional life. In today's world, the self is not only scenically revealed as one thing or another in relation to the daily rhythms of the work place, but it appears more and more in scenes whose central concern is the self itself, especially in troubled form.

For many years, Gubrium has studied the descriptive organization of personal troubles, focusing in part on the question of how the working context of description in settings such as clinics, nursing homes, psychiatric hospitals, and counseling centers mediates the identities of those in treatment. Staff members in these settings assessed problems ranging from physical disability, dementia, and mental illness to behavioral and emotional difficulties, in effect by doing practical readings of the self. Selves, of course, were not directly accessible to those concerned (social workers, nurses, doctors, psychologists, speech therapists, individual and family counselors, support group facilitators, relatives, and the troubled persons themselves), but were considered to be more or less hidden in the private, inner worlds of those in treatment. What was directly available—as indicators for, symbols of, and testaments to troubled lives—were situated representations of experience, and it is to these we turn to illustrate the scenic presence of troubled selves.

Take the seemingly trivial objects surrounding therapeutic activity at Fairview Hospital as a case in point (Gubrium 1992). We focus on the material mediations of patients' selves, even while the subjectivity of staff members is discursively implicated in the broader scheme of things. The hospital applies a gamut of treatment modalities, including the Twelve Steps, parenting skills, "toughlove" strategies, and assertiveness training. Fairview offers both inpatient and outpatient counseling for behavioral and substance abuse problems for individuals of various ages, and family members are encouraged to be involved in treatment. Besides counseling staff and individual patients of record (sometimes called "identified patients" or IPs because the family is typically viewed as the "actual" patient), sessions usually include relatives, friends, and significant others.

Let's enter a meeting room on the chemical dependency unit, which is scheduled for multifamily counseling. The therapist accompanying us has commented that there will be a gathering of approximately six to eight patients in treatment for various substance abuses. Concerned family members, intimates, and a few others will also attend. The therapist stops short before entering the room and states, in obvious exasperation, "This is gonna be a three-boxer." Sighing, she turns around and heads for a nearby supply cabinet and searches for something among the large packages and plastic containers. After what seems to be an interminable delay, she locates three "family-size" boxes of tissues, and jokes, "You need family-size for family therapy." One or two won't do, because, she explains, "I know this group."

While it might not be evident at the moment what tissue boxes have to do with the forthcoming proceedings, let alone the self, it will soon be clear that the staff will discern the group's success in admitting to spoiled identities from the amount of tissues used to wipe away tears. Tissue usage will be part of the material mediations of identity in the drama about to unfold. Among other things, usage will represent participants' denial or surrender to what they have become—unrepentant or recovering addicts, codependents, or dysfunctional families, as the case might be. The therapist is not about to actually see selves in tissue usage, but she does figure that usage signals both what she's up against and what she is about to accomplish, all bearing on the identities in question.

We enter the room and greet those in attendance. The therapist places two tissue boxes across the room from her and keeps one at her side. She herself won't weep during the session, but she expects to offer tissue to several participants who will. She'll use about a fourth of a box for that purpose and, while it might seem trivial to point that out, that fact will be a credit to her success, when she responds to questions such as "How did the multifamily session go yesterday?"

with references to how much weeping transpired and tissue usage there was as a result. Indeed, on one occasion, after a lively and "really heartrending" session, a member of the custodial staff, a long-time employee who was well acquainted with the therapists on the chemical dependency unit, commented as she emptied the wastebaskets in the room in which the session was held, "That musta been quite a session you had there, Connie. [Nods toward the wastebasket] Lots of tears I can see."

Another therapy room down the hall is a bit larger, with the usual chairs, lamps, tables, tissue boxes, and assorted literature, but there's a significant difference in the surroundings. Along one of the walls near the windows is a bookcase with a few books, pamphlets, and two shelves lined with teddy bears. There's nothing extraordinary about the teddy bears. They're brownish, over a foot tall, and fuzzy. But this is still the chemical dependency unit and it seems strange to find teddy bears here. It would be understandable in the adolescent services unit, but this is adult space, indeed therapy space for adults who are having deep and abiding anxieties about life, not to mention their addictions. Families here are said to be "dysfunctional." Some of those in treatment have lost jobs or are in serious jeopardy of being fired. Health risks abound. Can the teddy bears be just toys? What can they possibly have to do with the self?

Tissues. Tissue boxes. Teddy bears. Tears. All are located in a space where selves are in question and identity is ostensibly in shambles. It's a space formally designated for healing egos "reduced to nothing" and "self-esteem at rock bottom," as a pamphlet in the bookcase reads in bold print. Other pamphlets and books have similar telegraphic phrases splashed across their covers: "Dysfunctional families need help!" "Booze and drugs don't pay!" "Love can be a killer!" "Toughlove's the answer!" Exclamation points convey profound loss and personal urgency. It's clear that difficult problems lurk about the room. Their material texts convey this to us in concise and visible terms. This, too, is a healing place; it's Fairview Hospital. Can we surmise that the teddy bears are part of the material apparatus of recovery? What about the tissues? They couldn't possibly relate to the teddy bears? Teddy bears don't weep. Or do they?

Looking around the room, we find other items that, at first blush, seem out of place. There are several hand mirrors laid face down on a corner table. The backs of the mirrors are decorated with floral designs. One has roses, another has pansies. Again, this seems odd, because this is a hospital, not a boudoir. Browsing along, we spot other pamphlets and several copies of paperback books whose titles speak of love, loving, and women's lives. The general topic is evident: the texts are about women in love. Their message quickly becomes clear: this is a healing place for "women who love too much," a phrase that appears on a few books and pamphlets. But how do the mirrors and teddy bears figure in? How do they scenically mediate the topic, the messages, and the selves in question?

Fast forward a bit in time. The room is now filling with women in their twenties and thirties, a few older. As each settles down in her place, we notice that most of the teddy bears have been taken from the bookcases and are now placed on the women's laps. A few bears are on the floor next to a chair. The conversation is chatty, with little or no reference at the moment to the teddy bears. As the therapist enters the room, one of the women mentions to another whose chair is located next to the table with the hand mirrors, "Kitty, don't forget the mirrors." Kitty gets the mirrors and places them on a table in the middle of the room; she apparently knows where they should go. No one mentions the mirrors for the time being. The women continue to chat among themselves; a few adjust their blouses and freshen their makeup. It's hot and humid outdoors and some are evidently cooling down. The therapist, who has just gotten one of the few remaining bears for herself, is about to speak. One of the women in the room whispers sharply to her neighbor, "Karen! Quick! Get your teddy!" Karen openly feigns forgetfulness, softly striking her forehead with the open palm of her hand, and reaches behind her chair to retrieve one of the remaining teddy bears in the bookcase.

The room quiets. Everyone's waiting for the proceedings to begin. Nothing's been said yet that deals directly with the women's problems, selves, or healing. Love hasn't even been mentioned, nor has the apparent fact that these women, in their fashion, love too much. Yet there now seems to be a well-established scenic presence to that effect. Our impression is that an emotional drama is about to unfold. This isn't a playroom. Children aren't hugging the teddy bears. Right now, in this place, adult women have the bears on their laps, seemingly waiting. Play doesn't wait in that fashion, at least not in this locale.

If little has been said, we've nonetheless already witnessed some important factors relating to self construction. If we weren't sensitive to the discursively artful side of self construction, we might be tempted to conclude at this point that the scene in the room will "speak" a particular discourse for its occupants, playing itself and its selves out in the women's forthcoming talk, gestures, and emotional expression—and be done with it. The momentary stillness in the room seems to be a prefatory testament to what is about to transpire. Everyone has taken her place, the props have been arranged, and the action is about to roll. The scene, it would seem, is set to "do" therapeutically available selves. In this context, Karen's feigned forgetfulness and her last-minute scramble to get her bear were remarkably telling, having tacitly signaled for the women that what they are about to perform and become is as much a matter of proper staging, as it is part of the serious business of self narration.

Fast forward again. It's mid-session. Women all around the room are softly crying. Some of them hug their teddy bears, a few others bend over in their chairs weeping with their teddy bears pressed into their laps. Some have tossed their teddy bears into the corner and are now attending to others, affectionately comforting them and helping to wipe away tears. One women, seated next to Karen, encourages her to cry, whispering kindly, "That's okay, baby. Go ahead and bawl. It'll do ya good." Another women picks up one of the hand mirrors to see "what the damage is," referring to her makeup and general appearance. Many are speaking to their teddy bears, some cursing, one actually punching the bear for all the heartache he's caused her over the years. It's apparent that these teddy bears are male, former or current lovers who have wrought a great deal of pain and distress, in part because the women love them too much.

A few women address their bears more sympathetically, calling them by their own names, stroking them, telling the bears that they understand what they've been through. One of the women admonishes her weeping bear to wake up and realize that her problem is as much her own as her boyfriend's. (Evidently, teddy bears do cry, too.) These teddy bears are female; indeed in momentary talk and interaction with the bears, they are the women themselves, women who love too much and who need the firm but sympathetic understanding of their holders.

Suddenly, there's a crescendo of tears, shouting, and animated handling of teddy bears and hand mirrors. The din and activity in the room are gradually setting a scene for dramatic realization. Nothing's been fully expressed in words yet, but in the context of the discourse at play and materials at hand, the selves the women have been deliberating are about to be put into discursive practice. Karen is the most expressive, and others turn their attention to her interactions with her teddy bear. She speaks to the bear about the hard times she's had being overly devoted to him. "No matter what I do, no matter how much I give, you gimme shit, just shit," she blurts out through tears and choking sobs. The therapist asks one of the women to hand Karen a mirror. Karen peers into the looking glass, sees herself, and notes, "Yeah, that's me, all right. Dumb, goofy Karen."

All eyes are now on Karen, just as they can focus on any woman who appears ready to "open her heart" to some form of self realization, which happens time and again in these sessions. While commonplace, the drama is instructive because its particular combination of material objects and actions seems to embody, in a matter of moments, the very discourse and experiential contours of the entire setting. Karen is silent for a while, but she sits uneasily, repeatedly adjusting herself in her chair. She holds the mirror in her right hand, about a foot away from her face. It's the mirror with the roses on the back. She holds the teddy bear by the neck in her left hand, steadying it on her knee. Tears glisten on her cheeks. The other women in the room and the therapist look on. An institutional mission, a formal therapy group, a room full of meaningful props, a gathering of sorrowful yet angry women, and a set of highly visible and poignant gestures combine to silently, yet palpably, present the momentary object of concern—Karen's deeply hurt and discredited self.

Within this materially larded and emotionally charged circumstance, Karen then speaks at length about herself, intermittently prompted by others in the room. As she does, we hear Karen's identity oscillate between being simply referenced and described, on the one hand, and being passionately charged, evaluated, and redeemed, on the other. Looking into the mirror, she affirms, "Yeah, that's me all right, sad, pitiful shithead." A woman seated a few chairs to her right declares, pointing to the back of the mirror, "Yeah, you're second-hand rose all right." There are a few chuckles as others take notice of the word play related to the roses on the back of the mirror. The therapist counsels, "Crying your heart out is good, but it ain't gonna make you face up to your co-dependency. You're doin' it to yourself and you gotta realize that. Take that next step or, bang, you're dead in the water." Karen responds, addressing the mirror and shaking it as she speaks, as if she were actually shaking herself,

Get it through you head, dipshit, you're the problem. Own the goddamn problem, girl! He's just the same ol' prick. He ain't the problem. You're the problem.
Look at you. Ya ain't worth the pot you piss in. Face it, girl, you sure as shit ain't
smellin' like a rose right now. Stop hanging onto those feelings. Get a hold of
yourself!

As Karen rails against herself, her actions seem to become the literal embodiment of Cooley's looking-glass self. In so many words, she tells those gathered
around her who she is—part of the problem, if not all of it. She evaluates her conduct, what she has been, and she feels degraded by what she's described and
judged. The looking glass (the hand mirror) materializes that for her. Here is a
self with distinct emotional contours, one that she needs to re-engage ("Get a hold
of yourself!"). It is a self, too, that the therapist has just warned her is likely to
ruinously collapse onto itself if Karen doesn't take the "next step," which we eventually learn is one of the Twelve Steps of recovering from emotional addiction.

Karen turns to the teddy bear and speaks on, alternately calling out her own
and her boyfriend's name, in the process commenting on her immediate feelings.
At one point, she declares, ostensibly speaking to the boyfriend, "I'm feeling right
about this; I ain't your doormat, I ain't!" She intermittently looks into the mirror
and speaks with herself, promptly responding to every comment. She occasionally addresses the bear as if he (the boyfriend) were casting aspersion on her
emerging realizations, which she also halfheartedly questions as she sobs, "Did
ya hafta make it so hard, 'cause it didn't hafta be like this?" Quickly spotting her
image in the mirror again, Karen gains her composure and interjects, "Hey, Karen
Cousins, there ain't no excuse for this shit." The other women clap. Several egg
her on, one encouraging her with, "That's right, baby. You tell that ol' bear a thing
or two." Which Karen proceeds to do, articulating her own version of the step
she seems to have taken as she addresses her teddy bear, inserting further difference into the discourse of recovery.

Look, fuzzbutt. You got me steppin' in the wrong direction. I'm not gonna, fucking step anymore. I'm hot to trot the 12 steps right outta here and away from *you,*
man. [Gives the bear a hard shake and turns to the mirror] And away from you,
too, girl. I'm gonna skip right over a lotta steps getting away from you, girl. [Elab-
orates] I don't like you. You're not very nice to me. You really hurt me. You bet
your sweet patootie you did and you know it.

Again, the women clap, as Karen finishes the dialogical soliloquy with both her
self and herself.

Scenes like these play themselves out daily at Fairview Hospital, some in this
room with its props, others in different rooms with their distinct paraphernalia.
All ultimately bear on the self. The scenic presence of feelings is continually at
hand, embedded in a discourse about the source and the course of troubled lives
and mediated—apparently materialized—by particular objects on the premises.
What is played out and what materializes is not simply reproduced as these dramas unfold; patient, therapist, and significant other all put their own biographical stamps on the shape and substance of the troubled self in question. Certainly,
the scenic presence of paraphernalia doesn't wholly constitute the web of mean-

ings being spun, but it's evident in the scheduled gathering together of people in such places that objects can be arranged to represent a common sense of who we are. Indeed, the personas in question might vanish into thin air (as in the joke in Chapter 2) in the absence of their scenic presence. In places like Fairview, the storied environs virtually "materialize" identity.

Embodiment

Embodiment connotes personification, but it also can refer to the body itself as the materialization of otherwise invisible qualities. Bodily features literally objectify the self when we say things like "he's really got a big head" to specify a person's egotism. The pseudoscience of phrenology and early positivist criminology attest to the body's historical utility as a surface of material signs for inner worlds. From the currently popular interest in body language and artistic adornment, to the well-known connotations of assertive posture and direct eye contact, the body continues to be an omnipresent material mediator of who we are or hope to be.

Paralleling hotel doors and work life, the use of the body to signify subjectivity is probably as old as bodies themselves; it's the complex institutionalization of embodiment that's a recent phenomenon. Of course, not all institutions are concerned with troubled selves, as the proliferation of health and fitness clubs and other self-improvement organizations indicates. Troubled or not, the twentieth century has witnessed an explosion of material technology for interpreting the body as a way of constructing the self. Who and what we are in our innermost being is now made technically visible all over the body or, as we sometimes say, "It's written all over the face." It is the stock-in-trade of many professionals whose business it is to "read" the body in order to treat the self. From eye movements and voice modulation, to emotional displays, posture, seating demeanor, tactile responses, and frailty, we apprehend the body as a very revealing practical surface for communicating identity. Like the material mediation of physical objects, circumstantial usage specifies embodied selves.

Yet as Dorothy Smith comments on "texts," until recently sociologists paid little attention to the material body. If the self was related to the body at all, it was commonly discounted as stereotyping. In his book *The Body and Social Theory*, Chris Shilling (1993) refers to the body as an "absent presence" in sociology, explaining that if the body is a taken-for-granted condition of action, it is seldom given much attention in its own right. Sociologists usually treat it as the subject matter of other disciplines or, if it is considered, it's viewed as ancillary to more traditional concerns such as social control. Bryan Turner (1991) explains that if classical theorists such as Marx, Weber, and Durkheim paid attention to embodiments of the relations of production, rationalization, and social solidarity, they overlooked the ontological status of the lived body. Human agency was equated with consciousness and the mind; it wasn't considered in relation to the body as a corporeal entity.

Since the 1980s, however, there has been a rush of interest in embodiment, centered on the material body as a mediating feature of everyday life. Approaching the body as a social project has swept away the old body-mind duality, situating both body and mind in the interpretive practices by which meaning is assigned to experience. Many now view body and mind as alternative surfaces for signifying identity. Informed by the work of Pierre Bourdieu (1984, 1985), Norbert Elias (1978, 1991), Michel Foucault (1977, 1978a), Harold Garfinkel (1967), Anthony Giddens (1984, 1991) and Bryan Turner (1984, 1992), a leading sociological question has emerged: How does the body as a primary material presence in life serve as surface for the narrative embodiment of subjectivity?

The Schoolchild's Signifying Body

By way of answering, consider the way the body signifies the subject in the context of an institution whose mission it is to treat schoolchildren's learning and emotional deficits. Cedarview is a residential treatment center for the emotionally disturbed (Buckholdt and Gubrium 1979). It is a private vendor under contract with local public school systems and county welfare departments to improve children's learning skills, behavior management, and emotional control. While the average length of stay for children in such facilities has lessened over the years, Cedarview's therapeutic regimen, based on two-year placements at the time, is still typical of institutions of its kind.

Cedarview is committed to behavioral programming, which is centered, in part, on an elaborate token economy. The children collect tokens for appropriate behaviors, which they can redeem for valued items at a facility store, or they can trade them for a variety of privileges, such as participating in extracurricular activities. This is linked with a complex assessment system and treatment regimen in which targeted conduct such as "swearing behavior," "teasing behavior," and "off-task fantasizing" is measured before treatment (called "baselining") and at various intervals during and after treatment ("postbaselining"). The token economy, assessment system, and treatment program are major components of the prevailing therapeutic discourse and the local technology of self construction.

The child's body is of special interest to staff members, because it poignantly signifies to them his or her therapeutic needs and progress in treatment. It is, in effect, a well articulated surface of signs for the purpose of interpreting children's selves. The typical baselining assessment is illustrative. The case we consider centers on Maurice Clay's so-called teasing behavior. Maurice is elementary school age and has been referred to Cedarview for an attention deficit disorder with strong emotional overtones. The baseline will establish a point of reference for comparison with subsequent measures, indicating Maurice's progress in managing his conduct.

Baselining is conducted both in and out of the special education classrooms that line the center's main hallway. Maurice is to be baselined while in teacher Sally Meath's classroom. Before the children arrive, two staff members, Joe Julian and Francine O'Brien, inform Meath about the assessment and take their places in the observation room at the back of the classroom. All classrooms have observation rooms, outfitted with sound equipment and one-way mirrors. When an observation room is darkened and the classroom is full of light, the one-way mirror is transparent only from inside the observation room out, although savvy children in the classroom occasionally do cup their hands around their eyes immediately in front of the mirror, attempting to peek through the glass to see if anyone is watching. This effectively turns the "panopticon" in the other direction.

The observer joins the assessment team in the observation room and together they wait for the children to take their seats and settle down before the baselining begins. Julian and O'Brien are to tally how often Maurice teases (exhibits "teasing behavior") in a predesignated time period. The following conversation soon unfolds. Note the extent to which Maurice's body figures in quantifying the self in question. While, in this case, the body's designation is eventually considered failed, the process entailed clearly ties the local discourse-in-practice to discursive practice.

OBSERVER: Who are you baselining today?
JULIAN: Maurice Clay. I'm getting his teasing behavior.
OBSERVER: What's teasing behavior?
JULIAN: Look at these categories [gives rating sheet to the observer]. It's considered teasing if he hits, touches, makes faces or negative comments, or does any name-calling during work time. (Buckholdt and Gubrium 1979, p. 137)

Julian and O'Brien then turn to the classroom but say very little. There's a long pause as they focus their attention on Maurice. Julian eventually expresses his disappointment that "nothin' " has happened and that, instead, Maurice is fantasizing. This prompts the following exchange.

JULIAN: Damn! I should have done fantasizing this week and teasing last week. He was teasing a lot then, but nothin' now. Just look at him staring into space—that's fantasizing if I ever saw it.
OBSERVER: How do you know what fantasizing is?
JULIAN: Good point. I guess I really couldn't count staring into space like that. We only count verbal stuff for that. He may be staring into space, but is really thinking about his work. Who knows? So we only count verbal stuff like when he talks about Mr. Greaso, Spiderman, or Superwhat's-his-name. (P. 137)

Note how a possible shift in attention from teasing to fantasizing behavior positions Maurice's body to signify a different self. Concurrently, the institutional discourse of behavior deficits, treatment, and progress is crafted in the colorful terms of what Julian takes to be locally understood, particularizing the meaning of fantasizing.

One of the boys in the classroom, Jamie Edwards, walks up to the one-way mirror, cups his hands around his eyes, and peers into the observation room. In response, Julian and O'Brien further designate a rule for interpreting Maurice's body, which takes shape in the course of its possible application.

JULIAN: [Referring to Jamie] There's a little shit. I tried to baseline him last week and got nothin'. He must have known I was in here lookin' at him. He's a real bastard. I know what he's really like from working with him in the cottage [Maurice's dormitory].
O'BRIEN: Look! Maurice is givin' the finger to Sally [the teacher, who has her back to the classroom]. Can we count that?
JULIAN: Naw, only if he does it to another kid. (P. 138)

There's a pause in the assessment process as team members chat about Jamie and a few other children, exchanging anecdotes about mischief and misbehavior. Several minutes pass before the team's attention again turns to Maurice, who now gets out of his chair and stands behind the boy seated to his left, peering over the boy's shoulder at his school work. Interpretive rules again emerge in reflexive response to body observations.

JULIAN: Now we may get some action. Come on, touch him or something! If he really gets going, we could see a lot [of teasing behaviors] in a few minutes.
O'BRIEN: Can't we count what he's doing?
JULIAN: No, not unless he really bothers him, like touches him or makes faces. (P. 138)

It's evident that the significations of Maurice's body and its locally pertinent self-revealing meanings evolve at a parallel pace. The task at hand is to translate bodily signs into designated behavioral episodes. But the resulting rules ("only if he does it to another kid," "not unless he really bothers him," etc.) reflexively guide what team members consider themselves to be observing in the very same (baselining) process. Language games are hardly on holiday in this circumstance.

As Maurice heads back to his seat, he ruffles the hair of the boy whose shoulder he was peering over, prompting Julian to comment, "Good! Good! Now we're getting somewhere. Too bad he started so late. [Looks at his watch] Time's almost up." The baselining session ends as other assessments in this and other similar places sometimes do, with the knowledge that, had things gone differently, Maurice might have shown up for what he really is.

The Signifying Body in Old Age

Bodies of all ages are used to signify subjectivity, but they may be storied differently in the context of varied going concerns, whose discourses-in-practice distinctly mediate the life course (see Bertaux 1981; Dannefer 1984a, 1984b, 1992). The aging body, like that of the growing child, has been a perennial surface of signs for identity. Institutions such as convalescence centers, rehabilitation hospitals, adult day care facilities, and support groups for the caregivers of the elderly are now ubiquitous venues differentially linking the self and the body in old age.

The nursing home provides a now commonplace institutional venue for self construction, bringing both the body and the self into focus as interpretive projects. While there is both therapeutic and palliative interest in the condition of the body as a physiological entity, the body also is monitored for what it can reveal about a gamut of related concerns, from the nursing home resident's personal identity to family caregivers' lingering sense of responsibility after institutionalization.

Drawing upon Sacks's (1974) idea of a membership categorization device (MCD), which we considered earlier, we can think of the nursing home as a complex discursive mechanism for narratively cataloging and evaluating characteristics of the body (see Gubrium 1986a, 1993, 1997[1975]). As an MCD, the term *nursing home* conjures up all kinds of descriptive linkages, narratively configured within the expanding discourse of aging in contemporary society. The term topically guides body talk to disease, decrepitude, dementia, helplessness, nursing, caregiving, and death. It encourages persons to story the body—and its self—in relation to aging, rather than to talk of other matters, such as asceticism or the intergenerational resemblances of bodily traits.

Before an individual is placed in a nursing home, the home may be a relatively distant discursive anchor for linking the body and the self, yet it still can cast a narrative shadow on personal meaning. For example, in an in-depth home interview with the adult daughter of a frail, elderly mother, the mother's future is linked with thoughts of when "it's time" (to seek institutional care). In the following extract from the interview, the nursing home serves as an MCD for making meaningful linkages with the mother's deteriorating body.

> When ya think ahead—I try not to think too far ahead—ya can't help feeling what might happen to her [the frail mother]. She's getting pretty frail. You can see for yourself. And she's becoming a real burden to me. She's my mother, of course, and ya can take a lot because of that, you know what I mean? What makes me nervous, though, is thinking about what's ahead, you know, with it's time [for nursing home placement] and after that. Everyone keeps telling me not to get myself all riled up and sick caring for her and I know—better than anyone, don't ya know—what that can mean. Ya think too, about what those places are like. Sure, they take care of 'em, but do they *really* take care of 'em? She's declining, but she might decline all that much faster if I put her in one of them. When I think about her becoming a bunch of bones there in one of those beds, with three others in the same room, it's frightening. They say they decline fast in those places, don't they?

Note how the nursing home not only is considered a looming possibility, given the difficulty of continued home care, but it is also presented as a source of anxiety centered on what it signifies about the selves of anyone living there. According to the daughter, because of what "they say" about "those places," the nursing home risks turning the mother into a "bunch of bones," a skeletal self, so to speak. It descriptively anchors the daughter's narrative about her mother's body because it is a widely recognized care venue under the circumstances, as well as being ostensibly predictive of what will become of the mother after placement. The daughter's anxiety is admittedly drawn from what the care site tells her in this regard, something which she infers from what "they" say, implicating the broader discourse of contemporary frailty and aging.

The nursing home continues to be a basis for forming meaningful bodily linkages with the self after placement. For example, as repugnant as the term *vegetable* might be to some, it can come alive and reflexively construct the identity of its users, as nonvegetative as they might be. In the following conversation between two wheelchair-bound African-American nursing home residents, the identity indexed by bed location serves as a basis for interpreting more than the selves of others.[2]

MURIEL: Don't know how you stand it, girl. Why you go over there, down there by those rooms? I saw you lookin' in there.

RUBY: What you mean? I was just passin'. That Miss Casey, the one just over yonder, couple doors over there? Oh my, she is a bag of bones. Oh, wee! She's just in there in bed and she's on her back. You be hardly knowin' she's alive. They got her hooked up to all kinds of stuff. Her mouth's hangin' open, like that. [Imitates Casey] Oh, wee!

MURIEL: That one's a vegetable. Sweet Jesus, I don't know why they keep 'em alive. What good are they? The bags of bones they have in the place, it gives me the chills when I see 'em. I don't know how you can stand it, Ruby. Why do you look there, girl?

RUBY: Who you talkin' to?

MURIEL: You, girl. [Chiding Ruby] You thinkin' of bein' one of them there vegetables? You look like you gettin' pretty skinny. I'll get me one of those pills that knock me dead before I get like that!

RUBY: I'm no vegetable! Look at you, girl. That nappy hair look like ol' dried up corn silk. You better watch out, in a place like this here I can see you in one of those beds down there, like ol' Miss Casey. I be comin' down that hall and look in there and there you is, mouth open like this [imitates Casey], like an ol' dried up melon, oozin' and bruisin'.

MURIEL: Now look at you, Ruby. You already a bag of bones. You *all* skin and bones! You no vegetable, you a skeleton!

RUBY: Oh, wee! What you talkin' about, girl? You got no behind!

MURIEL: I'm leavin' this ol' place tomorrow. This here is bonetown. Ain't gonna be one of them vegetables like you Ruby. You gonna look at 'em so much, you gonna be one of 'em. [Laughing] You turnin' green already!

As the women banter and laugh about the "bags of bones," Muriel describes how chilling it is to wheel past "the vegetables," asserting that she would take a suicide pill before she'd let herself come to that. Joking with each other, their own bodies become a complex surface of related signs. Note, in particular, how these residents use and cleverly embellish what they know about their neighbor "Miss Casey" to concretely describe what they themselves could become. As they tell their stories, the two women's own bodies and selves discursively materialize out of both locally relevant and broadly recognized linkages, signifying who and what they themselves could become "in a place like this here." Their humor uses the material body in the same way that more serious talk about the self does.

Talk of nursing home life can conjure up the body even after a resident has died or otherwise left a facility. This is especially poignant when the body appears in retrospect to have been "near perfect" despite an illness. It's well known that cognitively incapacitating illnesses such as Alzheimer's disease do not necessarily result in visible bodily markings. Still, family members wonder how it could be that someone can "look so good" and, at the same time, have completely lost his or her mind to become the "shell of a former self." A surprisingly supple body is especially unsettling in the context of the nursing home, because residents' bodies are assumed to be frail, and are typically deployed in the discourse of decline and decrepitude.

The range and adaptability of body talk in relation to self construction was evident in one of the support groups observed as part of research on the caregivers of Alzheimer's disease sufferers (Gubrium 1986a). Here, two participating wives state that they "made it a point" to keep attending group meetings even after their husbands have died, because others benefited from their experience. The husbands, both in their eighties when they passed away, had been placed in nursing homes because of worsening dementia that made it too difficult to care for them at home. During a meeting of the support group, an animated discussion formed around the issue of how sufferers sometimes "look" despite their cognitive impairment. The received wisdom, available in advice books, pamphlets for families, and the visual media, is that Alzheimer's dementia may develop full-blown in a relatively healthy body. The discussion eventually settled on the "unfairness" of death in such cases, the reasoning being that it is not fair for individuals to be taken by death when they "look so good" and are "so healthy."

Compare the body talk in two different parts of the discussion as the term *nursing home* serves to differentially embellish their speakers' narratives. In the following extract from the first part, in which the demented body, not nursing homes, is under consideration, Nick's wife, whose husband had Alzheimer's disease and recently died, recalls that Nick "looked really good," especially in comparison with two other patients who recently died. She never mentions nursing homes and there are no related categorical inducements to elaborate the mind-body fairness doctrine in her account.

> Nick [her deceased husband] looked really good. He wasn't all there [cognitively], but he looked really good, seemed so healthy. Ask Sarah [another participant, who nods and elaborates]. I think, like you said, Prue, it's really unfair. The poor man could walk around and he was able to get out of bed everyday. [Elaborates] If you looked at him, you'd think he was really fit, just like a guy enjoying retirement. I'm not kidding. That's the truth. That's the way it is with this thing. You just never would think it, really. Remember when Richard [a recent participant's spouse] died? Now he was really bad, just eaten away. How about Rita? That gangrene got her whole body. Not Nick. [Pause] I don't know. It just isn't fair.

In another part of the same discussion, the bodily condition of nursing home residents has been reviewed and is now poignantly in the background. In this part, even the floor plan of a facility is made discursively relevant and used to formulate bodily descriptions and related self constructions. This sharpens the perceived irony of the mind-body linkage for the individuals in question. The speaker in this case is the spouse of a resident named Andy, who lived in a nursing home for a number of years before his death. Andy's wife constructs her account using what the nursing home resident's body typically signifies to contrastingly story the unfairness of Andy's death.

> I'm not saying I haven't accepted it. Andy's gone. I know that and I think I've accepted that. [Elaborates] He lived a good life for an 81-year-old man. But when you think about it—if you just looked at him in that room of his at Parkview [nursing home] or saw him walking down the hall—you'd think, what's he doing in here? He doesn't belong in here, right? That's that damned Alzheimer's. Ya look around and ya see this one next door [in the adjacent room] and ya see a vegetable. He's in bed and looks, well, dead. No color. And on the other side— Mrs. Korski I think her name was—was she ever bad off. When I went in there, I couldn't believe she was alive! But she lived a long time like that. It's a shame really, when you think about it. [Draws comparisons with residents on another unit.] Andy wasn't even in that there skilled care area, either. Now that's a doozy. Those are the ones really dyin'! Gosh, what a sight that is. I'd go through there to get to the smoking room and wonder why I didn't faint. I couldn't imagine those people were still alive. [Elaborates] It just didn't seem right that Andy was in that place. It really makes me wonder. I could write a book about it, I guess. And Andy goes [dies], just like that. [Snaps her fingers] You can't say that was really fair, was it? Like in comparison? [Pause] To this day, I can't understand it, but I think I've made my peace with it.

The nursing home, of course, is not a discursive template that designates exactly what will be said about bodies considered and described in relation to it. It is not as if the personal meaning of the body is specified wholesale through related linkages with the nursing home. The biographical particulars that enter into talk and interaction also describe the relevancies of the body's material mediations of the selves in question. As we saw in the preceding extracts, the nursing home can be used to signify the elderly body both fairly and unfairly, both sadly and humorously, depending on the working narrative context and its biographical particulars. At the same time, once the nursing home is made topical, it provides a discourse of its own for the embodiment of the elderly self, and this, while not definitive, nonetheless helps to story who and what people are as their bodies grow old.

Textual Mediation

Our attention to how the body is "read" for signs of the self leads us to consider how individuals interpret more literal texts of identity. Years ago, literary theorists including Mikhail Bakhtin, Roland Barthes, and Julia Kristeva revolutionized thinking about the meaning of textual material. Bakhtin (see Todorov 1984) seriously questioned the idea that a text had a final meaning. The meaning of a text, he argued, existed in a complex relationship with how it was read. The author was not the ultimate arbiter of meaning, but, having written it, became one among many other interpreters of "his" text. In an important statement aptly entitled "The Death of the Author," Barthes (1977) expanded this theme: "To give a text an Author is to impose a limit on that text, to furnish it with a final signified, to close the writing" (p. 175). For Barthes, the text was a "galaxy of signifiers" (1974, p. 5), the significances of which extended to an open horizon of readings. As Barthes succinctly put it, "A text's unity lies not in its origin but in its destination," in its usage (1977, p. 148). Kristeva (1973) developed the related concept of "intertextuality," the leading idea of which was that texts drew their meanings from other texts, in an unending interplay of readings and interpretations.

This is now familiar territory and it has come to have an important application to self construction. The view contributes to the notion that a centered self— even a multifaceted and presented self—has been displaced, if not disparaged. The self now rests in narratives derived from the related regions and concerns of the contemporary identity landscape. From one region or site to another, it's apparent that what we are has no final resting place. Who we are ultimately taken to be as individuals derives as much from the way we story ourselves, the textual material available for storytelling, and the ways in which stories are "read" and "heard," as from who and what we might ostensibly be in our own rights. These, of course, are the intertextual contours of the self we live by. The machinery of talk and interaction itself plays a part, even while we were reminded in Chapter 8 that what is thereby constructed is continually subject to the circumstantial resources—the discourses—available for storying selves. All of this doesn't make the self any less real or meaningful as a beacon of experience, but, rather, shifts reality and meaning from individual presence to the textual practices of self construction.

If we appreciate developments in literary criticism, we nonetheless aren't saying that selves are literally texts, any more than we have said that storytellers construct selves out of whole cloth in the process of narration. Rather, we use the term *text* to focus attention on the concretely textual ways that selves are narratively assembled and formed, with particular themes, subjectivities, and story lines in tow. Knowledge of the institutional availability of texts gives us a sense of the selves we need to be, or that we risk being, at certain times and places. Whether texts of identity are personal documents like diaries or personnel files, written tomes such as Alcoholics Anonymous' "Big Book," or take the form of advice pamphlets, such as those available to women who love too much, they shape identity above and beyond the pure give-and-take of talk and interaction.

As we use, or are encouraged to consult, the texts that are available in a particular setting to formulate who we are, we draw upon what others before us have been advised to do. These texts provide concrete presence for us long before we individually come on the scene. The related selves we construct and convey can come to have a kind of life of their own in other texts such as files and case records, which perpetuate our presence long after we have departed a setting. Taken together, such texts can be organized into chains of self construction, becoming virtual rivers of identity construction (Emerson 1991). As Franz Kafka's (1937) character Joseph K discovered in the novel *The Trial*, such rivers can flow unimpeded in time, carrying away our identities on their own.

Selves on File

Far from being boldly present in our daily affairs, textual mediation often emerges in quite subtle form, such as the occasional notes from teachers that children bring home from school or annual letters of evaluation from our employers, all of which carry messages between the lines. A brief annual letter of evaluation, which we browse and file away for future reference, seems innocuous enough. Its contents may confirm what we already know, although surprises are always possible and could, in the short run, have devastating effects on our self-esteem, if not our jobs and careers. But just as importantly, such seemingly innocuous texts are more or less independently filed away in institutional archives, with perhaps nothing being made of them at all at the time. Yet they can lurk about a going concern, just waiting to be activated to assert their self-constituting powers. In the future, they may be resurrected to support new assessments of our person or performance. Retrospectively, they can be read as linked together or as "adding up" to a formal documentation of some identity, which is then taken to be "the" record of who or what we were, have become, or will be for all practical purposes (see Wheeler 1969).

Such filed texts literally "get out of hand" because the circumstances that dictate their consultation may have little or no connection in practice with the circumstances that generate them. The files that textually represent who we are in various organizations lurk about our everyday lives, because, while we are in some sense ever-present in these organizations as a result of being "on file," who we are, according to file contents, becomes practically relevant only where and when the files are consulted and their contents interpreted. File contents, then, are narrative resources for whomever's business it eventually is to assemble and represent their subjects' identities. They don't continually or consistently represent who we are, even while they flow about our lives; they have to be actively consulted and storied to have meaning for us (Gubrium, Holstein, and Buckholdt 1994).

When the occasion arises for file contents to be assembled into a self story, such as for a promotion decision or to justify firing an employee, whatever occasions originally prompted the creation of file contents now become the retrospective formulations of a new circumstance. A document long on file may, in the future context of a firing decision, be questioned as to its authenticity or accuracy, but the questions are entertained against the background concerns of the situation at hand. The current context serves to "read" the meaning of the file and its documents. In turn, the occasioned identity of its subject is assembled, not the original identity that might have been intended by those who authored the documents in question. As Barthes might put it, those (original) authors are dead. Having written and filed documents, the original author moves on to become one of many other interpretively distantiated readers of the products of their own labors. While the rhetoric of original authorship has persuasive force in our society, the sense of "original" itself is nonetheless rhetorically challengeable. For example, readers might effectively argue that an "original" author could not have known what he or she was doing in relation to later readings, nor could the author have understood the consequences of his or her actions for future evaluations.

Textual Mediations as Relations of Ruling

Texts come into use in a variety of ways to figure identity, not the least of which is their mediating influence in institutional encounters. Dorothy Smith (1987) is especially concerned with the contrast between the attributed identities often embedded in institutional documents and the sometimes glaringly different identities of the intended readers of those documents, especially those socially positioned in institutionally unacknowledged ways. Smith focuses on mothers in relation to their children's schooling and considers the mediating influence that school documents can have on the construction of mothers' identities.

Smith explains that mothers' identities in relation to schooling are not so much directly influenced by figures of authority such as teachers and administrators as they are tacitly, yet effectively, "ruled" by the texts and related discourses that mediate mothers' relations to schooling. She refers to this in general as "relations of ruling." A simple note to a parent from a teacher may not directly implicate a mother's identity as a good or bad parent, but may assign identity in terms of what it takes for granted about parents and schools. For example, a note may take it for granted that parents are an integral, if not an expressly moral, part of the schooling team, and be composed accordingly. As such, a note's ordinary wording becomes a message that constitutes a parent's subjectivity in a particular way, in this case negatively implicating nonparticipatory parents. In effect, the relations of ruling—in this case, the institutional practice of including parents on the schooling team—exert self control *through* such texts.

Paralleling Foucault, Smith argues that textual messages combine institutional discourses with prevailing discursive practices to become the actual everyday sites of engagement with power. Smith puts it in the following way, emphasizing the socially relational character of ruling and implicating the identities of any and all who enter into such relations.

> When I write of "ruling" in this context I am identifying a complex of organized practices, including government, law, business and financial management, professional organization, and educational institutions as well as the discourses in texts that interpenetrate the multiple sites of power. . . . We are ruled by forms of organization vested in and mediated by texts and documents, and constituted externally to particular individuals and their personal and familial relationships. The practice of ruling involves the ongoing representation of the local actualities of our worlds in the standardized and general forms of knowledge that enter them into the relations of ruling. It involves the construction of the world in texts as a site of action. (1987, p. 3)

Describing her own experience as a single parent in relation to the textual mediation of identity in matters of schooling, Smith sets the stage for portraying the

seemingly minor, yet significant, "minidramas" that unfold in the matter of successfully completing homework, for example. The setting for the minidramas is
the household she and her children live in. Smith stresses the ordinariness of it
all by showing how matters of identity strike home in the most routine ways. Indeed, until the minidramas unfold, she admittedly hasn't given much thought to
the fact that she is a *single* parent; that self doesn't even occur to her. She is just
a parent in a world of others much like herself, or so she figures.

> I was for several years a "single parent." That concept provides for me a method
> of analyzing my biographical experience. That experience itself was situated in
> actual settings in which its minidramas went on—the home we lived in with its
> untidiness, the fruit trees, blackberries in the hedge between garden and lane, the
> view of the mountains from the kitchen window, the kitchen floor that would
> never come clean, the roads to and from the various schools my children attended.
> The children themselves as they were then are more difficult to re-envisage, over-
> laid as their images have been by their more recent being. I remember them play-
> ing soccer in the front yard and complicated games of fantasy in the back. In these
> fragmentary memories, there is no experience of *being* a single parent, though the
> work processes through which I engaged with those settings and relationships
> surely had that distinctive character because I was alone in charge of my children
> in a world of two-parent families. (Pp. 167–68)

Just as some who once lived in dire poverty often recount that they never figured
they were poor, Smith didn't much think about being a single parent. She does
suggest, however, that while she was not phenomenologically a single parent,
her relations with her children and their schooling nonetheless had its distinct
characteristics, perhaps centered on the daily burdens of combining work and
mothering in the same role.

This starts to unravel, revealing a "new" identity, when one of her children
begins to have difficulty learning to read. The difficulty not only presents the
question of how to get her child up to speed, but also how Smith herself contributes to the process. It occurs to Smith that the question of how she contributes
can easily transmute into the issue of how she contributed to the difficulty in the
first place. She realizes, in uncovering reasons for reading difficulties, that a child's
reading problem can spill over onto the mother's identity as a parent. It is an inevitable outcome of a parent's institutional relations with his or her children's
schooling in the context of an educational discourse that presumes that, in the
normal course of things, parents effectively parent, while single parents can cause
problems in children's schooling. If Smith's child is having difficulty learning to
read, who or what is the source of the problem? What kind of parent is Smith,
after all?

In schooling's relations of ruling, Smith risks becoming identified as a "single parent," a negatively charged commodity in this institution's economy of
subjectivity. It isn't as if this role and identity were simply there all along, featuring the real self that Smith actually was and apparently is; rather, they retroactively emerge from related interpretive practices, as the following extract suggests.

Other women in similar situations know what this problem is. One woman I know who is a teacher and a "single parent" has concealed this information from her child's school. A child's problem in school, when it is made accountable in terms of the concept of the single parenthood of her or his mother, marshals procedures entering child, parent, teacher, and school administration into courses of action specialized to this category of "problem." This concept then becomes a basis on which the work of mothering is organized and interpreted in relation to the schooling process. It does so not merely in providing for school staff a method of analyzing, assembling, and describing how a child is a problem and how that problem ties in to his or her home background. Provided the mother is competent in its conceptual methods, it gives her a procedure for analyzing her own work practices as a mother in terms of how their defects produce the child's problems in the school setting. (P. 168)

Smith finds herself tensely sandwiched between a routine domestic understanding of who she is, on the one side, and a possible new identity institutionally linked with a causal culture of learning deficiency, on the other. It's important to underscore how the self emerges out of these relations of ruling. It isn't clear at what exact point a new self consciously crops up out of identity-producing circumstances such as the one under consideration here. Smith argues, like Foucault, that the institutional apparatus linking parents with their children's schooling tacitly deploys various subjectivities for parents, and these are the conditions of possibility for who and what those parents will be to themselves and concerned others. This gets sorted out as circumstances unfold and as biographical particulars are assigned their identities. How any self will be defined is far from automatic, but definitions will emerge in relation to the institutional ways of conceptualizing parents, children, and schools. We get a general glimpse of this when we hear one teacher casually explain to another, "Your single parent is typically a big part of the problem, so keep an eye on that." The school, in effect, is prepared to construct the single parent's self out of a discourse of school troubles, but who is subjected to the discourse is not fully determined locally, as concealment practices suggest.

Smith makes the further point that very ordinary texts highlight the identities involved in the problem. As noted earlier in the chapter, Smith views textual material of various kinds as increasingly endemic to self construction in today's world. She argues that we learn who and what we are as much from what textual material conveys line by line or assumes between the lines, as we do from actual talk and social interaction. What's between the lines may be silent or invisible, but it can be glaringly evident when one's experiences contrast with what texts tacitly assume. In this regard, Smith cites a pamphlet for parents published by the Ontario Ministry of Education, which contains suggestions about "how parents (but in fact mothers) can improve their/her child's reading and writing."

> Have a place where your children can paint and crayon or cut-and-paste without having to worry about making a mess. It will take them a while to develop the co-ordination required to make small letters. Give them large sheets of paper to work with at first so that they'll have space for large printing.

> Examine photographs and works of art with your children. Discuss what they
> see. Extend the parts of their vocabulary that deal with shape, colour, and form.
> Use home-made puppets. Have your children dramatize stories they have read.
> They can write scripts and put on their own shows, but they need an audience—
> you! (Pp. 168–69)

These suggestions take for granted a distinctive understanding of "the" parent, casting his or her subjectivity in a particular way. As Smith explains, this parental identity presupposes expenditures of parental time and effort. In a word, "the" parent (in practice, the mother) is identified as someone available to participate in the activities. Not only are children to be encouraged to paint, cut-and-paste, and dramatize stories, but parents are expected to have the time to participate in these activities on a continuing basis. Proper parents in effect become students themselves, encouraging colearners, an audience for the child's school-related undertakings, and, on occasion, teachers in their own right. What's more, the pamphlet assumes that the materials described are available and that the parent will be able to do the considerable preparatory work of making a homemade puppet, not to mention other objects pertinent to what is expected under the circumstances.

Now, add this to all the ancillary domestic functions that schooling entails, including the competing job activities of the single parent. Smith's description of the result is poignant and worth quoting at length, because in the context of the relations of ruling, it emphasizes what is written between the lines for the single parent, not only what is assumed in a simple pamphlet message. Consider what the suddenly self-conscious (single) parent reads between the lines and not in the pamphlet about her identity as the following goes through her mind.

> Along with the work involved in "developing the child," there is work involved
> in scheduling the comings and goings of different family members in relation to
> their external commitments. The providing of household services facilitating the
> child's working schedule, supervising homework, providing cultural activities
> such as visits to museums, movies, and the like, taking care of emotional stresses
> arising in the schooling process, covering for a child so that minor delinquencies
> such as being late or missing school do not appear as defects on her or his record,
> helping with the school library, baking a cake for the bake sale, driving the car
> when the team plays another school, and so forth—all these along with the rou-
> tine and basic housework (feeding, clothing, health care, etc.) contribute to the
> child's capacity to function normally at school. (P. 169)

The last few words are key. "To function normally," of course, refers directly to the child's normal functioning at school, but, in the context of the roles and interactions involved in its relations of ruling, the words implicate the subjectivities of participants, pointedly including parents (mothers). When the child functions normally, the parent, for all practical purposes, is taken to be a normal parent. Indeed, why would anyone even think about or question this parental identity? Normal schooling and normal identities don't need explanation, their opposites do. Thus, the normal parent who reads the text of the pamphlet issued by the Ontario Ministry of Education reads about parents, not especially about himself or herself. More to the point, that parent isn't likely to wonder at all why the textual description portrays what he or she actually is as it does.

But how does the "problem" parent read the pamphlet? What about the parent who is or has been made aware of the difference that single parenting ostensibly can make in children's schooling? We can imagine that the text potentially, if not actually, informs her, in black and white, of what she can easily fail at, again and again, in trying to correct her child's reading deficit. We can imagine that she thinks about the possible aspersion that can be cast on her responsibility for what her child has become. This may be accentuated when her child's teacher ever so casually and sympathetically prefaces a comment to her at a parent-teacher conference with "We all know what you're up against as a single parent." In this institutional context, we can see how the seemingly straightforward text of a simple note or pamphlet can deploy a whole discourse and psychology of single parenthood as it relates to children's schooling. An apparently unassuming text becomes a material mediator of parental self construction, storying institutional identity in a most ordinary way.

Conclusion

CHAPTER TEN

The Moral Climate of the Self We Live By

T he story of the social self has come a long way in a short hundred years. Building on countless narratives and reflecting myriad institutional developments, the self is now distinctively appropriated and deployed virtually everywhere. Far from being a grand narrative settled at or near the center of personal experience, the self now materializes in myriad nooks and crannies of everyday life, reflecting one sense of who we are in one site, turning a second option for personal definition in another one. If the story is now complex and socially dispersed, the self still isn't lost in a "wilderness of mirrors." Rather, the many looking glasses we peer into themselves are built into the experiential projects of endless going concerns with narrative auspices of their own, providing discernible circumstances for assembling identity.

In this environment, does the self lose its direction along with its grand narrative? Can we continue to consider it in terms of choice, of right and wrong, of responsibility and decision-making? A beacon of experience observes, reconnoiters, weighs alternatives, and prudently directs itself along the way. It's a moral entity because, in part, it propels itself on its own and makes choices. In a postmodern world, the self's story forges ahead, but also follows in its own wake. Both before and after we set out on the proverbial path of life, the self is informed by diverse discourses. As Goffman (1959, p. 13) again informs us, "We must not overlook the crucial fact that any projected definition of the situation also has a distinctive moral character." Many discourses center on familiar themes of personal responsibility, surrounded by a heady philosophical sense of the good life we might realize. Simultaneously, these discourses deploy just the opposite, narratives of squandered opportunities, botched choices, and paths not taken, all adding up to tales of lives shorn of proper meaning. Of course, there's an element of fate, too, as the unwitting forces of existence themselves are inserted into the picture and then taken to sort our destinies according to their own devices. In that story, we can be false heroes and tragic figures despite ourselves. In this world, the grand no longer stands over and above the local, but instead is one more body of accounts alongside the many other narratives we use to construct ourselves.

What becomes of traditional moral matters when the grand narrative of the self devolves into multiple stories, pared down, circumscribed, and dispersed to myriad locations of everyday life? What is the moral climate that informs this restoried ending? What could responsibility, choice, decision-making, and the like possibly mean in this new context?

The Expansion of the Particular

A few years ago, while doing fieldwork at Cedarview, the residential treatment center we mentioned earlier, Gubrium overheard the following conversation between a 9-year-old emotionally disturbed child named Tina and Margaret, her psychiatric social worker (see Buckholdt and Gubrium 1979). Their ostensible chit-chat became morally telling only when viewed against a background of institutionally dispersed identities, which then highlighted the increasing importance of the role played by local understandings in defining who we are. Like other children in treatment, Tina attended daily individual counseling sessions. Tina and her social worker had been seeing each other for over a year and the child eagerly looked forward to visiting with Margaret. Tina not only "got outta class," as the children put it, but she also thought Margaret was "lots of fun." They played games as they talked about themselves and there was plenty of affection to go around. Tina often sat on Margaret's lap during the sessions, their exchanges literally wrapped in Margaret's comforting arms.

In this particular session, with Tina seated on Margaret's lap, facing away from her, their conversation moved along rather unremarkably. The two talked about Tina's thoughts and feelings. "So how was your day so far, Tina?" Margaret asked. Tina, playing with her fingers, muttered something incoherent. Margaret interrupted, explaining that she couldn't hear what Tina was saying and that she should take care to speak clearly and with lots of eye contact, as Margaret often reminded the children. (Could eye contact be a form of moral specification?) Margaret then asked Tina if she was being a good girl today. Snickering, Tina turned her head to look directly into Margaret's eyes and answered that she was always a pretty good girl. Margaret hugged Tina and responded, "I really like good girls." Still looking directly at Margaret, Tina ever so earnestly asked, "You think I'm a good girl, right Peggy?" using Margaret's pet name. Margaret assured Tina that she indeed did think that Tina was a good girl, repeating that she liked all good girls. Tina continued, holding Margaret's arms tightly around her, "And you really like me, too, don't you Peggy?" Margaret reassured her that she did and Tina again asked, "You think I'm a really good girl, too, don't you?" Margaret once more responded affectionately, "Yes, of course I do. I really like good girls."

Like many conversations at Cedarview, this one centered very globally on topics of local interest: right and wrong, children's "goodness," their self-control, whether or not they were being "bad," and the like. Tina and Margaret presumably were talking about Tina, but in many ways the conversation was also about "good girls" in general, who, in the moral scheme of things, were persons to like or "really like," according to the strength of one's convictions. Tina didn't expect "her" Peggy to respond that she didn't like good girls, nor did Margaret expect to answer otherwise. The issue of "goodness" was general enough to be automatically considered a moral imperative. Who, after all, was to deny "the good" in principle, to call to task the good boy or girl?

Centered universalistically, if not grandly, Tina and Margaret's conversation was agreeable, indeed even mutually affectionate. If it had developed in a different direction, there would have been equal agreement that being bad was undesirable, that cheating, fighting, or being "unfair" was far from praiseworthy. In general, as a matter of local interest, the discussion of good versus bad hummed along like this at the crest of cosmic consensus, presenting the broad moral contours of institutional life dedicated to producing good girls and boys.

Tina and Margaret also took it for granted that children who were "being bad," were obviously not being good and thus were not very nice or in some other way generally discredited. Rarely did such characterizations produce disagreement. Everyone, it seemed, was for "the good" and against "the bad," including the children, their parents, and the staff, echoing on a small scale an ethic as old as ancient philosophy. The children, their parents, and the staff regularly referred to the inappropriate, to "today's bad kids," to the behavior "we're up against," and so-called bad influences. In their own brief exchange, Tina and Margaret built an implicit consensus regarding the bad as well as the good. Tina asked about herself with great certainty of what good meant generally, as well as what it generally didn't mean. In turn, Margaret "of course" agreed that she liked good girls, implying that "of course" no one would like their opposite. Who, after all, would side with immorality?

The articulation of traditional standards wasn't all there was to such exchanges, however, and this is how they became locally telling. Discussions almost always grew more specific, raising questions about the particulars involved. Usually, in time, it became apparent that the meaning of things like "the good" and "the bad" was deeply entangled with institutional discursive technology at many levels, from the local culture that specified what goodness and badness concretely were in relation to the current situation, to the conversational machinery through which such matters were communicated. It was in the local specification of cosmic issues that selves were actually fleshed out, always with an eye to moral accountability in relation to the circumstances at hand. The moral order was perennially clarified in the details of social interaction; moral "ordering," in effect, was always in progress. As we showed in the last chapter, in the context of Joe Julian's and Francine O'Brien's baselining efforts, if the specific contours of teasing were elusive, the morality (or lack of it) of teasing was nonetheless institutionally mandated and locally sought in its biographical particulars, even if that wasn't always figured as effectively as it could have been. In practice, the pursuit of morally accountable assessments was conducted in relation to the immediate cultural and material horizons of classroom observation.

The good child. The good parent. The good life. Aren't these all worth being, worth living for? Their stories are so grand as to be unimpeachable. But isn't any cosmic moral order always so abstract as to be problematic when put into practice? Isn't moral consensus empty until it is grounded in the particulars of daily living? This has always been the philosophical rub of grand narratives of moral order. They serve to organize our selves in their own terms, over and above the equally imperative moral considerations of the circumstances of their application, as the early pragmatists were painfully aware. Still, grand moral narratives of the self surely have not disappeared; as Tina and Margaret's exchange echoed, grand narratives are regularly given voice in everyday life. They seem to have always been with us.

What was telling about Tina and Margaret's conversation was that, unarticulated in their exchange, the grandly moral was being referenced in the context of a particular setting, one whose rules of moral specification would not necessarily be the same as they would be in another site. The morally familiar, and timeless, would eventually be cast in locally accountable terms, as we now realize that the comment about eye contact hinted it would. It is the abundance and diversity of such practical, local environments of accountability that are new, having grown at a dizzying pace, transforming the moral contours of the familiar in the process. We are now more entangled in the relation between the grand and the particular than ever before and it is this social fact that makes Tina and Margaret's otherwise undistinguished exchange morally remarkable.

As we were writing this book, yet another narrative for the self resounded across the identity landscape. Like Tina and Margaret's exchange, this self-implicating story was unremarkable in the abstract, but it eventually became more complex and interesting when viewed as a discourse-in-practice. In a quest for spiritual renewal, thousands of Christian men gathered one Saturday on the National Mall in Washington D.C. to pray and sing about masculine responsibility. Some estimate that close to a million men, calling themselves "Promise Keepers," were seeking redemption and renewal in front of the nation's Capitol. Their goal was to "reverse the moral and social deterioration caused by men abandoning their family responsibility" (*New York Times*, Oct. 5, 1997, p. A14). This is a social movement that has bought into the masculine identity business in a big way.

Just as Tina and Margaret's small-scale discussion of the good girl was very general, the Promise Keepers movement describes the contemporary man's self in cosmic terms. This self needs renewal. It's made the wrong choices, become irresponsible. It no longer functions properly. The director of that Saturday's mass gathering, Dale Schlafer, suggested that men, as moral agents, have no one to blame but themselves. They're responsible for not being the proper men they should have been.

> We gather not to point fingers at society. We're not here to say that the government has failed. We're here to say that the problem is with us, with us men who are in the church. We are coming to confess our sins. (*New York Times*, p. A14)

Broadly speaking, the Promise Keepers are raising the issue of who men are now and who they need to be, as men. Women's identities aren't at stake, not even children's, although some vigorously claim that these are implicated in the wider scheme of things. The issue centers on what it means to "be a man," to actually take familial responsibility, and to thereby redeem oneself from the sin of failed promises and negligence. Failed promises and negligence are very global irresponsibilities, generally to be discouraged. Most of us detest negligence. No one likes failed promises. They are fairly consensual moral signposts.

But the devil is in the details, or so they say. The particulars of moral choice with regard to self construction definitely complicate the moral climate of this self. In a world of socially organized particulars, what it means to be a man can produce conflicting moral positions. Being a man, in relation to women, for example, is a going concern fraught with practical and moral tension. Most women probably support "family life," as long as such support isn't tied to a particular domestic arrangement (see Thorne and Yalom 1982; Gubrium 1993). But what could men's moral redemption possibly mean in the specific context of the "fictive families" that Carol Stack (1974), for example, observed in an African-American community where mutually supportive "kin" formed on the basis of domestic faithfulness regardless of gender? What could it mean for the nontraditional domestic partnerships that now populate the familial landscape? What might it imply for the domestic arrangements that many view as familial even though they eschew the breadwinner/homemaker division of household responsibility so earnestly endorsed by the Promise Keepers? Such are the practical questions to be answered in relation to moral redemption.

The *New York Times* report on the Promise Keepers rally was itself telling, appearing as it did on a page juxtaposed with a companion story featuring various observers' attempts to "divine the politics" (or set of particulars) of the occasion. The juxtaposition begins to teach us about the very practical dimensions of sin and redemption. The observers' opinions are not privileged truths, of course, no more truthful than Promise Keepers' views in the grand scheme of things. But the opinions point to the going concerns that regularly tug at the moral heartstrings of identity in today's world. As if to say that being good is no longer what it used to be, the various commentators insist on looking under and around the cosmically moral to see what "really" is behind the rally. For some, it was symbolic that the rally was held in Washington D.C., the political, but not necessarily the moral, capital of the nation. Patricia Ireland, president of the National Organization for Women, explains:

> I think it's disingenuous of the Promise Keepers' leadership to say the group is non-political. There is a reason that Promise Keepers is having their rally in Washington with the Capitol as the backdrop. If they were looking for visibility, why didn't they hold it in New York City, the media capital of the world? When members of Congress look out onto the Mall, they see the same thing I see—hundreds of thousands of constituents and voters. (*New York Times*, Oct. 5, 1997, p. A14)

Whether it's as nondescript as an ordinary discussion of the good girl or as visible as a national rally, moral discourse repeatedly centers on who and what we are as moral agents, increasingly implicating the narrative horizons of specific going concerns. Local rights and wrongs, local goods and bads, and locally credited and discredited identities diversely constitute the contemporary moral climate of the self. The morally abstract is thoroughly embedded in the mundane details of daily life. From selves who love too much, are not task oriented enough, or need spiritual renewal, to selves who have grown too fat, too thin, too irresponsible, or too indulgent, we find answers to who we are in the extraordinary minutiae of our everyday going concerns—in their available hand mirrors and teddy bears, in tissue boxes, eye contact, and voice modulation, in the machinery of institutional narratives, in the mere openness or reserve we show to others. The grand narrative of the self is now replete with the small tales of myriad distinct storytelling occasions, which leap out of diverse and variegated discourses and texts. From the *Diagnostic and Statistical Manual of Mental Disorders* of the American Psychiatric Association—which rationalizes virtually every conceivable action into too much of this trait or too little of that—to the multiplicity of support groups that stand ready to "talk out" every imaginable trouble, we've become a *self-articulating society*, collectively author(iz)ing particular selves.

Indeed, these selves that are authorized are no longer even embedded within traditional experiential borders, as Arlie Hochschild maintains in her book *The Time Bind* (1997). In the family-friendly company in which she did her fieldwork, called Amerco, a Total Quality (TQ) management system has displaced a top-down calculus of scientific management, purportedly "empowering" workers to make decisions on their own. But with its resulting cognitive and emotional intrusions into workers' personal lives, TQ inadvertently turns the work place into another home, encouraging a different kind of work place surveillance: an institutional gaze that places a premium on the expression of feelings, the sharing of emotional labor, and the cooperative spirit of family-like corporate responsibility.

Originally formulated by W. Edwards Deming (see Walton 1986), TQ principles have turned many corporate work places into experiential grounds that compete with the home for storying the self. The "time bind" that results from the cognitive and emotional engrossments of such work places blurs the work-family balance. A "third shift," according to Hochschild, has emerged for these workers that entails keeping the increasingly time-pressured and culturally rationalized household at bay so that workers can devote themselves to the evidently attractive emotional enticements of the work place. For many of Hochschild's informants at Amerco, the work place is often more of an experiential haven than they find at home; the work place offers emotional relief and emotional sustenance away from the rush and turmoil of the domestic front, ironically reversing Christopher Lasch's (1977) argument about the selves and the private family (haven) that are increasingly besieged by the (heartless) public sphere.

The implication for the self of this shift in the work-family balance further particularizes who and what we are; oddly, it locates some of our identities in sites of corporate domesticity. The company's work narrative has effectively changed from paternalistic to maternal accounts, not only nurturing but also healing the selves employees work by. According to Hochschild,

> At Amerco, employees are invited to feel relaxed while on the job. Frequent recognition events reward work but also provide the context for a kind of play. Amerco's management has, in fact, put thought and effort into blurring the distinction between work and play (just as that distinction is so often blurred at home) . . . there are even free Cokes, just as at home, stashed in refrigerators placed near coffee machines on every floor.
>
> Amerco has also made a calculated attempt to take on the role of helpful relative in relation to employee problems at work and at home, implicating the social selves in question. The Education and Training Division offers employees free courses (on company time) in "Dealing with Anger," "How to Give and Accept Criticism," "How to Cope with Difficult People," "Stress Management," "Taking Control of Your Work Day," and "Using the Myers-Briggs Personality Test to Im-

prove Team Effectiveness." . . . Amerco is also one of about a hundred companies that enrolls its top executives in classes at the Corporate Learning Institute. . . . One can, at company expense, attend a course on "Self-Awareness and Being: The Importance of Self in the Influence Process." (Pp. 205–6)

Still, as Hochschild explains, these sites do not homogenize employee selves. While Amerco's work environment has been "culturally engineered" away from scientific to TQ management principles, the work-family balance and a prevailing discourse of emotionality are nevertheless articulated in distinctive ways by different employees. Hochschild points out that "we need to recognize at least four other models of family and work life, each based on the relative emotional magnetism of home and work" (p. 202). The many accounts she presents make it clear that TQ is not the whole story, even while it is the prevailing narrative resource. As Hochschild shows, what Amerco has put in place wends its way through a variety of constitutive adjustments, as different individual employees and working couples convey their lives in relation to what the company expects them to be.

We don't mean to suggest that these developments and discoveries in the identity landscape are all bad, by any means, even though they do complicate and further localize the moral order. Rather, conceiving of identity in terms of the local and the particular provides us analytic purchase on the multiplicity of selves and the question of individualized agency, not to mention offering a moral position on diversity. In an important article on the storying of experience, anthropologist Lila Abu-Lughod (1991, 1993) writes that we must give special attention to small stories in studying culture, because culture doesn't designate our identities automatically, from the top down. In practice, culture works through the little, local stories we tell about who and what we are. Abu-Lughod (1993) contends that the analysis of stories of the self helps to work against a totalized cultural mold, presenting members of society as active agents of culture. Her material underscores the particular in the representation of culture, along with the related moral diversity of engaging the cosmic in the ordinary. She goes on to urge us to "write against culture" not as a way of abandoning culture, but as a means of making visible how culture lives in and through the ways we communicate identity as culture's agents. She argues, as we do, that, in this way, subjectivity is not homogenized into the moral generalizations of "the" culture in question, but is permitted to come through in living color, so to speak, in the ways its identities are used in everyday life.

In this book, we have adopted a version of Abu-Lughod's concern for the particular to call attention to a sociology of the mundane as it applies to selves in our society. To this, we've added a strong institutional dimension, reflecting the growing number of going concerns that populate the contemporary identity landscape. This landscape specifies the moral climate we live in.

Revisiting Multiphrenia

Does this necessarily produce the multiphrenia that Kenneth Gergen describes in *The Saturated Self*? Recall that Gergen's understandably busy professional life led to a feeling of decenteredness, the sense of being pulled in so many different and equally compelling directions at once that his "moral career," to borrow Erving Goffman's (1961) phrase, became directionless. In multiphrenia, an internal, grandly decisive beacon devolves into a thousand possible I's and me's, whose local articulations scatter us every which way. Buffeted about the self-construction terrain by diverse narratives, the self's compass spins wildly out of control, ostensibly losing its ability to pick and choose its own moral course.

Gergen experiences multiphrenia in even the most commonplace settings. The moral spectrum of contemporary life he portrays is so diverse that the competition of its elements for his attention leaves him with little choice but to virtually fold up and wither away. Gergen (1991) presents this "vaguely familiar" anecdote to make his point:

> It is a sunny Saturday morning and he finishes breakfast in high spirits. It is a rare day in which he is free to do as he pleases. With relish he contemplates his options. The back door needs fixing, which calls for a trip to the hardware store. This would allow a much-needed haircut; and while in town he could get a birthday card for his brother, leave off his shoes for repair, and pick up shirts at the cleaners. But, he ponders, he really should get some exercise; is there time for jogging in the afternoon? That reminds him of a championship game he wanted to see at the same time. To be taken more seriously was his ex-wife's repeated request for a luncheon talk. And shouldn't he also settle his vacation plans before all the best locations are taken? Slowly his optimism gives way to a sense of defeat. The free day has become a chaos of competing opportunities and necessities. (P. 73)

According to Gergen, this is social saturation, what he also calls "the populating of the self." As we noted earlier, the result is not a disease; it's the syndrome or *dis-ease* of multiphrenia. The end product is a new sensibility, a disheartening self-consciousness about the self itself. One would surmise that in unsaturated circumstances, the moral horizons of one's world would be clear, allowing one to make prudent decisions about manageable alternatives. In such a world, one's attention would be less on the self than on the choices at hand. But when the options begin to overpopulate, indeed, saturate the self, the self, rather than the options, comes into focus as the heart of the matter. This spirals into the full-blown state of multiphrenia when "technologies of self-expression" expand exponentially, in effect overwhelming the moral agent with too many choices and confronting it with endless possibilities for identity. The self, according to Gergen, experiences a "vertigo of the valued," an "expansion of inadequacy," and a sense that "rationality is in recession."

But, hold on! What's wrong with this picture? Are the possible options of a sunny Saturday morning all that unusual or demanding? Haven't people been confronted by such daily options ever since "weekends" sprang onto the moral horizon? Does the anecdote present anything new, anything especially "postmodern," as Gergen suggests it does? In our view, the picture is skewed because it gives little or no credit to the lived circumstantiality and variable topicality of the self, let alone to the self-constructing agent. We have no way of knowing whether that sunny Saturday morning's self is the self it will be on Sunday or, perhaps more decisively, on Monday morning when the self promptly gets back to business, so to speak. While the self one addresses from the breakfast table on a Saturday may be overpopulated by the day's possible chores, it may very well seem *underpopulated* on Monday morning at the office when an expected invitation to lecture in Rome fails to come through. The point is that the social self is practiced, not just cosmically experienced or entertained, and its related circumstantial character brings it into one's purview in manifold and distinct ways.

The self doesn't live all its circumstances at once. It hasn't since James located it in everyday life. It finds itself concretely here, there, or somewhere else in time and space. If it didn't, we would have no choice but to view it as transcending our lives, relocated, perhaps, in the philosophical venue it occupied before the pragmatists grounded it. Certainly, the self we live by faces increasingly complex and diverse circumstances. But whereas the multiphrenic self may very well be the topic of a philosophically pensive and chore-ridden Saturday morning, it isn't necessarily the topic of another day or even of that Saturday night, when a nice meal, a glass of wine, and the warm company of friends may materially mediate another self, more "at one" with itself. The very scenes of everyday life topicalize and inform the possibilities, of who and what we are in the immediate schemes of things. The resulting narratives don't collapse into each other in practice, because their practice is lived out, indeed, it is anchored in the contemporary geography of self definition.

In practice, we take the moral order in circumstantial doses, not all at once as if it were a universal life elixir or a hemlock cocktail, as the case might be. (Albeit there are circumstances in which the life-giving and the life-threatening do confront us wholesale.) In today's world, there are many self-topicalizing circumstances whose local doses of morality present the self to itself in distinct ways, which, indeed, within the contexts of particular going concerns, can confront us in bold relief. Multiphrenia or something resembling it might describe conditions of moral engagement in many going concerns, but its moral consequences are anything but homogeneous across the identity landscape.

In this regard, compare the moral horizons of Fairview Hospital's therapeutic regimen with the moral order informing therapeutic intervention at Westside House, two agencies offering individual and family counseling for personal troubles and addictions (Gubrium 1992). "Dis-eases" resembling multiphrenia were frequently topicalized at Fairview Hospital, where they were entertained and considered in relation to the emotional stresses of life in today's world. While multiphrenia wasn't named as such, it wasn't unusual to hear patients speak of, and therapists respond to, a syndrome with the characteristics Gergen describes. The syndrome came in the vernacular of emotional helplessness and indecisiveness in response to the "pressure cooker" of contemporary living that made oppressive demands on people. Pressure cookers, as we all know, sometimes "blow their tops" and this was said to happen to people when they simply couldn't "keep up" or "meet expectations." The solution in this setting was for people to learn how to manage their feelings in response to the rapid pace of life. The operating rule was to learn to be satisfied and happy with what one can accomplish under the circumstances by containing the emotional damage.

In contrast, consider Westside House's therapeutic agenda, which advocated authoritative strategies for families with similar problems. At Westside, patients were told not to emotionally despair or adjust their feelings to the problems and pressures of contemporary life. To the extent emotional dis-ease came up, it was to be overcome by taking the bull by the horns, so to speak, and asserting personal power over it. One didn't resign oneself to an overbearing, complex, and irrational world but, instead, one coped by firmly establishing one's place in it. No postmodern-like quandary here. No endless indecisiveness. If contemporary life populated the self, saturating it with endless expectations, it was because it was perhaps faster paced than ever, but otherwise, it was much as it has always been—a system of rights and obligations that needed to be confronted and dealt with on its own terms, not inundated with affective blather. Westside House's moral horizons were distinctly modern and rational, not romantic. A moral discourse of power and decisiveness circumstantially articulated its selves in anything but postmodern terms.

The comparison of these settings suggests that the dis-ease of a saturated self can lead to quite distinct interpretations and moral sensibilities, depending on the particular discourse within which its characteristics are brought to light. Indeed, in the unlikely event that someone would organize a Twelve Step group for "philosophical addiction to postmodernism," one might be discursively called to hit multiphrenic "bottom," surrender to a higher signifying power, and move ahead one hyperreal step at a time. Like postmodernism, the personal dis-eases of postmodernity themselves come in diverse discursive formulations, articulated in the contexts of their own going concerns and competing ideological vintages (see Best and Kellner 1991, Denzin 1991, Kumar 1995, Miller 1997a). Varied moral orders can be brought to bear on the diverse angsts of contemporary life—personal decisiveness, the power of love, even the redemption of Christian Promise Keepers. Each provides its own narrative for telling troubles, formulating related selves, and asserting moral imperatives.

One thing is evident. In revisiting multiphrenia or other quasi-philosophical malaises of contemporary life, we cannot simply consider that "the" self is under siege, that "it" is plagued, experiences overpopulation, or is variably saturated. While such symptoms or syndromes may indeed be considered by some to be the experiential signs of the times, what those signs convey cannot be understood separate from the varied circumstances in which they are narratively addressed. It is only within particular discourses that the condition of the self is discerned and its consequences evoked. We don't present our selves or risk who we are wholesale, in some ethereal location, as if our troubles or our achievements could be evaluated or judged once and for all. Each context for addressing such matters provides for a limited moral engagement, the result being that there are few complete heroes or thoroughly tragic figures in the ongoing dramas of self. We deal with each context on its own terms and, in contemporary life, we have considerable choice about the ones in which we immerse ourselves.

Panopticism Revisited

The relation between moral and institutional orders and identity invites us to re-visit the panopticon that Michel Foucault (1977) discussed in conjunction with the construction of subjectivity. The panopticon, we recall, was an actual building devised by Jeremy Bentham to keep prisoners under surveillance efficiently. With the guard tower always in view, but not the tower's occupants, prisoners had little choice but to keep themselves under control because they had no way of knowing when, or even if, they were being watched. Foucault argued that this sort of surveillance represents a regimen of power and knowledge increasingly pervading contemporary life. Panopticism is part of the varied discourses we share which, in use, articulate and regulate our subjectivity. Designating the sum and substance of our inner worlds and social relationships, these discourses also constitute the moral horizons of the self.

Foucault is careful to describe the institutional groundings of discourses. From the prison to the hospital and clinic, panopticism operates not only in word but in deed. Grounding is practical, suffused in the myriad acts, interactions, and material markers of the language games we apply in communicating to ourselves and to each other who and what we are, not to mention what we do and how we feel. As we noted earlier, because Foucault's project was to document historical constructions as they coalesced in different institutional domains, he did not provide us with much evidence of discursive technology. This, of course, has been part of our own project in this book, to forge an analytics of both discourses-in-practice and discursive practice and thus introducing Foucault and ethnomethodology to one another.

What is the moral flavor of panopticism as it applies to the self in discursive practice? Is the self morally implicated or marginalized? What degree of choice does panopticism leave for self construction? The grand view of panopticism, in which discourse is seen as a totalized deployment of subjectivity, leaves actors with little or no separate moral will. In a totalized panopticism, in which we not only unwittingly imagine others as discerning us in a particular way but discern ourselves likewise, what we do, say, or feel isn't a matter of choice. In a grand scheme of things, such as the broad sweep of new subjectivities that came with the Enlightenment to rationalize and individualize experience, who and what we are is an impersonal matter. The self is massively indebted to a prevailing discourse and has no recourse to alternative vocabularies of subjectivity. In this framework, discourse fully speaks the moral subject, in which case the self is morally immersed in its discourse.

Our view is less grand and confining; we see panopticism operating in relation to the particular. Recall, for example, that Foucault described how prisoners effectively became particular kinds of subjects by virtue of their articulation of a disciplinary regimen, which in turn produced its own moral order and respective selves. While Foucault doesn't describe this in lived detail, we might envision prisoners' identities emerging from the way their conduct was understood in relation to the local scheme of things. If we had ethnographic access to the scenes to which Foucault alerts us, we might see the prisoners, their guards, and other participants in prison life gazing upon each other in the very terms that the daily regimen specifies. These "gazes" not only provide a way of orienting to a schedule but also impose self definition and self discipline. The gazes virtually confer individual identities, according to the language games the regimen provides (Foucault, in effect, giving shape to Wittgenstein). The reflexive power of panopticism has the prisoners themselves discursively joining the ranks of the guards as they figure themselves in terms of the local rhythms and discourse of surveillance, speaking of each other in its vocabulary and deploying their identities in the same terms that a figurative tower guard might.

The institutionalization of the regimen involves everyone in the production of subjectivity. The gaze is universal. Even the savvy prisoner who refuses to adhere to the regimen on principle—not just because he or she is a backslider—is nonetheless looked upon in disciplinary terms. But matters of principle are not merely cosmic issues. They are raised at a specific time and place; in this case it is the confines of a prison or some related setting and the discourse in place is one of regimented confinement, not some other gaze. Both what is known and what is construed reflexively realize each other in terms of the prevailing discourse.

The situation is complicated because a sited panopticism, such as this prison's regimental system, deploys local, not universal, knowledge and power. The moral climate surrounding subjects such as who is a model prisoner, a trustee, or other prison identities is articulated in *prison* talk and interaction. Of course, what one prison puts into place is likely to be part of what all prisons deploy, a broad discourse of rationalized regimentation constituting related subjectivities. In turn, this may itself be part of a grand narrative of institutional rationalization, which Max Weber (see Bendix 1960), well before Foucault, made the centerpiece of his view of modernity. In that case, we're right back to square one, to the grand scheme of things and totalized discourse.

But there are features of everyday talk and action that limit the experiential penetration of totalized discourses and their pervasive moral orders. Thus, we can ask, how does everyday life provide a kind of moral leverage against totalized discourse? Ethnographic analyses of everyday institutional life have shown repeatedly that participants express different levels of awareness about the moral fragility of gazes (e.g., Buckholdt and Gubrium 1979; Edgarton 1967; Giallombardo 1966; Haas and Shaffir 1987; Holstein 1993; Loseke 1992; Miller 1991, 1997a; Perrucci 1974; Pollner and Stein 1996; Sykes 1958). The everyday talk of institutional participants indicates that some are keenly aware that local discourses are not etched in stone but provide *useful* moral options for defining, judging, and cataloging conduct and identity (Wittgenstein, in effect, giving shape to Foucault). As Goffman has indicated in his poignant analyses of the moral order of institutional environments, one can manage to "go through the motions" without thoroughly succumbing to the operating gaze of a going concern. Discourse-in-practice is seldom perfect.

At both Fairview Hospital and Westside House, for example, there were patients who had been ordered by the courts to receive treatment, as well as others whose employers had required, in effect, that they undergo therapy or lose their jobs. According to some of these patients, they were in treatment because they "had to be." To the chagrin of staff members, this could sometimes be glibly elaborated in administratively annoying terms during therapy sessions. It wasn't uncommon for Westside's counseling staff to complain about the lack of conviction of some of these clients. At Fairview Hospital, the inpatient facility, "going through the motions" was sometimes discussed by patients in afternoon recreational periods and during free time in the evening before retiring for bed. In these discussions, what "had to be" was often followed by discussions of "what you have to do because of what you have to do," underscoring the dramaturgical character of the local moral order, and its discourse.

One evening at Fairview Hospital, during a discussion of "[doing] what ya gotta do," a 28-year-old male patient animatedly explained why he decided to undergo treatment for an allegedly "bad crack [cocaine] habit." In the following reconstruction of his comments from ethnographic fieldnotes, notice how he dramaturgically distances himself from the locally applicable discourse of addiction, juxtaposing it to his "own" sense of the "problem" as merely recreational. He eventually reproduces the institutional gaze itself and the related subjectivities of the therapeutic regimen, in which everyone, including the therapists, are simply "doing their job." Initially, the speaker responds to an older patient's complaint about the "shit" the older patient received for smoking "a coupla joints" at work, which, the complainer adds, "ain't nowhere as bad as those fuckin' pillheads who pop all day long and no one knows it because they ain't smellin' it." The younger man responds:

That's cool. What they don't know, they don't know, right? You gotta pop off, pop. Better for your lungs.

Hey, we all get shit, man. I got real shit. You do some crack and ya get high. Who ain't gettin' high? They said I got a bad crack habit. Shit! That's a joke. Hey, man, I'm doin' my job! No one's kickin' about that, right? I'm doin' my fuckin' job. They like what I do. Yeah, they like it! Can ya beat that? Then they comes up with this counseling shit. [Snidely imitating his boss] "I gotta go to the shrink." Some fucker decides that my head ain't on straight. From a few hits!! So here I am. In the fucking nuthouse.

[Responding to a comment about "being set up"] Naw, I ain't been set up, man. Fucking boss just came over and right out in my face he says that it's either dry out or get axed. Simple as shit, man. Says I'm addicted. Can't afford to lose this job, either, you know what I mean?

But hey, dudes, you do what ya gotta do, right? [Several listeners nod] That disclosure shit [referring to his disclosure group], I just tell 'em what they wanna hear. Whatever ya wanna hear, boys and girls. Listen up, boys and girls, I got lots of head troubles. Real troubles. I'm down on my luck. Real bad luck story. Real bad. Been into drugs real bad. Bad ass, bad. Ruinin' my life. Fuckin' up my head. Got a bad attitude. I ain't got control over shit, not me, not my life, not the stuff, nothin'. I'm addicted. Face it, man. I know that song and dance. [Launches into plantation lingo] I'z a drughead. Yessa, I admit it. I'z alearnin'. Okay, massa. You the man. I'z alistenin'. Just like The Man say, you gotta do what ya gotta do. You do their thang, coupla or four weeks in the nutcake, pickin' at yo' head. So what's new? Nice vacation, job's safe, no big time hard time [prison].

[Responding to a comment about being therapeutically harassed] Come on, man, they got a job to do. No fuckin' way they ain't gonna do their job. You better believe it. I got my job in here, too. You gotta be sick, man. I'm sick. Real sick. And they the doctor. Hey, what you expect 'em to do? Lighten up, Lightnin'. [Laughter] They ain't harassing you. They just doin' their thang. We all doin' their thang. Take the steps, boys, one day at a time, like the Man say. This ain't no crack house. This here's treatment time, brothers.

Such comments and sentiments cast a particular moral light on the hospital's therapeutic gaze. While Foucault's panopticon sheds light throughout prisoners' cells, Goffman would suggest that prisoners can "see the light" and more or less consciously attend to their own circumstances in response, weighing the variety of selves at stake in matters at hand, thus figuratively bending the light in various directions as they move about the setting. As if to ask himself what self can be afforded under the circumstances, the prisoner more or less "chooses" to play out what the gaze intends, articulating the watchtower's subjectivity and playing out the local values in question. The prevailing discourse is thus *put* into practice, even if it is done humorously, or in bad faith.

The ability to dramaturgically navigate a discursive environment provides a moral space that can be exploited for other purposes, such as the recovery and reproduction of another self. The simple awareness by participants of alternative discursive strategies opens the moral horizons of gazes and discourses-in-practice. Of course, such awareness does not nullify the practical production of locally preferred subjectivities. Discourse is both power and knowledge. If one thinks in self-conscious terms, he or she does not cause the panopticon to vanish into thin air simply because of that. As we suggested earlier, even the savvy prisoner who disattends the relevancies in place on alleged principle is relegated to a working category within the institutionalized discourse; he is a type of dissenting *prisoner*, not a dissenter. Still, the awareness of alternatives is a basis for resisting the degree to which the categorical imperatives of a going concern can penetrate experience. The patient (or even the staff member) who explains that he's putting in his time until he goes back to work (or gets off work, as the case might be), isn't so much putting a self *at risk* as he is putting it *on hold* until the time and the place are suitable to his or her purposes. Of course, not everyone acts or speaks in this way, but the dramaturgic possibility indicates that the panoptic presence of everyday life is more variegated and disjoint than it is uniform and total. The self may be circumstantially saturated, but knowledge of the moral discourse of other occasions can hold that self at a distance, at the dramaturgic surface of talk and social interaction. Time, place, and memory can combine to short-circuit the moral penetration of life's dominating gazes, even while they continue to specify socially organized subjectivities.

Not only do the awareness of options and the knowledge of alternative sites soften the moral imperatives of self construction, but the alternatives actually can be weighed and worked against each other. The postmodern condition, to recall Jean-François Lyotard's (1984) assessment, locates the self at "crossroads" or "nodal points" of discourses-in-practice. This means that self construction takes place in relation to diverse moral vectors; its moral environment is layered with options, sometimes compatible, sometimes countervailing. While this complicates the self-construction process, to be sure, it also provides conditions that are ripe for interpretive slippage and artful, situationally accountable practical reasoning which, while complicated, can be morally empowering at the same time. Following Lyotard, we find that such conditions make it essentially impossible for social actors to be "powerless" in the face of discursive or moral imperatives, since such forces must always be played out in and through their local and particular applications—through discursive practice. They virtually require the assertion of individual agency—if only for the present—to deal with the competing demands of that moment and its social circumstances.

We can see alternatives at work as local narratives of identity are assembled from the moral hardware of their respective going concerns—in sites such as Metropolitan Court, Westside House, or Fairview Hospital that provide multiple possibilities for accounts of who and what we are. Two important real-life plots that often compete with each other for designating the moral horizons of troubled identities are respectively contained in narratives of crime and sickness. Arthur Kleinman's book *The Illness Narratives* (1988), for example, presents the experience of illness and recovery in stories of suffering and healing, while Jack Katz's book *Seductions of Crime* (1988), published the same year, describes criminality through stories of the "moral and sensual attractions of doing evil." Their narrative horizons compete to specify the etiological and moral bases for human problems in countless everyday situations, including places such as the two family therapy agencies we've discussed (see Conrad and Schneider 1980).

Patients' and family members' troubles would occasionally be discussed at Westside House and Fairview in relation to such alternative narrative paths, sometimes in these very terms. Alternative moral careers were interjected into treatment to exemplify the course that patients' lives would have taken had they not come to the therapeutic attention of the institution. For instance, a counselor at Fairview once ended an especially emotional disclosure session by saying, "I know it's real hard to disclose your feelings like we've done this afternoon but, just think, you could have been spilling your guts behind bars and there all you'd hear is shut up and stop bellyaching." Family members, too, cited the ominous alternatives their children might have faced as they railed against the children for not taking their treatment regimens seriously, pointing to how much worse off they would have been if they had gone to juvenile detention, say. On the other hand, it wasn't unusual to hear a patient complain about all the "mind games" they play in therapy, adding that he or she might have been better off just "doing time."

However real such alternatives were in practice, there was no mistaking their competing rhetorical, and moral, value. Time and again, staff members, patients, and significant others looked back and either portrayed or recalled what might have been, had a therapeutic alternative not been selected. Therapists attempted to convince patients that seeking treatment or being "forced to" go through therapy was "the best option," the "only choice you had," or "the right path to full recovery," among other ways of retrospectively justifying therapeutic identities. Patients and family members used similar rhetorical strategies to raise each other's morale. They looked ahead and portrayed the future in similar terms, as personal narratives that would likely have been told otherwise in stories of "hard time" or of becoming further "jail bait" had they not entered treatment. For better or worse, there also was the rhetorical value of being able to convince oneself or others of the excitement the future could still hold if one didn't let all "this shit go to [one's] head," as a 19-year-old drug abuser advised his friends.

Alternative discourses for the self are present throughout contemporary society, as integral parts of, and surrounding, the moral horizons of select institutions. While one discourse may be regularly pitted against another, the possibilities for competition are seemingly endless. For example, in his studies of interpretive practice and involuntary mental commitment, Holstein (1993) showed how the moral discourse operating in the court environment oscillated between binary narratives of sickness and ordinary living, of care and management versus custody and control, depending on the practical interests of judges, lawyers, psychiatrists, candidate patients, and witnesses to the "craziness" in question. Similarly, Gubrium and Buckholdt's (1982) research at Wiltshire Hospital, a physical rehabilitation facility, illustrated how educational narratives were used to describe patients' progress in treatment. Therapists addressed patients in educational terms, describing them as "pupils" and "learners" who would go as far as their "motivation" would take them. They were told, time and again, that physical rehabilitation was not a matter of being cured, but of achieving one's maximum potential. In sharp contrast, progress in rehabilitation—called "learning" when speaking to patients—was reported to third-party payers and to families in medical terms, communicating the details of "cure" and "recovery." Success was a medical accomplishment in this discourse. Failure to make progress, on the other hand, was descriptively retrenched to the vocabulary of motivation and learning, the lack of progress being the result of poor motivation, for example, reasserting an educational discourse.

To revisit panopticism in these terms is not to question the usefulness of Foucault's formulation for understanding the moral climate of the self. Rather, it is to put it in its everyday working places, as Foucault's broad institutional analyses started to do. In today's world, the morality of discourse-in-practice must necessarily be tied to an increasing expansion of the particular. This, of course, implicates discursive practice, as individuals work locally to construct and deploy accountable subjectivities. Despite the recent resurgence of romanticist impulses that suggest there are more authentic selves beneath or beyond the many language games through which we now communicate who and what we are, identity remains what local interpretive practice makes us out to be (see Gubrium and Holstein 1997, Chapter 4).

The self survives because we continue to refer to *it*, speak of *it*, and act toward the *entity* that we take to be at our moral core. At the same time, we do so in and through its complex and disciplined narrative technology. The selves we produce are the very same selves to which we turn in moral considerations of the selves we are. As we story ourselves, those stories provide the moral horizons for evaluating who and what we've become. There are plenty of options for self construction and self assessment. For some, this is frightening, as it conjures up moral recklessness and an associated proliferation of diversity that they can't abide. This hints at the fear of responsibility for self production that comes with the opening of new moral territory. Others, of course, find this morally refreshing because it presents us with worlds and identities of our own making, the narrative particulars of which are as limitless as our imaginations.

The Moral Significance of the Local

The theoretical tension between grand narratives and particular renditions of self is an old one. Over the years, we have seen repeated forays into totalizing social theory, systems of social thought so abstractly and broadly conceived that they leave virtually nothing to the agency and nuanced conduct of everyday actors (see Parsons 1951, for example). But, from the pragmatists' rejection of a philosophically transcendent self, to Garfinkel's repudiation of the cultural dope and to Foucault's specification of discourses-in-practice, we also can trace a complex stream of thought that has insinuated the particular into social theory. The groundings of interpretive practice—from the I's and me's of ordinary social interaction, to the machinery of conversation, and into the various going concerns we enter as we go about our lives—highlight the foundations of a less totalizing and determinant approach.

Its strength lies in its refusal to theorize away the lived morality of the self. Practice remains open to view; the moral climate of the self remains simultaneously and continually under construction. The self is not completely predefined; it's not the byproduct of a totalized and totalizing cultural or social system; it isn't what some grand narrative—some monolithic panopticon—might designate. Totalized, perfectly articulated conceptual systems leave little space for local modification. Yet, this is precisely what we see when we look at the practical production of the self, as we did when we observed Joe Julian and Francine O'Brien in Chapter 9 actually work at discerning the moral order applicable to Maurice Clay's teasing behavior. What Julian and O'Brien assumed to be universally and automatically applicable was bound to its practical realization.

We have chosen to locate self construction at the doorstep of the particular, in the varied self stories that populate the identity landscape. None of these is simply there for the telling. We've conceptualized these stories as narratives-in-the-making. Selves, we have argued, are constituted and received in relation to the complex machinery of telling, local ways of knowing and hearing, and the scenic presence of their performances. We accent the moral significance of the local, which is as varied and diverse as the circumstances of contemporary life.

This isn't a radical localism, however. The dividing practices that Foucault pointed to as increasingly constructive of contemporary subjectivity are not bereft of their discourses nor insensitive to their institutional horizons. The conversational machinery that Harvey Sacks introduced to us serves to articulate methodically the storying of the self, but it doesn't work in a cultural vacuum. In inventing conversation analysis, Sacks repeatedly came around to both the immediate and broader conditions of communication that bear on narrativity, as narrative practice invariably does.

For us, the moral significance of the local derives from "where people are," as Dorothy Smith reminds us. This is not meant to resurrect a positivistic naturalism, nor to romanticize a deeply hidden, genuine self. Instead, it points us in the direction of the *working* horizons of identity. As such, the moral significance of the local rests on the methods people themselves apply to construe who and what they are. It entails a concerted alertness to the many and diverse ways that self can be assembled and articulated in the midst of its always compelling operating locales.

The moral climate of the self we live by is located at the working crossroads of institutional discourses and everyday life, in the interplay of discursive practice and discourses-in-practice. It's a space where the self has multiple signposts, directed in various ways by what is both locally shared and broadly consequential. If there is anything grandly narrative about this, it lies in that which "everyone knows" as it is uniquely and specifically brought to bear on issues of immediate concern. We see this in the "sick" selves detected by Joe Julian and Francine O'Brien at Cedarview as opposed to the "traumatized" selves that Alan Young's Vietnam veterans reconstruct in group therapy. It may be the "spiritually lost" souls who seek to regain their manhood in Promise Keepers as opposed to those who search for redemption taking AA's Twelve Steps. Curiously enough, we even see this in the "haven" that work, not home, now provides for selves bound in time to both worlds.

The linkages between who and what we are and the various big and little stories of what we could be are enormously complex. This isn't a grand language game, which we might theorize as a mosaic of conceptual associations and dissociations. Nor is it reducible to the ethno-methods of folk fabrication. The age-old issues of responsibility, choice, and decision-making still apply, but they are anything but totalized or purely discursive. These are moral engagements we share with others—engagements that are informed by the circumstances in which we all find ourselves.

Our aim in this book has been to make these engagements visible, a goal realized through our own form of panopticism—a surveillance of surveillances, the discursive scrutiny of deployed subjectivities. Just as selves reflexively grow out of the diverse stories we can tell, our own restorying brings us to the junction of everyday accounts and the going concerns that mediate reflection on those accounts. If there is an inventiveness at this location and a related hope for the potential selves we might be, it is the natural creativity of any crossroads, where there is direction, yet the paths are unclear, where the signposts are a bit confusing and the crossing itself precarious and in need of continuous definition. As all panopticons do, the panopticon we have ourselves brought to bear on the self establishes its own moral climate. It opens individuals to view as subjects who are reflexively working out who and what they are as they articulate and ramify the myriad self narratives of contemporary life. It points out that, however much this figures in storying the self we live by, there are always new stories to spin, tell, and become. The going concerns of postmodernity assure us of it.

Notes

Chapter 1

1. As we will argue, these stories are grounded in a multiplicity of sites and settings, implicating the increasingly varied circumstances of institutional life and electronic communication. Our argument also has implications for the daily materialization of race, class, ethnicity, gender, sexuality, and a gamut of other categories of membership and identity (see Andersen and Collins 1998, Anzaldúa 1987, Buchbinder 1994, Butler 1990, Chow 1993, Connell 1995, Marcus 1992, Seidman 1997).
2. Richard de Mille (1980) has raised questions about the veracity of Schneebaum's account, especially regarding the reports of cannibalism and homosexuality. This skepticism, however, doesn't extend to the descriptions of Akarama subjectivity and the penchant for absorbing individuals into the collectivity.

Chapter 2

1. Two additional and important early pragmatists were John Dewey and Charles Sanders Peirce, who variously influenced, and were influenced by, the others both personally and intellectually. We focus on James, Cooley, and Mead because these thinkers' ideas about the social self most shaped subsequent social psychological formulations, even while this influence has been claimed by some commentators to have been assimilated into social psychology, especially into symbolic interaction, in mythic proportions (see note 6 below).
2. In our view, one can best understand the significance of the early pragmatists' contribution by considering their efforts in relation to what came before them, not what came afterward. A half century later, symbolic interactionists, for example, regularly made connections with early pragmatist thought and, certainly, there were many parallel concerns. But these were already in the pragmatist cards, so to speak; these were important, albeit not revolutionary, extensions, especially of Mead's contributions. The contrast with transcendental philosophy, however, was a sea change in perspective, launching the self as the empirical project it came to be for the behavioral and social sciences, as well as for its subjects.
3. As commentators Larry Reynolds (1990), David Miller (1973), and Gary Cook (1993) note, Hegelian idealism, with its absolutely transcendent self, was an important part of the Cartesian philosophical background for James's, Cooley's, and Mead's pragmatist reaction. What Descartes launched centuries earlier continued to lurk in the pragmatists' philosophical background as they turned away from a Hegelian and transcendental self to an empirical one.
4. Self is part of the "variable" human nature that Cooley is attempting to link with social order, as the title of his book indicates. In contrast to "metaphysicians and moralists' " universalized approach to human nature, Cooley's sense of human nature, like that of the other pragmatists, works against a singular view. For him, it's in the nature of man to have as many natures as the social order reflects who or what he is.

5. Were it not for Mead's assiduous liberalism, his emphasis on communicative practice and his concept of "game" might have been a precursor of Ludwig Wittgenstein's (1953, 1958) idea of the "language game" (see Miller 1973, Chapter 4). This would raise a number of questions related to the play/game distinction Mead makes. Before an overall sense of the game is in place, how does play transpire at its stage? Do children merely "pass from one role to another just as a whim would take [them]," as Mead puts it? Or does play itself have a certain whimsical game plan? In the world of everyday life, can we not help playing one (language) game or another, along with its respective selves, as Wittgenstein might have argued? Is it possible to conceive of life without its particular game plans or social logics, in particular a stage of human development preparatory to the playing of games? Even in play, isn't the sharedness of language at work organizing our actions? Are we not always discursively "imprisoned" in one game or another (Jameson 1972)? Mead did not pose such questions, of course, but they are suggested in the neopragmatism that is influenced by poststructuralist ideas (see, for example, Rorty 1982 and Saatkamp 1995). As we will see in Chapter 4, these are the kinds of critical questions raised at century's end in relation to both the transcendental self that Mead dismissed and the social self he so ingeniously helped to formulate.

6. There has been considerable debate over the relationship of the Chicago school, especially Blumer's intellectual connection, to early pragmatist thought (see Blumer 1977; Lewis 1976, 1977). In their controversial book *American Sociology and Pragmatism: Mead, Chicago Sociology, and Symbolic Interaction*, J. David Lewis and Richard L. Smith (1980) argue that the lines of intellectual development between Chicago sociology before and just after World War II and the early pragmatists are less clear and distinct than Blumer and other "Blumerians" would have them be. Lewis and Smith explain that, even while Blumer claimed a Meadian heritage, what Blumer called "symbolic interactionism" has greater intellectual affinities with the social nominalism of James and Dewey than with Mead's social realism. Lewis and Smith also cast doubt upon the intellectual coherence of a Chicago school centered on symbolic interactionism, claiming instead that the Meadian social psychology of the Chicago "school" is retrospective myth (also see Janowitz 1966).

   In raising the question of whether there was a second Chicago school in the decades following World War II, Gary Alan Fine (1995) and his contributors cast further doubt on the coherence of Chicago sociology. While the pragmatist roots of Blumer's thought are not so much the focus of the commentaries, it is suggested nonetheless that Blumer himself may have had considerable influence on formulating the idea (myth?) of a coherent body of ideas based on Mead's thought as being the primary inspiration of Chicago social psychology and on what Blumer coined "symbolic interactionism."

   Our own discussion of the differences between the Chicago and Iowa forms of symbolic interaction is not meant to take a stand in the debate, but rather is part of our attempt to trace several lines of thinking stemming from the idea of a social self. Whatever the ultimate pedigree of these lines is, our view is that the really big story is the empirical grounding the early pragmatists gave the self regardless of whether it comes in more or less realist form. It was this that opened a brand new horizon of thinking for that entity called the self, which, at century's turn, some say has exhausted itself.

7. Such neopositivist impulses continued to challenge symbolic interactionism throughout its history. See Joan Huber (1973), Clark McPhail and Cynthia Rexroat (1979), and Sheldon Stryker (1980) for a lively debate that developed in the 1970s around the issue of how to orient to patterning or "structure" in social life.

8. Goffman's own methodological position is sprinkled throughout his writing and it's easy enough to read his work as sympathetic to naturalistic inquiry, as is Blumer's. This

is evident, for example, when Goffman (1961) comments on his studies of the lives and selves of mental hospital inmates:

> My immediate objective in doing fieldwork at St. Elizabeth's [psychiatric hospital] was to try to learn about the world of the hospital inmate, as this world is subjectively experienced by him. . . . It was then and still is my belief that any group of persons—prisoners, primitives, pilots, or patients—develop a life of their own that becomes meaningful, reasonable, and normal once you get close to it, and that a good way to learn about any of these worlds is to submit oneself in the company of the members to the daily round of petty contingencies to which they are subject. (Pp. ix–x)

But as much as this resonates with Blumer's symbolic interactionist premises, Goffman distanced himself from symbolic interactionism, preferring not to be associated with any sociological "isms" (see Platt 1995).

Chapter 3

1. The image of the other-directed self, bombarded with radar messages from an ever-expanding and intrusive social world, is presciently similar to Kenneth Gergen's view of the "saturated self," to which we turn in Chapter 4. Even more remarkable is Riesman's anticipation of the social conditions that might lead to such "saturation," given that he was writing nearly a half century before Gergen.

2. Here Riesman anticipates postmodern analyses, including those by Baudrillard (1983) and Gergen (1991), in seeing the media onslaught on, if not simulacra of, the self. This is quite amazing given that Riesman wrote his book before the ubiquitous popularity of television. In general, in Riesman's opinion, the more advanced the technology—especially communications technology—the greater the possibility for people "to imagine being somebody else" (p. 292). Given the ability to "take the role of the other" and increasingly to take up myriad roles, the amount of social input into the self, according to Riesman, is all but overwhelming, even at mid-century.

3. Whyte's argument is strikingly similar to Riesman's, although he limits his account to the corporate and suburban worlds of the middle-class 1950s. While the Organization Man seems to be the corporate version of other-directedness, Whyte cites Riesman only once, in passing, in this regard.

4. Indeed, Hochschild sees a ray of hope for the real self in a heightened awareness of how much we engage in emotion work. As feelings and their management are increasingly commercialized, she suggests that we are developing an appreciative skepticism concerning their commodification and management. Because we are more and more aware that we interact constantly with others who display selves and feelings that are dictated by circumstance or organizational mandate, we are developing a culturally transmitted tendency to discount that which we see on the surface as merely (or falsely) "acting" as opposed to "being" in both others and ourselves. At the same time, Hochschild believes that a cultural appreciation is growing for the "sincere" and the "authentic," for the "true" self that is not a mere commercial product. She argues that as the value placed on the "natural," the "authentic," or the "individual" grows, there are increased attempts to manifest the true self. We may work harder at staying in touch with "who we really are." Hochschild concludes that "the more the heart is managed, the more we manage the unmanaged heart" (p. 192), which of course implicates the self.

5. While Becker is often credited with the creation of the labeling perspective, Edwin Lemert foreshadowed the essence of the approach over a decade before the publication of *Outsiders* (Becker 1973[1963]). Indeed, while Becker's is an imaginative and convincing statement of the approach, it fails to pursue many of its crucial implications, especially in relation to the self. More comprehensive and nuanced statements quickly

emerged that elaborated the perspective, pursued important ramifications, and located it more securely in the symbolic interactionist tradition. See, for example, Lemert (1950, 1967), John Kitsuse (1962), and Edwin Schur (1971, 1979).

6. Instead, Becker focuses on the changing social contexts of labels and the political environment of the so-called moral entrepreneurs that promote labeling. He and other labeling theorists are typically inattentive to the detailed interactional work that is necessary to attach labels to actions and individuals. See Virginia Gill and Douglas Maynard (1995) and James Holstein (1993).

7. Of course there are other chapters of the story that might be told. Perhaps the most notable competitor to the one we summarize has a chapter with the self turning inward, rather than outward. This chapter is eloquently presented, for example, in *The Fall of Public Man* by Richard Sennett (1974) and in *Habits of the Heart* by Robert Bellah and associates (1996[1985]). Like Christopher Lasch's book *The Culture of Narcissism* (1979), mentioned earlier, these books are twists of the plot in which the self retreats from the public scene, all but rejecting the social. Indeed, Sennett explicitly counters the accounts Riesman and Whyte offer: "I am turning around the argument David Riesman made in *The Lonely Crowd....* Riesman believed American society ... was moving from an inner- to an other-directed condition. The sequence should be reversed" (p. 5). Rather than passively responding to social demands and blandly reflecting social values, argues Sennett, people are becoming increasingly self-absorbed, leading to the demise of the public domain and the fall of public man. Bellah and his associates convey a similar message. Radical individualism plagues the self, leading to a crisis of commitment and the dissipation of civic responsibility.

While these descriptions reflect varied interpretations of changing times and conditions, the story of the *social* self remains. If Bellah and his associates write of the rampant individualism sweeping America, they nonetheless insist that the individualistic, autonomous self is not the opposite of the self determined completely by the social situation (p. 80). Rather, they argue, the "unencumbered" self is an educational, scientific, philosophical, and theological mistake. According to these authors, Americans have been falsely captivated by the discourse of individualism, leading them to erroneous beliefs about, and characterizations of, the self. "There are truths we do not see," they write, when we see the self in individualistic terms. "We find ourselves, not independently of other people and institutions but through them. We never get to the bottom of ourselves on our own. We discover who we are face to face and side by side with others in work, love, and learning"(p. 84). As if to preview a narrative understanding of self construction (including our own view), they argue that the discourse of individualism is merely a "cultural pattern of meaning," a collective way of characterizing our lives, selves, and experiences. The radically individualistic self, then, is a denial of the fundamentally social character of humanity. To speak of life in its terms poses a crucial problem, extracting a "high price" from those adopting this view. These authors conclude that we need an awareness of the social side of our selves "if we are not to have a self that hangs in the void, slowly twisting in the wind" (p. 84). By implication, they argue that the critical contemporary problem for the social self is that its social character is not sufficiently recognized or appreciated. Theirs is more a variant on the theme of the "embattled" social self than a rejection of the social.

Sennett also allows that it is the social conditioning of the self that, in his view, has driven it inward. Calling the turn inward a "romantic quest for personality," Sennett suggests that it is the conditions of ordinary life that propel people into this search for selves within. Once again, it is the social that influences people to characterize their lives and selves in individualistic terms. The social remains essential to this account of the self, even as that self dons the guise of individualism.

Chapter 4

1. Charles Lemert (1994) refers to Gergen's view as "pseudo-postmodern." Gergen's perspective doesn't introduce a brand new vocabulary for understanding ourselves, but instead pummels an old terminology with a cacophony of meanings.

2. Baudrillard is often taken to be the high priest of radical postmodernism, yet he denies the label "postmodern," which is nonetheless commonly applied to his position (Gane 1993).

3. The scenario had already been anticipated by Larry Beinhart's novel *American Hero* (1993), a fictional account of the Bush Administration's concoction of a media war to raise its flagging public opinion ratings. The book became the basis for the popular Hollywood film *Wag the Dog*, which reflexively filmed the filming of the staged reality.

4. For some, the parallel with television is overdrawn (see Best and Kellner 1991; Featherstone 1988; Lash and Friedman 1992; Poster 1988; Seidman and Wagner 1992). Mike Featherstone (1988, p. 200), for example, cautions that while Baudrillard attempts to describe hyperreality as a site epitomized by television, he offers few clues to how the hyperreal relates to practice: "For all the alleged pluralism and sensitivity to the Other talked about by some theorists one finds little discussion of the actual experience and practice of watching television by different groups in different settings." Referring to the postmodern penchant for situating experience in channel hopping and multiphrenic imaging, Featherstone adds that "evidence of the extent of such practices, and how they are integrated into, or influence, the day-to-day encounters between embodied persons is markedly lacking." In the *Introduction to Selected Writings from Baudrillard*, Mark Poster (1988) is also critical, even while he later appreciates Baudrillard's contributions to our understanding of the impact of electronic media on society:

   [Baudrillard's] writing style is hyperbolic and declarative, often lacking sustained, systematic analysis when it is appropriate; he totalizes his insights, refusing to qualify or delimit his claims. He writes about particular experiences, television images, as if nothing else in society mattered, extrapolating a bleak view of the world from that limited base. (P. 7)

5. In hyperreality, we no longer experience things in the way we once did in the modern world. There's no point in being nostalgic, because we can immediately produce the simulacrum of that for which we long. We can't be charmed by how well we mirror or reproduce reality; nor can we be critical of how reality is overshadowed by images alien to itself. There's no warrant for emotions or basis for ideological analysis. If Madonna's rendition of "Don't Cry for Me Argentina" weren't so mournful, we might similarly advise ourselves not to cry over reality; it's no longer there to weep (or sing) for. If anything, we can only be sensually playful in hyperreality, as the postmodern carnival and Baudrillard's writing intimate.

6. Even the possibility that the accounts are rehearsed and later staged is obviated by the equally real possibility that the accusation of fraud is itself a publicity stunt—part of the staged reality and not commentary on it.

7. It's been said that Baudrillard's writing is prone to exaggeration, especially after 1980 when he adopts and elaborates the vocabulary of postmodernism (Best and Kellner 1991). The stem "hyper" not only references Baudrillard's sense of postmodern reality, but also seems to describe his approach. Douglas Kellner (1989, p. 174) indicates that "the novelty and indetermination [of hyperreality] bring with them the now familiar Baudrillardian experiences of giddiness and vertigo and a rejection of previous

views, including his own, which fail to take into account the novelty of the situation." Baudrillard's post-1980 writing seems fueled both by its own internal logic and the universe it constructs.

   Lest we judge hyperreality to be gratuitous exaggeration, with Baudrillard's writing its accomplice, we need to focus on the serious implications of his project (if we can refer to "seriousness" in hyperreality). Baudrillard not only describes a new and rapidly developing world, one that features novelty and indetermination, but he also takes seriously his place in it. As his writing must, it highlights novelty and playfulness. Baudrillard refuses to merely write in a somber, linear, objectivistic, modern expository fashion; indeed, he needs to write against this. When Baudrillard describes hyperreality—an increasingly "fantasmagoric" America, the simulacra, and their implosion—he writes reflexively. His writing itself is fantasmagoric, placing Baudrillard squarely in the center, so to (ironically) speak, of what Kellner (1989) calls "the postmodern carnival." The writing itself reproduces the novelty and indetermination of hyperreality; the reader experiences a version of hyperreality as he or she reads along. In hyperreality, the reader needn't go elsewhere; reality is literally at hand. What Baudrillard has imagined and given a name becomes its/his own subject matter.

8. Norbert Wiley (1994) asks the same questions, but in relation to the "inner conversation" that George Herbert Mead calls "mind." Wiley tries to find a way to decenter this interior side of the self without eliminating it. He extends Mead's dyadic I-me self, which is reflexive and past oriented, by adding to it pragmatist Charles Sanders Peirce's I-you dyad, which is future oriented. The resulting triad (I-me-you; present-past-future), in its interior reflexivity or inner conversation, preserves the empirical or social self in the subject's ongoing reflection on itself from the point of view of the other, while also opening the self to the possible "you's" it could be and by which it has the potential to address itself. Thus, the inner conversation is real enough, but is always in the process of displacing itself from a central location because it is constantly being addressed from positions of possibility, not actuality.

   This provides an intriguing complement to our own view, which also attempts to decenter the social self without eliminating it. Our approach focuses on the ongoing practical work of constructing existing and potential selves in the varied contexts of everyday life; it is a distinctly "exterior" or public view of the social self. But it is concerned with a parallel issue: how to incorporate the contemporary diversity of self-constructive language games, which serve multiple subjectivities (postmodern), while at the same time sustaining the (modern) working self of everyday life.

9. The conflation of the individual and the individual's social roles and status is apparently common cross-culturally. The realizations of such selves, however, are quite varied. The Gahuku-Gama of highland Papua New Guinea, for example, eschew stylized ceremonial performance for more "bodily" idioms. Their concept of the person is highly particularized; the self becomes a unique combination of roles. Rather than transcending individual lives as Balinese dramatis personae do, individual role combinations/selves cease at death. But, while the Gahuku-Gama lack a generalized concept of personhood, individuals develop a strong sense of self—of who they are—in terms of their unique role combinations (see Shweder and Bourne 1984).

10. Compare Gergen's (1991, p. 1) orientation to the respite of "seclusion, restoration, and recentering," which we discussed earlier in the chapter. Clearly, for Gergen, "privacy," if not the private sphere, is the space where the modern self can be restored so that it can continue to withstand the relentless onslaught of public life. Indeed, the differentiation of the public and the private spheres is a virtual semiotic for a distinct individuality and the related meaning of authenticity. The public sphere presents the mul-

tiphrenic selves we must often be in a saturated world, while the private sphere is increasingly elusive as a space for sustaining the semblance of an individualized subjectivity.

Chapter 5

1. The term *work* has been carried forward in this practical sense by a number of contemporary constructionist researchers, although their particular angles on practice vary considerably. From J. William Spencer's (1994) and Amir Marvasti's (1998) research on "client work" and identity among the homeless, to Jaber Gubrium and James Holstein's (1995a) and Gubrium and Robert Lynott's (1985) analysis of "biographical work," David Snow and Leon Anderson's (1987) focus on "identity work," and Holstein and Gale Miller's (1993b) considerations of "social problems work," the orientation is to everyday language at work doing the social forms and entities in question.
2. Later, Marvin B. Scott and Stanford Lyman (1968) and John P. Hewitt and Randall Stokes (1975) further distinguished vocabularies of motive into "accounts" and "disclaimers," important devices for managing the self in social interaction. See Terri Orbuch (1997) for a review of the sociology of accounts and Gubrium and Holstein (1998) for a consideration of such vocabularies in the context of narrative practice.
3. John Heritage (1997) makes a similar point in distinguishing two forms of conversation analysis (CA). Formal CA focuses on the internal organization of talk and interaction, which, from Mills's perspective, could hardly be the whole story. In contrast, studies of what is called "institutional talk" take into account the institutional arrangements within which ongoing talk and interaction unfold, pointing to the (external) social distribution of language games. Putting less emphasis on the "outside" than Mills does, but still acknowledging that this plays into the articulation of language games, Heritage writes, "The assumption is that it is fundamentally through interaction that institutional imperatives originating from *outside* the interaction are evidenced and made real and enforceable for the participants" (p. 163, emphasis added).
4. In Michel Foucault's (1982) afterword to Hubert Dreyfus and Paul Rabinow's (1982) book about his system of thought, Foucault describes his work as the history by which human beings are made subjects in our culture. Foucault notes that his work has dealt with three modes of objectification that transform individuals into subjects, the second of which involves the practical application of binary distinctions, which is a form of "dividing practice." Foucault explains that dividing practices set the subject either against himself or against others. In thus locating who they are in relation to themselves and each other, they create difference.
5. Whatever its content, social order is ineluctably created, because its associated practical reasoning is indexical and reflexive. Harold Garfinkel's (1967) so-called breaching experiments—which entail disrupting the "normal" course of everyday life, such as acting like a stranger at the dinner table or endlessly pursuing why someone did an otherwise trivial act—can, in the final analysis, devolve angrily, impatiently, even jokingly into talk and interaction focused on the experiment itself. The point is that it never devolves into nothing, even while we may not be able to discern what it devolves into on the basis of principles of practical reasoning or conversational practice alone. Social order, even jocular games that consciously play on social order, are invariably reflexive in that they integrally form their own sense of orderliness, whose jokes index the order produced. Thus, as long as there is talk and interaction, the *hows* of everyday life are at play constructing social order. For an empirical demonstration of the construction of meaningful order from "randomness," see Garfinkel's (1967,

Chapter 3) research on the "documentary method of interpretation in lay and professional fact finding."

6. Tapes are transcribed to reproduce the fine-grained details of speech exchanges (see Atkinson and Heritage 1984). Occasionally, neither tape-recording nor videotaping is possible and some researchers have then relied on fieldnotes gathered expressly for the purpose of capturing the organization of talk and interaction (see Holstein 1993; West 1996).

7. Heritage (1997, p. 179) points out that a number of scholars have noted the parallel between Foucault's conception of power/knowledge and ethnomethodological considerations of the indexical and reflexive character of everyday language in use (see Gubrium and Holstein 1997; Miller 1994, 1997b; Miller and Holstein 1996; Potter 1996; Prior 1997; Silverman 1993).

8. There is even a certain terminological parallel, for example, for the reflexivity of practice (reflexivity/indexicality versus power/knowledge), for language use (practical reasoning versus dividing practices), and for configurations of available meaning (MCDs versus discourses).

9. In formulating a poststructuralist/feminist approach that "subverts" the phallocentric and, more generally, modern conception of identity, Judith Butler (1990) offers what she calls a "performative" view, in which identity is less an essentially interior feature of subjectivity than it is a way of playing out or performatively realizing our identities for ourselves and for others. For Butler, interiority is constructed, not an emergent result of human development. The upshot of the approach is that we become in our innermost being who and what we and others construct for us.

Robert Dunn (1998) suggests that this invites a comparison to Goffman (1959, 1967), who, according to Dunn, "stressed the dramatistic or theatrical character of social behavior, albeit while retaining a conception of an interior identity" (p. 192). Echoing Friedrich Nietzsche (1956, pp. 178–79), Butler writes, "My argument is that there need not be a 'doer behind the deed,' but that the 'doer' is variably constructed in and through the deed" (p. 142). Leaving aside Goffman's assumption of experiential interiority, he, more than Butler, nonetheless provides us with a view of the social organization of the construction of interiority, siting the construction process in the social situation. This would suggest that various social situations construct interiority differently. (However, with a few exceptions, such as Goffman's concern with the moral careers of mental patients, he gives us little sense of the social distribution of these situations and their construction processes, or of the social distribution of related identities.) As Dunn points out, like many theories of identity formation today, Butler's is too discursive and provides no theory of social practice at all. The result is that while identity is set free of essentialist moorings, we are offered nothing by which to discern its social organization (see also Weeks, 1998, p. 128). Dunn explains that "[Butler] remains entrapped in a theory of discourse bereft of any conceptualization of the manifold social and individual sources of meaning, identity, and agency" (p. 193).

At the risk of disciplinary snideness, we might add that such is also the risk of theory formation in the humanities and literary criticism, where orienting "texts" are primarily textual rather than viewed in the social arenas of everyday life. There's a danger in conceptualizing these arenas as texts. Social arenas, in contrast to texts, present their participants with more than reading challenges for constructing the meanings of things, including the construction of subjectivity; they can actually present risks to participants' dignity, jobs, health, if not to their very lives, when things are not constructed in particular ways. Our point is that there may be a disciplinary bias to the conceptualization of the construction process, which is likely to be "fixed" more toward the social in the social sciences and "freed" from it in the humanities. Siting the social construction process in going concerns tames the often rampant fluidity and sense of "anything goes" in some poststructuralist formulations. The social siting reappropriates a "modern," scientific sense of the regularities of the construction process.

10. The rubric "discourse analysis" has come to refer to such a large category of activities as to become virtually meaningless. Jonathan Potter (1996, 1997) has helped to sort some of the differences. We borrow from his descriptions to describe in Foucauldian terms our orientation to the analytic interplay between discursive practice and discourses-in-practice. While Potter subsumes conversation analysis (CA) under Anglo-American discourse analysis (DA), he isn't clear about what that difference is in its own right. Our sense is that with the possible exception of the growing research on talk-at-work or institutional talk, CA has been much more oriented than DA to the sequential machinery of talk and interaction; DA focuses more on substantive concerns in relation to practical reasoning. (See Heritage 1984, 1997 for a discussion of the distinction between "formal" and "institutional" CA.)

There also is the matter of empirical register. From the start, CA has worked at the level of real-time talk and interaction, while discursively oriented ethnographers have instinctively taken a more expansively scenic view of equally real-time talk and interaction (see Atkinson 1995; Buckholdt and Gubrium 1979; Gubrium 1992; Maynard 1989a; Miller 1991, 1997a; Wieder 1974). Given their historical proclivities, Foucauldian discourse analysts understandably focus less on real-time talk and interaction than on varieties of texts to document their constitutive and subjectivizing elements (for example, Donzelot 1980; Hacking 1981, 1982; Rose 1990). Alec McHoul and Wendy Grace (1993) and Teun van Dijk (1997) provide useful accounts of other distinctions.

11. We originally conceived of analytic bracketing as a procedural move devoted to preserving the tension at the center of an increasingly self-conscious qualitative inquiry and at the lived border of reality and representation. Eventually, we figured that it not only served the fuller exploration of everyday life, but was a *critically* reflexive move as well. Analytic bracketing makes us critically aware of the hallmark tension at the heart of interpretive practice. It is a way of integrally reminding ourselves that in the civilization in which we live, both structure and agency have always mattered and continue to matter, even while it also warns us that too great an emphasis on one or the other, or their reifications, can destroy the practical enterprise upon which it is balanced.

Chapter 6

1. The "newer" narrative studies are quite diverse. For a sampling of the alternate perspectives on narrative, narration, and "storied lives," see Berger (1997); Bertaux (1981); Bruner (1986); Gubrium (1993); Josselson and Lieblich (1993, 1995); Lieblich and Josselson (1994); Lowenthal, Thurner, and Chiriboga (1975); Maines (1993); Maines and Ulmer (1993); Meyerhoff (1992); Plummer (1983, 1995); Richardson (1990, 1991); Runyan (1982); Sarbin (1986); Thompson (1978); and Thompson, Itzin, and Abendstern (1990), among others.

2. It is becoming increasingly fashionable to argue for the social and moral elasticity of the self. Certainly, our own view harbors this sentiment (see Chapter 10), as we have traced the particularization of identity through a plethora of going concerns and attempted to make visible the complex technology of self construction in contemporary life. But this has not ignored the need to formulate a *general* sociological understanding of particularization, along with the forms and everyday functioning of difference.

What we object to is the current particularization of theory itself, considering this to be a disservice to the ongoing debate surrounding difference. When every conceivable experience is viewed as in need of its own theory, conceptualization and analysis can easily devolve into wholesale political correctness and analytic balkanization. While we applaud and very much appreciate the theoretical contributions, empirical enlightenment, and useful ideological "uncoverings" that formulations such as feminist thought and queer theory have provided in response to mainstream sociological thinking, the challenge is not to displace general sociological understanding, but to reformulate it to accommodate diversity and difference in theory, method, and our sense of the empirical. Carefully reading the many current particularizations of social theory for their similarities and differences shows clear overlaps at many levels, from preferred theoretical formulations (often constructionist and historical or institutional in form), to desired methodological directions (often qualitative and comparative in design). We believe it is from the overlaps that a general sociological understanding of narrative identity should take its inspiration.

3. Sometimes options are not apparent until subsequent metanarratives indicate that what has transpired in talk and interaction was a shift from one set of related linkages or language games to another. Implicit shifts are broached, for example, when a listener eventually asks a storyteller, "What [or who] are you talking about now?" Implicit shifts represent another occasion for narrative slippage. The degree of slippage a researcher might discern ultimately rests on his or her analytic orientation. Focused as ethnography is on the institutional environments and situational patterning of storytelling, there is warrant for entertaining hypotheses about locally likely, but conversationally absent, options. Discourse or conversation analysis, on the other hand, tends to engage only hearable options and reveals the actual work that related transitions do in producing narrative coherence and difference.

4. "Prefacing" is a key feature of the conversational analysis of storytelling, which we discuss in greater detail in Chapter 7. Harvey Sacks (1992b), for example, points to the massive work done by story prefaces in producing the interactional environment within which an extended narrative may emerge. Among other things, he suggests that prefaces provide for the recognizability of stories' beginnings and ends, serving as virtual instructions for when and how listeners should respond to forthcoming narrative material and, by implication, to the narrative borders of selves in personal stories.

5. We have chosen to see discourses-in-practice as evidenced in everyday articulations of identity and, accordingly, note the slippage manifested in drawing narrative linkages and making meaning. As we noted earlier, this has been inspired in part by Foucault's important studies of the technical apparatus of institutional discourses. At the same time, we suggest that Foucault's panoptical imagery in this regard may be overdrawn, a point to which we will return in Chapters 8 and 9. Yes, "power/knowledge" works through speech, action, and systems of related thought, which, when articulated in talk and interaction, display subjectivities without the metaphorical surveillance of the guard tower. The institutional apparatus within which we participate makes us into our own disciplinary agents, so to speak. But this doesn't mean that adherents are the mere puppets of the discourses that operate from within talk and interaction. They more or less reflexively attend to the discourses organizing their actions from various footings, always located within language, of course, but nonetheless free enough to use language in relation to local needs and understandings. In practice, we are more or less aware that the guard tower is within us. As such, part of power/knowledge extends to the ordinary work done to manifest discourse as power/knowledge in the various nooks and crannies of everyday life, which is now, according to Foucault, more disciplined than ever.

6. Marvin Scott and Stanford Lyman (1968) and John Hewitt and Randall Stokes (1975) distinguish "accounts" and "disclaimers" as important devices for managing meaning-making, but they do not provide a broader analytic framework for usage. Here, we take accounts and disclaimers to be two types of narrative editing, focused primarily on the content of stories, which, along with narrative linkage and other aspects of storytelling practice, serve to show some of the ways in which coherence is built up, reworked, and reproduced in social interaction.
7. See Steven Seidman's (1998) discussion of privacy in the context of "the closet" as a leit-motif in gay and lesbian narrativity.
8. These before-and-after stories resemble the redemption tales that Amir Marvasti (1998) has documented as identity-building practices in his study of homelessness. Marvasti also argues that the establishment of the degraded "before" identity is an instance of stigma management in which, ironically, "stigma-in-use" serves as a resource and technique for *positive* self construction.

Chapter 7

1. In this chapter, we present illustrations of storytelling using transcribed conversational extracts. These data are taken from a variety of sources, including our own empirical materials (some of it already published, some taken from unpublished notes and/or transcripts), others' publications, and many extracts taken from public lectures (see Sacks 1992a, 1992b).

   Conversation analysis and other forms of close analysis of talk-in-interaction utilize rigorously designed transcription conventions to reproduce on the printed page as much of the hearable (and sometimes visual) detail of the conversation as is possible. Gail Jefferson has developed a system of transcript notation that is commonly employed by conversation analysts (see Atkinson and Heritage 1984, Button and Lee 1987), but the system continues to evolve in response to expanding research interests. Because the extracts presented here come from sources spanning four decades, there is considerable variety in their notational systems. Most, but not all, have used some variant of Jefferson's system. Much of the variation derives from the purposes for which the extracts were originally transcribed. Less complex transcription does not necessarily indicate compromised rigor; most transcripts present the level of conversational detail appropriate to the original analysis.

   Generally, we've attempted to present the transcripts in their original form, so we use the transcription conventions employed in the originals. We indicate when we've simplified some transcriptions for the sake of readability. Briefly summarized below are some of the conventions employed in the illustrations in this book. (See Atkinson and Heritage 1984 or Button and Lee 1987 for more complete discussions of transcription conventions.)

   1. **Simultaneous utterances** are linked together with either double or single left-hand brackets ([ ). Double slashes (//) are also used to indicate the onset of simultaneous talk.
   2. **Overlapping utterances** are marked by a left-hand bracket at the point in the talk at which simultaneous speech begins. The point at which overlapping utterances stop is indicated with a single right-hand bracket.
   3. **Contiguous** (or latching) **utterances**, where there is no interval between adjacent utterances, are marked with equal (=) signs.
   4. **Silences** within and between utterances are timed in tenths of a second and are inserted within parentheses, either within or between utterances (e.g., (0.7)).

Approximations of the length of silences may be inserted within double parentheses (e.g., ((one second silence))).

5. **Prolongation or stretching** of sounds is indicated by the use of colons within
   or at the end of words (e.g., I ju : st can't. I'm so :: sorry.) Multiple colons indicate prolonged stretch.
6. **Rising inflection** is indicated by a question mark. This does not necessarily indicate a question.
7. **Emphasis** on a particular word or syllable is indicated by underlining.
8. Words **spoken louder** than surrounding talk are indicated with capital letters
   (e.g., Would you PLEASE sit down).
9. Items enclosed within **single parentheses** indicate that the transcriber is unsure about the words enclosed, but is offering the enclosed speech as a "best
   guess" at what was heard.
10. Sentences and phrases enclosed in single brackets indicate summaries of talk
    that transpires at a particular location in conversation (e.g., [Edith continues
    her story about the shopping trip.]). Single brackets may also be used to en-
    close characterizations of talk (e.g., [Spoken sarcastically to Mira.]).
11. **Ellipses points** (e.g., " . . .") are used to indicate that some intervening talk has
    been omitted.

2. This extract, and some others to follow, are reconstructed from fieldnotes made of observed social interaction. As such, they are less precise and detailed than transcriptions
made from tape-recorded conversation. Such transcripts rely upon the researcher's
hearing and memory, and thus may conform to what might have been expected to be
heard as well as to what was actually heard. Candace West (1996) offers an excellent
review of the strengths, weaknesses, and possibilities of using fieldnotes and reconstructed conversations to analyze talk-in-interaction. As West suggests, as long as reconstructed conversational data are used to appropriately address phenomena that are
observable under such conditions, they provide a useful tool for analyzing interaction.
It is inappropriate, however, to attempt to analyze features of the flow of talk that are
not precisely notable in, or recallable from, a single, real-time hearing of a conversation (e.g., conversational silences of less than one second or the exact point at which
overlapping talk ceases).

3. This extract is reconstructed from a single hearing of the televised exchange. See note
2.

4. This extract is reconstructed from fieldnotes of the conversation. See Holstein (1988,
1993) for details of how transcriptions were constructed. See West (1996) for commentary on this technique. Also see note 2 above.

5. This extract is reconstructed from notes of the observed conversation. See note 2 above.

6. This extract is reconstructed from notes of the observed conversation. See note 2 above.

7. See Gale Miller's (1997a) discussion of the conversational techniques used in brief therapy to get clients to elaborate on their domestic troubles.

8. See Chapter 9 for a consideration of the intertextuality of accounts.

9. See note 4 above.

10. See note 4 above.

11. This extract is reconstructed from notes of the observed conversation. See note 2
above.

12. This extract is reconstructed from notes of the observed conversation. While it is not
indicated in the transcript, perceptible silences followed each of Kate's utterances—
small but noticeable gaps in the conversation that might not be tolerated as "normal"
in other conversational sequences. Also, see note 2 above.

Chapter 8

1. There are clear affinities between Goffman's rich and elaborate descriptions of self presentation and our discussion of self construction. At the same time, there are significant differences in the approaches. Most importantly, Goffman is primarily concerned with the *management* of the moral order, not its construction or the reflexive availability of constitutive discourses or resources. His interests lie in the ritual and performance that address the social order, but he does not deal explicitly with how social order and structure come about in the first place. In many ways, Goffman follows a Durkheimian path into social interaction, illustrating for us in bold detail how the solidarity of social forms—especially that of the self—is managed and maintained, but not how it is interactionally produced.

   A second difference lies in Goffman's situational emphasis. While we also emphasize the situated construction of selves, our aim is to capture more than the evanescent influences of temporarily salient, situated interaction orders. Although Goffman does address the institutional constraints on self presentation (especially those of total institutions), he generally has little to say regarding the myriad going concerns that shape the possibilities for self construction. Again, his focus is more on the momentary and the managerial, rather than on the enduring and the constitutive, as far as the self and the social order are concerned.

   A third difference lies in the image of agency in Goffman's work. Again, while we underscore the constitutive, Goffman's model is more performative. Goffman's agent is active, to be sure, and, when he is savvy, knows the tricks of the trade that control the moral order around him or her. But it is a managerial competence that the actor displays, not a reality-constituting agency. Goffman's dramaturgic language of performance, role, and the like signals more an actor than a construction worker or bricoleur.

   Despite our differences, however, Goffman has pointed the way for many of the developments in this book. His situational focus, for example, leads us headlong into the need to assess the scenic presence of self production. This pushes us analytically beyond discursive practice and its conversational machinery, as well as past the narrow picture of available discursive structures. In an important way, he alerts us to the fact that talk-in-interaction takes place somewhere in time and place, to the fact that discourses must always be activated in lived circumstances, not just spoken. We more fully address this and related issues in Chapter 9.

2. The extent to which conversation analysts who study institutional talk are willing to argue that *particular* variations from the speech exchanges of ordinary conversation specify institutions is open to question. While we would agree that specific going concerns have typical conversational formats, it is another matter altogether whether these formats are also specific to particular institutions, definitively distinguishing them from other going concerns. For example, the typical clipped courtroom exchanges that occur between witnesses and lawyers can be produced in angry parents' "interrogation" of their misbehaving children at home, with all the associated prefacing and procedural control mechanisms in place. Indeed, the idea that "ordinary" conversation itself presents conversation's basic systematics is also debatable, as it implies that some conversations are foundationally noninstitutional, essentially beyond meaning. Harvey Sacks (1992b) himself argued that the ordinary per se was something that needed "doing" and thus was also a going concern. See note 5 from Chapter 2 for a related discussion bearing on the issue of foundationalism in George Herbert Mead's work.

3. The normative and legal expectations for question-answer exchanges in court lend themselves to strategic manipulation on behalf of the varied interests in interrogation. As we can see from this example, the PD controls the emerging picture of the client by reclaiming turns at talk at the earliest possible point, doing what might be called "damage control." Opposing attorneys also manipulate conversational expectancies to their advantage, shaping preferred selves in the process. For example, in Chapter 7, in an extract from the case of Lisa Sellers, we saw that the narrative of her encounter with a rocketship was *allowed* to emerge as the district attorney questioned Sellers. The DA's refusal to terminate Sellers's possibly complete turns at talk by reclaiming speakership virtually induced an extended story that culminated in damaging testimony from the point of view of Sellers's case for release.

4. Highly structured interviews with fixed-choice response formats more closely approximate courtroom proceedings, offering little or no opportunity for narrative elaboration. Many construct selves needed for what C. Wright Mills (1959, p. 55) some time ago called "abstracted empiricism," which is less the product of a direct interest in experience, according to Mills, than it is methodological inhibition.

5. Fictional TV sitcom psychologist Bob Hartley, played by comedian Bob Newhart, offers the quintessential version of such technique. His "patients" would routinely complain of paying for an hour-long session, only to find that Hartley had literally nothing to say.

6. This transcript has been simplified and slightly modified to facilitate the present analysis.

7. This transcript has been simplified and slightly modified to facilitate the present analysis.

8. It's important to point out here that local culture also draws from broader cultural metaphors. In certain instances, we might presume that the men of Tally's Corner would make use of related public images of gendered differences in self-control, for example, to bolster the theory of manly flaws.

9. We can also see that while racial identity is important in these two communities, it is neither a straightforward nor omnipresent issue. If race were made topical, it's likely that men on Tally's Corner or persons in Stack's neighborhood would have somehow asserted its relevance to their identities. However, as with Chase's school superintendents, the salience of such matters was circumstantially variable and contingent— itself a matter of construction. Race (or other categories of membership) shapes identity not through grand racial narratives so much as through locally accountable usage, however broadly the "local" and "accountable" are socially mediated.

10. Interestingly enough, Miller's study also shows how the usual modern/postmodern divide can be *used* to reconstruct subjectivity. At Northland, postmodernism was not viewed so much as a crisis of confidence as it signified positive therapeutic opportunities. Somewhat in parallel to our own response to the challenge of a postmodern world as a chance to entertain and design new forms of subjectivity, Northland transformed their approach into a new discourse with an explicit emphasis on the generation of new language games that figured as solutions for the clients.

11. As mundane as this might be, "the ordinary" is not bereft of "theory." It is as much an interpretive invention as is the extraordinary (see Gubrium 1993; Gubrium and Holstein 1994, 1995b; Silverman and Gubrium 1994). By and large, social scientists do not theorize the ordinary. Rather, they separate out and center their explanatory interest on particular differences—deviance, psychopathology, and rapid social change, among other forms of ostensibly extraordinary conditions—as if these were not ordinary. It is

to Sacks's credit that he alerted us to the need to theorize the ordinary across its range of differences.

12. Since this story has become part of the AA literature (and legend), it has served as a model for subsequent AA storytelling. It stands, then, as an example of both the storyteller's use of AA culture and as a local cultural icon in its own right.

Chapter 9

1. A number of commentators (see Holstein and Miller 1993a) have emphasized the need to keep the material world center stage in considerations of processes of social construction, arguing that these processes are not to be conceived as separate and distinct from everyday life and its material conditions. M. R. Bury (1986) complains that a social constructionist perspective cannot adequately deal with the constraining role of material reality, which Paul Atkinson (1995, p. 43) succinctly corrects:

> In effect, this implies that social constructivism is a purely idealist posture, that acknowledges no reality independent of its socially organized representations. There is, however, absolutely no need for a constructivism to adopt a naive idealism any more than there is for Bury or other critics to endorse a vulgar materialism. There is, in fact, no major problem, for a constructivist view does not imply that social actors whimsically conjure reality out of thin air. Equally (and this is often overlooked) it certainly does not mean that it is simply and solely a mental product. It is necessary to remind oneself that the "social construction of reality" does indeed refer to *social* processes; that it refers to collective acts, not to individual, much less private cognition. It is not a solipsistic view of reality construction. It is sometimes less easy, however, to remind oneself, or critics like Bury, that the collective acts of reality construction are themselves material. Socially organized transactions with the physical world are themselves real.

2. The following extract is reconstructed from fieldnotes of the observed conversations. See note 2, Chapter 7.

References

Abel, Emily K. and Margaret K. Nelson (eds.). 1990. *Circles of Care: Work and Identity in Women's Lives*. Albany, N.Y.: SUNY Press.

Abu-Lughod, Lila. 1991. "Writing Against Culture." Pp. 137–62 in *Recapturing Anthropology: Working in the Present*. Santa Fe, N.M.: School of American Research Press.

Abu-Lughod, Lila. 1993. *Writing Women's Worlds: Bedouin Stories*. Berkeley: University of California Press.

Ahrne, Goran. 1990. *Agency and Organization*. London: Sage.

Alasuutari, Pertti. 1997. "The Discursive Construction of Personality." Pp. 1–20 in *The Narrative Study of Lives*, volume 5, edited by Amia Lieblich and Ruthellen Josselson. Thousand Oaks, Calif: Sage.

Alcoholics Anonymous. 1953. *Twelve Steps and Twelve Traditions*. New York: Alcoholics Anonymous World Services.

Alcoholics Anonymous. 1967. *As Bill Sees It: The AA Way of Life. Selected Writings of AA's Co-Founder*. New York: Alcoholics Anonymous World Services.

Alcoholics Anonymous. 1976. *Alcoholics Anonymous*. New York: Alcoholics Anonymous World Services.

Allport, Gordon W. 1942. *The Use of Personal Documents in Psychological Science*. New York: Little, Brown & Company.

Andersen, Margaret L. and Patricia Hill Collins (eds.). 1998. *Race, Class, and Gender*. Belmont, Calif.: Wadsworth.

Anzaldúa, Gloria. 1987. *Borderlands/La Frontera: The New Mestiza*. San Francisco: Aunt Lute Books.

Ariès, Philippe. 1962. *Centuries of Childhood*. New York: Knopf.

Atkinson, J. Maxwell and Paul Drew. 1979. *Order in Court*. Atlantic Highlands, N.J.: Humanities Press.

Atkinson, J. Maxwell and John Heritage (eds.). 1984. *Structures of Social Action*. Cambridge: Cambridge University Press.

Atkinson, Paul. 1988. "Ethnomethodology: A Critical Review." *Annual Review of Sociology* 14: 441–65.

Atkinson, Paul. 1995. *Medical Talk and Medical Work*. London: Sage.

Atkinson, Paul. 1997. "Narrative Turn or Blind Alley?" *Qualitative Health Research* 7: 325–44.

Atkinson, Paul and David Silverman. 1997. "Kundera's *Immortality*: The Interview Society and the Invention of the Self." *Qualitative Inquiry* 3: 304–25.

Baker, Carolyn. 1997. "Membership Categorization and Interview Accounts." Pp. 130–43 in *Qualitative Research: Theory, Method and Practice*, edited by David Silverman. London: Sage.

Barthes, Roland. 1974. *S/Z*. New York: Hill & Wang.

Barthes, Roland. 1977. *Image, Music, Text*. New York: Hill & Wang.

Baudrillard, Jean. 1983. *Simulations*. New York: Semiotext(e).

Baudrillard, Jean. 1995. *The Gulf War Did Not Take Place.* Bloomington, Ind.: Indiana University Press.

Bauman, Richard. 1986. *Story, Performance, and Event: Contextual Studies of Oral Narrative.* Cambridge: Cambridge University Press.

Becker, Howard S. (ed.). 1964. *The Other Side.* New York: Free Press.

Becker, Howard S. 1967. "Whose Side Are We On?" *Social Problems* 14: 239–47.

Becker, Howard S. 1973[1963]. *Outsiders.* New York: Free Press.

Beinhart, Larry. 1993. *American Hero.* New York: Pantheon.

Bellah, Robert N., Richard Madsen, William M. Sullivan, Ann Swidler, and Steven M. Tipton. 1996[1985]. *Habits of the Heart.* Berkeley: University of California Press.

Bendix, Reinhard. 1960. *Max Weber: An Intellectual Portrait.* New York: Doubleday.

Berger, Asa. 1997. *Narratives in Popular Culture, Media, and Everyday Life.* Thousand Oaks, Calif.: Sage.

Berger, Peter. 1963. *Invitation to Sociology.* Garden City, N.Y.: Doubleday.

Berman, Marshall. 1992. "Why Modernism Still Matters." Pp. 33–58 in *Modernity and Identity,* edited by Scott Lash and Jonathan Friedman. Oxford: Blackwell.

Bertaux, Daniel (ed.). 1981. *Biography and Society: The Life-History Approach in the Social Sciences.* Beverly Hills, Calif.: Sage.

Best, Steven and Douglas Kellner. 1991. *Postmodern Theory.* New York: Guilford.

Blumer, Herbert. 1969. *Symbolic Interactionism: Perspective and Method.* Englewood Cliffs, N.J.: Prentice-Hall.

Blumer, Herbert. 1977. "Comment on Lewis' 'The Classic American Pragmatists as Forerunners to Symbolic Interaction'." *Sociological Quarterly* 10: 275–91.

Boden, Deirdre and Don Zimmerman (eds.). 1991. *Talk and Social Structure.* Cambridge, England: Polity.

Bogdan, Robert and Steven Taylor. 1989. "Relationships with Severely Disabled Persons: The Social Construction of Humanness." *Social Problems* 36: 135–48.

Bourdieu, Pierre. 1984. *Distinction: A Social Critique of the Judgment of Taste.* London: Routledge.

Bourdieu, Pierre. 1985. "The Social Space and the Genesis of Groups," *Theory and Society* 14: 723–44.

Bourdieu, Pierre. 1986. "L'illusion biographique." *Actes de la Recherche en Sciences Sociales* 62/63: 69–72.

Bruner, Jerome. 1986. *Actual Minds, Possible Worlds.* Cambridge, Mass.: Harvard University Press.

Buchbinder, David. 1994. *Masculinities and Identities.* Carlton, Victoria: Melbourne University Press.

Buckholdt, David R. and Jaber F. Gubrium. 1979. *Caretakers: Treating Emotionally Disturbed Children.* Newbury Park, Calif.: Sage.

Bury, M. R. 1986. "Social Constructionism and the Development of Medical Sociology." *Sociology of Health and Illness* 8: 137–69.

Butler, Judith. 1990. *Gender Trouble: Feminism and the Subversion of Identity.* New York: Routledge.

Button, Graham and J. R. E. Lee (eds.). 1987. *Talk and Social Organization.* Clevedon, England: Multilingual Matters.

Cain, Carole. 1991. "Personal Stories: Identity Acquisition and Self-understanding in Alcoholics Anonymous." *Ethos* 19: 210–53.

Carrithers, Michael, Steven Collins, and Steven Lukes (eds.). 1985. *The Category of the Person.* Cambridge: Cambridge University Press.

Cazden, Courtney and Dell Hymes. 1978. "Narrative Thinking and Story-Telling Rights: A Folklorist's Clue to a Critique of Education." *Keystone Folklore Quarterly* 22: 21–36.

Chase, Susan E. 1995. *Ambiguous Empowerment: The Work Narratives of Women School Superintendents.* Amherst: University of Massachusetts Press.

Chow, Rey. 1993. *Writing Diaspora: Tactics of Intervention in Contemporary Cultural Studies.* Bloomington, Ind.: Indiana University Press.

Christopher, James. 1988. *How to Stay Sober: Recovery Without Religion.* Buffalo, N.Y.: Prometheus Books.

Clayman, Steven E. 1988. "Displaying Neutrality in Television News Interviews." *Social Problems* 35: 474–92.

Clayman, Steven E. 1992. "Footing in the Achievement of Neutrality: The Case of News Interview Discourse." Pp. 163–98 in *Talk at Work*, edited by Paul Drew and John Heritage. Cambridge: Cambridge University Press.

Collins, Patricia Hill. 1990. *Black Feminist Thought: Knowledge, Consciousness, and the Politics of Empowerment.* Boston: Unwin Hyman.

Conley, John M. and William M. O'Barr. 1990. *Rules and Relationships.* Chicago: University of Chicago Press.

Connell, Robert W. 1995. *Masculinities.* Berkeley: University of California Press.

Connor, Steve. 1989. *Postmodernist Culture.* Oxford: Blackwell.

Conrad, Peter and Joseph W. Schneider. 1980. *Deviance and Medicalization: From Badness to Sickness.* St. Louis, Mo.: Mosby.

Cook, Gary A. 1993. *George Herbert Mead: The Making of a Social Pragmatist.* Urbana: University of Illinois Press.

Cooley, Charles Horton. 1964[1902]. *Human Nature and the Social Order.* New York: Scribner's.

Cortazzi, Martin. 1993. *Narrative Analysis.* London: Falmer Press.

Couch, Carl J. 1962. "Family Role Specialization and Self-Attitudes in Children." *Sociological Quarterly* 3: 115–21.

Crunden, Robert M. 1982. *Ministers of Reform: The Progressive's Achievement in American Civilization, 1889–1920.* New York: Basic Books.

Czarniawska, Barbara. 1997. *Narrating the Organization: Dramas of Institutional Identity.* Chicago: University of Chicago Press.

Dannefer, Dale. 1984a. "Adult Development and Social Theory: A Paradigmatic Reappraisal." *American Sociological Review* 49: 100–116.

Dannefer, Dale. 1984b. "The Role of the Social in Life-Span Developmental Psychology, Past and Future: A Rejoinder." *American Sociological Review* 49: 847–50.

Dannefer, Dale. 1992. "On the Conceptualization of Context in Developmental Discourse: Four Meanings of Context and Their Implications." Pp. 83–110 in *Life-Span Development and Behavior*, volume 11, edited by David L. Featherman, Richard M. Lerner, and Marion Perlmutter. Hillsdale, N.J.: Lawrence Erlbaum Associates.

Dégh, Linda. 1995. *Narratives in Society.* Helsinki: Academic Scientarum Fennica.

De Mille, Richard (ed.). 1980. *The Don Juan Papers.* Santa Barbara, Calif.: Ross-Erikson.

Demos, John. 1970. *A Little Commonwealth: Family Life in Plymouth Colony.* New York: Oxford University Press.

Demos, John. 1979. "Images of the Family, Then and Now." Pp. 43–60 in *Changing Images of the Family*, edited by Virginia Tufte and Barbara Myerhoff. New Haven, Conn.: Yale University Press.

Denzin, Norman K. 1970. "The Methodologies of Symbolic Interaction: A Critical Review of Research Techniques." Pp. 447–65 in *Social Psychology Through Symbolic Interaction*, edited by Gregory P. Stone and Harvey A. Farberman. Waltham, Mass.: Ginn and Company.

Denzin, Norman K. 1986. *Treating Alcoholism*. Newbury Park, Calif.: Sage.

Denzin, Norman K. 1987a. *The Alcoholic Self*. Newbury Park, Calif.: Sage.

Denzin, Norman K. 1987b. *The Recovering Alcoholic*. Newbury Park, Calif.: Sage.

Denzin, Norman K. 1989. *Interpretive Biography*. Newbury Park, Calif.: Sage.

Denzin, Norman K. 1991. *Images of Postmodern Society: Social Theory and Contemporary Cinema*. Newbury Park, Calif.: Sage.

Denzin, Norman K. 1997a. *Interpretive Ethnography: Ethnographic Practices for the 21st Century*. Thousand Oaks, Calif.: Sage.

Denzin, Norman K. 1997b. "The Standpoint Epistemologies and Social Theory." *Current Perspectives in Social Theory* 17: 39–76.

Dingwall, Robert. 1980. "Orchestrated Encounters." *Sociology of Health and Illness* 2: 151–73.

Dollard, John. 1935. *Criteria for the Life History*. New Haven, Conn.: Yale University Press.

Donzelot, Jacques. 1980. *The Policing of Families*. London: Hutchinson.

Douglas, Mary. 1986. *How Institutions Think*. Syracuse, N.Y.: Syracuse University Press.

Drew, Paul and John Heritage (eds.). 1992. *Talk at Work*. Cambridge: Cambridge University Press.

Dreyfus, Hubert L. and Paul Rabinow. 1982. *Michel Foucault: Beyond Structuralism and Hermeneutics*. Chicago: University of Chicago Press.

Drucker, Peter F. 1993. *Post-Capitalist Society*. New York: Harper.

Dunn, Robert G. 1998. *Identity Crisis: A Social Critique of Postmodernity*. Minneapolis: University of Minnesota Press.

Durkheim, Emile. 1961. *The Elementary Forms of the Religious Life*. New York: Collier Books.

Eder, Donna. 1995. *School Talk: Gender and Adolescent Culture*. New Brunswick, N.J.: Rutgers University Press.

Edgarton, Robert B. 1967. *The Cloak of Competence: Stigma in the Lives of the Mentally Retarded*. Berkeley: University of California Press.

Elias, Norbert. 1978. *The Civilizing Process*. Oxford: Blackwell.

Elias, Norbert. 1991. *The Symbol Theory*. London: Sage.

Ellison, Ralph. 1947. *The Invisible Man*. New York: Random House.

Emerson, Robert M. 1991. "Case Processing and Interorganizational Knowledge: Detecting the 'Real Reasons' for Referrals." *Social Problems* 38: 198–212.

Ezzy, Douglas. 1998. "Theorizing Narrative Identity: Symbolic Interactionism and Hermeneutics." *Sociological Quarterly* 39: 239–52.

Featherstone, Mike. 1988. *Postmodernism*. Special issue of *Theory, Culture and Society*, Vol. 5.

Featherstone, Mike. 1992. "Postmodernism and the Aestheticization of Everyday Life." Pp. 265–290 in *Modernity and Identity*, edited by Scott Lash and Jonathan Friedman. Oxford: Blackwell.

Feffer, Andrew. 1993. *The Chicago Pragmatists and American Progressivism*. Ithaca, N.Y.: Cornell University Press.

Fields, Belden A. 1988. *Trotskyism and Maoism: Theory and Practice in France and the United States*. New York: Praeger.

Fine, Gary Alan (ed.). 1995. *A Second Chicago School? The Development of a Postwar American Sociology*. Chicago: University of Chicago Press.

Fish, Stanley. 1980. *Is There a Text in This Class? The Authority of Interpretive Communities*. Cambridge, Mass.: Harvard University Press.

Foucault, Michel. 1973. *Madness and Civilization: A History of Insanity in the Age of Reason*. New York: Vintage.

Foucault, Michel. 1975. *The Birth of the Clinic*. New York: Vintage.

Foucault, Michel. 1977. *Discipline and Punish: The Birth of the Prison*. New York: Vintage.

252   References

Foucault, Michel. 1978a. *The History of Sexuality, Volume 1.* New York: Vintage.
Foucault, Michel (ed.). 1978b. *I, Pierre Rivière, having slaughtered my mother, my sister, and my brother. . . : A Case of Parricide in the 19th Century.* Lincoln: University of Nebraska Press.
Foucault, Michel. 1980. *Power/Knowledge: Selected Interviews and Other Writings 1972–1977.* London: Harvester.
Foucault, Michel. 1982. "Afterword: The Subject and Power." Pp. 208–26 in *Michel Foucault: Beyond Structuralism and Hermeneutics,* by Hubert L. Dreyfus and Paul Rabinow. Chicago: University of Chicago Press.
Foucault, Michel. 1988. *Technologies of the Self.* Amherst: University of Massachusetts Press.
Fromm, Erich. 1944. "Individual and Social Origins of Neurosis." *American Sociological Review* 9: 380–91.
Gane, Mike (ed.). 1993. *Baudrillard Live: Selected Interviews.* New York: Routledge.
Garfinkel, Harold. 1967. *Studies in Ethnomethodology.* Englewood Cliffs, N.J.: Prentice-Hall.
Garfinkel, Harold and Harvey Sacks. 1970. "On the Formal Structure of Practical Actions." Pp. 338–66 in *Theoretical Sociology,* edited by John C. McKinney and Edward A. Tiryakian. New York: Appleton-Century-Crofts.
Geertz, Clifford. 1973. *The Interpretation of Cultures.* New York: Basic.
Geertz, Clifford. 1983. *Local Knowledge.* New York: Basic.
Geertz, Clifford. 1984. " 'From the Native's Point of View': On the Nature of Anthropological Understanding." Pp. 123–37 in *Culture Theory,* edited by Richard Shweder and Robert LeVine. Cambridge: Cambridge University Press.
Gergen, Kenneth J. 1991. *The Saturated Self: Dilemmas of Identity in Contemporary Life.* New York: Basic.
Gergen, Kenneth J. and Mary M. Gergen. 1986. "Narrative Form and the Construction of Psychological Science." Pp. 22–44 in *Narrative Psychology,* edited by Theodore R. Sarbin. New York: Praeger.
Giallombardo, Rose. 1966. *Society of Women: A Study of a Women's Prison.* New York: Wiley.
Giddens, Anthony. 1984. *The Constitution of Society.* Berkeley, Calif.: University of California Press.
Giddens, Anthony. 1991. *Modernity and Self-Identity.* Stanford, Calif.: Stanford University Press.
Giddens, Anthony. 1992. *The Transformation of Intimacy: Sexuality, Love and Eroticism in Modern Societies.* Stanford, Calif.: Stanford University Press.
Gill, Virginia T. and Douglas W. Maynard. 1995. "On 'Labeling' in Actual Interaction: Delivering and Receiving Diagnoses of Developmental Disabilities." *Social Problems* 42: 11–37.
Goffman, Erving. 1959. *The Presentation of Self in Everyday Life.* New York: Doubleday.
Goffman, Erving. 1961. *Asylums.* Garden City, N.Y.: Doubleday.
Goffman, Erving. 1963. *Stigma: Notes on the Management of Spoiled Identity.* Englewood Cliffs, N.J.: Prentice-Hall.
Goffman, Erving. 1967. *Interaction Ritual: Essays on Face-to-Face Behavior.* Garden City, N.Y.: Doubleday.
Gouge, William. 1622. *Of Domestic Duties.* London.
Gubrium, Jaber F. 1986a. *Oldtimers and Alzheimer's: The Descriptive Organization of Senility.* Greenwich, Conn.: JAI Press.
Gubrium, Jaber F. 1986b. "The Social Preservation of Mind: The Alzheimer's Disease Experience." *Symbolic Interaction* 6: 37–51.
Gubrium, Jaber F. 1988. *Analyzing Field Reality.* Newbury Park, Calif.: Sage.

Gubrium, Jaber F. 1992. *Out of Control: Family Therapy and Domestic Disorder*. Newbury Park, Calif.: Sage.

Gubrium, Jaber F. 1993. *Speaking of Life: Horizons of Meaning for Nursing Home Residents*. Hawthorne, N.Y.: Aldine de Gruyter.

Gubrium, Jaber F. 1997[1975]. *Living and Dying at Murray Manor*. Charlottesville: University Press of Virginia.

Gubrium, Jaber F. and David R. Buckholdt. 1982. *Describing Care: Image and Practice Rehabilitation*. Cambridge, Mass.: Oelgeschlager, Gunn, and Hain.

Gubrium, Jaber F. and James A. Holstein. 1990. *What Is Family?* Mountain View, Calif.: Mayfield.

Gubrium, Jaber F. and James A. Holstein. 1993. "Family Discourse, Organizational Embeddedness, and Local Enactment." *Journal of Family Issues* 14: 66–81.

Gubrium, Jaber F. and James A. Holstein. 1994. "Grounding the Postmodern Self." *Sociological Quarterly* 35:685–703.

Gubrium, Jaber F. and James A. Holstein. 1995a. "Biographical Work and New Ethnography." Pp. 45–58 in *Interpreting Experience: The Narrative Study of Lives*, edited by Ruthellen Josselson and Amia Lieblich. Newbury Park, Calif.: Sage.

Gubrium, Jaber F. and James A. Holstein. 1995b. "Individual Agency, the Ordinary, and Postmodern Life." *Sociological Quarterly* 36: 555–70.

Gubrium, Jaber F. and James A. Holstein. 1995c. "Qualitative Inquiry and the Deprivatization of Experience," *Qualitative Inquiry* 1: 204–22.

Gubrium, Jaber F. and James A. Holstein. 1997. *The New Language of Qualitative Method*. New York: Oxford University Press.

Gubrium, Jaber F. and James A. Holstein. 1998. "Narrative Practice and the Coherence of Personal Stories." *Sociological Quarterly* 39: 163–87.

Gubrium, Jaber F., James A. Holstein, and David R. Buckholdt. 1994. *Constructing the Life Course*. Dix Hills, N.Y.: General Hall.

Gubrium, Jaber F. and Robert J. Lynott. 1985. "Alzheimer's Disease as Biographical Work." Pp. 349–68 in *Social Bonds in Later Life*, edited by Warren A. Peterson and Jill Quadagno. Newbury Park, Calif.: Sage.

Hass, Jack and William Shaffir. 1987. *Becoming Doctors*. Greenwich, Conn.: JAI Press.

Hacking, Ian. 1981. "How Should We Do the History of Statistics?" *Ideology and Consciousness* 8: 15–26.

Hacking, Ian. 1982. "Bio-Power and the Avalanche of Printed Numbers." *Humanities in Society* 5: 279–95.

Hall, Stuart. 1985. "Signification, Representation, Ideology: Althusser and the Poststructuralist Debates." *Critical Studies in Communication Inquiry* 10: 45–60.

Hazelrigg, Lawrence. 1989. *Social Science and the Challenge of Relativism: A Wilderness of Mirrors: On Practices of Theory in a Gray Age*. Gainesville: University Press of Florida.

Heath, Christian. 1997. "The Analysis of Activities in Face to Face Interaction Using Video." Pp. 183–200 in *Qualitative Research: Theory, Method and Practice*, edited by David Silverman. London: Sage.

Heritage, John. 1984. *Garfinkel and Ethnomethodology*. Cambridge, England: Polity.

Heritage, John. 1997. "Conversation Analysis and Institutional Talk." Pp. 161–82 in *Qualitative Research: Theory, Method and Practice*, edited by David Silverman. London: Sage.

Heritage, John and David Greatbach. 1991. "On the Institutional Character of Institutional Talk." Pp. 93–137 in *Talk and Social Structure*, edited by Deirdre Boden and Don Zimmerman. Cambridge, England: Polity.

Heritage, John and D. R. Watson. 1980. "Aspects of the Properties of Formulations in Natural Conversation." *Semiotica* 3/4: 245–62.

Hewitt, John P. 1997. *Self and Society: A Symbolic Interactionist Social Psychology.* Boston: Allyn and Bacon.

Hewitt, John P. 1998. *The Myth of Self-Esteem: Finding Happiness and Solving Problems in America.* New York: St. Martin's Press.

Hewitt, John P. and Randall Stokes. 1975. "Disclaimers." *American Sociological Review* 40: 1–11.

Hinchman, Lewis P. and Sandra K. Hinchman. 1997. *Memory, Community, Identity: The Idea of Narrative in the Human Sciences.* Albany, N.Y.: SUNY Press.

Hochschild, Arlie Russell. 1983. *The Managed Heart.* Berkeley: University of California Press.

Hochschild, Arlie Russell. 1997. *The Time Bind: When Work Becomes Home and Home Becomes Work.* New York: Henry Holt and Company.

Hodder, Ian. 1994. "The Interpretation of Documents and Material Culture." Pp. 393–402 in *Handbook of Qualitative Research,* edited by Norman K. Denzin and Yvonna S. Lincoln. Thousand Oaks, Calif.: Sage.

Holstein, James A. 1988. "Court Ordered Incompetence: Conversational Organization in Involuntary Commitment Hearings." *Social Problems* 35: 458–73.

Holstein, James A. 1993. *Court-Ordered Insanity: Interpretive Practice and Involuntary Commitment.* Hawthorne, N.Y.: Aldine de Gruyter.

Holstein, James A. and Jaber F. Gubrium. 1994. "Phenomenology, Ethnomethodology, and Interpretive Practice." Pp. 262–71 in *Handbook of Qualitative Research,* edited by N. Denzin and Y. Lincoln. Thousand Oaks, Calif.: Sage.

Holstein, James A. and Jaber F. Gubrium. 1995a. *The Active Interview.* Thousand Oaks, Calif.: Sage.

Holstein, James A. and Jaber F. Gubrium. 1995b. "Deprivatization and Domestic Life: Interpretive Practice in Family Context." *Journal of Marriage and the Family* 57: 607–22.

Holstein, James A. and Gale Miller (eds.). 1993a. *Reconsidering Social Constructionism: Debates in Social Problems Theory.* Hawthorne, N.Y.: Aldine de Gruyter.

Holstein, James A. and Gale Miller. 1993b. "Social Constructionism and Social Problems Work." Pp. 151–172 in *Reconsidering Social Constructionism: Debates in Social Problems Theory,* edited by James A. Holstein and Gale Miller. Hawthorne, N.Y.: Aldine de Gruyter.

Huber, Joan. 1973. "Symbolic Interaction as a Pragmatic Perspective: The Bias of Emergent Theory." *American Sociological Review* 38: 278–84.

Hughes, Everett C. 1984[1942]. *The Sociological Eye.* New Brunswick, N.J.: Transaction Books.

Husserl, Edmund. 1970. *Logical Investigation.* New York: Humanities Press.

Hyvärinen, Matti. 1996. "Explaining Problematic Experiences: The Methods of Narrative Coherence." Paper presented at the Fifth International Conference on Narrative, University of Kentucky, Lexington.

James, William. 1961[1892]. *Psychology: The Briefer Course.* New York: Harper & Brothers.

Jameson, Frederic. 1972. *The Prison-house of Language.* Princeton, N.J.: Princeton University Press.

Janowitz, Morris. 1966. "Introduction." Pp. vii–viii in *W.I. Thomas. On Social Organization and Social Personality,* edited by Morris Janowitz. Chicago: University of Chicago Press.

Jefferson, Gail. 1978. "Sequential Aspects of Storytelling in Conversation." Pp. 219–48 in *Studies in the Organization of Conversational Interaction,* edited by Jim Schenkein. New York: Academic Press.

Joas, Hans. 1987. "Symbolic Interactionism." Pp. 82–115 in *Social Theory Today,* edited by Anthony Giddens and Jonathan Turner. Stanford, Calif.: Stanford University Press.

Josselson, Ruthellen and Amia Lieblich (eds.). 1993. *The Narrative Study of Lives,* vol. 1. Thousand Oaks, Calif.: Sage.

Josselson, Ruthellen and Amia Lieblich (eds.). 1995. *Interpreting Experience: The Narrative Study of Lives*, vol. 3. Thousand Oaks, Calif.: Sage.

Kafka, Franz. 1937. *The Trial*. New York: Knopf.

Katz, Jack. 1988. *Seductions of Crime*. New York: Basic Books.

Kellner, Douglas. 1989. *Jean Baudrillard: From Marxism to Postmodernism and Beyond*. Stanford, Calif.: Stanford University Press.

Kellner, Douglas. 1992. "Popular Culture and the Construction of Postmodern Identities." Pp. 141–77 in *Modernity and Identity*, edited by Scott Lash and Jonathan Friedman. Oxford: Blackwell.

Kenyon, Gary M. and William L. Randall. 1997. *Restorying Our Lives: Personal Growth Through Autobiographical Reflection*. Westport, Conn.: Praeger.

Kinch, John. 1963. *Social Psychology*. New York: McGraw-Hill.

Kitsuse, John I. 1962. "Societal Reactions to Deviant Behavior." *Social Problems* 9: 247–56.

Kleinman, Arthur. 1988. *The Illness Narratives: Suffering, Healing, and the Human Condition*. New York: Basic Books.

Krieger, Susan. 1983. *The Mirror Dance: Identity in a Women's Community*. Philadelphia: Temple University Press.

Kristeva, Julia. 1973. "The System and the Speaking Subject." *Times Literary Supplement*, October 12, p. 1249.

Kuhn, Manford. 1960. "Self-Attitudes by Age, Sex, and Professional Training." *Sociological Quarterly* 1: 38–55.

Kuhn, Manford. 1964. "Major Trends in Symbolic Interaction Theory in the Past Twenty-five Years." *Sociological Quarterly* 5: 61–84.

Kuhn, Manford and Thomas S. McPartland. 1954. "An Empirical Investigation of Self-Attitudes." *American Sociological Review* 19: 68–72.

Kumar, Krishan. 1995. *From Post-Industrial to Post-Modern Society: New Theories of the Contemporary World*. Oxford: Blackwell.

Labov, William. 1972. "The Transformation of Experience in Narrative Syntax." Pp. 352–96 in *Language in the Inner City*, edited by William Labov. Philadelphia: University of Pennsylvania Press.

Labov, William. 1982. "Speech Actions and Reactions in Personal Narrative." Pp. 219–47 in *Analyzing Discourse: Text and Talk*, edited by Deborah Tannen. Washington, D.C.: Georgetown University Press.

Lakoff, George and Mark Johnson. 1980. *Metaphors We Live By*. Chicago: University of Chicago Press.

Lasch, Christopher. 1977. *Haven in a Heartless World*. New York: Basic.

Lasch, Christopher. 1979. *The Culture of Narcissism*. New York: Norton.

Lash, Scott and Jonathan Friedman (eds.). 1992. *Modernity and Identity*. Oxford: Blackwell.

Lather, Patti. 1994. "Staying Dumb? Feminist Research and Pedagogy With/in the Postmodern." Pp. 101–32 in *After Postmodernism: Reconstructing Ideology Critique*, edited by Herbert W. Simons and Michael Billig. London: Sage.

Lazlett, Peter. 1965. *The World We Have Lost*. New York: Scribner's.

Lee, Dorothy. 1950. "Lineal and Nonlineal Codifications of Reality." *Psychosomatic Medicine* 12: 89–97.

Lemert, Charles. 1994. "Dark Thoughts About the Self." Pp. 100–130 in *Social Theory and the Politics of Identity*, edited by Craig Calhoun. Cambridge, Mass.: Blackwell.

Lemert, Edwin M. 1950. *Social Pathology*. New York: McGraw-Hill.

Lemert, Edwin M. 1967. *Human Deviance, Social Problems, and Social Control*. Englewood Cliffs, N.J.: Prentice-Hall.

Lévi-Strauss, Claude. 1966. *The Savage Mind*. Chicago: University of Chicago Press.

Lewis, J. David. 1976. "The Pragmatic Foundation of Symbolic Interactionism." *Sociological Quarterly* 17: 347–59.

Lewis, J. David. 1977. "Reply to Blumer." *Sociological Quarterly* 19: 291–92.

Lewis, J. David and Richard L. Smith. 1980. *American Sociology and Pragmatism: Mead, Chicago Sociology, and Symbolic Interaction.* Chicago: University of Chicago Press.

Lieblich, Amia and Ruthellen Josselson (eds.). 1994. *Exploring Gender: The Narrative Study of Lives,* vol. 2. Thousand Oaks, Calif.: Sage.

Liebow, Elliot. 1967. *Tally's Corner.* Boston: Little, Brown & Company.

Linde, Charlotte. 1993. *Life Stories: The Creation of Coherence.* New York: Oxford University Press.

Lindesmith, Alfred R., Anselm L. Strauss, and Norman K. Denzin. 1988. *Social Psychology.* Englewood Cliffs, N.J.: Prentice-Hall.

Loseke, Donileen R. 1992. *The Battered Woman and Shelters.* Albany, N.Y.: SUNY Press.

Lowenthal, Marjorie, M. Thurner, and David Chiriboga. 1975. *Four Stages of Life: A Comparative Study of Women and Men Facing Transitions.* San Francisco: Jossey-Bass.

Lynch, Michael and David Bogen. 1994. "Harvey Sacks's Primitive Natural Science." *Theory, Culture, and Society* 11:65–104.

Lyotard, Jean-François. 1984. *The Postmodern Condition: A Report on Knowledge.* Minneapolis: University of Minnesota Press.

Maines, David R. 1993. "Narrative's Moment and Sociology's Phenomena: Toward a Narrative Sociology." *Sociological Quarterly* 34: 17–38.

Maines, David R. and Jeffrey T. Ulmer. 1993. "The Relevance of Narrative for Interactionist Thought." *Studies in Symbolic Interaction* 14: 109–24.

Malcolm X. 1965. *The Autobiography of Malcolm X.* New York: Random House.

Manis, Jerome G. and Bernard N. Meltzer. 1967. *Symbolic Interaction: A Reader in Social Psychology.* Boston: Allyn and Bacon.

Marcus, George E. (ed.). 1992. *Rereading Cultural Anthropology.* Durham, N.C.: Duke University Press.

Marvasti, Amir. 1998. " 'Homelessness' as Narrative Redemption." Pp. 167–82 in *Perspectives on Social Problems,* vol. 10, edited by Gale Miller and James A. Holstein. Greenwich, Conn.: JAI Press.

Maynard, Douglas W. 1980. "Placement of Topic Change in Conversation." *Semiotica* 30: 263–90.

Maynard, Douglas W. 1989a. "On the Ethnography and Analysis of Discourse in Institutional Settings." Pp. 127–46 in *Perspectives on Social Problems, vol. 1,* edited by J. Holstein and G. Miller. Greenwich, Conn.: JAI Press.

Maynard, Douglas W. 1989b. "Perspective-Display Sequences in Conversation." *Western Journal of Speech Communication* 53: 91–113.

Maynard, Douglas W. 1991a. "Interaction and Asymmetry in Clinical Discourse." *American Journal of Sociology* 97: 448–95.

Maynard, Douglas W. 1991b. "The Perspective-Display Series and the Delivery and Receipt of Diagnostic News." Pp. 164–92 in *Talk and Social Structure,* edited by Deirdre Boden and Don H. Zimmerman. Cambridge, England: Polity.

Maynard, Douglas W. and Steven E. Clayman. 1991. "The Diversity of Ethnomethodology." *Annual Review of Sociology* 17: 385–418.

McHoul, Alec and Wendy Grace. 1993. *A Foucault Primer: Discourse, Power and the Subject.* London: UCL Press.

McLuhan, Marshall. 1967. *The Medium Is the Message.* New York: Random House.

McPartland, Thomas S. and John H. Cumming. 1958. "Self-Conception, Social Class, and Mental Health." *Human Organization* 17: 24–29.

McPartland, Thomas S., John H. Cumming, and Wynona S. Garretson. 1961. "Self-Conception and Ward Behavior in Two Psychiatric Hospitals." *Sociometry* 24: 111–24.

McPhail, Clark and Cynthia Rexroat. 1979. "Mead vs. Blumer: The Divergent Methodological Perspectives of Social Behaviorism and Symbolic Interactionism." *American Sociological Review* 44: 449–67.

Mead, George Herbert. 1934. *Mind, Self and Society.* Chicago: University of Chicago Press.

Mehan, Hugh. 1979. *Learning Lessons.* Cambridge, Mass.: Harvard University Press.

Meltzer, Bernard N. 1967. "Mead's Social Psychology." Pp. 15–27 in *Symbolic Interaction,* edited by Jerome G. Manis and Bernard N. Meltzer. Boston: Allyn and Bacon.

Meltzer, Bernard N., John W. Petras, and Larry T. Reynolds. 1975. *Symbolic Interactionism: Genesis, Varieties and Criticism.* London: Routledge.

Merleau-Ponty, Maurice. 1964. *Signs.* Evanston, Ill.: Northwestern University Press.

Meyerhoff, Barbara G. 1992. *Remembered Lives: The Work of Ritual, Storytelling and Growing Older.* Ann Arbor: University of Michigan Press.

Miller, David L. 1973. *George Herbert Mead: Self, Language, and the World.* Austin: University of Texas Press.

Miller, Gale. 1991. *Enforcing the Work Ethic.* Albany, N.Y.: SUNY Press.

Miller, Gale. 1994. "Toward Ethnographies of Institutional Discourse." *Journal of Contemporary Ethnography* 23:280–306.

Miller, Gale. 1997a. *Becoming Miracle Workers: Language and Meaning in Brief Therapy.* New York: Aldine de Gruyter.

Miller, Gale. 1997b. "Building Bridges: The Possibility of Analytic Dialogue Between Ethnography, Conversation Analysis and Foucault." Pp. 24–44 in *Qualitative Research: Theory, Method and Practice,* edited by David Silverman. London: Sage.

Miller, Gale and James A. Holstein. 1996. *Dispute Domains and Welfare Claims.* Greenwich, Conn.: JAI Press.

Mills, C. Wright. 1940. "Situated Actions and Vocabularies of Motive." *American Sociological Review* 5: 904–13.

Mills, C. Wright. 1959. *The Sociological Imagination.* New York: Grove Press.

Mills, C. Wright. 1963. *Power, Politics and People.* Edited by Irving Louis Horowitz. New York: Ballantine.

Mulford, Harold A. and Winfield W. Salisbury II. 1964. "Self-Conception in a General Population." *Sociological Quarterly* 1964: 36–46.

Murray, Henry. 1938. *Explorations in Personality.* New York: Oxford University Press.

Nietzsche, Friedrich. 1956. *The Birth of Tragedy* and *The Genealogy of Morals.* Garden City, N.Y.: Doubleday.

Orbuch, Terri L. 1997. "People's Accounts Count: The Sociology of Accounts." *Annual Review of Sociology* 23: 455–78.

Parsons, Talcott. 1951. *The Social System.* New York: Free Press.

Perrucci, Robert. 1974. *Circle of Madness: On Being Insane and Institutionalized in America.* Berkeley: University of California Press.

Pfohl, Stephen. 1997. "Review Essay." *Contemporary Sociology* 26: 138–41.

Pfuhl, Erdwin H. 1986. *The Deviance Process* (2nd ed.) Belmont, Calif.: Wadsworth.

Platt, Jennifer. 1995. "Research Methods and the Second Chicago School." Pp. 82–107 in *A Second Chicago School? The Development of a Postwar American Sociology,* edited by Gary Alan Fine. Chicago: University of Chicago Press.

Plummer, Ken. 1983. *Documents of Life.* London: George Allen & Unwin.

Plummer, Ken. 1995. *Telling Sexual Stories.* London: Routledge.

Polanyi, L. 1979. "So What's the Point?" *Semiotica* 25: 207–41.

Pollner, Melvin. 1987. *Mundane Reason.* New York: Cambridge University Press.

Pollner, Melvin and Lynn McDonald-Wikler. 1985. "The Social Construction of Unreality: A Case Study of a Family's Attribution of Competence to a Severely Retarded Child." *Family Process* 24: 241–54.

Pollner, Melvin and Jill Stein. 1996. "Narrative Mapping of Social Worlds: The Voice of Experience in Alcoholics Anonymous." *Symbolic Interaction* 19: 203–24.

Poster, Mark. 1988. "Introduction." Pp. 1–9 in *Jean Baudrillard, Selected Writings*. Stanford, Calif.: Stanford University Press.

Potter, Jonathan. 1996. *Representing Reality: Discourse, Rhetoric and Social Construction*. London: Sage.

Potter, Jonathan. 1997. "Discourse Analysis as a Way of Analysing Naturally Occurring Talk." Pp. 144–160 in *Qualitative Research: Theory, Method and Practice*, edited by David Silverman. London: Sage.

Potter, Jonathan and Margaret Wetherell. 1987. *Discourse and Social Psychology*. London: Sage.

Presthus, Robert. 1978. *The Organizational Society*. New York: St. Martin's Press.

Prior, Lindsey. 1997. "Following in Foucault's Footsteps: Text and Context in Qualitative Research." Pp. 63–79 in *Qualitative Research: Theory, Method and Practice*, edited by David Silverman. London: Sage.

Psathas, George. 1995. *Conversation Analysis*. Newbury Park, Calif.: Sage.

Quiroz, Pamela Anne and Tommie Lee Ragland. 1998. " 'A Rose by Any Other Name': Latino and Anglo Teachers Constructing Chicago School Reform." *Journal of Contemporary Ethnography* 27: 137–68.

Randall, William Lowell. 1995. *The Stories We Are: An Essay on Self-Creation*. Toronto: University of Toronto Press.

Reynolds, Larry T. 1990. *Interactionism: Exposition and Critique*. Dix Hills, N.Y.: General Hall.

Richardson, Laurel. 1990. "Narrative and Sociology." *Journal of Contemporary Ethnography* 19: 116–35.

Richardson, Laurel. 1991. "Postmodern Social Theory: Representational Practices." *Sociological Theory* 9: 173–79.

Riesman, David. 1950. *The Lonely Crowd: A Study of the Changing American Character*. New Haven, Conn.: Yale University Press.

Riesman, David. 1968. "On Autonomy." Pp. 445–62 in *The Self in Social Interaction*, edited by Chad Gordon and Kenneth Gergen. New York: John Wiley & Sons.

Riessman, Catherine Kohler. 1990. *Divorce Talk: Women and Men Make Sense of Personal Relationships*. New Brunswick, N.J.: Rutgers University Press.

Riessman, Catherine Kohler. 1993. *Narrative Analysis*. Thousand Oaks, Calif.: Sage.

Rorty, Richard. 1982. *Consequences of Pragmatism: Essays 1972–1980*. Minneapolis: University of Minnesota Press.

Rosaldo, Renato. 1994. "Race and Other Inequalities." Pp. 213–25 in *Race*, edited by Steven Gregory and Roger Sanjek. New Brunswick, N.J.: Rutgers University Press.

Rose, Arnold M. (ed.). 1962. *Human Behavior and Social Processes: An Interactionist Perspective*. Boston: Houghton Mifflin & Co.

Rose, Nikolas. 1990. *Governing the Soul: The Shaping of the Private Self*. London: Routledge.

Rose, Nikolas. 1997. *Inventing Ourselves: Psychology, Power, and Personhood*. Cambridge: Cambridge University Press.

Rosen, Lawrence (ed.). 1995. *Other Intentions: Cultural Contexts and the Attribution of Inner States*. Santa Fe, N.M.: School of American Research Press.

Rosenau, Pauline Marie. 1992. *Post-modernism and the Social Sciences*. Princeton, N.J.: Princeton University Press.

Rosenthal, Robert and Lenore Jacobson. 1968. *Pygmalion in the Classroom*. New York: Holt, Rinehart and Winston.

Rosenwald, George C. and Richard L. Ochberg. 1992. *Storied Lives*. New Haven, Conn.: Yale University Press.

Rucker, Egbert Darnell. 1969. *The Chicago Pragmatists*. Minneapolis: University of Minnesota Press.

Runyan, William M. 1982. *Life Histories and Psychobiography: Explorations in Theory and Method*. New York: Oxford University Press.

Ryle, Gilbert. 1949. *The Concept of Mind*. Chicago: University of Chicago Press.

Saatkamp, Herman J., Jr. (ed.). 1995. *Rorty and Pragmatism: The Philosopher Responds to His Critics*. Nashville, Tenn.: Vanderbilt University Press.

Sacks, Harvey. 1974. "On the Analyzability of Stories by Children." Pp. 216–32 in *Ethnomethodology*, edited by Roy Turner. Harmondsworth, England: Penguin.

Sacks, Harvey. 1992a. *Lectures on Conversation, vol. I*. Oxford: Blackwell.

Sacks, Harvey. 1992b. *Lectures on Conversation, vol. II*. Oxford: Blackwell.

Sacks, Harvey and Emanuel A. Schegloff. 1979. "Two Preferences in the Organization of Reference to Persons in Conversation and Their Interaction." Pp. 15–21 in *Everyday Language Studies*, edited by G. Psathas. New York: Irvington.

Sacks, Harvey, Emanuel Schegloff, and Gail Jefferson. 1974. "A Simplest Systematics for the Organization of Turn-Taking for Conversation. *Language* 50: 696–735.

Sandywell, Barry, David Silverman, Maurice Roche, Paul Filmer, and Michael Phillipson. 1975. *Problems of Reflexivity and Dialectics in Sociological Theory: Language Theorizing Difference*. London: Routledge & Kegan Paul.

Santayana, George. 1957. *Winds of Doctrine* and *Platonism and the Spiritual Life*. New York: Harper & Brothers.

Sarbin, Theodore R. 1986. *Narrative Psychology: The Storied Nature of Human Conduct*. New York: Praeger.

Schegloff, Emanuel A. 1980. "Preliminaries to Preliminaries: 'Can I Ask You a Question?'" *Sociological Inquiry* 50: 104–52.

Schegloff, Emanuel A. 1982. "Discourse as an Interactional Achievement." Pp. 73–91 in *Georgetown University Roundtable on Languages and Linguistics*, edited by D. Tannen. Washington, D.C.: Georgetown University Press.

Schegloff, Emanuel A. 1984. "Some Questions and Ambiguities in Conversation." Pp. 28–52 in *Structures of Social Action*, edited by J. Maxwell Atkinson and John Heritage. Cambridge: Cambridge University Press.

Schegloff, Emanuel A. and Harvey Sacks. 1973. "Opening Up Closings." *Semiotica* 7: 289–327.

Schenkein, Jim. 1978. "Identity Negotiations in Conversation." Pp. 57–78 in *Studies in the Organization of Conversational Interaction*, edited by Jim Schenkein. New York: Academic Press.

Schneebaum, Tobias. 1969. *Keep the River on Your Right*. New York: Grove.

Schneider, Joseph. 1991. "Troubles with Textual Authority in Sociology." *Symbolic Interaction* 14 296–319.

Schur, Edwin M. 1971. *Labeling Deviant Behavior*. New York: Harper & Row.

Schur, Edwin M. 1979. *Interpreting Deviance*. New York: Harper & Row.

Schutz, Alfred. 1962. *The Problem of Social Reality*. The Hague: Martinus Nijhoff.

Schutz, Alfred. 1964. *Studies in Social Theory*. The Hague: Martinus Nijhoff.

Schutz, Alfred. 1967. *The Phenomenology of the Social World*. Evanston, Ill.: Northwestern University Press.

Schutz, Alfred. 1970. *On Phenomenology and Social Relations.* Chicago: University of Chicago Press.

Schrag, Calvin O. 1997. *The Self After Postmodernity.* New Haven, Conn.: Yale University Press.

Scott, Joan W. 1995. "Multiculturalism and the Politics of Identity." Pp. 3–14 in *The Identity in Question,* edited by John Rajchman. New York: Routledge.

Scott, Marvin B. and Stanford Lyman. 1968. "Accounts." *American Sociological Review* 33: 46–62.

Seidman, Steven (ed.). 1996. *Queer Theory/Sociology.* Cambridge, Mass.: Blackwell.

Seidman, Steven. 1997. *Difference Troubles: Queering Social Theory and Sexual Politics.* New York: Cambridge University Press.

Seidman, Steven. 1998. "Are We All in the Closet? Notes Towards a Sociological and Cultural Turn in Queer Theory." *European Journal of Cultural Studies* 1: 177–92.

Seidman, Steven and David G. Wagner (eds.). 1992. *Postmodernism and Social Theory.* Oxford: Blackwell.

Sennett, Richard. 1974. *The Fall of Public Man.* New York: Vintage.

Shaw, Clifford. 1930. *The Jack Roller: A Delinquent Boy's Own Story.* Chicago: University of Chicago Press.

Shaw, Clifford. 1931. *The Natural History of a Delinquent Career.* Chicago: University of Chicago Press.

Sheridan, Alan. 1980. *Michel Foucault: The Will to Truth.* London: Tavistock.

Shilling, Chris. 1993. *The Body and Social Theory.* London: Sage.

Shore, Bradd. 1996. *Culture in Mind: Cognition, Culture, and the Problem of Meaning.* New York: Oxford University Press.

Shorter, Edward. 1975. *The Making of the Modern Family.* New York: Basic Books.

Shotter, Jonathan and Kenneth Gergen. 1989. *Texts of Identity.* London: Sage.

Shweder, Richard A. and Edmund J. Bourne. 1984. "Does the Concept of the Person Vary Cross-culturally?" Pp. 158–99 in *Culture Theory,* edited by Richard Shweder and Robert LeVine. Cambridge: Cambridge University Press.

Sica, Alan. 1993. "Does PoMo Matter?" *Contemporary Sociology* 22: 16–19.

Silverman, David. 1993. *Interpreting Qualitative Data.* London: Sage.

Silverman, David. 1998. *Harvey Sacks: Social Science and Conversation Analysis.* New York: Oxford University Press.

Simons, Herbert W. and Michael Billig. 1994. *After Postmodernism: Reconstructing Ideology Critique.* London: Sage.

Skidmore, William. 1975. *Theoretical Thinking in Sociology.* Cambridge: Cambridge University Press.

Smith, Dorothy. 1974. "Women's Perspective as a Radical Critique of Sociology." *Sociological Inquiry* 44: 7–13.

Smith, Dorothy. 1987. *The Everyday World as Problematic: A Feminist Sociology.* Boston: Northeastern University Press.

Smith, Dorothy. 1990. *Texts, Facts, and Femininity: Exploring the Relations of Ruling.* London: Routledge.

Snow, David and Leon Anderson. 1987. "Identity Work Among the Homeless: The Verbal Construction and Avowal of Personal Identities." *American Journal of Sociology* 92: 1336–71.

Solomon, Robert C. 1988. *Continental Philosophy Since 1750: The Rise and Fall of the Self.* Oxford: Oxford University Press.

Spencer, J. William. 1994. "Homeless in River City: Client Work in Human Service Encounters." Pp. 29–46 in *Perspectives on Social Problems, vol. 6*, edited by James A. Holstein and Gale Miller. Greenwich, Conn.: JAI Press.

Stack, Carol B. 1974. *All Our Kind: Strategies for Survival in a Black Community*. New York: Harper & Row.

Stone, Gregory P. and Harvey A. Farberman (eds.). 1970. *Social Psychology Through Symbolic Interaction*. Waltham, Mass.: Ginn and Company.

Stryker, Sheldon. 1980. *Symbolic Interactionism: A Social Structural Version*. Menlo Park, Calif.: Benjamin/Cummings.

Sykes, Gresham. 1958. *The Society of Captives*. Princeton, N.J.: Princeton University Press.

Tannenbaum, Frank. 1938. *Crime and the Community*. Boston: Ginn.

Taylor, Charles. 1989. *Sources of the Self: The Making of the Modern Identity*. Cambridge, Mass.: Harvard University Press.

ten Have, P. 1990. "Methodological Issues in Conversation Analysis." *Bulletin de Methodologie Sociologique* 27: 23–51.

Thomas, W. I. and Florian Znaniecki. 1927[1918–1920]. *The Polish Peasant in Europe and America*. New York: Knopf.

Thompson, Paul. 1978. *The Voice of the Past: Oral History*. Oxford: Oxford University Press.

Thompson, Paul, Catherine Itzin, and Michelle Abendstern. 1990. *I Don't Feel Old: The Experience of Later Life*. Oxford: Oxford University Press.

Thorne, Barrie and Marilyn Yalom (eds.). 1982. *Rethinking the Family: Some Feminist Questions*. New York: Longman.

Todorov, Tzvetan. 1984. *Mikhail Bakhtin: The Dialogical Principle*. Minneapolis: University of Minnesota Press.

Trinh Minh-ha. 1991. *When the Moon Waxes Red: Representation, Gender and Cultural Politics*. New York: Routledge.

Trinh Minh-ha. 1992. *Framer Framed*. New York: Routledge.

Tufte, Virginia and Barbara Myerhoff (eds.). 1979. *Changing Images of the Family*. New Haven, Conn.: Yale University Press.

Turner, Bryan S. 1984. *The Body and Society*. Oxford: Blackwell.

Turner, Bryan S. 1991. "Recent Developments in the Theory of the Body." Pp. 1–35 in *The Body: Social Process and Cultural Theory*, edited by Mike Featherstone, Mike Hepworth, and Bryan S. Turner. London: Sage.

Turner, Bryan S. 1992. *Regulating Bodies*. London: Routledge.

Turner, Stephen Park and Jonathan H. Turner. 1990. *The Impossible Science: An Institutional Analysis of American Sociology*. Newbury Park, Calif.: Sage.

van Dijk, Teun A. 1993. "Stories and Racism." Pp. 121–42 in *Narrative and Social Control*, edited by Dennis K. Mumby. Newbury Park, Calif.: Sage.

van Dijk, Teun A. (ed.). 1997. *Discourse Studies: A Multidisciplinary Introduction*. London: Sage.

Vernon, Glenn M. 1962. "Religious Self-Identification." *Pacific Sociological Review* 5: 40–43.

Vila, Pablo. 1997. "Narrative Identities: The Employment of the Mexican on the U.S.-Mexican Border." *Sociological Quarterly* 38: 147–83.

Waisanen, Fred B. 1962. "Self-Attitudes and Performance Expectations." *Sociological Quarterly* 3: 208–19.

Walton, Mary. 1986. *The Deming Management Method*. New York: Dodd, Mead.

Warren, Robert Penn. 1959. *All the King's Men*. New York: Bantam.

Weeks, Kathi. 1998. *Constituting Feminist Subjects*. Ithaca, N.Y.: Cornell University Press.

West, Candace. 1996. "Ethnography and Orthography: A (Modest) Methodological Proposal." *Journal of Contemporary Ethnography* 25: 327–52.

Whalen, Jack. 1992. "Conversation Analysis." Pp. 303–10 in *Encyclopedia of Sociology, vol. 1*, edited by E. Borgatta. New York: Macmillan.

Wheeler, Stanton (ed.). 1969. *On Record: Files and Dossiers in American Life*. New York: Russell Sage Foundation.

Whyte, William H. 1956. *The Organization Man*. Garden City, N.Y.: Doubleday.

Wieder, D. Lawrence. 1974. *Language and Social Reality*. The Hague: Mouton.

Wiley, Norbert. 1985. "Marriage and the Construction of Reality: Now and Then." Pp. 21–32 in *The Psychosocial Interior of the Family*, edited by G. Handel. New York: Aldine de Gruyter.

Wiley, Norbert. 1994. *The Semiotic Self*. Chicago: University of Chicago Press.

Winnicott, D. W. 1965. *The Maturational Process and the Facilitating Environment*. New York: International Universities Press.

Wittgenstein, Ludwig. 1953. *Philosophical Investigations*. New York: Macmillan.

Wittgenstein, Ludwig. 1958. *The Blue and Brown Books*. Oxford: Blackwell.

Wuthnow, Robert. 1994. *Sharing the Journey: Support Groups and America's New Quest for Community*. New York: Free Press.

Young, Allan. 1995. *The Harmony of Illusions*. Princeton, N.J.: Princeton University Press.

Zimmerman, Don. 1988. "On Conversation: The Conversation-Analytic Perspective." Pp. 406–32 in *Communication Yearbook II*, edited by J. A. Anderson. Newbury Park, Calif.: Sage.

Zimmerman, Don H. and Melvin Pollner. 1970. "The Everyday World as a Phenomenon." Pp. 80–103 in *Understanding Everyday Life*, edited by Jack D. Douglas. Chicago: Aldine.

Zurcher, Louis A. 1977. *The Mutable Self*. Beverly Hills, Calif.: Sage.

Author Index

Subject Index